Time series models for business and economic forecasting

The econometric analysis of economic and business time series is a major field of research and application. The last few decades have witnessed an increasing interest in both theoretical and empirical developments in constructing time series models and in their important application in forecasting. In *Time series models for business and economic forecasting*, Philip Hans Franses examines recent developments in time series analysis.

The early chapters of the book focus on the typical features of time series data in business and economics. Chapter 3 is concerned with the discussion of some important concepts in time series analysis; the discussion focuses on the techniques which can be readily applied in practice. Chapters 4–8 suggest different modeling methods and model structures. Chapter 9 extends the concepts in chapter 3 to multivariate time series. Chapter 10 examines common aspects across time series.

Time series models for business and economic forecasting

Philip Hans Franses

CAMBRIDGE
UNIVERSITY PRESS

PUBLISHED BY THE PRESS SYNDICATE OF THE UNIVERSITY OF CAMBRIDGE
The Pitt Building, Trumpington Street, Cambridge CB2 1RP, United Kingdom

CAMBRIDGE UNIVERSITY PRESS
The Edinburgh Building, Cambridge CB2 2RU, United Kingdom
http://www.cup.cam.ac.uk
40 West 20th Street, New York, NY 10011-4211, USA http://www.cup.org
10 Stamford Road, Oakleigh, Melbourne 3166, Australia

© Cambridge University Press 1998

First published 1998

Printed in the United Kingdom at the University Press, Cambridge

Typeset in 10/12pt Times New Roman   [SE]

A catalogue record for this book is available from the British Library

Library of Congress Cataloguing-in-Publication data

Franses, Philip Hans, 1963–
      Time series models for business and economic forecasting / Philip
Hans Franses.
         p.   cm.
      Includes bibliographical references (p.   ) and indexes.
      ISBN 0 521 58404 3 (hb)   0 521 58641 0 (pb)
         1. Time-series analysis.   2. Social sciences – Statistical methods.
      3. Business forecasting.   4. Economic forecasting.   I. Title.
      HA30.3.F7   1998
      338.5′442′0151955–dc21   97–47490
                                                                            CIP

ISBN 0 521 58404 3 hardback
ISBN 0 521 58641 0 paperback

To my wife Gabrielle and my son Tobias

Contents

Preface

The econometric analysis of economic and business time series is a major field of research and application. The last few decades have witnessed an increasing interest in both theoretical and empirical developments in constructing time series models and in their important application in forecasting. Examples of the many novel aspects of today's practice are unit roots, cointegration, GARCH, changing seasonality, aberrant observations, and nonlinearity. Although not for all these aspects it has been convincingly shown that better forecasts can be obtained, many of these are here to stay and will belong to the tool kit of the practical forecaster in the next decade. This book aims at reviewing several recent developments within the context of forecasting business and economic time series.

A full-blown textbook on all aspects of time series analysis will cover thousands of pages. For example, the field of unit root analysis has expanded with such a pace and variation that a book only on this topic would take more pages than the current book does. This book is not intended to be a survey of all that is available and that can be done in time series analysis. Obviously, such a selection comes with a cost, that is, the discussion will sometimes not be as theoretically precise as some readers would have liked. In fact, the discussion can sometimes be very sketchy. Merely, it is my purpose that the readers should be able to generate their own forecasts from time series models that adequately describe the key features of the data, to evaluate these forecasts, and to come up with suggestions for possible modifications if necessary. In some interesting cases, though, I also recommend further reading. To attain this, I make a selection between all the possible routes to constructing and evaluating time series models, between all the possible estimation methods and between all the various tests that can be used. Basically, my choice is also often motivated by the availability of methods in such statistical packages as MicroTSP (version 7.0) or Eviews (version 2.0), while sometimes a little bit of Gauss or Matlab programming is needed. In fact, all empirical results in this book are thus obtained. An additional motivation for my choice is given by my own practical experience in forecasting business and economic time series. This experience is also based on supervising projects of our econometrics undergraduate students during their internships at banks, investment companies, and consultancy agencies. Needless to say that, since such experience is always limited, this book should not be interpreted as a statement against the possible usefulness of alternative approaches.

My second purpose with this book is that the reader will be able to get some understanding of novel approaches reported in recent and future issues of, say, the *Journal of Time Series Analysis, Journal of Econometrics, Journal of Business and Economic Statistics, Journal of Forecasting, International Journal of Forecasting, Journal of Applied Econometrics*, and the *Journal of the American Statistical Association*. It is hoped that the reader finds the material in this book helpful to understand why such new methods can be useful for forecasting.

Although this book amounts to an introduction to the field of time series analysis and forecasting, it is necessary that the reader has knowledge of introductory econometrics. Specifically, regression analysis, matrix algebra, and various concepts in estimation should be included in that knowledge. This book should then be useful to advanced undergraduate students and graduate students in business and economics, but also to practitioners and applied economists who wish to obtain a first, but not too technical, impression of time series forecasting. In fact, most of the material has already been used in "Time Series Analysis" courses for third year under-graduate students at the Econometric Institute in Rotterdam in the Fall of 1996 and 1997. Several students made useful suggestions for modifications and corrections. In particular, I am grateful to Olav Beruto, Peter Brouwer, Johan Duyvesteyn, Roy Kluitman, and Erik Pennings.

This book was written during my affiliation with the Econometric Institute at the Erasmus University Rotterdam. This Institute is a very stim-ulating teaching and research environment. I wish to express my gratitude to my colleagues Dick van Dijk, Teun Kloek, Andre Lucas, Marius Ooms, and an anonymous referee for their kind willingness to comment on some or all chapters. My special thanks go to Christiaan Heij, who, as a fellow teacher of our "Time Series Analysis" course, read all chapters with great precision and suggested many ways for modification and improvement.

Rotterdam, January 1998

1 Introduction and overview

This book concerns the construction of time series models to be used for out-of-sample forecasting. The time series are observations on economic variables, which can originate from various fields of economics and business. Examples of such variables are inflation rates, stock market indices, unemployment rates, and market shares. Out-of-sample forecasts for such variables are often needed to set policy targets. For example, the forecast for next year's inflation rate can lead to a change in the monetary policy of a central bank. A forecast of a company's market share in the next few months may lead to changes in the allocation of the advertising budget. The models in this book can be called econometric time series models since we use econometric methods for analysis.

Time series data can display a wide variety of patterns. Typically, many macroeconomic aggregates such as industrial production, consumption, and wages show upward trending patterns. Tourism data and retail sales display a pronounced seasonal pattern, that is, tourism spending is usually large in the summer and retail sales tend to peak around Christmas. Stock markets can crash with decreases in daily returns that can be as large as −20 percent, while such markets do not tend to boom with similarly sized increases in returns. Another feature is that some observations on economic data can be aberrant data in the sense that these rarely occur and do not seem to "belong" to the variable. For example, if new car registrations are almost zero in a certain month because of a computer breakdown, this does not reflect the true sales of new cars.

It seems obvious that there is not a single time series model that can be used to describe all of the above features and that is also reasonably precise in out-of-sample forecasting. In fact, there are several models to describe each of these features, and all these models can be used to generate forecasts. It is the key purpose of this book to survey several of these various possible models, and to discuss how these models can be constructed and how their possible merits for forecasting can be evaluated. It is my opinion

1

that just as that there is no true descriptive model, there is also no uniformly best forecasting model. Therefore, I restrict myself to presenting guidelines for the selection between available models for forecasting. As will become apparent from the graphs in chapter 2, the specific features of economic time series often lead to an *a priori* selection of possibly useful models. For example, there are time series models that explicitly deal with seasonality, and such models may be less useful for data that do not display seasonal variation.

An important requirement for the model construction methods discussed in this book is that the practitioner takes some time to construct his or her forecasts. If it is necessary to generate forecasts 1,000 times every day, it is better to rely on the many automatic extrapolation schemes that are available, such as smoothing algorithms and exponentially weighted moving averages. I do not wish to claim that such methods are less useful, not the least because it appears in forecasting competitions that these automatic schemes can outperform the various models below, see, for example, Makridakis *et al.* (1982). I do claim, however, that the decisions involved in constructing a descriptive time series model for a time series with specific features that is also useful for out-of-sample forecasting may be difficult to formalize in automatic routines.

Model building

The modeling strategies to be reviewed in this book exploit the obvious important property of an economic time series, which is that the sequence of the data is determined by calendar time. This implies that an observation on unemployment in 1989 always precedes observations in 1990 and later, and, naturally that the observation in 1990 is somehow influenced by that in 1989. In turn this leads to a consecutive analysis of time series data while leaving their sequence intact. When a time series is denoted by y_t, where the time index runs from 1 to n, that is, y_t is short-hand for observations y_1, y_2, y_3 to y_n, the key property of time series data is that observation y_t always comes after y_{t-1}. Therefore it makes sense to analyze y_{t-1} prior to analyzing y_t. This is in sharp contrast to cross-sectional data where the sequence of data points does not matter. In order to measure, say, the average age of all family members, it does not matter if we start with the oldest and end with the youngest or the other way round, that is, the average age will be the same.

Given that y_{t-1} is always measured prior to y_t, it is likely that part of the value of y_{t-1} is reflected in the value y_t. For example, it seems unlikely that if this month's inflation rate is 10 percent, it will be -5 percent next month. In fact, it is more likely that it will be, say, between 8 percent and 12 percent.

Again, this is in contrast to cross-sectional data. If one person is 80 years old, the next observed person may well be 25 years old or may also be 80 years old. For many time series data, we can say that the observations at any time t and $t-1$, that is, y_t and y_{t-1}, are likely to be correlated. Since these observations are measurements of the same variable, we say that y_t is correlated with itself. This concept is called autocorrelation. If there is such autocorrelation between for example y_t and y_{t-1}, and may be with y_{t-i} for some i, with $i = 2,3,4,\dots$, we can exploit this correlation for forecasting. If it holds that y_t equals $0.8y_{t-1}$ for all $t = 2,\dots,n$, and y_t is again the inflation rate with a value of 10 percent in the nth month, we may forecast next month's rate y_{n+1} as 8 percent.

Time series data can be characterized by a set of autocorrelations. Given a certain time series at hand, we can estimate these correlations. The key feature of the time series models discussed in this book is that such estimated autocorrelations can be exploited to obtain a first impression of possibly useful models to describe and forecast the time series. This is because those time series models imply certain autocorrelation properties of time series that we would generate from these models in case these were the true data generating processes. For example, the so-called autoregressive model of order 1 for a non-trending time series y_t, of which more details will be given in chapter 3, implies that y_t is mainly correlated with y_{t-1} and less correlated with y_{t-2}. In practice, we can estimate these correlations, and if the implied relationship seems to hold, we may be inclined to consider such a first order model in the first round of specification analysis. In brief, certain features of observed time series data suggest the possible adequacy of corresponding time series models. Notice that again this does not hold for a sample of cross-sectional data which do not depend on time.

In this book I focus on five key features of economic and business time series data. These features are trends, seasonality, aberrant observations, conditional heteroskedasticity, and non-linearity. Each of these features points toward the possible usefulness of certain classes of time series models. In order to keep matters simple, I restrict the attention to regression-based models like

$$y_t = \beta x_t + \varepsilon_t, \quad t = 1,2,\dots,n, \tag{1.1}$$

where y_t and x_t are observed time series, ε_t is an unobserved error time series, and β is an unknown parameter. Commonly, the x_t variable contains the past of y_t. Needless to say that (1.1) is an overly simplified version of the models considered later, but here it serves as an illustration. When there are n data points, and the current observation is made at time n, it is often the case that we will wish to forecast h steps out of sample, that is, to estimate y_{n+h}. Usually, the y_t variable, which is the variable of focal interest is known.

However, the x_t variable usually has to be selected, and it will become clear in later chapters that, for example, autocorrelations can be helpful to decide on the most appropriate form of x_t. In this book, these x_t variables (or functions thereof) are usually assumed to be observable. There are also classes of time series models where x_t should be estimated as well. In these so-called unobserved components models such x_t variables can be labeled as "trend" or "seasonal fluctuations," see Harvey (1989) for an excellent treatment of these models. Furthermore, also in order to limit the exposition, I confine myself to cases where the function that relates y_t to x_t is known and can be characterized by a few parameters. In (1.1) this relationship is linear. In chapters 7 and 8, I will discuss some non-linear time series models. For a detailed treatment of non-parametric methods which allow for flexible functional relations between y_t and x_t, the interested reader is referred to, for example, Härdle, Lütkepohl, and Chen (1997) and Fan and Gijbels (1996).

Statistical method

There are two dominant approaches in analyzing time series. One of these is called spectral analysis. The key assumption within this approach is that any non-trending time series can be decomposed into a certain number of cyclical patterns. The length of these cycles can be of interest and can be exploited to characterize a time series. For example, a cycle of infinite length corresponds with a trend, see Granger (1966), while a cycle of four quarters corresponds with a seasonal pattern. Although such spectral techniques can be useful to obtain a visual impression of time series properties and to describe, for example, business cycle properties, these are not often explicitly considered for out-of-sample forecasting. For a thorough treatment of spectral techniques, see, for example, Priestley (1981).

The second approach to analyzing time series, which is common in economics, is called the time-domain approach. In this case, the fact that time series observations are measured in a sequence is exploited. Within this time-domain approach, the autocorrelation function plays a crucial role. Important work on this type of time series analysis is Box and Jenkins (1970), of which a third edition recently appeared in Box, Jenkins, and Reinsel (1994). Although the field of time series analysis has expanded widely since 1970, the main ideas underlying Box and Jenkins's work are still valid. In the present book I confine the discussion to this time-domain approach, also since it is most commonly used even in more complicated non-linear and specific seasonal models. In fact, in those last cases, the application and interpretation of spectral techniques is not at all trivial.

A final remark on the statistical method concerns Bayesian and classical statistical methods. Without taking a standpoint toward favoring one of these two contrasting approaches (which sometimes yield similar inference), in this book I will use only classical statistical methods. For treatments of Bayesian methods in statistics, see Bernardo and Smith (1994), Zellner (1970), and Poirier (1995).

The data

An obvious first step when forecasting economic and business time series is to collect the relevant data for model construction. Sometimes this is easy, but in many cases we have to make many decisions before a useful set of data is available. For example, how to define market share when only the information of about 50 percent of the market is available? Or, how should we define the unemployment rate? Does unemployment also include persons who work less than five hours per week?

In this book I use several empirical sample series for the illustration of the various concepts and models. The relevant data are presented in the data appendix. Some data, which are constructed by myself, appear in specific chapters. The sources of the data are given below each table. Of course, in some cases different data can be obtained for the same phenomenon, but here I assume that the data are properly measured. Examples of the series used in this book for illustration are annually observed production indices in China, the weekly Dow-Jones index, quarterly unemployment in Germany, weekly observed market and distribution shares for a fast-moving consumer good, monthly retail sales, and four-weekly advertising expenditures on television. These data can be used by the reader to verify the empirical results and also to try out alternative modeling strategies and to evaluate the properties of other out-of-sample forecasts.

Forecasting

From a methodological point of view it is important to be precise about the goal of econometric time series modeling. In this book, I focus on time series models that give an adequate description of the available data, and that are useful for out-of-sample forecasting. The concept of adequate description will be discussed in chapter 3. When it comes to forecasting, a crucial assumption is that the data in the model specification sample are somehow similar to the out-of-sample data. If not, there is of course no point in spending much time on the construction of high-brow time series models. Hence, it is crucial that we evaluate the stability of the forecasting model. For example, if all forecasts are too high or too low, we would obviously wish to re-specify our forecasting model.

A useful empirical strategy that can be helpful to assess the stability of the model and the modeling environment is the following. Suppose there are $n + m$ observations for a variable y_t, then the first n observations can be used to construct a model and to estimate its parameters, and we can use the last m observations to evaluate out-of-sample forecasting performance. Hence, we have the forecasts y_{n+h}, where $h = 1,2,\ldots,m$, from a model that is constructed for n observations on y_t, where $t = 1,2,\ldots,n$. When the forecasting performance is satisfactory, we may want to generate forecasts for the unknown observations at times $n + m + 1$ to $n + m + l$. Obviously, these forecasts can only be evaluated once the corresponding l observations at those dates have become available.

The selection of m, the number of forecasts, is not trivial and there is no specific rule for it. It is important, though, that n is large enough to have some precision for the parameter estimates, and m should also be large enough to compare various models. To illustrate how to generate forecasts, I sometimes re-estimate the models for the first n observations while keeping the model structure fixed. The reader can use the data in the data appendix to evaluate alternative strategies.

Outline of this book

The contents of this book are as follows. Chapter 2 surveys typical features of time series data in economics and business. I limit this discussion to five such features: trends, seasonality, aberrant data, time-varying variance, and non-linearity. The treatment of these features corresponds with a decreasing source of variation in economic time series. The most dominant source of variation is often the trend. The next dominant source is seasonal variation, while the smallest amount of variation often tends to be due to non-linearity. There is no explicit treatment of a "business cycle" here since this sometimes corresponds with cyclical dynamics in the time series itself, sometimes with short-term deviations from a trend, and sometimes it can be viewed as a non-linearity or outlier aspect of the data. Each of the five features suggests different modeling methods and model structures, and hence I return to each of these features in chapters 4 to 8. Before that, chapter 3 is concerned with a discussion of some important concepts in time series analysis. Intentionally, this discussion is far from being as technically rigorous as T.W. Anderson (1971), Fuller (1976), and Hamilton (1994). The focus is instead on discussing those techniques which can be readily applied in practice. When necessary, I give references to studies that include proofs of formal asymptotics and other results. Most of this discussion in chapter 3, as well as that in chapters 4 to 8, deals with univariate time series. In chapter 9 some of the concepts in chapter 3 are extended to multivariate time series. In chapter 10 the focus is on common aspects across economic time series such as common trends. Most chapters contain also current research topics. The research area of time series analysis is very active, and we can expect many new developments in the not too distant future.

2   Key features of economic time series

In this chapter the focus is on key features of typical business and economic time series. It also serves to introduce several of the empirical sample series which will be used throughout this book as running examples. The relevant data are given in the data appendix.

The five key features of economic and business data can be (i) trends, (ii) seasonality, (iii) somehow influential data points, (iv) a variance that changes because of past observations (conditional heteroskedasticity), and (v) non-linearity. Typically, an economic time series displays at least one, but usually two or three of these features. To keep matters simple, however, in this chapter each series is analyzed for only one of these five features. In later chapters, the application of various possible models for each of these features will be sometimes combined to illustrate the practice of time series modeling.

Each of the five data features in this chapter will be illuminated using simple regression-based calculations. This should not imply that these models are also the best models we can use; these models are merely helpful to show the properties of the data. In chapters 4 to 8, more sophisticated models will be presented that can describe and forecast the observed features. A second important tool in this chapter is a graphical analysis. In most cases it is already quite helpful to put the data just in a graph with the values of the observations on the vertical axis and time on the horizontal axis. However, in case of, for example, many data or data with a large variance, it may sometimes be more insightful to rely on scatter or correlation plots. The latter shows the correlation between y_t and another variable x_t. Since time series analysis is our focus here, x_t is often replaced by, for example, y_{t-1}. In a practical situation, I would advise to construct each of the graphs as well as to quantify each of the simple regressions in order to obtain some overall insight in the specific data properties. Here, quantification means the estimation of the unknown parameters in the relevant regression.

The data in the appendix are all in their original format, that is to say, these data have not been transformed. In empirical time series analysis it is common practice to analyze data after the natural logarithmic transformation has been applied. Hence, if the raw data are denoted by w_t, we usually model and forecast $y_t = \log(w_t)$, where log denotes the natural logarithm. If forecasts are needed for w_t, it is usual to re-transform using $w_{n+h} = \exp(y_{n+h})$, preferably with some correction. One of the reasons for the log-transformation is that an exponential trend becomes linear. Although there are recent empirical and theoretical studies that question the validity of this automatism, for the moment I assume that y_t is the time series considered for modeling, and hence y_t usually denotes $\log(w_t)$. In cases where the data are already in relative format, as the unemployment rate, inflation rate or market share, the log transformation is usually not applied.

2.1 Trends

One of the dominant features of many economic and business time series is the trend. Such a trend can be upward or downward, it can be steep or not, and it can be exponential or approximately linear. Since a trend should definitively somehow be incorporated in a time series model, simply because it can be exploited for out-of-sample forecasting, an analysis of trend behavior typically requires quite some research input. The discussion in chapter 4 will show that the type of trend has an important impact on forecasting.

To illustrate the presence of trends in economic data, consider the five graphs in figure 2.1, which are the annual indices of real national output (in logs) in China in five different sectors for the sample period 1952–1988. These sectors are agriculture, industry, construction, transportation, and commerce.

From this figure it can be observed that the five sectors have grown over the years at different growth rates, and also that the five sectors seem to have been affected by the, likely, exogenous shocks to the Chinese economy around 1958 and 1968. These shocks roughly correspond to the two major political disturbances in China, that is, the Great Leap Forward around 1958 until 1962 and the Cultural Revolution from 1966 until 1976. It also appears from the graphs that these disturbances may not have affected each of the five sectors in a similar fashion. For example, the decline of the output in the construction sector in 1961 seems much larger than that in the industry sector in the same year. It also seems that the Great Leap Forward shock already had an impact on the output in the agriculture sector as early as 1959.

To quantify the trends in the five Chinese output series, consider the following simple regression model

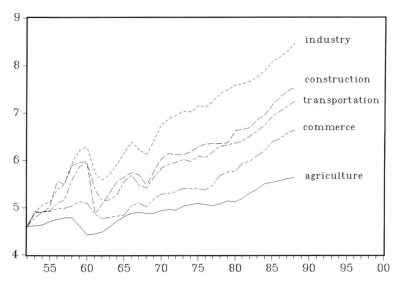

Figure 2.1 *Annual indices of real national output in China, 1952–1988*

$$y_t = \alpha + \delta t + u_t, \quad t = 1, 2, \ldots, n, \tag{2.1}$$

where α and δ are unknown parameters and where u_t is an unknown residual error time series. Since the graphs in figure 2.1 show some cyclical behavior, indicating that u_t may be correlated with u_{t-1}, and hence suggesting dynamic misspecification of (2.1), the standard errors in table 2.1 should be treated with care.

The left-hand panel of table 2.1 displays the estimates of δ in (2.1). It is clear that the upward trend is steepest for the industry sector (0.094) and that such growth is smallest for agriculture (0.028).

The simple regression model in (2.1) assumes that the trend in y_t can be represented by a linear trend $t = 1, 2, 3, \ldots$ An alternative method to obtain insight in the trend pattern is to consider the growth rate of the variable. In case $y_t = \log(w_t)$, it follows that

$$
\begin{aligned}
y_t - y_{t-1} &= \log(w_t/w_{t-1}) \\
&= \log[1 + (w_t - w_{t-1})/w_{t-1}] \\
&\approx (w_t - w_{t-1})/w_{t-1} \qquad \text{when } (w_t - w_{t-1})/w_{t-1} \text{ is small.}
\end{aligned}
$$

In industrialized countries, the growth rate of macroeconomic aggregates is in between -0.01 and 0.10, which can be considered as small relative to unity. Hence, the first differences of y_t can approximately correspond to the growth rate of w_t. Below in section 2.3, we will see that such correspondence

Table 2.1. *The significance of trends in real national output in China*

Variable	$\hat{\delta}$ in regression: $y_t = \alpha + \delta t + u_t$		$\hat{\mu}$ in regression: $y_t - y_{t-1} = \mu + u_t$	
Agriculture	0.028	(0.002)	0.029	(0.011)
Industry	0.094	(0.003)	0.107	(0.028)
Construction	0.064	(0.004)	0.082	(0.042)
Transportation	0.060	(0.004)	0.074	(0.027)
Commerce	0.047	(0.003)	0.056	(0.016)

Note:
The numbers in parentheses are estimated standard errors.

does not always hold. Notice that the growth rate can also be useful to obtain interpretable numbers. Usually it is less important to know that the Dow-Jones index is 6,000 or so, than that it is to know that the rate of change with respect to the week before is, say, 2 percent.

A trending pattern in economic data will be reflected by a significant average growth rate. Alternative to (2.1), we can therefore consider the regression

$$y_t - y_{t-1} = \mu + u_t \quad t = 2,3,\ldots,n. \tag{2.2}$$

Notice that, just as in (2.1), we have effectively removed the trend in the regression (2.2), although now by differencing the data. A result of this operation is that there are now $n - 1$ observations that can be used to estimate μ. When it is possible to get rid of the trend by differencing the data, we say that y_t has a stochastic trend. If regression (2.1) is more adequate, we say that y_t has a deterministic trend. This illustrates that the concept of a trend is defined only in the context of a model. In chapter 4, I will return to this issue of modeling trends, and the important choice between (2.1) and (2.2).

The second panel of table 2.1 displays the estimates of μ in (2.2). It appears that μ parameters are slightly larger than the δ parameters in (2.1), although again the growth rate of the industry sector of about 10 percent by far exceeds the growth in the other sectors. Notice also that the estimated standard error of $\hat{\mu}$ in (2.2) is much larger than that of $\hat{\delta}$ in (2.1).

Changing trends

The trends in figure 2.1 are all of the familiar type, that is, many economic time series display an upward moving trend. It is however not necessary for

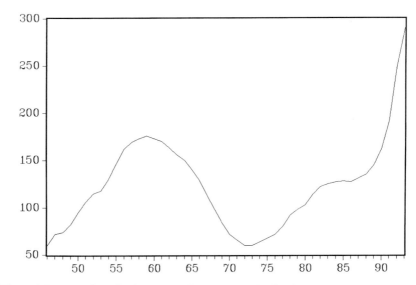

Figure 2.2 *Annual stock of motor cycles in The Netherlands, 1946–1993*

a trend to move upwards to be called a trend. It is also possible that a trend is less smooth and may display slowly changing tendencies which once in a while change directions.

An example of such a trending pattern is given in figure 2.2 where the annual stock of motor cycles in The Netherlands is displayed, for 1946–1993. From 1946 to about 1960, there is an increasing trend due to the increasing popularity of motor cycles because of their successful use in World War II. From 1960 to 1973 the stock of motor cycles tends toward zero because of the increasing willingness to own a car. From 1974 onwards there is again a trend upwards, which in the last few years seems to explode. This can be attributed to the fact that car owners may want to have a motor cycle as an additional leisure vehicle. In sum, for this time series we can observe several gradual changes in the trend. In chapter 4 it will appear that time series such as in figure 2.2 may have a so-called double stochastic trend, that is, the direction of trend itself is in turn a stochastic trend.

The motor cycles example in figure 2.2 highlights one possible approach to describing changing trends. An alternative method is allow the parameters in either (2.1) or (2.2) to change over time. Usually we consider such an approach in cases where it is reasonable to assume that certain exogenous shocks may have changed the direction of the trend. For example, the oil price shock in 1979.4 may have changed the direction of the trend in macroeconomic variables, see, e.g., Perron (1989). This can be illustrated by the

Table 2.2. *The significance of trends in US industrial production*

Sample	$\hat{\delta}$ in regression: $y_t = \alpha + \delta t + u_t$		$\hat{\mu}$ in regression: $y_t - y_{t-1} = \mu + u_t$	
1960.1–1991.4	0.825	(0.016)	0.818	(0.167)
1960.1–1979.4	1.023	(0.030)	1.007	(0.216)
1980.1–1991.4	0.758	(0.041)	0.507	(0.256)

Note:
The numbers in parentheses are estimated standard errors. All numbers are multiplied by 100.

(log of) industrial production index in the US (quarterly, seasonally adjusted), for which some regression results for (2.1) and (2.2) for different samples are presented in table 2.2.

The first panel again considers regression (2.1), of which the parameters are estimated for the complete sample 1960.1–1991.4 and for the sub-samples 1960.1 to 1979.4 and 1980.1 to 1991.4. Clearly, the estimated trend parameter $\hat{\delta}$ in the first sample (1.023) exceeds that of the second sample (0.758). A similar conclusion holds for regression (2.2) in the second panel of table 2.2 where growth in the period before the oil crisis is about 1 percent per quarter while it is only about 0.5 percent per quarter after that crisis. Again, the estimated standard error of $\hat{\mu}$ exceeds that of $\hat{\delta}$. The change in trend is visualized in figure 2.3.

A second example of changing trends is given in figure 2.4, which gives the monthly retail sales in The Netherlands. Until about 1979 we can observe a much steeper trend than after that period. A second feature of these data is the pronounced seasonal variation, a feature which will be discussed in the next subsection.

To conclude this introduction on trends in economic time series, it should be mentioned that there is no unique way to describe a trend. There are several different approaches, and each of these has a different impact on forecasting. When comparing figures 2.3 and 2.4 with figure 2.2, it is also clear that it may not be easy to make a proper choice between the versions of trend descriptions. Some of the selection methods will be discussed in chapter 4. The issue of breaking or changing deterministic trends will be treated in chapter 6.

2.2 Seasonality

When economic time series are observed each month or quarter, it is often the case that such a series displays a seasonal pattern. Similar to the feature

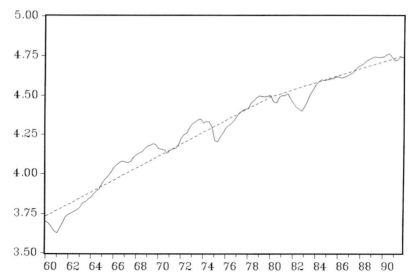

Figure 2.3 *Quarterly index of industrial production in the US, 1960.1–1991.4 (seasonally adjusted), with changing deterministic trend after 1979.4*

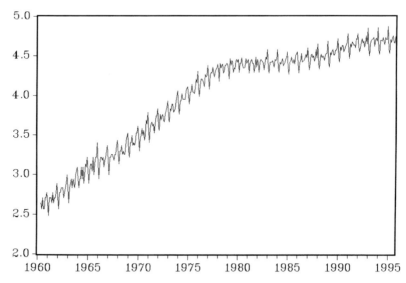

Figure 2.4 *Monthly index of retail sales in The Netherlands, 1960.05–1995.09 (not seasonally adjusted)*

of a trend, where the definition of a trend depends on the model used to describe the trend, there does not exist a very precise definition of *seasonality*. Usually we refer to seasonality when observations in certain seasons display strikingly different features to those in other seasons. For example, when retail sales are always large in the fourth quarter (because of Christmas spending) as can be observed from figure 2.4 where the peaks occur in December, we can say that retail sales display seasonality. It may also be that seasonality is reflected in the variance of a time series. For example, for daily observed stock market returns the volatility seems often highest on Mondays, basically because investors have to digest three days of news instead of only one day.

The number of seasons is denoted by S. When a calendar year is considered the benchmark, which is the case in this book, this S equals 4 for quarterly data. In case there are N years of observations y_t, the number of observations n equals SN. Of course, other benchmarks can also be considered. For example, in empirical finance it may be relevant to consider daily observations with a week as the benchmark, that is, N refers to weeks and $S = 5$, or even higher frequency data like minutes within a day.

Seasonality is often noticeable rightaway from a simple graph of the time series, as in figure 2.4. In other cases, more experience is needed to spot the seasonal variation. For example, in figure 2.5, where $y_t - y_{t-1}$ of the logs of US industrial production index (seasonally unadjusted) is given, it may not be evident how relatively important seasonality is. On the other hand, it seems that the pattern after, say, 1975 is different from the pattern before that year. Notice also the dip in 1975.1, which seems an irregular observation.

In case simple graphs are not informative enough to highlight possible seasonal variation, we can rely on the following regression, which is a modification of (2.2)

$$y_t - y_{t-1} = \mu_1 D_{1,t} + \mu_2 D_{2,t} + \ldots + \mu_S D_{S,t} + u_t \quad t = 2,3,\ldots,n, \qquad (2.3)$$

where $D_{s,t}$ is a seasonal dummy variable with

$$D_{s,t} = 1 \quad \text{when } t = (T-1)S + s, \quad \text{with } s = 1,2,\ldots,S \qquad (2.4)$$
$$\text{and } T = 1,2,\ldots,N$$

$$D_{s,t} = 0 \quad \text{otherwise.}$$

In case the u_t process does not contain any information on seasonality, we may also consider the R^2 of (2.3) as giving an indication of the "amount of deterministic seasonality," see, for example, Miron (1996).

Given the tentative evidence in figure 2.5 of possibly changing patterns in the growth rates of US industrial production, it is often useful to fit a

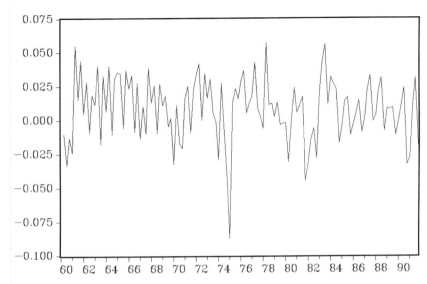

Figure 2.5 *First differences of the (log of) the industrial production index in the US (not seasonally adjusted)*

model like (2.3) for different subsamples. Here, S equals 4, and when the sample of 1960.1 to 1991.4 is divided into 1960.1–1975.4 and 1976.1 to 1991.4, the estimates of the parameters μ_1 to μ_4 are given in figure 2.6.

The R^2 values for these two samples are 0.269 and 0.254, respectively. From figure 2.6, we can observe that the growth rates in quarters 2 and 4 are largest in the first subsample (0.027 and 0.016), while quarters 2 and 3 are important in the second sample (0.017 and 0.017). In other words, it seems that seasonality has changed in the sense that the fourth quarter observations have become less important in more recent years.

Another example of a time series that displays marked seasonality is the log of quarterly consumption of non-durables in the UK for 1955.1–1988.4, which is depicted in figure 2.7.

Next to an upward moving trend, which seems to lose strength around 1973 but regains its path after 1985, there seems clear visual evidence of seasonality. This is confirmed by the results of regression (2.3), where for the subsamples 1955.1–1971.4 and 1972.1–1988.4 we obtain R^2 values of 0.971 and 0.965, respectively.

The two sets of estimates of the parameters μ_1 to μ_4 for this quarterly series are given in figure 2.8, from which it can be observed that relative to the first sample, the second quarter becomes less important and the fourth quarter becomes more important in the second subsample. In contrast to

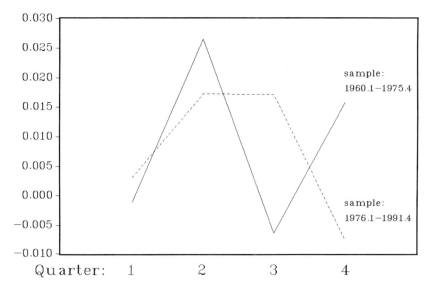

Figure 2.6 *Changing seasonality in US industrial production*

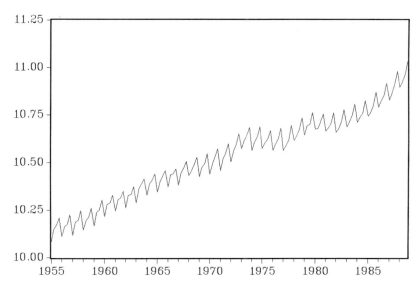

Figure 2.7 *Quarterly consumption of non-durables in the UK, 1955.1–1988.4*

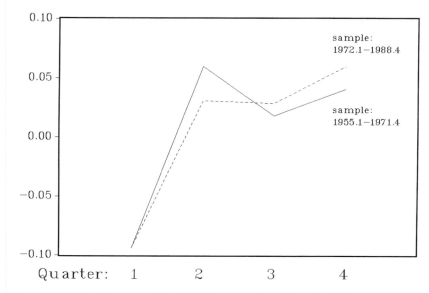

Figure 2.8 *Changing seasonality in UK consumption of non-durables*

figure 2.6, the changes in the seasonal pattern for consumption of non-durables are less substantial than those for US industrial production.

A final example of time series with pronounced seasonality is given in figure 2.9, where I depict (logs of the) four-weekly advertising expenditures on radio and television in The Netherlands for 1978.01–1994.13.

For these two marketing time series it is clear that television advertising displays quite some seasonal fluctuation throughout the entire sample, where possibly there are some changes toward the end of the sample, and that radio advertising has seasonality only in about the last five years. This last period corresponds to the period where an additional commercial network (RTL-4) was introduced in The Netherlands. Furthermore, there seems to be a structural break in the radio series around observation 53. This break is related to an increase in radio broadcasting minutes in January 1982. Additionally, there is some visual evidence that the trend changes over time. In chapter 6, I return to analyzing the consequences of such mean shifts on time series modeling.

To investigate the effect of the introduction of RTL-4 on seasonality in television advertising, consider again the results of the regression in (2.3) for two subsamples, which are depicted in figure 2.10.

It is clear from figure 2.10 that seasonality seems to increase in the second subsample since then the estimates of μ_s, $s = 1,2,\dots,13$ show more volatility.

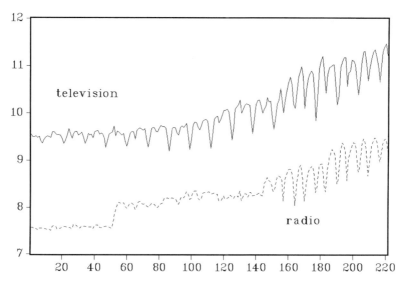

Figure 2.9 *Four-weekly advertising expenditures on radio and television in The Netherlands (1978.01–1994.13)*

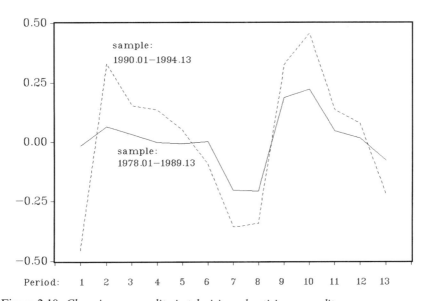

Figure 2.10 *Changing seasonality in television advertising expenditures*

Generally, it appears that many seasonally observed business and economic time series display seasonality in the sense that the observations in certain seasons have properties that differ from those data points in other seasons. A second feature of many economic time series is that seasonality changes over time. Sometimes these changes appear abrupt, as is the case for advertising on the radio in figure 2.9, and sometimes such changes occur only slowly, as is the case for UK non-durables. In chapter 5, I will review methods to describe and forecast economic time series with changing seasonality.

2.3   Aberrant observations

The radio advertising series in figure 2.9 indicates that time series may be subject to so-called regime shifts. The mean of the observations in the first part of the sample is smaller than that in the second part of the sample, and in the third part there even emerges a seasonal pattern that was previously absent. Obviously, account should be taken of such changing patterns when forecasting out of sample. For example, if we were to analyze the entire sample of the radio advertising series with a model that does not allow for seasonality, it is likely that inaccurate forecasts would be made for certain seasons. Furthermore, when the mean shift around observation 53 is neglected, we would also expect a systematic bias in forecasts. This implies that account should be taken for the possibility that there are periods or subsamples that can make time series modeling difficult.

Possibly distorting observations do not necessarily come in a sequence as in the radio advertising example. It may also be that only single observations have a major impact on time series modeling and forecasting. Such data points are called aberrant observations. As an illustration, consider the differenced y_t, that is, $y_t - y_{t-1}$, where $y_t = \log(w_t)$, with w_t the price level, and the inflation rate $(w_t - w_{t-1})/w_{t-1}$ in Argentina, for the sample 1970.1–1989.4 in figure 2.11.

The first obvious feature of these graphs is that in the case where the quarterly inflation rate is high (as is the case in 1989.3 where it is about 500 percent), the differenced y_t series is not a good approximation to the inflation rate (since the 1989.3 observation would now correspond to about 200 percent). For convenience I analyze $y_t - y_{t-1}$ in the sequel, since it smooths the variance of the time series, although of course preference could be given to modeling the inflation rate itself.

A second obvious feature of the graphs in figure 2.11 is that the data in 1989 seem to be quite different from those observations the years before. In fact, if there is any correlation between $y_t - y_{t-1}$ and $y_{t-1} - y_{t-2}$, such a

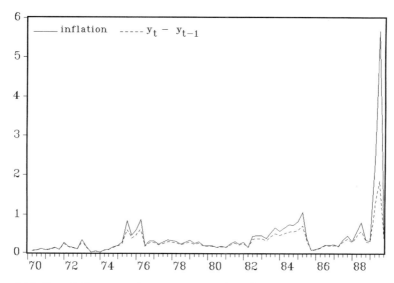

Figure 2.11 *First differences in log prices versus the inflation rate: the case of Argentina, 1970.1–1989.4*

correlation may be affected by these observations. In other words, when considering the following simple regression

$$y_t - y_{t-1} = \alpha + \rho(y_{t-1} - y_{t-2}) + u_t, \quad t = 3,4,\dots,n \tag{2.5}$$

we would expect that an estimate of ρ is influenced by the data points in the last year. It should be mentioned that a model as in (2.5) is called a first order autoregressive model [AR(1)] for $y_t - y_{t-1}$, see chapter 3. It reflects the possible occurrence that this quarter's price change is likely to be correlated with the price change in the previous quarter.

When the model in (2.5) is quantified for $n-2$ observations (which is 78 here since the estimation sample runs from 1970.3 to 1989.4), the estimated value of ρ equals $\hat\rho = 0.561$ (0.094), where the estimated standard error is in parentheses. This regression result is summarized in figure 2.12, where the slope of the regression line equals 0.561.

As is obvious from this graph, there are at least three observations that are far away from the regression line. These three observations are 1989.2, 1989.3, and 1989.4. At first sight, it is difficult to get a clear picture of how each of these observations affects the regression line and hence $\hat\rho$. Therefore, ρ in (2.5) is estimated again, while now deleting the 1989 observations. The result is displayed in figure 2.13.

It seems that the regression line is somewhat steeper than that in figure

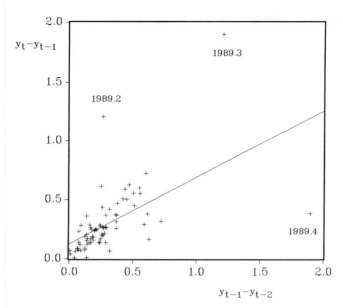

Figure 2.12 *Regression of first differences in log prices in Argentina at time t on differences at time t-1: all observations*

2.12. Indeed, the ρ is now estimated as $\hat{\rho} = 0.704$ (0.082). Even though this value may not differ significantly from the $\hat{\rho}$ for all data, we may expect the forecasts from both models to differ. The fact that in figure 2.13 all observations seem to correspond more to the regression line as they are in figure 2.12 is reflected by the smaller standard error (0.082 versus 0.094). In sum, it appears that only a few observations can affect the correlation in a time series y_t, and also the precision of an estimate of such a correlation. In chapter 6, I will return to a discussion of the effect on modeling and forecasting of such aberrant data points.

Needless to say, such aberrant data points do not necessarily appear in easily identifiable groups or years. Consider for example the relative price of a fast-moving consumer good (observed during 103 weeks, see the data appendix) in figure 2.14.

Since these so-called scanning data concern weekly observations, aberrant observations are more likely since such data points are not averaged out as in the case with, say the quarterly data for the same series. Clearly, there seem to be at least five or six (but probably more) observations that are somehow likely to have an impact on time series modeling of this series. Such observations may for example be due to price changes in competitive products and promotional activities, see Blattberg, Briesch, and Fox (1995)

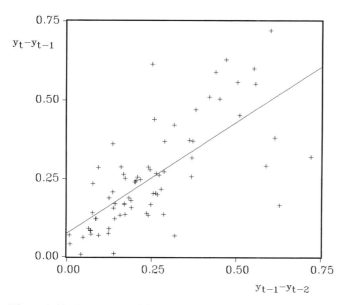

Figure 2.13 *Regression of first differences in log prices in Argentina at time t on differences at time t-1: all observations without 1989.1–1989.4*

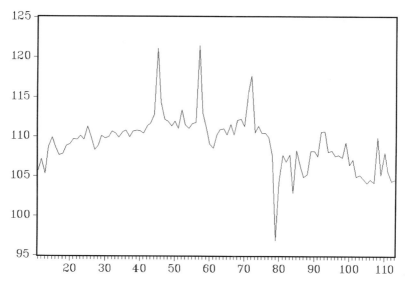

Figure 2.14 *Weekly relative price of a fast moving consumer good (week 11 in 1989 to week 8 in 1991)*

and Leone (1987) on the effects of promotions on price levels. Chapter 6 discusses methods to detect several types of aberrant observations, and also methods to take account of such data for forecasting. An important issue in that chapter is the effect of such observations on the selection of models for trends and seasonality.

2.4   Conditional heteroskedasticity

A fourth feature of economic time series, and in particular of financial time series, is that aberrant observations tend to emerge in clusters. Intuitively, if on a certain day news arrives on a stock market, we may react by selling or buying many stocks, while the day after the news has been digested and valued more properly, we may wish to return to the behavior of before the arrival of the news. This pattern would be reflected by (a possibly large) increase or decrease in the returns on one day followed by an opposite change on the next day. In a sense, we can interpret these two observations as two aberrant observations in a row. On the other hand, we may assume that the second sharp increase or decrease in returns is caused by the first, and hence that the two sudden changes in returns are correlated.

Consider for example the 770 consecutive returns on the Dow-Jones index, from week 1 in 1980 to week 39 in 1994, as they are given in figure 2.15.

These returns concern the end-of-the-week returns, where a week is assumed to run from Thursday to Wednesday. Observation 408 corresponds to the week commencing Monday, October 19, 1987. Around that so-called Black Monday, the returns on the Dow-Jones index decreased by about 17 percent. Immediately after that observation, we can find several data points that are large in absolute value. Additionally, in other parts of the sample, we can observe "bubbles," i.e., clusters of observations with large variances. This phenomenon is called volatility clustering or, otherwise, conditional heteroskedasticity.

Allowing for the possibility that high volatility is followed by high volatility, and that low volatility will be followed by low volatility, where volatility is defined in terms of the returns themselves, we can consider the presence of so-called conditional heteroskedasticity. This time series feature can be put forward by the simple regression

$$(y_t - y_{t-1})^2 = \alpha + \rho(y_{t-1} - y_{t-2})^2 + u_t, \quad t = 3,4,\dots,n, \tag{2.6}$$

where $(y_t - y_{t-1})^2$ represents the variance of the returns. For the sample of 768 data points (770 minus 2 starting values), we obtain $\hat{\rho} = 0.292$ (0.035), where the estimated standard error is given in parentheses. This suggests that there is positive correlation between the variances of the returns.

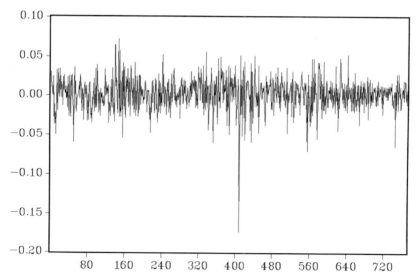

Figure 2.15 *Returns on the weekly Dow-Jones index (week 1 in 1980 to week 39 in 1994)*

Additionally, when $(y_t - y_{t-1})^2$ is replaced by $|y_t - y_{t-1}|$, the absolute value of the return, the regression in (2.6) yields $\hat{\rho} = 0.213$ (0.035). This result also points toward the presence of volatility clustering.

In case of volatility clustering, we may wish to exploit this in order to forecast future volatility. Since this variable is a measure of risk, such forecasts can be useful to evaluate investment strategies. Furthermore, it can be useful for decisions on buying or selling options or other derivatives. Time series models for conditional volatility are often applied in practice, and some of these models will be discussed in chapter 7.

2.5 Non-linearity

The fifth and final feature of several economic time series that is treated in this book is non-linearity. Although the best definition of non-linearity may perhaps be "everything other than linearity," for economic time series we usually rely on concepts such as regime switches or so-called state dependency. The latter indicates that the behavior of a time series is different depending on its current state. Such a state may be a volatile period for a financial market, as discussed in the previous section, or it may be a recession. When the behavior of a time series is different across such discrete states, we can also call this regime-switching behavior. It should be

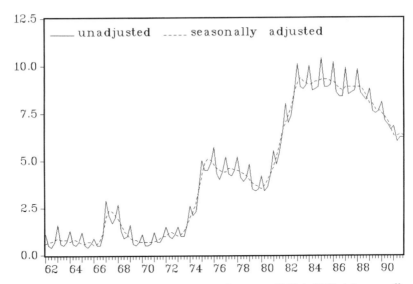

Figure 2.16 *Quarterly unemployment rate in Germany, 1962.1–1991.4 (seasonally adjusted and not seasonally adjusted)*

mentioned that such a state (as a recession) may concern only a few observations. Furthermore, in case there are regime switches, there must also be so-called thresholds, which mark the differences between the regimes. Finally, notice that regime switching can show similarity with structural breaks. For example, the oil crisis in quarter 4 of 1979 may have changed the trend in US industrial production, see figure 2.3.

Non-linear behavior is often quite obvious for certain macroeconomic time series in case the growth rate $(y_t - y_{t-1})$ or the change $(w_t - w_{t-1})$ takes different average values across states. Consider for example the unemployment rate in Germany for 1962.1 to 1991.4 in figure 2.16.

Clearly, unemployment sometimes rises quite rapidly, usually in the recession years 1967, 1974–1975, and 1980–1982, while it decreases very slowly, usually in times of expansions. This asymmetry can be formalized by estimating the parameters in the following simple regression

$$y_t - y_{t-1} = \mu_1 I_t[\text{expansion year}] + \mu_2 I_t[\text{recession year}]$$
$$+ u_t, \quad t = 2, 3, \ldots n, \tag{2.7}$$

where $I_t[.]$ is an indicator variable, which allows the absolute value of the rate of change to vary across the two states, say, "decreasing y_t" and "increasing y_t" from μ_1 to μ_2, where μ_1 may be different from $-\mu_2$. For the German seasonally adjusted unemployment rate, we find that $\hat{\mu}_1 = -0.040$

and $\hat{\mu}_2 = 0.388$, indicating that when the unemployment rate increases (in recessions), it rises faster than when it goes down (in expansions). This regression result seems to confirm the visual impressions from figure 2.16.

A second example is given by seasonally adjusted industrial production in the US, as depicted in figure 2.3. This time series is often considered to be non-linear, in the sense that the drop in this variable during recessions is larger than its increase in other periods. The regression in (2.7) yields for this variable that $\hat{\mu}_1 = -0.017$ and $\hat{\mu}_2 = 0.016$, hence on average the decrease is slightly larger than is the increase. Notice that the so-called threshold value for $y_t - y_{t-1}$ equals 0. In practice we can allow for more flexibility in this choice, for example by estimating μ_1 and μ_2 simultaneously with c, the unknown value of the threshold. Additionally, we can if we wish allow for more than two regimes.

When a non-linear time series model is used to describe and forecast an economic variable, much more effort is usually needed to specify the model and to estimate its parameters. A key reason is that this option leads to a wide variety of possible models. In practice therefore we start with a diagnostic measure to obtain a first and tentative impression of what type of non-linear model could be useful. In chapter 8, I will discuss several non-linear time series models that are often used in practice. Furthermore, I will review diagnostics that can guide model selection.

2.6   Common features

Many time series in economics and business usually have at least one of the above five features. For example, the graphs for the German unemployment rate in figure 2.16 show that this variable displays seasonality, non-linearity, and possibly also some aberrant observations. As another example, the advertising expenditure series in figure 2.9 seems to display structural breaks, changing seasonality, and trends. Finally, the Dow-Jones index may be heteroskedastic, but there may also be aberrant observations (such as perhaps the week around Black Monday).

In case of univariate time series modeling, that is, when we only analyze and forecast y_t given its own past pattern, it is important to take account of all of the observed features, which are illuminated by simple auxiliary regressions and specific insightful graphs. In case we want to incorporate past patterns of variables as, say, x_t and z_t to describe and forecast y_t, and possibly to use the past of y_t to describe and forecast x_t and z_t, the so-called multivariate time series models are considered. Some of the important aspects of these models are discussed in chapter 9.

Given all the possible features and also given the possible wish to use multivariate models, it is likely that many decisions will have to be made.

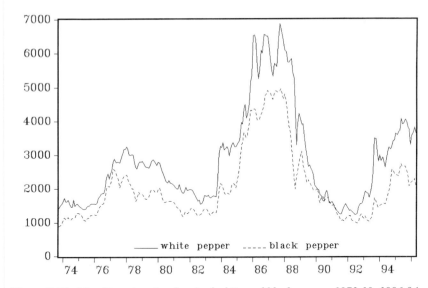

Figure 2.17 *Monthly prices (no logs) of white and black pepper, 1973.10–1996.04*

One way to reduce the number of decisions is to search for the presence of common features across univariate time series. Additionally, such common features may themselves be the focus of interest. For example, a relevant question for the output in the five sectors in China, as displayed in figure 2.1, is whether these have common growth or whether the industry sector significantly outgrows the other four sectors. For the same five variables, we may wonder whether the transportation and commerce sectors have in fact the same trend.

Figure 2.17 displays the monthly prices of black and white pepper over more than two decades. Given that these two products can be substitutes, it would be reasonable to expect the prices of these commodities to move together over time. Because of international pricing agreements, temporary overproduction, or failure of crops, prices can display trending behavior, although the direction of these trends may not be constant over time. This expectation is reflected by the graphs in figure 2.17 where pepper undergoes some periods with increasing prices, while also (as for example between 1977 and 1982) the prices tend downwards for longer periods. Furthermore, there are sequences of months with very large increases or decreases in prices. Hence, as well as trends pepper prices display volatility clustering. The graphs in figure 2.17 clearly suggest common patterns across pepper prices, such as common trends and common conditional volatility. The common feature can then be interpreted as that the risk

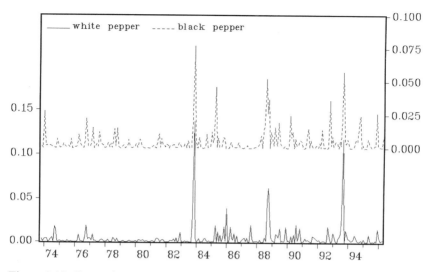

Figure 2.18 *Squared returns on white and black pepper*

involved in buying or selling black or white pepper is about the same. When again the time series $(y_t - y_{t-1})^2$ is taken as a measure of this risk, the graphs of these time series for the two commodities in figure 2.18 clearly suggest such common risk.

A final example of possibly common features is given by the series of advertising expenditures on radio and television in figure 2.9. Since the launch of a new commercial network in The Netherlands (in October 1989, which is about observation 154), it is noticeable that radio and television advertising seem to display common seasonality. This common feature is visualized in figure 2.19, where the growth rates $y_t - y_{t-1}$ of each of these series for the sample 157 to 221 (that is, the last five years) are presented.

Except for a few observations, it seems that the growth rates of both series match quite well. I will test for this common feature in chapter 10.

Chapter 10 of this book is mainly dedicated to common trends (which is also called cointegration) and common seasonality. The simple framework that is often used to investigate common features is

$$y_t = \beta x_t + u_t, \tag{2.8}$$

where y_t and x_t have a certain feature and the residual time series u_t does not have this feature. For example, y_t and x_t may both have a trend, while u_t does not show trending behavior. Key topics of chapter 10 are how to find a proper value of β and how to investigate the features of the unobserved u_t time series.

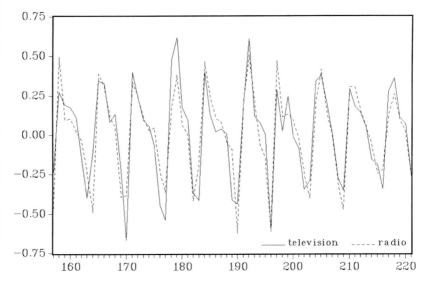

Figure 2.19 *Common seasonality in radio and television advertising expenditures 1990.01–1994.13*

Conclusion

In this chapter I have illustrated through several examples (and more examples will follow in later chapters) that business and economic time series tend to display such features as trends, seasonality, aberrant observations, conditionally varying variance, and/or non-linearity. Before we can construct sensible out-of-sample forecasts of such time series, each of these features can best be described by a time series model that is specifically designed for that purpose. In chapters 4 to 8, I will consider several such models. Needless to say, in practice such models are usually combined into a single model that deals with more than one feature. The discussion in these five chapters is limited to univariate time series models. Before I turn to these chapters, I first give an overview in chapter 3 of some of the key concepts in univariate time series analysis in general. Chapter 9 extends this chapter 3 to multivariate models, and chapter 10 discusses common features. The empirical sample series already used in this introductory chapter will also be used in illustrative examples below.

3 Useful concepts in univariate time series analysis

In this chapter I discuss several concepts which are in principle useful for the analysis of such time series as depicted in the previous chapter. Examples of these concepts are autoregressive moving average models, autocorrelation functions, estimation, diagnostic measures, model selection and forecasting. In this chapter these concepts are treated within the context of non-seasonal, linear and non-trending univariate time series with constant variance. Even although none of the features in chapter 2 will be explicitly dealt with, the above concepts are generally useful and often can be modified to allow for the apparent empirical features of the time series at hand.

The technical level in this chapter is kept at a moderate level. The main focus is on explaining why the concepts are useful, how the relevant methods can be calculated in practice, and how the outcomes can be interpreted. Needless to say that there will be many different opinions on, for example, how best to explain the origin of ARMA models (see section 3.1), how to estimate certain autocorrelation functions (see section 3.2), and how to select a useful model (see section 3.4). Also, there are several concepts that I do not treat in detail here. The content of the present chapter merely reflects what should be a useful basis for modeling real-life time series such as those given in the previous chapter. It is not my intention to downplay the importance of formal asymptotic results for the practical techniques we use in small samples, but it is the intention to keep matters simple. I recommend the interested reader to consult more advanced time series textbooks such as T.W. Anderson (1971), Box and Jenkins (1970), Fuller (1976), Abraham and Ledolter (1983), Granger and Newbold (1986), Hamilton (1994), etc. It is my experience that with the tools outlined in this chapter, it is possible to construct a time series model for forecasting and to understand how such models can be enlarged so that features such as seasonality and non-linearity can be incorporated.

3.1   Autoregressive moving average models

As before, the univariate time series of interest is denoted by y_t, where y_t can be log (w_t), with w_t being the originally observed time series. The y_t data are observed for $t = 1,2,...,n$. The key aspect of time series, which contrasts with cross-section data, is that the y_t data are observed in a sequence, that is, at time $t-1$ the observation at time t is yet unknown, while all observations until and including $t-1$ are known. Formally, we may denote this as Y_{t-1}, the information set at time $t-1$. The fact that time series data are observed in a sequence implies that there can be information in the set Y_{t-1} that can be exploited to explain or forecast y_t. In fact, if the stock of motor cycles is 200,000 this year, and it was 180,000 last year, it is likely that next year's stock will be closer to say 220,000 than to 100,000.

In case the observations y_{t-k} for $k = 1,2,...$ are not informative for the value of this variable at time t, and if the best prediction or expectation $[E]$ for y_{n+h} is equal to zero, such a time series is called a white noise time series. In this book a white noise time series will be denoted by ε_t. A more formal definition of this series is given by

$$E(\varepsilon_t) = 0 \qquad t = 1,2,...,n \qquad (3.1)$$

$$E(\varepsilon_t^2) = \sigma^2 \qquad t = 1,2,...,n \qquad (3.2)$$

$$E(\varepsilon_s \varepsilon_t) = 0 \qquad s,t = 1,2,...,n \text{ and } s \neq t, \qquad (3.3)$$

which means that the mean of ε_t equals zero, that all observations ε_t have the same variance σ^2, and that there is no (linear) correlation between any past, current, and future ε_t observations. It should be mentioned here that this definition allows that ε_{n+h} can be forecasted using non-linear functions such as $\varepsilon_{t-1}\varepsilon_{t-2}$, but a discussion of such so-called bilinear models is postponed to chapter 8.

Autoregressive [AR] model

In many cases, however, it occurs that the observations at time t depend on observations at $t-1$, $t-2$, and so on. Because the latter observations involve a time lag between t and $t-k$, with $k = 1,2,...$, we usually say that y_t depends on its lagged values $y_{t-1}, y_{t-2},...$, or briefly, on its lags. In order to keep notation simple, it is convenient to write this lagging of y_t in terms of the so-called lag operator L. This operator is defined by

$$L^k y_t = y_{t-k} \quad \text{for } k = ... -2, -1, 0, 1, 2, ... \qquad (3.4)$$

Hence, $L^{-2}y_t$ means y_{t+2} and $L^0 y_t$ means y_t. The algebra of the L operator is discussed in, for example, Dhrymes (1981, pp. 19–24). It is shown that the algebra of polynomials $R\,(L)$, where $R\,(L)$ is defined as the set of all finite linear combinations of elements of the set $\{L^k;\ k=\ldots-2,-1,0,1,2,\ldots\}$ is isomorphic to the algebra of polynomial functions $R(z)$. An implication of this formal statement is that, in a sense, we can use L in products and ratios, and in adding and subtracting operations. For example, when $0<\alpha<1$, we can write

$$(1-\alpha L)^{-1}=1+\alpha L+\alpha^2 L^2+\alpha^3 L^3+\ldots \tag{3.5}$$

As another example, we have

$$(1+L^2)\,(1-L^2)=1-L^4 \tag{3.6}$$

which can be useful for summarizing complicated time series models.

Suppose now that the observations in the time series y_t depend on p of its lagged observations, that is, that y_t can be described by the linear model

$$y_t-\phi_1 y_{t-1}-\phi_2 y_{t-2}-\ldots-\phi_p y_{t-p}=\varepsilon_t \quad t=p+1,p+2,\ldots,n, \tag{3.7}$$

where ϕ_1, ϕ_2 to ϕ_p are unknown parameters. In practice, the observations on ε_t are not directly observed and have to be estimated from the data, based on the presupposed model for y_t. In case of (3.7), y_t can be described by a regression model that includes only lagged y_t variables, and hence this model (3.7) is usually called an autoregressive model of order p [AR(p)], or an autoregression of order p. With the lag operator, the expression in (3.7) can be abbreviated as

$$\phi_p\,(L)y_t=\varepsilon_t \tag{3.8}$$

where

$$\phi_p\,(L)=1-\phi_1 L-\ldots-\phi_p L^p \tag{3.9}$$

which is called the AR-polynomial in L of order p. The weights on the lags are the parameters ϕ_1 to ϕ_p, and these express to what extent y_t depends on its past. Since the observation at any time t depends on the past p observations, it is clear that, strictly speaking, (3.7) assumes that y_t somehow depends on all past observations. In order to forecast y_{n+h}, it should first of all hold that this dependence on the past is constant. Indeed, if for any time t this dependence would differ, there is no point in trying to forecast y_{n+h} since for any horizon h the forecast function may differ. Furthermore, in order to make sensible statements about y_{n+h}, it should hold that the immediate past is more important than the less recent. In other words, if we were to measure the impact of the observation at time $t=10$, y_{10}, we would want it to be less large for, say, y_{80} than for y_{11}. Since y_{10} involves a white noise observation ε_{10}, or, as commonly said, a shock at time 10, we can also rephrase this by stating that the impact of the shock at $t = 10$ should be less important for the observation y_{80} than for y_{11}.

In terms of (3.7), this can be put somewhat more formally by imposing on the parameters ϕ_1 to ϕ_p that when this equation is rewritten as

$$y_t = [\phi_p (L)]^{-1} \varepsilon_t \cong \sum_{i=0}^{n-1} \theta_i \varepsilon_{t-i} + y_0, \tag{3.10}$$

where y_0 summarizes a function of pre-sample starting-values and parameters ϕ_1 to ϕ_p, the values of θ_i converge toward zero when $n - 1$ gets larger, or better, the effect of shocks dies out when $\sum_{i=1}^{\infty} |\theta_i| < \infty$. To attach some interpretation to this statement, consider the first order autoregression

$$y_t = \phi_1 y_{t-1} + \varepsilon_t, \quad t = 2,3,\ldots,n. \tag{3.11}$$

Since (3.11) implies that

$$y_1 = \phi_1 y_0 + \varepsilon_1, \tag{3.12}$$

where y_0 is a pre-sample starting value (which is usually unknown, and hence in practice is set equal to the first observation in case of an AR(1) model), and furthermore since (3.11) implies that

$$y_2 = \phi_1 y_1 + \varepsilon_2 = \phi_1 \phi_1 y_0 + \phi_1 \varepsilon_1 + \varepsilon_2$$
$$y_3 = \phi_1 y_2 + \varepsilon_3 = \phi_1 (\phi_1 \phi_1 y_0 + \phi_1 \varepsilon_1 + \varepsilon_2) + \varepsilon_3$$
$$\ldots$$
$$y_t = (\phi_1)^t y_0 + (\phi_1)^{t-1} \varepsilon_1 + (\phi_1)^{t-2} \varepsilon_2 + \ldots + \varepsilon_t$$

(3.11) can be rewritten as

$$y_t = (\phi_1)^t y_0 + \sum_{i=0}^{t-1} (\phi_1)^i \varepsilon_{t-i}, \quad t = 1,2,\ldots,n. \tag{3.13}$$

Clearly, the parameters in (3.13) for the observations ε_t converge to zero with increasing i when $|\phi_1| < 1$. Also, $\sum_{i=0}^{\infty} (\phi_i)^i < \infty$. When ϕ_1 exceeds 1, (3.13) shows that the time series is explosive, which is a feature that does not often occur in practice. In case of explosive data, it is usual to transform these by taking the natural logarithms once or twice. In this book, I exclude this explosive case. When ϕ_1 is equal to 1, (3.13) simply becomes

$$y_t = y_0 + \sum_{i=0}^{t-1} \varepsilon_{t-i} \quad t = 1,2,\ldots,n \tag{3.14}$$

for which it is obvious that the effects of, say, ε_1 and ε_{10} on y_{20} are both equal to 1.

In a sense, when y_t is as in (3.14), it is clear that it can undergo wild fluctuations since if by any chance a value of, say, ε_{10} is very large and all its sequential values are small, the direction of the time series after time $t = 10$

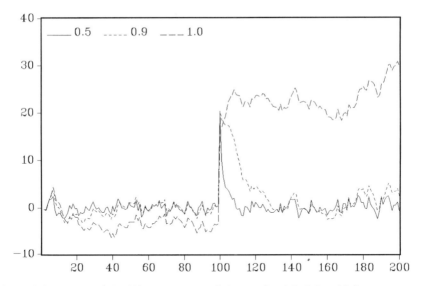

Figure 3.1   *Generated AR(1) time series with ϕ_1 equal to 0.5, 0.9 and 1.0*

can change quite dramatically. Put otherwise, such a time series is highly unpredictable. An AR(1) model with $\phi_1 = 1$ is therefore called a *random walk* model. To illustrate the impact of the value of ϕ_1 on the pattern of y_t, consider the three simulated time series for 200 observations in figure 3.1.

These data are generated as follows. First, 200 numbers are generated from 200 independent standard normal distributions, denoted as $N(0,1)$. These are white noise observations since these are independently drawn from distributions with the same variance $\sigma^2 = 1$. Next, the observation ε_{100} is replaced by $\varepsilon_{100} + 20$. Thirdly, y_1 is set equal to zero. Finally, 199 observations y_t are generated by $y_t = \phi_1 y_{t-1} + \varepsilon_t$ for t running from 2 to 200. The values of ϕ_1 are set at 0.5, 0.9, and 1.0, yielding three different time series, which are all constructed from the same error time series ε_t. The solid line in figure 3.1 corresponds with $\phi_1 = 0.5$, and it shows a large spike at observation 100. The effect of ε_{100} dies out fairly quickly, as can be observed from the fact that the time series does return quickly to its average level. The effect of the added value of 20 to ε_t at time 100 is 10 at $t = 101$, 5 at $t = 102$, and is negligible at $t = 110$. This is not the case when $\phi_1 = 0.9$, as can be seen from the graph of the relevant time series in figure 3.1. Indeed, it takes some time before $(0.9)^i$ times 20 becomes reasonably small. However, in both these cases, the data have a tendency of mean reversion. Finally, and most obvious from the third graph in this figure 3.1, the time series does not return to its original average level after observation 100 when $\phi_1 = 1.0$.

Hence, this shock seems to have changed the direction of the time series, that is, this shock seems to have a permanent effect. This is in contrast to the other two cases where shocks appear to have only transitory effects.

In this chapter I confine the discussion to time series where shocks have only transitory effects. In the case where a variable displays permanent effects of shocks, the series is usually transformed to a time series with transitory effects by taking first differences of the time series y_t. This is related to the concept of stationarity, which will be discussed in some detail in chapter 4. We then proceed with the analysis of $y_t - y_{t-1}$ instead of y_t. The motivation is that when y_t is a random walk time series as in (3.14), that is

$$y_t = y_{t-1} + \varepsilon_t \qquad (3.15)$$

all shocks have a permanent effect, as can observed from (3.14) and figure 3.1. However, for the transformed time series $z_t = y_t - y_{t-1}$, which can be described by the simple white noise model, that is

$$z_t = y_t - y_{t-1} = \varepsilon_t \qquad (3.16)$$

the past shocks ε_t have only transitory effects. In other words, while, say, ε_{100} can change the direction of y_t after $t = 100$ permanently, it does not do so for the direction of $y_t - y_{t-1}$ in (3.16). Note again that when y_t is $\log(w_t)$, the z_t variable in (3.16) approximately equals the growth rate of w_t.

It may be the case that it is necessary to difference y_t twice to obtain the desired result. Again, in order to keep the notation simple the differencing filter or differencing operator Δ_j is often used, which is defined by

$$\Delta_j^d = (1 - L^j)^d \quad \text{for } d,j = \ldots, -2, -1, 0, 1, 2, \ldots \qquad (3.17)$$

In practice it is usual to consider the cases where $j = 1$ or S (with S being the number of seasons) and d is equal to 0, 1, or 2. Notice that when d is 2, and $y_t = \log(w_t)$, the resultant second order differenced series is the change in the growth rate of w_t. In the case where a time series needs to be differenced d times, it is said that it is *integrated of order d*, abbreviated as I (d). When y_t is an I (d) time series, and after differencing d times it can be modeled using an AR(p) model, this model for y_t can be written as

$$\Delta_1^d y_t - \phi_1 \Delta_1^d y_{t-1} - \ldots - \phi_p \Delta_1^d y_{t-p} = \varepsilon_t, \quad t = p + d, p + d + 1, \ldots, n, \quad (3.18)$$

The estimation sample n decreases to $n - p - d$ observations since differencing a time series d times absorbs the first d data points. The model in (3.18) is usually abbreviated as an ARI(p,d) model.

Another terminology for permanent or transitory effects of shocks is based on the roots of the characteristic polynomial of an AR(p) model. Consider again the AR(1) model in (3.11). Its characteristic polynomial is

$$1 - \phi_1 z = 0, \tag{3.19}$$

and its solution (or root) is $(\phi_1)^{-1}$. When $\phi_1 = 1$, this solution equals 1, and hence, the relevant AR(1) polynomial is said to have a unit root. When ϕ_1 is smaller than 1, as is the case for two of the three time series in figure 3.2, the root of (3.19) exceeds 1. Since in higher order AR(p) models there may be complex roots, we say that with $\phi_1 < 1$, the solution to (3.19) is outside the unit circle. In chapter 5, when discussing seasonality, we will study the possibility of complex unit roots for seasonal time series. In this chapter, I confine the discussion to real unit roots.

It can be shown that a time series does not need to be differenced when the solutions to such characteristic polynomials as

$$1 - \phi_1 z - \ldots - \phi_p z^p = 0 \tag{3.20}$$

or equivalently

$$(1 - \alpha_1 L)(1 - \alpha_2 L)\ldots(1 - \alpha_p L) = 0 \tag{3.21}$$

are outside the unit circle, see, for example, Fuller (1976). In practice this can be hard to verify, especially because the ϕ_i parameters have to be estimated from the available data. Since we are mainly interested to know whether we need to difference or not, it is usual to check only whether one or more of the solutions of the characteristic polynomial are exactly equal to 1. For example, the ARI($p,\bar{a}$) model (3.18) with characteristic polynomial

$$(1-z)^d - \phi_1(1-z)^d z - \ldots - \phi_p (1-z)^d z^p = 0 \tag{3.22}$$

clearly has at least d solutions $z = 1$. In chapter 4, I continue with focusing on models with d possibly unequal to 0. In fact, in practice an estimate for d should be obtained, and it appears that this is not easy. Furthermore, when d equals 1, we say that the corresponding time series has a stochastic trend. For forecasting purposes it is quite important to make a proper choice between a stochastic trend (as in (2.2)) and a deterministic trend (as in (2.1)), and therefore I postpone this discussion to the next chapter.

Autoregressive moving average [ARMA] model

It may well occur that the value of p in the AR(p) model as in (3.7) is quite large, that is, many lags of y_t are needed in a regression model like (3.7) such that the residuals of the regression mimic the presumed white noise properties in (3.1)–(3.3). When p increases, the number of unknown parameters in (3.7) to be estimated increases as well. Making use of the properties of the L operator as in (3.5) and (3.6), it is possible to approximate a lengthy

AR polynomial by a ratio of two polynomials which in sum involve less parameters. Otherwise formulated, we may consider approximating the $\phi_p(L)$ in (3.7) by the ratio of a different $\phi_p(L)$ (with this p usually smaller than the previous one) and the polynomial $\theta_q(L)$. The resultant univariate time series model is then

$$[\phi_p(L)/\theta_q(L)]y_t = \varepsilon_t$$

or better

$$\phi_p(L)y_t = \theta_q(L)\varepsilon_t, \quad t = p+1, p+2, \ldots, n \tag{3.23}$$

with

$$\phi_p(L) = 1 - \phi_1 L - \ldots - \phi_p L^p,$$
$$\theta_q(L) = 1 + \theta_1 L + \ldots + \theta_q L^q,$$

where this last notational convention is chosen such that the model in (3.23) amounts to the regression model

$$y_t = \phi_1 y_{t-1} + \ldots + \phi_p y_{t-p} + \varepsilon_t + \theta_1 \varepsilon_{t-1} + \ldots + \theta_q \varepsilon_{t-q}. \tag{3.24}$$

This model is called an autoregressive moving average model of order (p,q), or briefly, ARMA(p,q). When the y_t series is replaced by $\Delta_1^d y_t$, we say that y_t is described by an autoregressive integrated moving average model of order (p,d,q), or briefly ARIMA(p,d,q). It is exactly this class of univariate time series models that became very popular with practitioners through the seminal work of Box and Jenkins (1970). The label moving average is assigned to this model since the right-hand side part of (3.23) is in a sense a moving average of ε_t terms.

It should be mentioned that for (3.24) to be useful in practice, it is usually required that $p+q$ in (3.24) is smaller than p in (3.7) for an AR(p) model. Furthermore, for many practical purposes consideration is usually given to the ARI model instead of the ARIMA model. The main reasons are that the parameters in ARI models can be easily estimated (see section 3.3), that any diagnostic measures can be easily calculated (see also section 3.3), and that such ARI(p,d) models can be easily extended to allow for seasonality, shifts in mean or trends, and non-linearity.

Moving average [MA] model

In some practical cases it may however be convenient to consider only a very simple variant of an ARMA(p,q) model, that is, the MA(q) model given by

$$y_t = \varepsilon_t + \theta_1 \varepsilon_{t-1} + \ldots + \theta_q \varepsilon_{t-q} \tag{3.25}$$

or

$$y_t = \theta_q(L)\varepsilon_t \tag{3.26}$$

with

$$\theta_q(L) = 1 + \theta_1 L + \ldots + \theta_q L^q. \tag{3.27}$$

An important feature of an MA(q) model, and hence also of an ARMA(p,q) model, is that the variables in (3.25), that is, ε_{t-1} to ε_{t-q}, are unobserved and have to be estimated using the available sample data. Since this may cause estimation problems, it is usual to keep q at a small value. In practice, this q is often set at 1 or 2 (or S in case of seasonal time series).

At first sight it seems that y_t does not depend on its own past when an MA(q) model describes this variable. However, similar to (3.10), (3.26) can be written as

$$[\theta_q(L)]^{-1} y_t = \varepsilon_t, \tag{3.28}$$

which shows that y_t depends on all previous values of y_t. For example, for the MA(1) model

$$y_t = \varepsilon_t + \theta_1 \varepsilon_{t-1}, \tag{3.29}$$

it can be derived that (assuming that ε_0 is 0)

$$\begin{aligned}
y_1 &= \varepsilon_1 \\
y_2 &= \varepsilon_2 + \theta_1 \varepsilon_1 = \varepsilon_2 + \theta_1 y_1 \\
y_3 &= \varepsilon_3 + \theta_1 \varepsilon_2 = \varepsilon_3 + \theta_1 (y_2 - \theta_1 y_1) \\
&\ldots
\end{aligned} \tag{3.30}$$

and so on. These expressions will become useful when estimating θ_1, as will be clear from section 3.3.

Similar to the concept of a unit root in the AR(p) polynomial, there can be one or more unit roots in the MA(q) polynomial. In case of an MA(1) model as (3.29) with its characteristic polynomial

$$1 + \theta_1 z = 0 \tag{3.31}$$

a unit root implies that $\theta_1 = -1$. If so, the MA(1) model is non-invertible. In general, MA(q) models are called invertible when the solutions to

$$1 + \theta_1 z + \ldots + \theta_q z^q = 0 \tag{3.32}$$

are all outside the unit circle.

Two simulated realizations of MA(1) processes with θ_1 equal to -0.5 and -2.0 are displayed in figure 3.2, where the 200 observations on ε_t are drawn from the same $N(0,1)$ distributions.

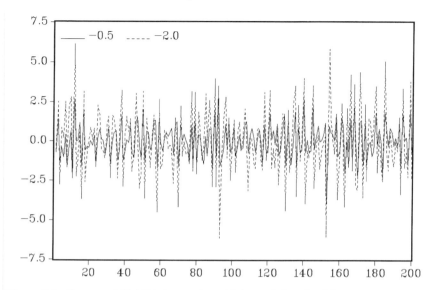

Figure 3.2 *Generated MA(1) time series with* $\theta_1 = -0.5$ *and* -2.0

Clearly, the impact of the values of the MA parameter is less clear-cut as in case of AR models. The key difference between the MA model with $\theta_1 = -0.5$ and -2.0 is that the latter seems to display more reaction to large values of one period lagged values of ε_t, that is, its variance is larger. Given that the impact of shocks ε_t becomes zero after one period by construction (since it is a moving average model of order 1), large shocks do not tend to change the direction of the time series. The graphs in figure 3.2 versus those in figure 3.1 clearly show that the impact of shocks is a much less important topic to study for MA models. Furthermore, since the ε_t are unobserved variables, the finding that, say, $\theta_1 = -1$, does not lead to the application of some form of a summation filter for y_t.

Sometimes, however, it may be important to test the hypothesis $\theta_1 = -1$. Usually the presence of a unit root in the MA polynomial is an indication of overdifferencing. In fact, when for the ARMA(1,1) model with $\phi_1 = 1$, which is in fact an IMA(1,1) model

$$y_t - y_{t-1} = \varepsilon_t + \theta_1 \varepsilon_{t-1} \tag{3.33}$$

holds that $\theta_1 = -1$, y_t has been erroneously differenced once too often since the polynomial $(1-L)$ cancels from both sides. Formal tests for overdifferencing are derived in Breitung (1994), Franses (1995), and Tsay (1993), among others. In theory, we want to difference a time series until the resultant time series can be described by an ARMA(p,q) model with neither of the components $\phi_p(L)$ and $\theta_q(L)$ containing the component $(1-L)$.

Mean of time series and intercept in model

Until now, it has been assumed that the mean μ of y_t is equal to 0. In case of a known $\mu \neq 0$, the y_t in the above expressions can be replaced by $y_t - \mu$, which implies that its mean is subtracted before any analysis. In that case, an AR(1) model can be written as

$$(y_t - \mu) = \phi_1(y_{t-1} - \mu) + \varepsilon_t. \tag{3.34}$$

In practice, however, this μ is unknown and has to be estimated from the data. A simple method for this is to rewrite for example (3.34) as

$$y_t = (1 - \phi_1)\mu + \phi_1 y_{t-1} + \varepsilon_t \tag{3.35}$$

which transforms the regression model (3.11) into the same model while it now includes an intercept term, that is

$$y_t = \delta + \phi_1 y_{t-1} + \varepsilon_t, \tag{3.36}$$

where δ equals $(1 - \phi_1)\mu$. For the general AR(p) model, this regression becomes

$$\phi_p(L)y_t = \delta + \varepsilon_t. \tag{3.37}$$

The mean μ of y_t can now be determined using

$$\begin{aligned}\mu &= (1 - \phi_1 L - \ldots - \phi_p L^p)^{-1}\delta \\ &= (1 - \phi_1 - \ldots - \phi_p)^{-1}\delta \\ &= [\phi_p(1)]^{-1}\delta.\end{aligned} \tag{3.38}$$

The inclusion of a constant in an AR regression is quite important in case of trending variables, as we will see in the next chapter (and also in chapter 10 where common trends are discussed). In case of an MA(q) model with an intercept, that is

$$y_t = \delta + \theta_q(L)\varepsilon_t \tag{3.39}$$

it is clear rightaway that the δ corresponds to μ since ε_t is a zero mean series.

In practice when using ARMA models, we usually consider a regression model which includes an intercept term. It may then occur that the t-ratio of the estimated value of δ suggests that it is insignificant and hence that δ can be deleted from (3.37). The expression in (3.35) shows, however, that the deletion of δ from an AR(1) model may not always be sensible. In fact, when μ is not zero, but $\delta = (1 - \phi_1)\mu$ is imposed to be zero, this restriction will make ϕ_1 to approach 1. With the estimation methods to be outlined in section 3.3, we can easily verify this by generating data with $\mu = 10$ and $\phi_1 = 0.5$, which yield an estimate $\hat{\phi}_1 \approx 1$ when δ is deleted from the AR(1) regression. For many practical applications, it is therefore better to include an intercept in the estimation model, even though it is not significant.

3.2   Autocorrelation and identification

The ARMA model discussed in the previous section has an important feature that makes it distinct from many other econometric models, and that is that in a sense the adequacy of such a model to describe a certain time series can be "recognized" by specific features of these empirical data. These features are summarized in so-called autocorrelations and partial autocorrelations. The process of recognizing a possibly appropriate model is called identification, see Box and Jenkins (1970). The idea is that if a time series is generated by an ARMA model, it should in theory have certain autocorrelation properties. In practice, where this ARMA model is unknown and its values for p and q have to be estimated from the data (see section 3.4), the estimated counterparts of these theoretical functions are then compared with the theoretical values to see whether these match certain regular patterns. In this section, I discuss two autocorrelation functions, and illustrate how these can be implemented to identify some simple ARMA time series models.

Autocorrelation

The autocorrelation function [ACF] of a time series y_t is defined by

$$\rho_k = \gamma_k / \gamma_0, \tag{3.40}$$

where γ_k is the kth order autocovariance of y_t, that is

$$\gamma_k = E[(y_t - \mu)(y_{t-k} - \mu)] \quad k = \ldots, -2, -1, 0, 1, 2, \ldots \tag{3.41}$$

Given (3.41), it is easily seen that for the autocorrelations it holds that $\rho_0 = 1$, $\rho_{-k} = \rho_k$ and that $-1 < \rho_k < 1$.

This ACF can be useful to characterize ARMA time series models. A simple example is the white noise series ε_t for which $E(\varepsilon_t) = 0$ and $\rho_k = 0$ for all $k \neq 0$. For the AR(1) model

$$y_t - \mu = \phi_1 (y_{t-1} - \mu) + \varepsilon_t, \quad t = 2, 3, \ldots, n \tag{3.42}$$

we can derive that

$$E(y_t) = \mu + \phi_1 E(y_{t-1} - \mu) + E(\varepsilon_t) \tag{3.43}$$
$$= (1 - \phi_1)\mu + \phi_1 E(y_{t-1}).$$

When $E(y_{t-i}) = E(y_t)$, which is the case for time series that correspond to

ARMA models for which there is no $(1-L)$ component in the AR part, which here implies that $|\phi_1|<1$, see below and also chapter 4, (3.43) can be written as

$$E(y_t)=(1-\phi_1 L)^{-1}(1-\phi_1)\mu=\mu. \tag{3.44}$$

In order to calculate the ACF, we start with

$$\gamma_0=E[(y_t-E(y_t))\,(y_t-E(y_t))]. \tag{3.45}$$

For the AR(1) model, the right-hand side [RHS] of (3.45) is

$$E[(y_t-\mu)\,(y_t-\mu)]=E[\phi_1(y_{t-1}-\mu)\phi_1(y_{t-1}-\mu)]+E(\varepsilon_t^2)$$
$$+2E[\phi_1(y_{t-1}-\mu)\varepsilon_t]. \tag{3.46}$$

The covariance of μ with a time series is of course equal to zero. Considering again (3.10), when the AR(1) model is written as

$$y_t=\varepsilon_t+\theta_1\varepsilon_{t-1}+\theta_2\varepsilon_{t-2}+\ldots+y_0, \tag{3.47}$$

where the parameters are scaled by θ_0, and in its one-period lagged version

$$y_{t-1}=\varepsilon_{t-1}+\theta_1\varepsilon_{t-2}+\theta_2\varepsilon_{t-3}+\ldots+y_0, \tag{3.48}$$

it is clear that $E(y_{t-1}\varepsilon_t)=0$. In fact, moving (3.48) even further back in time, it follows that $E(y_{t-j}\varepsilon_t)=0$ for any discrete $j>0$. With (3.47) and (3.48) it is also evident that $E(y_{t-j}\varepsilon_{t-j})=E(\varepsilon_t^2)=\sigma^2$. With these results, (3.46) can be seen to become

$$\gamma_0=(1-\phi_1^2)^{-1}\sigma^2. \quad\text{subject to } |\phi_1|<1. \tag{3.49}$$

The first order autocovariance for an AR(1) time series is

$$\begin{aligned}\gamma_1&=E[(y_t-\mu)\,(y_{t-1}-\mu)] \\ &=E[\phi_1(y_{t-1}-\mu)\,(y_{t-1}-\mu)]+E[\varepsilon_t(y_{t-1}-\mu)] \\ &=\phi_1\gamma_0.\end{aligned} \tag{3.50}$$

Hence, the ρ_1 for an AR(1) model simply becomes

$$\rho_1=\gamma_1/\gamma_0=\phi_1. \tag{3.51}$$

To calculate ρ_k, it is convenient to consider the following expression for an AR(1) model

$$E[(y_t-\mu)\,(y_{t-k}-\mu)]=E[\phi_1(y_{t-1}-\mu)\,(y_{t-k}-\mu)], \tag{3.52}$$

which again follows from the fact that $E(y_{t-k}\varepsilon_t)=0$. Dividing both sides by γ_0 results in

$$\rho_k=\phi_1\rho_{k-1} \quad\text{for } k=1,2,3,\ldots \tag{3.53}$$

For example, when $\phi_1 = 0.8$, the first four (theoretical) autocorrelations are 0.8, 0.64, 0.512, and 0.4096. In practice we can estimate such correlations for real data, and see whether this pattern matches with this sequence. If so, we can consider an AR(1) model for forecasting.

Given the requirement in (3.43) and (3.49), it is clear that the case $\phi_1 = 1$ is a special case. Earlier we saw that it corresponds with the case where the AR(1) polynomial has a unit root, and in chapter 4 we will see that this case can be usefully considered when modeling trends. To demonstrate its impact on the ACF, it is convenient to write the model

$$y_t = y_{t-1} + \varepsilon_t \tag{3.54}$$

as

$$y_t = \varepsilon_t + \varepsilon_{t-1} + \varepsilon_{t-2} + \ldots + \varepsilon_2 + \varepsilon_1 + y_0, \quad t = 1, 2, \ldots, n. \tag{3.55}$$

Since $E(\varepsilon_t) = 0$, $E(\varepsilon_{t-k} \varepsilon_t) = 0$ for all k except $k = 0$, and assuming that y_0 is a fixed constant, it follows that

$$\gamma_0 = E(y_t^2) = t\sigma^2. \tag{3.56}$$

Comparing (3.55) with its one-period lagged version

$$y_{t-1} = \varepsilon_{t-1} + \varepsilon_{t-2} + \ldots \varepsilon_2 + \varepsilon_1 + y_0, \tag{3.57}$$

we find that

$$\gamma_1 = E(y_t y_{t-1}) = (t-1)\sigma^2, \tag{3.58}$$

which, together with (3.56), results in

$$\rho_{1,t} = (t-1)/t, \tag{3.59}$$

where the index t for ρ_1 indicates that its value depends on time t. Because of the time-varying nature of ρ_1, it is not of much use to yield information on a possibly adequate ARMA model. In fact, at every time t we get another value, and this disables interpretation.

Results similar to (3.59) can be derived for any AR model which includes an $(1-L)$ component in its AR polynomial by replacing y_t in (3.54) by the filtered $\phi_{p-1}(L)y_t$ series, where $\phi_{p-1}(L) = \phi_p(L)(1-L)$. In other words, the ACF is not interpretable for AR models with unit roots. Hence, from now on it is assumed in this chapter that if there is such an $(1-L)$ component, that it has been removed by filtering the time series with the Δ_1 filter. To keep notation simple, I will still use y_t for the appropriately transformed data. Also, and for similar reasons, I set μ equal to zero from now on (except when otherwise indicated).

In principle, the determination of the autocorrelation coefficients for higher order autoregressive models proceeds along similar lines as for the AR(1) model. For example, consider the AR(2) model

$$y_t - \phi_1 y_{t-1} - \phi_2 y_{t-2} = \varepsilon_t \tag{3.60}$$

Multiplying both sides by y_{t-1}, taking expectations, and dividing them by γ_0 results in

$$\rho_1 - \phi_1 \rho_0 - \phi_2 \rho_1 = 0 \tag{3.61}$$

and since $\rho_0 = 1$, we obtain

$$\rho_1 = \phi_1/(1 - \phi_2). \tag{3.62}$$

To determine an expression for ρ_2, analogous operations are carried out on (3.60), yielding

$$\rho_2 - \phi_1 \rho_1 - \phi_2 \rho_0 = 0. \tag{3.63}$$

Substituting (3.62) into (3.63) gives

$$\rho_2 = \phi_1^2/(1 - \phi_2) + \phi_2. \tag{3.64}$$

Analogous to (3.61) and (3.63) we can derive that

$$\rho_k = \phi_1 \rho_{k-1} + \phi_2 \rho_{k-2}. \quad \text{for } k = 2,3,4,\dots \tag{3.65}$$

To find expressions for the ACF for AR(p) models with $p > 2$, we use the same techniques as above. In general it applies that the ACF of an AR process shows an exponentially decaying pattern.

Consider for example the theoretical autocorrelation function of an AR(2) model as (3.60) with parameters $\phi_1 = 0.5$ and $\phi_2 = 0.3$ (in figure 3.3) and $\phi_1 = 0.5$ and $\phi_2 = 0.49$ (in figure 3.4).

The ACFs in both graphs concern ρ_1 to ρ_{30}. Figure 3.3 clearly shows the decay in the values of the ACF when k increases, where ρ_{30} approaches zero. On the other hand, when ϕ_2 increases from 0.3 to 0.49, the ACF is figure 3.4 shows that it does not die out quickly at all. In fact, ρ_{30} still exceeds 0.8. This feature reflects the fact that the AR(2) polynomial $1 - 0.5z - 0.49z^2$ is almost equal to $(1-z)(1+0.5z)$, which contains the $(1-z)$ component. With such a $(1-z)$ component, the expression for $\rho_{1,t}$ in (3.59) suggests that (if we did not take account of the fact that this ρ_1 varies over time) its value is close to 1. Indeed, the first 30 ACF values are all very close to unity. Hence, a first tentative indication that a time series y_t can be described by an ARMA model of which the AR part contains the $(1-L)$ component, which should be removed by applying the first differencing filter Δ_1, is given by a very slow decay of the ACF values. Box and Jenkins (1970) recommend to use this visual evidence as an indication to opt for Δ_1 or not. By now, however, there exist testing procedures which enable us to make a more formal decision for a differencing filter or not, see chapter 4.

In case the solutions of the characteristic polynomial for an AR(2) model yield two complex solutions, that is, the solutions to $1 - \phi_1 z - \phi_2 z^2 = 0$ are

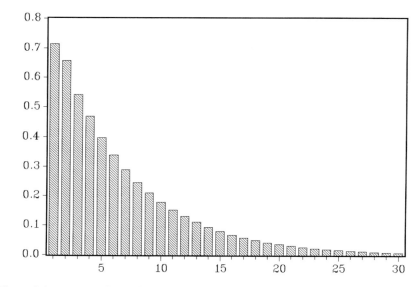

Figure 3.3 *Autocorrelation function of an AR(2) process with $\phi_1=0.5$, $\phi_2=0.3$*

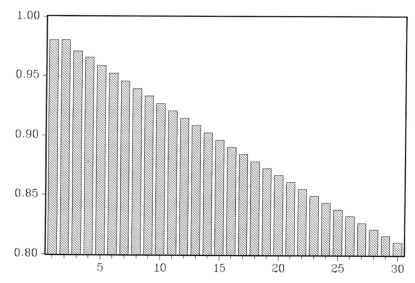

Figure 3.4 *Autocorrelation function of an AR(2) process with $\phi_1=0.5$, $\phi_2=0.49$*

$z_{1,2} = a \pm bi$, where i is the complex number with $i^2 = -1$, then the ACF shows a cyclical pattern. The corresponding time series y_t displays a cyclical pattern with cycle length

$$c = 2\pi/[\tan^{-1}(b/a)] \tag{3.66}$$

which is a result that follows from standard differential calculus. This cyclical pattern can be illustrated by the ACF values of AR(2) models with $\phi_1 = 1.2$ and $\phi_2 = -0.4$ (in figure 3.5) and with $\phi_1 = 1.0$ and $\phi_2 = -0.5$ (in figure 3.6).

With (3.66) we can show that c is larger for the series with the ACF as in figure 3.5 than for that in figure 3.6. From figure 3.6 it can be observed that positive and negative peaks in the ACF occur at lags 0, 4, 8, 12, and so on, respectively. Since the solutions to the polynomial $1 - z + 0.5z^2$ are $0.5 \pm 0.5i$, (3.66) gives that c is indeed exactly equal to 8.

Figures 3.3 to 3.6 show that the values of ρ_k for $k = 3,4,5,\ldots$ can still be quite large for an AR(2) model. Hence, the ACF may not be particularly useful to identify whether an AR of specific order is a suitable model. In fact, the ACF is more useful in case of MA(q) models. Consider for example the MA(2) model

$$y_t = \varepsilon_t + \theta_1 \varepsilon_{t-1} + \theta_2 \varepsilon_{t-2} \tag{3.67}$$

and its lagged versions

$$y_{t-k} = \varepsilon_{t-k} + \theta_1 \varepsilon_{t-k-1} + \theta_2 \varepsilon_{t-k-2}. \tag{3.68}$$

The variance γ_0 equals

$$\gamma_0 = (1 + \theta_1^2 + \theta_2^2)\sigma^2, \tag{3.69}$$

since all covariances between ε_t and its lags are equal to zero. With (3.67) and (3.68) it is fairly easy to see that

$$\gamma_1 = E(y_t y_{t-1}) = (\theta_1 + \theta_1 \theta_2)\sigma^2 \tag{3.70}$$

$$\gamma_2 = E(y_t y_{t-2}) = \theta_2 \sigma^2 \tag{3.71}$$

$$\gamma_k = 0 \qquad \text{for } k = 3,4,\ldots \tag{3.72}$$

and hence that $\rho_k = 0$ for $k = 3,4,\ldots$ This implies that when in practice the estimated ACF is available, and the values are zero after the qth lag, we may decide to analyze a MA(q) model for y_t. This follows from the fact that for a MA(q) model it holds that

$$\gamma_k = \left[\sum_{i=0}^{q-k} \theta_i \theta_{i+k}\right]\sigma^2 \quad \text{for } k = 0,1,\ldots,q \tag{3.73}$$

$$= 0 \qquad\qquad \text{for } k > q$$

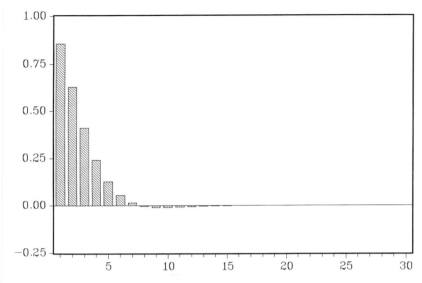

Figure 3.5 *Autocorrelation function of an AR(2) process with $\phi_1 = 1.2$, $\phi_2 = -0.4$*

with $\theta_0 = 1$, and hence this can be simply used to obtain a first indication for the value of q.

For ARMA($p,1$) models the pattern of the ACF is of course a mixture of the ACF pattern for pure AR and MA models. For example, consider the ARMA(1,1) model

$$y_t = \phi_1 y_{t-1} + \varepsilon_t + \theta_1 \varepsilon_{t-1}, \tag{3.74}$$

for which we can derive (along similar lines as for (3.61)) that

$$\begin{aligned}
\gamma_0 &= \phi_1 \gamma_1 + \sigma^2 + \theta_1 E(y_t \varepsilon_{t-1}) \\
&= \phi_1 \gamma_1 + [1 + \theta_1 (\phi_1 + \theta_1)]\sigma^2 \\
\gamma_1 &= \phi_1 \gamma_0 + \theta_1 \sigma^2 \\
\gamma_2 &= \phi_1 \gamma_1 \\
\gamma_k &= \phi_1 \gamma_{k-1} \quad \text{for } k = 3,4,5,\ldots
\end{aligned}$$

such that (after some algebra)

$$\rho_k = \phi_1^{k-1}(1 + \phi_1 \theta_1)(\phi_1 + \theta_1)/(1 + 2\phi_1 \theta_1 + \theta_1^2). \quad \text{for } k = 1,2,3,\ldots \tag{3.75}$$

From this expression it can be seen that ρ_k can take a wide variety of values for distinct choices of ϕ_1 and θ_1. This suggests that the identification of an ARMA time series model from the patterns of the ACF alone may be rather difficult. Notice that when $\phi_1 = -\theta_1$, the ρ_k become equal to 0 since (3.74) collapses to a white noise series.

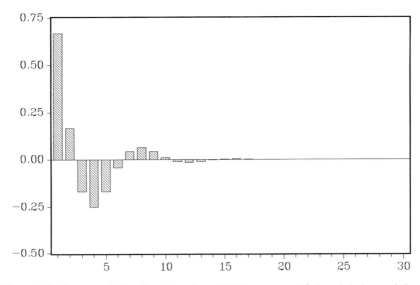

Figure 3.6 *Autocorrelation function of an AR(2) process with $\phi_1 = 1.0$, $\phi_2 = -0.5$*

Partial autocorrelation function

The ACF is helpful to identify that the MA model (of some order) is possibly useful to describe y_t, but it appears less useful to identify AR models. The reason for this is that for example for the AR(1) model

$$y_t = \phi_1 y_{t-1} + \varepsilon_t, \tag{3.76}$$

which can be written as

$$y_t = \phi_1^2 y_{t-2} + \varepsilon_t + \phi_1 \varepsilon_{t-1}, \tag{3.77}$$

the inclusion of y_{t-1} in a regression model for y_t, also allows y_t to depend on y_{t-2} (though slightly weaker since $\phi_1^2 < \phi_1$), as can be observed from the ACF in (3.53). What is helpful, though, to identify an AR model is to notice that adding y_{t-2} to the regression (3.76) would not help in explaining y_t, i.e., the corresponding parameter should equal zero. Loosely speaking, along these lines we can construct the so-called partial ACF [PACF]. The PACF value at lag 1, say ψ_1, is given by

$$y_t = \psi_1 y_{t-1} + u_t, \tag{3.78}$$

where u_t is only a white noise error time series when the model for y_t is indeed an AR(1). From (3.78) it follows that since ψ_1 equals γ_1/γ_0, by construction we have that $\psi_1 = \phi_1$ for all time series models. The second PACF value ψ_2 results from the regression model

$$y_t = \eta_1 y_{t-1} + \psi_2 y_{t-2} + u_t. \tag{3.79}$$

In case of an AR(1), this ψ_2 equals zero. In case of an AR(2) or higher, it is unequal to zero. For an AR(2) model, it holds that $\psi_3 = 0$ in the regression

$$y_t = \eta_1 y_{t-1} + \eta_2 y_{t-2} + \psi_3 y_{t-3} + u_t. \tag{3.80}$$

Hence, when ψ_{p+1} equals zero, while ψ_p is not, we may wish to consider an AR model of order p. More formal derivations of the PACF, where it is also shown that the ψ_k are functions of the ρ_k, can be found in Box and Jenkins (1970).

Overdifferencing

As shown in chapter 2, many economic time series display trending behavior, and, as will become clear in chapter 4, should be differenced using the Δ_1 filter to remove the $(1-L)$ component in the AR polynomial. It may however be that a mistake is made, and the Δ_1 filter is erroneously applied once too often such that the resultant time series is overdifferenced. For example, when the white noise series $y_t = \varepsilon_t$ is differenced, the model becomes

$$y_t - y_{t-1} = \varepsilon_t + \theta_1 \varepsilon_{t-1} \quad \text{with } \theta_1 = -1. \tag{3.81}$$

Defining $z_t = \Delta_1 y_t$, the first order autocorrelation of z_t equals -0.5. In general, it can be shown that overdifferencing results in a typical pattern of the ACF. Suppose the autocovariances of the series y_t are denoted as γ_k and those of $\Delta_1 y_t$ as g_k, then

$$g_k = E\{ (y_t - y_{t-1}) (y_{t-k} - y_{t-k-1})\} = 2\gamma_k - \gamma_{k-1} - \gamma_{k+1}. \tag{3.82}$$

Given this connection between γ_k and g_j, $j = k-1, k, k+1$, it follows that

$$\sum_{i=1}^{\infty} \rho_i = (\gamma_1 - \gamma_0)/(2\gamma_0 - 2\gamma_1) = -0.5, \tag{3.83}$$

where ρ_i is the ith autocorrelation of $\Delta_1 y_t$. In sum, if the ACF dies out only very slowly, we may think of differencing the time series, and if its values sum up to about -0.5, we may take this as evidence that we have differenced once too often.

Estimated autocorrelation functions

In practice, for a given economic or business time series y_t, the correlation functions have to be estimated. The ACF can be estimated by means of

$$\hat{\rho}_k = C_k / C_0 \tag{3.84}$$

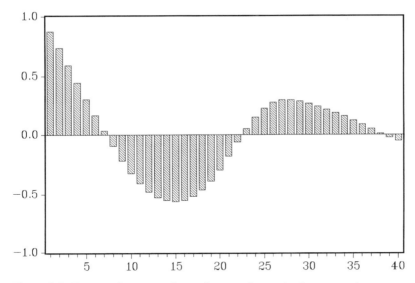

Figure 3.7 *Estimated autocorrelation function for stock of motor cycles*

where

$$C_k = \sum_{t=k+1}^{n} (y_t - \bar{y})(y_{t-k} - \bar{y}), \qquad (3.85)$$

where $\bar{y}$ denotes the relevant sample mean of y_t, $t = 1,2,3,\ldots,n$. The $\hat{\rho}_k$ for $k = 0,1,2\ldots$ form the estimated ACF [EACF]. As an illustration, consider $\hat{\rho}_1$ to $\hat{\rho}_{40}$ for the stock of motor cycles in The Netherlands, as these are given in figure 3.7. It is clear from this graph that the EACF values are still quite large at high lags, and also that there seems to be a cycle of about 15 years.

The sample equivalents of ψ_k, the estimated partial ACF [EPACF] can be obtained by applying ordinary least squares [OLS] to

$$y_t - \bar{y} = \hat{\psi}_1(y_{t-1} - \bar{y}) + \ldots + \hat{\psi}_k(y_{t-k} - \bar{y}) + v_t \qquad (3.86)$$

for any values of k, where v_t is not necessarily a white noise time series. Notice that (3.86) only concerns estimating the last ψ_k parameter.

In principle, we may consider the estimated t-statistics for the ψ_k in (3.86) to establish the significance of the EPACF values. For the EACF values we can derive the distribution of the $\hat{\rho}_k$. The latter distribution can be shown to depend on the underlying true model, see Box and Jenkins (1970) among others. Usually, we approximate the distribution of the $\hat{\rho}_k$ and $\hat{\psi}_k$ by setting their asymptotic standard errors at $n^{-\frac{1}{2}}$. Again, details of how good such an

Table 3.1. *Estimated (partial) autocorrelation functions for differences in log prices in Argentina*

Lag	1970.2–1989.4		1970.2–1988.4	
	EACF	EPACF	EACF	EPACF
1	0.560**	0.560**	0.703**	0.703**
2	0.214	−0.146	0.525**	0.061
3	0.227	0.255**	0.446**	0.112
4	0.215	−0.025	0.240	−0.246**
5	0.107	−0.019	0.135	0.019
6	0.038	−0.025	0.046	−0.086
7	0.020	−0.019	−0.042	−0.008
8	−0.044	−0.092	−0.100	−0.071
9	−0.072	0.006	−0.078	0.116
10	−0.055	−0.017	−0.043	0.044
11	−0.071	−0.036	−0.083	−0.104
12	−0.055	0.045	−0.009	0.123
13	−0.050	−0.043	0.081	0.095
14	−0.085	−0.045	0.032	−0.122
15	−0.061	0.036	−0.003	−0.129
16	0.072	0.143	−0.024	−0.037

Note:
** Significant at the 5% level. The estimated standard error for the sample 1970.2–1989.4 is 0.113, and that for the sample 1970.2–1988.4 is 0.115. The time series is $y_t = \Delta_1 \log(\omega_t)$, where w_t is given in the data appendix.

approximation is can be found in, for example, Granger and Newbold (1986). In this book, I follow the usual approach by assigning 95 percent confidence of ρ_k and ψ_k in case for their estimated values holds that $(\hat{\rho}_k - 2n^{-\frac{1}{2}}, \hat{\rho}_k + 2n^{-\frac{1}{2}})$ and $(\hat{\psi}_k - 2n^{-\frac{1}{2}}, \hat{\psi}_k + 2n^{-\frac{1}{2}})$ do not include zero.

As an illustration of the EACF and EPACF, consider their first 16 values as those given in table 3.1 for the differences of log prices in Argentina. The first obvious feature of the EACF in table 3.1 is that the last four data points have a large effect on the EACF. In fact, $\hat{\rho}_1$ is 0.560 for the complete sample, while it is 0.703 for the sample less one year, see also figures 2.12 and 2.13. Furthermore, for the shorter sample $\hat{\psi}_4$ is significant, while it is insignificant for the entire sample (for $\hat{\psi}_3$ it is the other way round). All in all, the EACF and EPACF patterns seem to suggest the possible adequacy of an AR(1) or may be an ARMA(1,1) model.

In practice, we usually do not go through all possible models that are indicated by the EACF and EPACF. In fact, the key issues are often (i) whether the EACF values die out sufficiently quickly, where sufficiency here is not a formal concept but merely a rule based on experience, (ii) whether the EACF signals overdifferencing, and (iii) whether the EACF and EPACF show any significant and easily interpretable peaks at certain lags. The main reason for this less formal approach in practice is that each variant of an ARMA model implies certain properties of the ACF and PACF, but, given the fact that these functions have to be estimated, a given set of EACF and EPACF values may suggest a wealth of possibly useful models. Hence, it is usual to select a seemingly reasonable set of tentative models, that is, with values for p and/or q, with parameters estimated and diagnostic checks applied to see whether the models capture the dynamics of the time series sufficiently. A choice has then to be made between the models.

3.3   Estimation and diagnostic measures

A useful specification strategy for ARMA time series starts with an inspection of the EACF and EPACF values, to check which values are significant such that reasonably simple ARMA model structures can be hypothesized, to estimate the parameters of the various models, and to investigate whether the estimated residuals can be said to be approximately white noise. This strategy amounts to a subtle interplay between identification, estimation, and modification, and quite some practical experience is needed to get some skill. Usually, it does not make much sense to start off with a very large ARMA model, and to delete all insignificant parameters. The reason for this is that we are likely to encounter a situation in which parts of the AR and MA components cancel out. Intuitively, if data are generated from an AR(1) model, but we estimate the parameters in

$$(1 - \alpha_1 L)\,(1 - \alpha_2 L)y_t = (1 - \theta_1 L)\varepsilon_t, \tag{3.87}$$

where α_1 (or α_2) should equal θ_1, we may expect estimation problems for the various parameters, and also problems with the distribution of the t-test statistics for α_1 and θ_1. Of course, when only AR models are considered, we may start off with an AR(p^*) with p^* large, and work downwards to p, a smaller value than the initial p^*. Notice that this puts forward an additional advantage of AR models over ARMA models.

Once the parameters have been estimated, the estimated residuals $\hat{\varepsilon}_t$ are usually inspected for the presence of some remaining autocorrelation. This is again in contrast to regression models based on cross-section data, since in case of ARMA models, the results of the diagnostic checks suggest modification possibilities. In this section, I discuss simple estimation methods for AR and ARMA models. Other estimation routines can be found in the advanced literature on ARMA models. Furthermore, I give two often applied tests for correlation in the $\hat{\varepsilon}_t$ time series.

Estimation of AR models

The parameters in the AR(p) model, where the choice for p is based on EPACF values that are significant, given by

$$y_t = \delta + \phi_1 y_{t-1} + \phi_2 y_{t-2} + \ldots + \phi_p y_{t-p} + \varepsilon_t \quad t = p+1, p+2, \ldots, n \quad (3.88)$$

can be estimated by OLS, where the observations y_1 to y_p are assumed to be the starting values. It can be shown that the OLS estimators of the parameters are consistent and asymptotically normal, and that standard t-statistics can be used to investigate their significance. The underlying mean μ can be estimated from

$$\hat{\mu} = (1 - \hat{\phi}_1 - \hat{\phi}_2 - \ldots - \hat{\phi}_p)^{-1} \hat{\delta} \tag{3.89}$$

and again it should be stressed that imposing δ to be zero while μ is not, forces the estimate $(1 - \hat{\phi}_1 - \hat{\phi}_2 - \ldots - \hat{\phi}_p)$ toward zero, and hence spuriously suggests the presence of a unit root, see (3.20).

Consider the following estimation results for an AR model of order 1 for $\Delta_1 y_t$ for log prices in Argentina, for the estimation sample 1970.3–1988.4

$$\Delta_1 y_t = 0.078 + 0.704 \Delta_1 y_{t-1} + \hat{\varepsilon}_t, \tag{3.90}$$
$$(0.026) \ (0.082)$$

where estimated standard errors are given in parentheses. Clearly, both $\hat{\delta}$ and $\hat{\phi}_1$ are significantly different from zero. Furthermore, $\hat{\phi}_1$ seems far enough from 1 to abstain from considering the Δ_1^2 transformation. The mean μ of $\Delta_1 y_t$ is estimated as $0.078/(1 - 0.704) = 0.264$. In figure 3.8, I present the graph of the time series, the fit from the regression (3.90), and the estimated residual time series. This figure illuminates a typical feature of the fit from linear time series models. It seems that the fitted line is approximately equal to the original time series, one period lagged. Given the expression in (3.90), this is not unexpected. Furthermore, it seems that the AR(1) model finds difficulties in fitting the more extreme observations. In other words, these observations cannot be predicted well given the past.

Estimation of ARMA models

There exists a wide variety of estimation routines for ARMA models. The main reason for this is the important feature that the lagged ε_t variables in

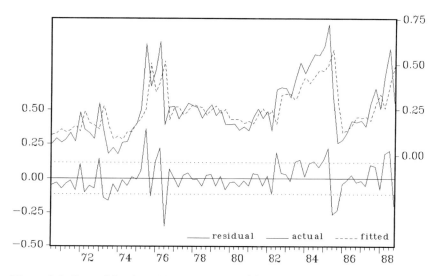

Figure 3.8 *Typical fit of an AR time series model*

the MA part are unobserved variables, and hence have to be estimated as well. For example, for the ARMA(1,1) model

$$y_t = \phi_1 y_{t-1} + \varepsilon_t + \theta_1 \varepsilon_{t-1}, \tag{3.91}$$

the parameters ϕ_1 and θ_1 are unknown, and also the ε_{t-1} variable is unknown. This ARMA model can be written as

$$(1 + \theta_1 L)^{-1} y_t = \phi_1 (1 + \theta_1 L)^{-1} y_{t-1} + \varepsilon_t. \tag{3.92}$$

Denoting $z_t = (1 + \theta_1 L)^{-1} y_t$ such that

$$z_t = y_t - \theta_1 y_{t-1} + \theta_1^2 y_{t-2} - \theta_1^3 y_{t-3} + \ldots \tag{3.93}$$

we have the observations (when assuming that $y_0 = 0$)

$$z_1 = y_1$$
$$z_2 = y_2 - \theta_1 y_1$$
$$z_3 = y_3 - \theta_1 y_2 + \theta_1^2 y_1$$
$$\ldots,$$

and so on. Given a value for θ_1, we can construct the time series z_t, and estimate ϕ_1 via OLS applied to (3.92). This regression gives an estimated $\hat{\varepsilon}_t$ series, which, when setting $\varepsilon_1 = 0$, can be used in (3.91) to give a value for θ_1 in a second step. A commonly applied optimization routine that yields final estimates for the ARMA parameters in not too many iterations is the Gauss–Newton routine.

As an illustration, consider the first differences of the monthly log prices of black pepper for which we obtain

$$\Delta_1 y_t = 0.003 + \hat{\varepsilon}_t + 0.390\hat{\varepsilon}_{t-1} \qquad (3.94)$$
$$\quad (0.004) \qquad (0.056)$$

for the estimation sample 1973.11–1996.04. Since this is an MA model, the mean of $\Delta_1 y_t$ does not differ significantly from 0. The θ_1 parameter is significant at the 5 percent level.

Diagnostic testing for residual autocorrelation

An obvious requirement for an ARMA time series model is that the estimated residual time series is approximately white noise. If not, we may have missed some dynamic structure in y_t that could have been incorporated in an ARMA model. The EACF of the estimated residuals is given by

$$r_k(\hat{\varepsilon}) = \left[\sum_{t=k+1}^{n} \hat{\varepsilon}_t \hat{\varepsilon}_{t-k} \right] \bigg/ \left[\sum_{t=1}^{n} \hat{\varepsilon}_t^2 \right] \qquad (3.95)$$

for $k = 1,2,3\ldots$ Given model adequacy, it can be shown that the population equivalents of $r_k(\hat{\varepsilon})$ are asymptotically uncorrelated and have variances that can be approximated by $(n-k)/(n^2+2n) \cong n^{-1}$. Hence, under the additional assumption of normality, a rough check at the 95 percent confidence level may be to test whether the estimated residual autocorrelations lie within the $\pm 2n^{-\frac{1}{2}}$ interval. Ljung and Box (1978) propose a joint test for the significance of the first m residual autocorrelations, which is given by

$$\text{LB}(m) = n(n+2) \sum_{k=1}^{m} (n-k)^{-1} r_k^2(\hat{\varepsilon}) \qquad (3.96)$$

which asymptotically follows a $\chi^2 (m-p-q)$ distribution under the hypothesis of no residual autocorrelation provided that m/n is small and m is moderately large. This type of test where the value of m is often set *a priori* and which should detect any kind of misspecifiation up to m, is usually called a portmanteau test. A drawback of this portmanteau test is that it may be helpful to detect whether the model is inadequate, but it is not useful in indicating how the model should be modified if necessary. Furthermore, if for example the m is selected too large, the LB test lacks power against low order residual autocorrelation.

An alternative is to consider the nested hypotheses tests developed in, for example, Godfrey (1979). With the Lagrange Multiplier (LM) principle, these tests are relatively easy to calculate. For example, to test an AR(p) model against an AR($p+r$) or an ARMA(p,r) model, the LM test is found by estimating

$$\hat{\varepsilon}_t = \alpha_1 y_{t-1} + \ldots + \alpha_p y_{t-p} + \alpha_{p+1}\hat{\varepsilon}_{t-1} + \ldots + \alpha_{p+r}\hat{\varepsilon}_{t-r} + v_t, \qquad (3.97)$$

where $\hat{\varepsilon}_t$ are the estimated residuals of the AR(p) model with $\hat{\varepsilon}_t$ set equal to zero when $t < p+1$. The test statistic is calculated as nR^2, where R^2 is the coefficient of determination from (3.97) and it is asymptotically $\chi^2(r)$ distributed under the hypothesis that the AR(p) model is adequate. I will denote the F-version of this LM test as $F_{AC,1-r}$. The simulation results in Hall and McAleer (1989), for example, indicate that this LM test often has higher power than the LB test.

For the AR(1) model for Argentinean prices, the auxiliary regression as in (3.97) for residual autocorrelation of order 1 results in

$$\hat{\varepsilon}_t = -0.016 + 0.065\Delta_1 y_{t-1} - 0.133\hat{\varepsilon}_{t-1} + \hat{v}_t \qquad (3.98)$$
$$\phantom{\hat{\varepsilon}_t =} (0.032)\ (0.118) (0.173)$$

for 1970.3–1988.4 (where $\hat{\varepsilon}_1$ is set equal to zero) with an R^2 of 0.008, where $n = 74$. The $F_{AC,1-1}$–test obtains a value of 1.347, which is not significant at the 5 percent significance level of the $F(1,72)$ distribution. Hence, the AR(1) model for this series does not need to be enlarged by including additional lags of y_t or of ε_t.

In case of an MA(1) model (and this applies naturally to higher order models), it is necessary to take account of the fact that the regressor $\hat{\varepsilon}_{t-1}$ cannot be added to the model, since that regressor is already included in the model. In that case, we construct new time series

$$y_t^* = y_t + \hat{\theta}_1 y_{t-1}^* \text{ with } y_0^* = 0$$
$$\hat{\varepsilon}_t^* = \hat{\varepsilon}_t + \hat{\theta}_1 \hat{\varepsilon}_{t-1}^* \text{ with } \hat{\varepsilon}_0^* = 0$$

and performs the auxiliary regression

$$\hat{\varepsilon}_t = \hat{\alpha}_1 \hat{\varepsilon}_{t-1}^* + \beta_1 y_{t-1}^* + \ldots + \beta_r y_{t-r}^* + \hat{v}_t \qquad (3.99)$$

in order to test against an MA($1+r$) or an ARMA(r,1) model.

For the black pepper example, the resulting $F_{AC,1-1}$-test against an MA(2) or an ARMA(1,1) model obtains the insignificant value of 0.030.

Diagnostic testing for normality of residuals

To facilitate the interpretation of, for example, parameter estimates and t-ratios, the estimated residuals should be approximately normal. The skewness [SK] can be calculated as

$$SK = \hat{m}_3 / \hat{m}_2^{\frac{3}{2}} \qquad (3.100)$$

and the kurtosis K as

$$K = \hat{m}_4 / \hat{m}_2^2, \qquad (3.101)$$

where

$$\hat{m}_j = n^{-1} \sum_{t=1}^{n} \hat{\varepsilon}_t^j. \tag{3.102}$$

Under the null hypothesis of normality (and no autocorrelation in $\hat{\varepsilon}_t$), we can construct the test statistics $SK^* = (n/6)^{\frac{1}{2}}SK$ and $K^* = (n/24)^{\frac{1}{2}}(K - 3)$, which are independent and have an asymptotic $N(0,1)$ distribution, see Lomnicki (1961). The well-known Bera–Jarque (1982) test is given by

$$JB = (SK^{*2} + K^{*2}) \sim \chi^2(2). \tag{3.103}$$

Rejection of the normality null hypothesis may indicate that there are some outlying observations, or that the error process is not homoskedastic, see chapters 6 and 7.

The 74 residuals from the AR(1) model for Argentinean prices have a value for SK of 0.060 and for K of 4.332. Even though the last value does not seem close to 3, the JB obtains the value of 5.512, which is not significant at the 5 percent level. On the other hand, the 270 residuals of the MA(1) model for black pepper prices have an SK of 0.460 and a K of 4.334. Given that here there are many more observations, the JB test now obtains the highly significant value of 29.562. Hence, the black pepper time series seems to display one or more outlying observations. In chapter 6, I will consider more formal methods to detect aberrant data points.

Other diagnostic tests

For out-of-sample forecasting, it is important to expect the time series to continue to behave similarly out-of-sample as it does within the estimation sample. If this is so, confidence in the possible usefulness of the time series model for forecasting is established. If the time series model suffers from structural breaks within sample, account for these breaks should be taken when generating forecasts. Such tests, as well as tests for specific types of outliers, will be discussed in chapter 6.

Other relevant diagnostic checks, which can point toward possibly suitable modification of the actual time series model, are presented in chapters 7 and 8. In chapter 7, I discuss diagnostic checks for the presence of conditional heteroskedasticity. In chapter 8, I will focus on tests for specific forms of non-linearity.

3.4   Model selection

The previously discussed identification, estimation, and diagnostic stages can result in a set of tentatively useful models, in the sense that these models cannot be rejected using the above diagnostic measures. We may now want to select between these remaining models, although we may also opt to consider all models for out-of-sample forecasting in order to decide on which performs best on some previously unseen data.

A survey of model selection criteria is given in, for example, De Gooijer *et al.* (1985). It seems sensible to assume that no model is *a priori* preferable, and hence that the models should be treated symmetrically. This corroborates with the views expressed in Granger, King, and White (1995). In general, this implies that a final model is selected which minimizes the value of a certain criterion function.

The standard coefficient of determination R^2 may be less useful for evaluating time series models. For example, for the AR(1) model $y_t = \phi_1 y_{t-1} + \varepsilon_t$, it follows, at least theoretically, that

$$
\begin{aligned}
R^2 &= 1 - \sigma^2/\gamma_0 \\
&= 1 - \sigma^2/[\sigma^2/(1 - \phi_1^2)] \\
&= \phi_1^2.
\end{aligned}
\tag{3.104}
$$

Hence, the R^2 depends solely on the AR parameter. This expression shows that the R^2 in case of $\phi_1 = 0.9$ is much larger than in case $\phi_1 = 0.2$, while both appear to be adequate, see also Nelson (1976). Modified R^2 criteria appear in Harvey (1989).

Two often applied criteria to select between time series models are the information criteria put forward by Akaike (1974) and Schwarz (1978) (and Rissanen, 1978). Both criteria evaluate the fit versus the number of parameters. When n now denotes the number of effective observations (which are the observations needed to estimate the parameters), and when k denotes the number of ARMA parameters to be estimated, the Akaike Information Criterion [AIC] is given by

$$
\text{AIC}(k) = n\log\hat{\sigma}_{ML}^2 + 2k,
\tag{3.105}
$$

where $\hat{\sigma}_{ML}^2 = \text{RSS}/n$, and RSS is the residual sum of squares. The value of k that minimizes AIC(k) is selected. The same decision rule applies for the Schwarz criterion, which is given by

$$
\text{SIC}(k) = n\log\hat{\sigma}_{ML}^2 + k\log n.
\tag{3.106}
$$

Comparing the expressions for AIC and SIC, it is clear that, when $n \geq 8$, the SIC criterion penalizes the inclusion of regressors (and thus of additional parameters) more than the AIC does. This means that the model order selected with the SIC criterion is usually smaller than the model order selected with the AIC.

As an illustration of the model selection procedure, consider the Chinese log transportation series (in first differences) for the estimation

Table 3.2. *Model selection for the growth of the annual index of output in the transportation sector in China*

Model	RSS	k	$F_{AC,1-1}$	AIC	SIC
AR(1)	0.7951	1	4.226	−88.67	−87.41
MA(1)	0.7495	1	0.057	−90.21	−88.95
MA(2)	0.7377	2	1.732	−88.62	−86.10
ARMA(1,1)	0.7501	2	2.301	−88.19	−85.67
AR(2)	0.6715	2	3.003	−91.06	−88.55
ARMA(2,1)	0.5117	3	4.398**	−96.03	−92.36
ARMA(1,2)	0.6050	3	7.888**	−91.78	−88.00
ARMA(2,2)	0.5153	4	3.719	−93.95	−88.92

Notes:
** Significant at the 5% level.
All models are estimated for the sample 1955–1980, i.e., using 26 annual observations. The observations in 1953 and 1954 are used as starting-values for the models which include $\Delta_1 y_{t-1}$ and $\Delta_1 y_{t-2}$.

sample 1955 to 1980, where observations before 1955 are used as starting values for the various models, and the observations for 1981 to 1988 will be used for evaluating the forecasts later on. The first four values of the EACF (for a sample of 26 observations) are 0.339, −0.240, −0.524, and −0.294, and the first four EPACF values are 0.339, −0.402, −0.368, and −0.081. With a standard deviation of 0.196, it is not immediately obvious which ARMA model would be a good starting point. Hence, we may decide to estimate eight different models, the key results of which are given in table 3.2.

For this $\Delta_1 y_t$ series, the AIC prefers the ARMA(2,2) model, while the SIC opts for the MA(1) model. Notice that the ARMA(2,1) and ARMA(1,2) models do not enter this final model selection stage since the $F_{AC,1-1}$-test values indicate that their errors are not approximately white noise. In the next section, we will see which of the selected models is preferred for forecasting (at least for 1981–1988).

3.5   Forecasting

Once one or more time series models have been selected we may generate one-step and h-step ahead forecasts for y_t (where y_t denotes a suitably differenced variable). The forecasts concern the observations y_{n+h} and hence will be denoted as $\hat{y}_{n+h}$, with $h = 1,2,...,m$. In general, a one-step ahead forecast is defined by $\hat{y}_{n+1}$, which is based on the information set Y_n. In the case where m observations have been recorded to evaluate one-step ahead fore-casts, we advance the information set with each forecast. For example, $\hat{y}_{n+2}$ is then based on Y_{n+1} and $\hat{y}_{n+3}$ is based on Y_{n+2}. The intuitive motivation behind this is that we may not always be able (or willing) to re-estimate the parameters of the time series model. In that case, we keep the estimates for the parameters fixed for the sample $t=1,2,...,n$, while making one-step ahead forecasts for y_{n+1} to y_{n+m}. If possible, we can also decide to estimate the parameters for each of the information sets Y_{n+h-1}. Furthermore, we may then delete the first h data points, such that the estimation sample has the same size for all the m forecasts. Finally, an h-step (or dynamic) forecast denotes a forecast of y_{n+h} (for $h=1,2,...,m$) which is based on Y_n. Obviously, when h is larger than the memory of the model (or, for example, the length of the AR polynomial), the forecasts $\hat{y}_{n+h}$ likely include forecasts for previous data points as $\hat{y}_{n+h-1}$ and also forecast errors tend to build up, as will become clear below.

The principle of forecasting from ARMA models is very simple, as will be clear from the next few examples. Consider the MA(2) model

$$y_t = \varepsilon_t + \theta_1\varepsilon_{t-1} + \theta_2\varepsilon_{t-2}, \quad t=1,2,...,n \tag{3.107}$$

for which it is easy to see that

$$y_{n+1} = \varepsilon_{n+1} + \theta_1\varepsilon_n + \theta_2\varepsilon_{n-1}. \tag{3.108}$$

At time n, the ε_{n+1} is unknown, and since for its expectation at time n holds that $E_n\varepsilon_{n+1}=0$, an unbiased forecast of y_{n+1} equals

$$\hat{y}_{n+1} = \theta_1\varepsilon_n + \theta_2\varepsilon_{n-1}. \tag{3.109}$$

In practice, θ_1, θ_2, ε_n, and ε_{n-1} should be estimated, but for convenience I assume that these estimates are given. Comparing the expressions for y_{n+1} and $\hat{y}_{n+1}$, the forecast error (or prediction error) appears to be equal to

$$y_{n+1} - \hat{y}_{n+1} = \varepsilon_{n+1} \tag{3.110}$$

and hence the squared prediction error [SPE] is σ^2. For two steps ahead, we have

$$y_{n+2} - \hat{y}_{n+2} = (\varepsilon_{n+2} + \theta_1\varepsilon_{n+2} + \theta_2\varepsilon_n) - (\theta_2\varepsilon_n) \tag{3.111}$$

since at time n, ε_{n+2} and ε_{n+1} are unknown, for which the SPE equals $(1+\theta_1^2)\sigma^2$. For three steps ahead, we get

$$y_{n+3} - \hat{y}_{n+3} = (\varepsilon_{n+3} + \theta_1\varepsilon_{n+2} + \theta_2\varepsilon_{n+1}) - (0) \tag{3.112}$$

and hence the SPE equals $(1+\theta_1^2+\theta_2^2)\sigma^2$. Similar to three steps ahead, there is no memory in the MA(2) model that can help to forecast y_t four steps ahead since

$$y_{n+4} - \hat{y}_{n+4} = (\varepsilon_{n+4} + \theta_1\varepsilon_{n+3} + \theta_2\varepsilon_{n+2}) - (0) \qquad (3.113)$$

which again yields an SPE of $(1 + \theta_1^2 + \theta_2^2)\sigma^2$.

In general, for an MA(q) model the h-step ahead forecast equals

$$\hat{y}_{n+h} = \sum_{i=0}^{q} \theta_{i+h}\varepsilon_{n-i} \qquad (3.114)$$

with $\theta_0 = 1$ and $\theta_{i+h} = 0$ for $i + h > q$, with an h-step error

$$\varepsilon_{n+h} = y_{n+h} - \hat{y}_{n+h} = \sum_{i=0}^{h-1} \theta_i\varepsilon_{n+h-i} \qquad (3.115)$$

Given the white noise assumption on ε_t it follows that

$$E(e_{n+h}) = 0, \text{ and} \qquad (3.116)$$

$$\text{SPE}(h) = E(e_{n+h}^2) = \sigma^2 \sum_{i=0}^{h-1} \theta_i^2. \qquad (3.117)$$

From (3.114) we can see that generally for a zero mean time series that can be described by a MA(q) model it implies that $\hat{y}_{n+h} = 0$ when $h > q$. Assuming normality, a 95 percent forecasting interval for y_{n+h} is bounded by $\hat{y}_{n+h} - 1.95\text{RSPE}(h)$ and $\hat{y}_{n+h} + 1.95\text{RSPE}(h)$, where RSPE denotes the square root of SPE(h).

Since for an AR(p) model it holds that y_t depends on all the previous observations, the h-step ahead forecasts have similar properties. Consider for example the AR(2) model

$$y_t = \phi_1 y_{t-1} + \phi_2 y_{t-2} + \varepsilon_t \qquad (3.118)$$

and the one-step ahead forecast at time n, that is

$$\hat{y}_{n+1} = \phi_1 y_n + \phi_2 y_{n-1}. \qquad (3.119)$$

Since

$$y_{n+1} = \phi_1 y_n + \phi_2 y_{n-1} + \varepsilon_{n+1} \qquad (3.120)$$

the SPE for one-step ahead, denoted as SPE(1), is σ^2. For two steps ahead, we obtain

$$\begin{aligned} \hat{y}_{n+2} &= \phi_1\hat{y}_{n+1} + \phi_2 y_n \\ &= \phi_1(\phi_1 y_n + \phi_2 y_{n-1}) + \phi_2 y_n. \end{aligned} \qquad (3.121)$$

Since

$$\begin{aligned} y_{n+2} &= \phi_1 y_{n+1} + \phi_2 y_n + \varepsilon_{n+2} \\ &= \phi_1(\phi_1 y_n + \phi_2 y_{n-1} + \varepsilon_{n+1}) + \phi_2 y_n + \varepsilon_{n+2} \end{aligned} \qquad (3.122)$$

it holds that

$$\text{SPE}(2) = (1 + \phi_1^2)\sigma^2. \tag{3.123}$$

For three steps ahead, we would have

$$
\begin{aligned}
\hat{y}_{n+3} &= \phi_1 \hat{y}_{n+2} + \phi_2 \hat{y}_{n+1} \\
&= \phi_1(\phi_1(\phi_1 y_n + \phi_2 y_{n-1}) + \phi_2 y_n) + \phi_2(\phi_1 y_n + \phi_2 y_{n-1})
\end{aligned} \tag{3.124}
$$

and since

$$
\begin{aligned}
y_{n+3} &= \phi_1 y_{n+2} + \phi_2 y_{n+1} + \varepsilon_{n+3} \\
&= \phi_1(\phi_1(\phi_1 y_n + \phi_2 y_{n-1} + \varepsilon_{n+1}) + \phi_2 y_n + \varepsilon_{n+2}) \\
&\quad + \phi_2(\phi_1 y_n + \phi_2 y_{n-1} + \varepsilon_{n+1}) + \varepsilon_{n+3}
\end{aligned} \tag{3.125}
$$

the forecast error variance is

$$\text{SPE}(3) = (1 + \phi_1^2 + \phi_2^2 + 2\phi_1^2\phi_2 + \phi_1^4)\sigma^2 \tag{3.126}$$

which shows that $\text{SPE}(3) > \text{SPE}(2)$. In general, it holds that for $\text{AR}(p)$ models $\text{SPE}(h) > \text{SPE}(h-1)$. The expression in (3.126) clearly shows that the expression for h-step ahead forecast errors can be notationally cumbersome. It is then more useful to write an $\text{AR}(p)$ model into MA format, and as such use similar formulas as (3.117). For example, the AR(2) model (3.118) can be written as

$$y_t = \varepsilon_t + \eta_1 \varepsilon_{t-1} + \eta_2 \varepsilon_{t-2} + \eta_3 \varepsilon_{t-3} + \ldots \tag{3.127}$$

for which it holds that

$$\text{SPE}(h) = \sigma^2 \sum_{i=0}^{h-1} \eta_i^2, \quad \text{with } \eta_0 = 1. \tag{3.128}$$

For the AR(3) model, it is easy to verify that $\eta_1 = \phi_1$ and $\eta_2 = \phi_1^2 + \phi_2$, which with (3.128) leads to (3.126).

The h-step ahead forecast for ARMA models are derived along similar lines as for AR and MA models. For example, for the ARMA(1,1) model we have

$$\hat{y}_{n+1} = \phi_1 y_n + \theta_1 \varepsilon_n, \tag{3.129}$$

with obviously again $\text{SPE}(1) = \sigma^2$, and

$$
\begin{aligned}
\hat{y}_{n+2} &= \phi_1 \hat{y}_{n+1} \\
&= \phi_1(\phi_1 y_n + \theta_1 \varepsilon_n)
\end{aligned} \tag{3.130}
$$

which compares with

$$
\begin{aligned}
\hat{y}_{n+2} &= \phi_1 y_{n+1} + \varepsilon_{n+2} + \theta_1 \varepsilon_{n+1} \\
&= \phi_1(\phi_1 y_n + \varepsilon_{n+1} + \theta_1 \varepsilon_n) + \varepsilon_{n+2} + \theta_1 \varepsilon_{n+1}
\end{aligned} \tag{3.131}
$$

such that $\text{SPE}(2) = (1 + \theta_1^2 + \phi_1^2 + 2\phi_1\theta_1)\sigma^2$. This last expression can also be derived by writing the $\text{ARMA}(1,1)$ model as

$$y_t = (1 - \phi_1 L)^{-1}(1 + \theta_1 L)\varepsilon_t = \varepsilon_t + \eta_1\varepsilon_{t-1} + \eta_2\varepsilon_{t-2}$$
$$+ \eta_3\varepsilon_{t-3} + \cdots, \tag{3.132}$$

where $\eta_1 = \phi_1 + \theta_1$.

A final remark about forecasting concerns forecasting w_t when a model has been made for $y_t = \log(w_t)$. Consider again the MA(2) process, and its one-step ahead forecast

$$\hat{y}_{n+1} = \theta_1\varepsilon_n + \theta_2\varepsilon_{n-1}. \tag{3.133}$$

If one wants to forecast w_{n+1} using

$$\hat{w}_{n+1} = \exp(\hat{y}_{n+1}) \tag{3.134}$$

it is easy to show that $\hat{w}_{n+1}$ is biased for w_{n+1} since

$$E(w_{n+1}) = E[\exp(\varepsilon_{n+1} + \theta_1\varepsilon_n + \theta_2\varepsilon_{n-1})] \tag{3.135}$$
$$= \exp(\sigma^2/2)E[\exp(\theta_1\varepsilon_n + \theta_2\varepsilon_{n-1})]$$
$$= \exp(\sigma^2/2)\hat{w}_{n+1}.$$

Hence, an unbiased forecast of w_{n+1} in case of a model for logs, is given by $\exp(\sigma^2/2)\hat{w}_{n+1}$, where $\hat{w}_{n+1}$ is called the naive forecast. For two steps ahead, we have that

$$E(w_{n+2}) = E[\exp(\varepsilon_{n+2} + \theta_1\varepsilon_{n+1} + \theta_2\varepsilon_n)] \tag{3.136}$$
$$= \exp[(1 + \theta_1^2)\sigma^2/2]E[\exp(\theta_2\varepsilon_n)]$$
$$= \exp[(1 + \theta_1^2)\sigma^2/2]\hat{w}_{n+2}.$$

When ARMA models are written in MA format as (3.127), we can derive proper expressions for the correction factor of the naive forecasts for w_{n+h}. See Granger and Newbold (1976) for additional derivations.

Comparing forecasts

A common practical procedure is to keep m observations to evaluate forecasts from models which are fitted to the first n observations. One possibility is to check whether 95 percent of the forecasts indeed lie within the 95 percent interval. If so, we gain confidence in the models. If not, it is likely that the variance of the data will be underestimated. Furthermore, we would want the forecast errors e_{n+h} to be about randomly positive or negative. If not, the models underestimate or overestimate the conditional mean of the time series. Usually, this can be interpreted as that the deterministic component in the model such as mean and trend are not adequately specified.

In many empirical studies it appears that the models that tend to do best for within-sample data do not necessarily forecast better out of sample. There is no strict rule for that, but empirical experience suggests that it may be better to select a few models based on the AIC and SIC, and to evaluate these on the m hold-out data. This last evaluation can be based on the (root) mean squared prediction error [(R)MSPE]

$$\text{MSPE} = (1/m) \left[\sum_{h=1}^{m} (\hat{y}_{n+h} - y_{n+h})^2 \right] \tag{3.137}$$

or the mean absolute percentage error [MAPE]

$$\text{MAPE} = (1/m) \left[\sum_{h=1}^{m} |(\hat{y}_{n+h} - y_{n+h})/y_{n+h}| \right] \tag{3.138}$$

although other criteria are also available. It should be mentioned that MAPE is not very useful for very small observations like growth rates.

Finally, if we want to decide whether, for example, the MSPEs of two models A and B are significantly different, a simple procedure is to create the new variable d_j, with $j = 1, 2, \ldots, m$, which equals 1 when the MSPE_A exceeds MSPE_B, and zero otherwise. We can now construct the sign test statistic S defined by

$$S = (m/4)^{-\frac{1}{2}} \left[\sum_{h=1}^{m} d_j - (m/2) \right] \sim N(0,1) \tag{3.139}$$

to decide whether there are significant differences between the MSPEs. The simulation results in Diebold and Mariano (1995) indicate that the S test is useful in practice, although for small values of m the asymptotic $N(0,1)$ distribution may not hold.

As an illustration, consider the empirical results for three models for the growth rates of the output in the transportation sector in China. Table 3.3 gives the RMSPEs and the number of times the forecasts exceed the true values for the AR(2), ARMA(2,2), and MA(1) models. These models seem preferable to using the AIC and SIC in table 3.2.

For one-step ahead, the MA(1) model is best, while for one to eight steps ahead the AR(2) has the lowest RMSPE. The number of positive forecast errors is large, suggesting that the mean of the time series may not be well estimated. Given the graphs in figure 2.1, this may be due to outlying observations. The final two columns give the estimates of two times the root mean squared prediction errors for one-step and eight-steps ahead (i.e., the 95 percent forecasting intervals). It appears that the MA(1) model is most precise for eight-steps ahead.

Table 3.3. *Forecasting the growth of the annual index of output in the transportation sector in China for 1981–1988, based on ARMA models with estimated parameters for 1955–1980*

| | 1-step ahead | | *h*-steps ahead | | forecast intervals | |
Model	RMSPE	# pfe	RMSPE	# pfe	1-step	8-step
AR(2)	0.060	7	0.063	7	0.174	0.200
ARMA(2,2)	0.086	6	0.067	7	0.168	0.204
MA(1)	0.052	7	0.065	7	0.180	0.195

Notes:
pfe denotes the number of positive forecasting errors, where the forecast error is defined by $y_{n+h} - \hat{y}_{n+h}$. The forecasting intervals for one and eight steps ahead are defined by two times the roots of the mean squared prediction errors for 1 or 8 steps ahead, see (3.117).

Conclusion

In this chapter I discussed some important concepts in univariate time series modeling and forecasting. These concepts should be useful when analyzing time series with the typical features reviewed in chapter 2. Some of these concepts can be readily extended to multivariate series as well. In many cases below I will confine myself to ARI(p,d) models. Such models have many advantages over ARIMA(p,d,q) models. For example, estimation routines are simple, the memory is longer and more useful for forecasting, these models are easy to identify, and can reasonably easily be extended to multivariate models (as we will see in chapters 9 and 10). Also, non-linearity and outliers are more easily handled in the ARI framework.

In the next chapter I start off with a discussion of trends. The adequacy of forecasts from economic and business time series models can largely depend on the appropriate form of the trend. The concept of unit roots in AR polynomials will be shown to play a crucial role.

4 Trends

The graphs in chapter 2 show that many economic and business time series have a trending pattern, where for macroeconomic time series such trends typically move upwards. Although many practitioners would be able to indicate roughly what a trend is ("an upward moving pattern"), a formal definition of a trend cannot be given otherwise than in the context of a model. In other words, when we have agreed upon a time series model that describes the data, we can define a trend within such a framework. In this book, the focus is on ARMA type time series models, and hence the current chapter deals with trends within this model class. In principle, such trends imply possible unbounded behavior of the time series. For many macro-economic data this may be sensible, but for business economic data, one may sometimes expect that there is some upperbound to the time series. In the case of such non-linear trends, we deal with growth curves.

It is important to investigate the precise formulation of the trend in a time series prior to putting effort in modeling and forecasting. Firstly, the trend will dominate long-run out-of-sample forecasts, although short-run fore-casts also can be affected, as we will see in section 4.4. Secondly, when time series display, say, an increasing trend, such series are non-stationary. With such an upward trend, a time series does not show a tendency of mean reversion. This implies that it can be difficult to estimate the mean of a trending time series with some degree of precision. Notice that we can always find a value for a mean for a given sample of data, but for trending time series this estimate does not converge to some value when the number of observations increases. Thirdly, and related to the second issue, with an increasing trend, the variance of the forecast errors increases with any new observation. Obviously, this implies that the autocorrelation function can also vary over time, since it depends on the variance. In sum, for the summary statistics mean, variance, and autocovariance to be interpretable, these three measures should be constant over time, and hence one has to exercise care when analyzing trending time series.

A more formal definition of stationarity is that for a given time series y_t it should hold that (given $t-k \geq 1$)

$$E(y_t) = \mu \qquad \text{for all } t = 1,2,\ldots,n \qquad (4.1)$$

$$E[(y_t-\mu)^2] = \gamma_0 \qquad \text{for all } t = 1,2,\ldots,n \qquad (4.2)$$

$$E[(y_t-\mu)(y_{t-k}-\mu)] = \gamma_k \quad \text{for all } t = 1,2,\ldots,n \qquad (4.3)$$
$$\text{and for all } k = \ldots,-2,-1,0,1,2,\ldots$$

where μ, γ_0, and γ_k are all finite-valued numbers. For a given time series it is usually difficult to verify whether these three conditions hold at the same time. Intuitively, to verify (4.1) with a certain test statistic, we need an estimate of the variance of y_t, which in turn should obey (4.2), which in turn depends on the validity of (4.1). Hence, for practical purposes (4.1)–(4.3) are not very useful.

One way to overcome the practical limitations of (4.1)–(4.3) while investigating the stationarity or trending behavior of a time series is to consider stationarity and trends within the framework of, for example, an $AR(p)$ time series model, possibly with deterministic components. Hence, it is possible to show which values of parameters in an $AR(p)$ model or which components in the deterministic part of the model correspond with a time series for which (4.1) to (4.3) do not hold. Obviously, when the deterministic component includes the variable t, $t = 1,2,\ldots,n$, the y_t series has a deterministic trend. And, when the $AR(p)$ part of the model contains the component $(1-L)$, we say that the y_t series has a stochastic trend. In practice, we proceed as follows. An $AR(p)$ time series model is fitted to y_t, and we test whether the trend t contributes to the explanation of y_t, and whether a $(1-L)$ component can be separated out from the $AR(p)$ part. Since $(1-L)$ concerns a solution 1 to the characteristic polynomial of the $AR(p)$ model, we say that in the stochastic trend case, we investigate the presence of a unit root. Notice that trends are only defined in the context of $AR(p)$ models (or ARMA models), see chapter 3. In fact, since a pure $MA(q)$ model only contains ε_t variables, it is easy to verify that the conditions (4.1)–(4.3) always hold.

In this chapter, I review various models for trends in section 4.1, and methods to check whether a time series is stationary or not in the sections 4.2 and 4.3. In section 4.2, I discuss the Dickey–Fuller (1979) method, and in section 4.3, I limit attention to the Kwiatkowski *et al.* (1992) method. The literature on this topic has expanded enormously in the last few decades, mainly because the statistical methods involved are non-standard. Of course, it is virtually impossible to treat all issues. The interested reader should consult more extensive surveys, which appear in Banerjee *et al.* (1993), Hamilton (1994), and Hatanaka (1996), amongst many others. The main aim of this chapter is to show how trends can be modeled, and how these decisions can affect out-of-sample forecasting, as will be discussed in section 4.4. In chapter 10 we will see that a decision on trends in univariate time series has an impact on how to proceed with modeling a set of time series in a multivariate model.

4.1 Modeling trends

To discuss the various possible representations of trends within the context of an autoregressive time series model, consider the AR(1) model for y_t, where y_t is considered in deviation of a possible deterministic trend, that is

$$y_t - \mu - \delta t = \phi_1(y_{t-1} - \mu - \delta(t-1)) + \varepsilon_t, \quad t = 2, 3, \ldots, n. \tag{4.4}$$

This expression can be rewritten as

$$y_t = (1 - \phi_1)\mu + \phi_1\delta + (1 - \phi_1)\delta t + \phi_1 y_{t-1} + \varepsilon_t, \quad t = 2, 3, \ldots, n. \tag{4.5}$$

or briefly as

$$y_t = \mu^* + \delta^* t + \phi_1 y_{t-1} + \varepsilon_t, \quad t = 2, 3, \ldots, n. \tag{4.6}$$

which corresponds with the model we would consider for the estimation of μ, δ, and ϕ_1, see also chapter 3 for the no trend case.

Defining $z_t = y_t - \mu - \delta t$, we can solve (4.4) by recursively substituting lagged z_t values as

$$z_t = (\phi_1)^t z_0 + \sum_{i=1}^{t} (\phi_1)^{t-i} \varepsilon_i, \tag{4.7}$$

where z_0 is a pre-sample starting value of z_t. When $|\phi_1| < 1$, (4.7) indicates that the impact of this z_0 decreases and that more recent shocks ε_t have more impact on z_t than less recent ones. In fact, the effect of such shocks dies out in the long run. In other words, such shocks are transitory. Since (4.4) can be written as

$$\Delta_1 z_t = (\phi_1 - 1)z_{t-1} + \varepsilon_t \tag{4.8}$$

it can be observed that when $|\phi_1| < 1$, positive values of z_{t-1} will lead to a decrease in z_t through $\Delta_1 z_t$, and negative values lead to an increase in z_t. Since positive and negative values of z_t correspond with y_t being larger or smaller than its mean $\mu + \delta t$, we say that when $|\phi_1| < 1$, the time series y_t display mean- (or trend-) reverting behavior. The results in chapter 3 on the ACF and PACF of an AR(1) model show that these functions take constant values when $|\phi_1|$ is smaller than 1. Since the deterministic trend variable t is included in (4.4), we say that when y_t can be described by (4.4) and $|\phi_1| < 1$, the y_t series is a trend-stationary time series and that it can be described by a deterministic trend model [DT model].

When $\phi_1 = 1$ there is no mean-reverting behavior since then (4.8) reduces to

$$\Delta_1 z_t = \varepsilon_t \tag{4.9}$$

or in terms of y_t, (4.5) becomes

$$y_t = \delta + y_{t-1} + \varepsilon_t. \tag{4.10}$$

This model is called a random walk with drift, where this drift equals δ. With $\phi_1 = 1$, it also holds that (4.9) can be written as

$$z_t = z_0 + \sum_{i=1}^{t} \varepsilon_i \tag{4.11}$$

or again in terms of y_t, that

$$y_t = y_0 + \delta t + \sum_{i=1}^{t} \varepsilon_i, \tag{4.12}$$

where y_0 is some function of the pre-sample observations and μ. The partial sum time series $S_t = \sum_{i=1}^{t} \varepsilon_i$ is now called the stochastic trend. Hence, when y_t can be described by (4.10) it has a deterministic trend and a stochastic trend. In order to avoid confusion, when $\phi_1 = 1$, y_t is said to be described by a stochastic trend model [ST model]. For a ST model it holds that shocks have a permanent effect. Since the AR(1) polynomial for (4.10) equals $(1-L)$, of which the solution to the characteristic equation $(1-z) = 0$ equals 1, this ST model corresponds with an AR model with a so-called unit root.

When ε_t in (4.4) is replaced by $\eta_t = [\phi_{p-1}(L)]^{-1} \varepsilon_t$, where $\phi_{p-1}(L)$ does not contain the component $(1-L)$, all above results continue to hold. Hence, when an AR(p) polynomial $\phi_p(L)$ can be decomposed as $\phi_{p-1}(L)(1-L)$, the time series y_t has a stochastic trend. When $\phi_p(L)$ does not contain $(1-L)$ and the deterministic part of the model includes a trend term t, y_t has a deterministic trend. In general it holds that an ST time series can be made stationary by applying the Δ_1 differencing filter. This means that we turn to analyzing an AR($p-1$) model for $(1-L)y_t$ instead of an AR(p) model for y_t. Therefore, we sometimes call y_t a difference-stationary time series.

To illustrate the differences between DT and ST models, consider the data depicted in figure 4.1, which are generated from

$$\text{DT: } y_t = 0.2t + \varepsilon_t \qquad t = 1,2,3,...,200 \tag{4.13}$$

$$\text{ST: } y_t = 0.2 + y_{t-1} + \varepsilon_t \quad t = 1,2,3,...,200 \text{ and } y_1 = 0, \tag{4.14}$$

where 200 observations for ε_t are drawn from the N $(0, 0.25)$ distribution, and which are used in both equations.

Clearly, the upward-moving trend in both time series is similar, as can be expected given (4.4) and (4.12). The key difference between the series is that

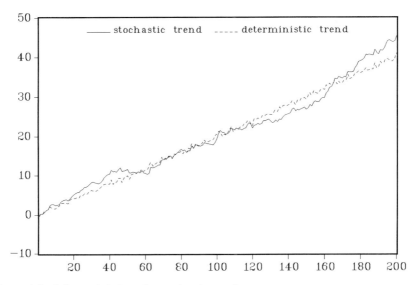

Figure 4.1 *A deterministic and a stochastic trend*

the ST time series can deviate from this trend for lengthy periods of time. This displays the lack of mean-reverting forces for ST time series. For values of δ that are small relative to the ε_t observations, we can in fact generate data which never seem to revert to some mean, see also figure 3.1. The ST time series displays features different from the DT time series because of the partial sum series $S_t = \Sigma^t_{i=1}\varepsilon_i$.

To illustrate that the patterns in figure 4.1 can reflect the behavior of truly observed time series, consider the results from the auxiliary regression

$$y_t = \hat{\tau} + \hat{\psi}t + \hat{u}_t \tag{4.15}$$

which was also used in chapter 2 for the USA industrial production series (seasonally adjusted) for the sample 1960.1–1991.4 in figure 4.2.

Figure 4.2 displays y_t, the fit $\hat{y}_t = \hat{\tau} + \hat{\psi}t$ from (4.15) and $\hat{u}_t$. Clearly, there is a trend in USA industrial production. Additionally, the residuals $\hat{u}_t$ seem to mimic the ST pattern in figure 4.1, and hence it may be that this variable can be described by an ST model.

The selection between ST and DT models for y_t may be important from an economic point of view. For example, it can be useful to know whether shocks to a certain time series have a permanent effect or not, as in the ST and DT model, respectively. From a forecasting perspective it is also important to consider the most appropriate model for forecasting. In fact, for

$$y_t = y_{t-1} + \gamma + \varepsilon_t, \tag{4.16}$$

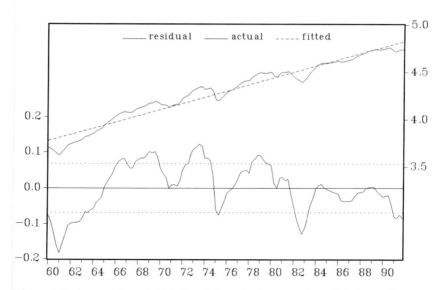

Figure 4.2 *A regression of US industrial production on a deterministic trend*

the two-step ahead forecast at time n is

$$\hat{y}_{n+2} = \hat{y}_{n+1} + \gamma = y_n + 2\gamma. \tag{4.17}$$

Since the true value y_{n+2} equals

$$y_{n+2} = y_{n+1} + \gamma + \varepsilon_{n+2} = y_n + 2\gamma + \varepsilon_{n+2} + \varepsilon_{n+1}, \tag{4.18}$$

the SPE(2) is $2\sigma^2$. For the DT time series

$$y_t = \gamma + \vartheta t + \phi_1 y_{t-1} + \varepsilon_t, \tag{4.19}$$

it is easily found that $\text{SPE}(2) = (1 + \phi_1^2)\sigma^2$. Obviously, when ϕ_1 is smaller than 1, the latter expression for SPE(2) is smaller than that for the random walk with drift model. Hence, the out-of-sample forecasts from the ST model are not as precise as those from the DT model. The higher level of uncertainty for the ST model, which is reflected by the fact that shocks have a permanent effect and thus can change the level of y_t permanently, is in turn reflected by wider forecasting intervals relative to the DT model.

In order to select between a ST and DT model for a given empirical time series y_t, there exists a wide variety of methods. These methods either pay close attention to the $(1-L)$ component in the AR(p) model for y_t or to the relative importance of the stochastic trend component $\Sigma_{i=1}^t \varepsilon_t$. The first set of methods are called tests for unit roots, and an often applied method in practice will be discussed in section 4.2. The second set of

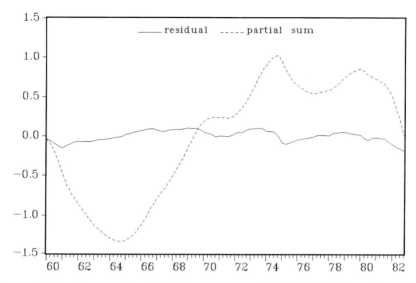

Figure 4.3 *Partial sums of residuals from regression (4.15) for US industrial production, 1960.1–1982.4*

methods are called stationarity tests, and one of these will be discussed in section 4.3. With respect to the latter, consider the residuals from the regression (4.15) for the same USA data (but now for the sample 1960.1–1982.4 since the last part is reserved for the evaluation of forecasts) and their partial sums

$$\hat{S}_t = \sum_{i=1}^{t} \hat{u}_t \qquad (4.20)$$

in figure 4.3. When such an $\hat{S}_t$ series takes large values, we may say that there is a large stochastic trend component in y_t. The graphs in figure 4.3 suggest that this is the case for USA industrial production. More formal test results appear in sections 4.2 and 4.3 below.

Integration

A time series y_t that requires the first differencing filter Δ_1 to remove the stochastic trend is called a time series that is integrated of order 1[I(1)]. There are also time series that even after first differencing contain a stochastic trend. An example is represented by

$$z_t = z_{t-1} + \delta + \varepsilon_t \qquad (4.21)$$

with $z_t = y_t - y_{t-1}$, such that $\Delta_1^2 y_t = \delta + \varepsilon_t$. In this case, y_t is an I(2) time series since it needs the Δ_1 filter twice to become stationary.

One way to understand the possible practical relevance of I(2) processes, which typically seem to occur for nominal monetary aggregates and price levels of rapidly growing economies, is by the following representation

$$\Delta_1 y_t = \delta_t + \varepsilon_t \tag{4.22}$$

$$\delta_t = \delta_{t-1} + \eta_t, \tag{4.23}$$

that is, the growth rate of y_t has a time-varying mean δ_t, which is again a random walk process, see Harvey (1989). When the mean and variance of η_t equal zero, the mean of $\Delta_1 y_t$ is constant, and hence $\Delta_1 y_t$ shows mean-reverting behavior. It should be mentioned that testing for this variance to be equal to zero is one other way to select between ST and DT models, as will become clear in section 4.3. The expressions in (4.22) and (4.23) can be combined into

$$\Delta_1^2 y_t = v_t, \tag{4.24}$$

where v_t is the MA(1) process given by $\eta_t + (1-L)\varepsilon_t$. The variance of the v_t series is $\sigma_\eta^2 + 2\sigma^2$ and $\gamma_1 = -\sigma^2$. When σ_η^2 is very small relative to σ^2, ρ_1 approximates -0.5, and hence it seems that the $(1-L)$ polynomial is redundant. However, when for example $\sigma_\eta^2 = 0.5\sigma^2$, the model becomes

$$\Delta_1^2 y_t = (1-0.5L)v_t \tag{4.25}$$

which can be derived from ρ_1 of v_t, with v_t a white noise error series. Notice that when δ_t does not change much, the resultant $\Delta_1^2 y_t$ series may easily seem overdifferenced. Furthermore, in the case where δ_t only changes slightly, which results in a time series model as (4.25) with a large MA component, it is difficult to select between Δ_1^2 and Δ_1 since the Δ_1 polynomial almost cancels out from both sides.

An I(2) time series has a growth rate which fluctuates randomly over time and hence has two stochastic trends. This can be observed from solving (4.21) as

$$z_t = z_0 + \delta t + \sum_{i=1}^{t} \varepsilon_i$$

such that

$$y_1 = z_1 = z_0 + \delta + \varepsilon_1$$
$$y_2 = z_1 + z_2 = z_0 + \delta + \varepsilon_1 + z_0 + 2\delta + \varepsilon_1 + \varepsilon_2$$
$$y_3 = z_0 + \delta + \varepsilon_1 + z_0 + 2\delta + \varepsilon_1 + \varepsilon_2 + z_0 + 3\delta + \varepsilon_1 + \varepsilon_2 + \varepsilon_3$$
$$\dots$$

$$y_t = y_0 + z_0 t + \delta t(t+1)/2 + \sum_{i=1}^{t}\sum_{j=1}^{i} \varepsilon_j. \tag{4.26}$$

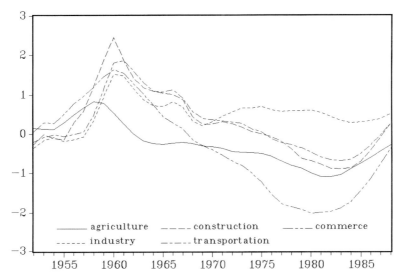

Figure 4.4 *Partial sums of residuals from regression (4.15) for five output sectors in China, 1954–1988*

This result shows that when δ is not equal to zero, we should be able to detect an I(2) time series from its graph, that is, it displays explosive growth through the $t(t + 1)/2$ component. Furthermore, the double stochastic trend appears in the $\Sigma^t_{i=1} \Sigma^i_{j=1} \varepsilon_j$ component, which needs double differencing to be removed.

Common stochastic trends

As mentioned earlier, it is important to analyze the quality of the trends in univariate time series also for multivariate modeling. The main reason is that there are occasions where several time series display common stochastic trends. As an example, it is unlikely that the trend in real disposable income is different from that in real consumption, simply because if this were not the case we would persistently consume too much or save too much. In fact, we may expect that an error of consuming too much will effect future consumption and hence that there will be some form of error correction. Later in chapter 10, we will see that common trends and error correction are linked in the sense that one implies the other, and vice versa.

As an illustrative example of the possible presence of common stochastic trends, consider the estimated partial sums of the residuals of the regression in (4.15) for the five Chinese output series in figure 4.4.

Given that these five sectors are part of one and the same economy, it is not unexpected that the S_t series seem to display common patterns. Hence, it may be that linear combinations of these S_t variables do not contain stochastic trend components. In fact, it seems from figure 4.4 that if there are any stochastic trends in construction, commerce, and transportation, they have a similar pattern. I will return to these data in chapter 10, when dealing with the concept of common trends in terms of its companion concept of common integratedness or, briefly, cointegration.

Growth curves

In principle, the ST and DT models allow the y_t series to be unbounded. This may imply that such models cannot be useful for variables such as the unemployment rate, because this variable is bounded by 0 and 100. However, in small samples we may decide to allow such ST and DT models to yield approximately adequate data descriptions, although we should exercise care when forecasting many periods ahead.

For many marketing time series, it is conceivable that the time series converge to a certain maximum or minimum as time passes by. The market penetration of durable consumer goods such as dishwashers may be 100 percent in the long-run. Sales may have been small initially, while they rise through the adoption of the new product by the majority, and ultimately sales may decrease such that penetration converges to some saturation level. Hence, for time series variables that characterize some product or market life-cycle, we may wish to modify the above trend models to allow for a saturation level.

An overview of such so-called growth curves is given in Mahajan, Muller, and Bass (1993), see also Meade and Islam (1995). Two frequently used growth curves in practice are the Gompertz growth curve, given by

$$y_t = \alpha \exp[-\beta \exp(-\gamma t)] \tag{4.27}$$

and the logistic growth curve, given by

$$y_t = \alpha/[1 + \beta \exp(-\gamma t)], \tag{4.28}$$

where α is the saturation level, and α, β, and γ are all positive parameters. An example of a typical growth curve pattern is given in figure 4.5, for a Gompertz curve with $\alpha = 100$, $\beta = 4$, and $\gamma = 0.05$ (and adding $\varepsilon_t \sim N(0,1)$).

The expressions in (4.27) and (4.28) show that when time proceeds (that is, when t increases), the y_t value approaches α. The key difference between the two growth curves is the rate of increase toward α when y_t has passed the point of inflection, say, τ. It is easily shown that for the Gompertz curve it holds that $\partial^2 y_t / \partial^2 t = 0$ at time $\tau = \log\beta/\gamma$, and that then $y_\tau = \alpha/e$. For the

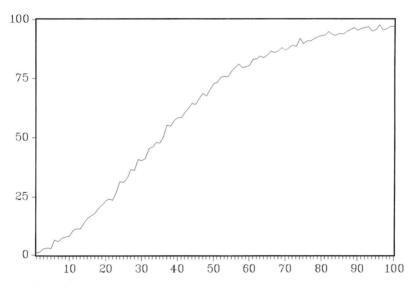

Figure 4.5 *A Gompertz curve*

logistic curve, we find that again the inflection point is at $\tau = \log\beta/\gamma$, though now $y_\tau = \alpha/2$. Hence, it takes longer to approach α for the Gompertz curve, say, after the sales have peaked.

Given that forecasts from logistic and Gompertz curves can differ because of their differing rates of convergence to α, it is important to be able to select between the two growth curves. Through simulations, Franses and Van der Nol (1997) show that taking one model while the other is appropriate can have dramatic effects on the estimate of the saturation level, which, of course, in turn dominates long-run forecasts. A simple selection method using only the data in the estimation sample is given by the recognition that the Gompertz curve can be rewritten as

$$\log(\Delta_1 \log y_t) = \beta^* + \gamma^* t \tag{4.29}$$

with β^* and γ^* being non-linear functions of β and γ, while the logistic model holds that

$$\log(\Delta_1 \log y_t) = \beta^{**} + \gamma_1 t + \gamma_2 t^2 + \gamma_3 t^3 + \dots \tag{4.30}$$

A simple regression-based test for the significance of γ_2, γ_3, and so on, can help to decide between (4.27) and (4.28), see Franses (1994).

As an illustration, consider the annual series in figure 4.6 of the millions of dollars that are paid for the rights to broadcast the Olympic Summer Games on USA television.

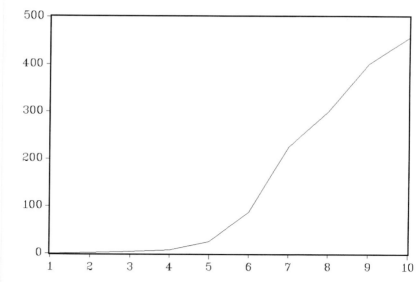

Figure 4.6 *US television rights (in million dollars) for Olympic Summer Games*

The first observation in figure 4.6 concerns Rome in 1960, while the last data point is that for Atlanta in 1996, see the data appendix. Comparing this graph with that in figure 4.5 shows that a growth curve may be useful. The t-ratio of γ_2 in (4.30), in which no additional powers of t are included because of the limited number of observations, equals -2.045, and hence I proceed with a logistic curve. There are many different estimation methods for growth curves, see Meade and Islam (1995), but here I use the non-linear least squares [NLS] routine in MicroTSP with starting-values 1,000, 0, and 0 for α, β and γ, respectively. The final estimation result is

$$y_t = 475.024/\,(1+2167.371\exp\,(-1.049t)) + \hat{\varepsilon}_t \qquad (4.31)$$
$$\;\;(21.850)\quad\;\;(1563.442)\qquad(0.111)$$

with an R^2 of 0.995. Hence, the estimated saturation level is 475 million dollars and the inflection point was reached at the Olympic Games in 1984 (Los Angeles).

Fractional integration

In a sense, the above growth curves, which are neither a linear DT nor an ST model, may be viewed as being integrated of an order unequal to 0, 1, or 2. Such time series do not return to their mean, but are also not unbounded. Loosely speaking, such time series seem somehow fractionally integrated.

The concept of fractional integration within the context of ARIMA models was first put forward by Granger and Joyeux (1980) and Hosking (1981). A fractionally integrated model appears useful to describe time series with very long cycles for which it is difficult to estimate their mean. Typically, the application of such a model concerns inflation rates and some other financial time series, see, for example, Hassler and Wolters (1995), Cheung (1993), and see also Baillie (1996) for a survey.

The simplest fractionally integrated time series model is defined as

$$(1-L)^d y_t = \varepsilon_t, \qquad 0 < d < 1, \tag{4.32}$$

where the differencing operator $(1-L)^d$ can be expanded infinitely as

$$(1-L)^d = 1 - dL - (1/2)d(1-d)L^2 - (1/6)d(1-d)(2-d)L^3 \tag{4.33}$$
$$- \ldots - (1/j!)d(1-d)(2-d)\ldots((j-1)-d)L^j - \ldots$$

which obviously becomes 1 for $d=0$ and $(1-L)$ for $d=1$. This expression shows that y_t can be described by an infinitely lengthy AR polynomial, of which the AR parameters never attain the value zero. When $0 < d < 0.5$, the time series is said to be long memory, and when $0.5 \le d < 1$, it is non-stationary.

Although much more accurate estimation methods for d are available, see, for example, Beran (1995) and Sowell (1992), we may exploit the fact that eventually the AR parameters do become very small, and also that (4.33) imposes a non-linear structure on the AR parameters. As an illustration, consider the $\Delta_1 y_t$ series, where $y_t = \log$ (prices in Argentina) for the sample 1972.1–1988.4, which can be described by an AR(1) model, which for this sample results in

$$\Delta_1 y_t = 0.090 + 0.674 \Delta_1 y_{t-1} + \hat{\varepsilon}_t \tag{4.34}$$
$$(0.028)\ (0.089)$$

with an RSS of 0.941. When the AR(∞) model implied by (4.33) is approximated by an AR(7) model, and the non-linear restrictions on the AR parameters that are implied by (4.33) are imposed, the ARFIMA model in (4.32) is quantified (using non-linear least squares) as

$$(1-L)^d \Delta_1 y_t = 0.046 + \hat{\varepsilon}_t, \qquad \text{with } \hat{d} = 0.583 \tag{4.35}$$
$$(0.024) \qquad\qquad\qquad (0.103)$$

with an RSS of 0.984. Notice that strictly speaking the intercept parameter in (4.35) is not identified when $d > 0.5$. Based on the residual sum of squares, the ARFIMA model does not seem to be preferrable. In case it would have, the estimation result for d suggests that price changes in

Argentina display non-stationary behavior, which cannot be detected using the simple AR(1) model in (4.34).

The above difficulty to show an in-sample improvement of an ARFIMA model over (possibly lengthy) AR models appears to pertain as well to out-of-sample forecasting. Crato and Ray (1996) show that simple AR models outperform ARFIMA models in out-of-sample forecasting, also because estimation of d can be quite complicated. Hence, further research of the empirical usefulness of ARFIMA models seems warranted.

4.2   Testing for unit roots

One of the specific features of a time series that is governed by a stochastic trend is that its AR representation (or the AR part of an ARMA model) contains the component $(1-L)$. In other words, the AR polynomial can be decomposed as

$$\begin{aligned}
\phi_p(L) &= 1 - \phi_1 L - \phi_2 L^2 - \ldots - \phi_p L^p \\
&= (1 - \alpha_1 L - \alpha_2 L^2 - \ldots - \alpha_{p-1} L^{p-1})(1-L) \\
&= \phi_{p-1}(L)\,(1-L)
\end{aligned} \tag{4.36}$$

When a time series is I(2), it holds true that

$$\phi_p(L) = \phi_{p-2}(L)(1-L)^2. \tag{4.37}$$

In case of an I(1) time series, it is easy to see using (4.36) that $(1-L)$ can be separated from the $\phi_p(L)$ polynomial when

$$\phi_p(1) = 1 - \phi_1 - \phi_2 - \ldots - \phi_p = 0 \tag{4.38}$$

and similarly for the I(2) series, it additionally holds that $\phi_{p-1}(1)=0$.

One unit root

In order to test for a single unit root in an AR(p) model, we may wish to test the restriction (4.38). A simple approach to this testing problem is proposed in Dickey and Fuller (1979). It is based on the fact that we can always write

$$\phi_p(L) = (1 - \phi_1 - \phi_2 - \ldots - \phi_p)L^i + \phi_{p-1}^*(L)(1-L) \tag{4.39}$$

for any $i = 1, 2, \ldots, p$. For example, consider the AR(2) model and setting i equal to 1 yields

$$1 - \phi_1 L - \phi_2 L^2 = (1 - \phi_1 - \phi_2)L + (\phi_0^* + \phi_1^* L)(1-L) \tag{4.40}$$

with $\phi_0^* = 1$ and $\phi_1^* = \phi_2$. When $\phi_2 = -1$ and ϕ_1 equals 2, (4.40) becomes $(1-L)^2$. The expression in (4.40) can be used to rewrite any AR(2) model

$$y_t = \phi_1 y_{t-1} + \phi_2 y_{t-2} + \varepsilon_t \tag{4.41}$$

into

$$\phi^*_{p-1}(L)\Delta_1 y_t = (\phi_1 + \phi_2 - 1)y_{t-1} + \varepsilon_t \tag{4.42}$$

with $\phi^*_{p-1}(L) = (\phi^*_0 + \phi^*_1 L)$. When $\phi_1 + \phi_2 - 1$ equals zero, (4.42) collapses to an AR(1) model for $\Delta_1 y_t$, that is, the AR(2) model becomes an ARI(1,1) model. Based on (4.39), the test for a unit root in an AR(p) polynomial proposed by Dickey and Fuller (1979) is then the t-test for the parameter ρ in the auxiliary regression

$$\Delta_1 y_t = \rho y_{t-1} + \alpha^*_1 \Delta_1 y_{t-1} + \ldots + \alpha^*_{p-1} \Delta_1 y_{t-(p-1)} + \varepsilon_t, \tag{4.43}$$

where $\alpha^*_i = -\phi^*_i$ defined in (4.39). The relevant null hypothesis is $\rho = 0$ and the alternative is $\rho < 0$. Hence, the test statistic is one-sided. Phillips (1987) derives the non-standard asymptotic distribution of the t-test statistic for ρ [$t(\hat{\rho})$]. Intuitively, under the null hypothesis of a unit root, the y_t series contains a stochastic trend, and hence its variance and autocovariances depend on time. The denominator of the t-test statistic includes a function of such variances, and therefore the distribution of $t(\hat{\rho})$ is not normal. Even though the variance is time dependent, Phillips (1987) shows that there exists an asymptotic distribution of $t(\hat{\rho})$. In the first panel of table 4.1, I display the critical values for $t(\hat{\rho})$ in the so-called augmented Dickey–Fuller regression (4.43) [ADF], which were obtained using Monte Carlo simulation. The null hypothesis of a unit root is rejected when the $t(\hat{\rho})$ value is lower than the critical value. If the null hypothesis cannot be rejected, the y_t series should be differenced with the $(1-L)$ operator prior to any further analysis.

Notice that the $t(\hat{\rho})$ test is a one-sided test since values of $\phi_1 + \ldots + \phi_p - 1$ which exceed 1 correspond with an explosive time series, for which a casual glance at the graph already indicates that it cannot be described by a DT model. The critical values shift slightly when the sample size increases.

Hall (1994) shows that when the order p in the AR(p) model for y_t is selected through t-tests on the α^*_1 to α^*_{p-1} parameters in (4.43) (or via an application of the AIC or SIC), the critical values in table 4.1 can still be used. Intuitively, this can be understood from the fact that in case of a single unit root, the $\Delta_1 y_t$ series does not have a stochastic trend component, while in the case where it is already stationary and the Δ_1 filter implies overdifferencing, the asymptotic normal distribution for the t-tests on the AR parameters still holds. Furthermore, Said and Dickey (1984) argue that when the data can better be described by an ARMA model then by a pure AR model, we should set $p-1$ in (4.43) at a higher value. Obviously, for such an ARMA model, the MA component should not be approximately similar to

Table 4.1. *Critical values for tests to select between deterministic trend and stochastic trend models, where the auxiliary test regression can contain a constant and/or a trend*

Auxiliary regression	Sample size	Critical value			
		10%	5%	2.5%	1%
Testing for unit roots with the Dickey–Fuller method (*t*-test)					
No constant, no trend	25	−1.60	−1.95	−2.26	−2.66
	50	−1.61	−1.95	−2.25	−2.62
	100	−1.61	−1.95	−2.24	−2.60
	250	−1.62	−1.95	−2.23	−2.58
	500	−1.62	−1.95	−2.23	−2.58
	∞	−1.62	−1.95	−2.23	−2.58
Constant, no trend	25	−2.63	−3.00	−3.33	−3.75
	50	−2.60	−2.93	−3.22	−3.58
	100	−2.58	−2.89	−3.17	−3.51
	250	−2.57	−2.88	−3.14	−3.46
	500	−2.57	−2.87	−3.13	−3.44
	∞	−2.57	−2.86	−3.12	−3.43
Constant and trend	25	−3.24	−3.60	−3.95	−4.38
	50	−3.18	−3.50	−3.80	−4.15
	100	−3.15	−3.45	−3.73	−4.04
	250	−3.13	−3.43	−3.69	−3.99
	500	−3.13	−3.42	−3.68	−3.98
	∞	−3.12	−3.41	−3.66	−3.96
Testing for stationarity with the KPSS test (accumulated partial sums)					
Constant, no trend	∞	0.35	0.46	0.57	0.74
Constant and trend	∞	0.12	0.15	0.18	0.22

Source: Fuller (1976) and Kwiatkowski et al. (1992).

the AR component. For example, we may expect difficulties in testing the null hypothesis $\rho + 1 = 1$ in the model

$$y_t = (\rho + 1)y_{t-1} + \varepsilon_t + \theta_1 \varepsilon_{t-1} \tag{4.44}$$

when θ_1 is very close to -1 since in that case the AR and MA polynomial are both approximately equal to $(1 - L)$. See Agiakloglou and Newbold (1992) for some simulation evidence which leads to the conclusion that only when, say, $\theta_1 > -0.5$, adding extra lags of $\Delta_1 y_t$ in (4.43) may yield appropriate results.

Notice that when the y_t series really is I(2), the $\Delta_1 y_t$ variable still has a stochastic trend. Haldrup (1994) shows that then the critical values to test one unit root versus no unit root in table 4.1 cannot be used anymore. In the case where the possible presence of two unit roots is suspected in the AR(p) part of the model, it is better first to investigate two unit roots versus one unit root, and, in case of rejection, proceed with one versus zero unit roots. The ADF test regression in the first round then becomes

$$\Delta_1^2 y_t = \rho^* \Delta_1 y_{t-1} + \alpha_1^{**} \Delta_1^2 y_{t-1} + \ldots + \alpha_{p-2}^{**} \Delta_1^2 y_{t-(p-2)} + \varepsilon_t. \qquad (4.45)$$

Dickey and Pantula (1987) show that critical values for $t(\hat{\rho}^*)$ are again as given in table 4.1.

Deterministic components

So far, the ADF test regressions in (4.43) and (4.45) do not include deterministic components as a constant and a trend. For illustration, consider again the AR(1) model in (4.4)

$$y_t - \mu - \delta t = \phi_1 (y_{t-1} - \mu - \delta(t-1)) + \varepsilon_t, \quad t = 2,3,\ldots,n \qquad (4.46)$$

which can be rewritten as

$$y_t = (1 - \phi_1)\mu + \phi_1 \delta + (1 - \phi_1)\delta t + \phi_1 y_{t-1} + \varepsilon_t. \quad t = 2,3,\ldots,n. \qquad (4.47)$$

When ϕ_1 is unequal to 1, (4.47) can be written as

$$y_t = \mu^* + \delta^* t + \phi_1 y_{t-1} + \varepsilon_t, \quad t = 2,3,\ldots,n \qquad (4.48)$$

with μ^* and δ^* unequal to zero. However, when $\phi_1 = 1$, (4.47) becomes

$$y_t = \delta + y_{t-1} + \varepsilon_t. \qquad (4.49)$$

This implies that in the ADF regression

$$\Delta_1 y_t = \mu^{**} + \delta^{**} t + \rho y_{t-1} + \alpha_1^* \Delta_1 y_{t-1} + \ldots + \alpha_{p-1}^* \Delta_1 y_{t-(p-1)} + \varepsilon_t. \qquad (4.50)$$

under the null hypothesis not only ρ equals zero but also δ^{**} is zero. Dickey and Fuller (1981) propose a joint F-test for the hypothesis $\rho = \delta^{**} = 0$, and in case of no trends, $\rho = \mu^{**} = 0$. Notice that the single t-test for $\delta^{**} = 0$ has an asymptotic distribution that mimics the one for the ρ, since δ^{**} is a function of this parameter, see Haldrup (1996) for some formal results on this matter and Nankervis and Savin (1987) for some simulation results.

A common practical procedure in case we want to consider (4.50) is to use the critical values in panels 2 and 3 of table 4.1, which are generated for a data generating process [DGP] of a random walk with no drift, and where $t(\hat{\rho})$ is calculated using (4.50) with p set equal to 1. Clearly, these critical values shift to the left. Intuitively, if the data are generated by a random walk model, the inclusion of a trend biases the estimate for ρ away from zero, and hence we need even larger values of the test statistic to be able to reject the null hypothesis at, say, the 5 percent level.

It should be mentioned that, when the DGP really is a random walk with drift μ, the asymptotic distribution of $t(\hat{\rho})$ in (4.50) approaches the standard normal distribution with increasing values of μ, see Hylleberg and Mizon (1989a). In practice, however, we never know for sure how big μ is (before knowing whether ρ equals 0 or not), and hence simply run the regression (4.50) in all cases where the data show an upward or downward trending pattern. Campbell and Perron (1991) show that erroneously neglecting deterministic terms is worse than including redundant variables.

Some applications

Given its relevance for modeling trends, and also since Nelson and Plosser (1982) find that almost all important annually observed USA macro-economic time series can be described by a ST model, there have appeared many studies on the size and power properties of the Dickey–Fuller test procedure. When an AR model is the DGP, it appears that the size of the test in small samples is reasonably accurate. In contrast, when an ARMA model is the DGP, with the MA component having a root close to the unit circle, the empirical size of the test becomes too large, see Agiakloglou and Newbold (1992). The power of the ADF test is not very high in small samples. As expected, it is not easy to distinguish between $\phi_p(1) = 0$ and $\phi_p(1) = 0.05$. However, when the sample size increases, the power appears to increase quite rapidly. For practical application, a simple guideline is to evaluate the ADF test not only at the 5 percent level, but also at, say, the 10 percent (or even the 20 percent) level. An additional, more theoretical feature of the ADF test is that the null hypothesis is a point hypothesis, while the alternative is an interval of parameter values. This observation has led to many alternative (including Bayesian) methods. The overall conclusion is that we should exercise care when evaluating the ADF test results, in the sense that in case of doubt, we may even be better off assuming the possible adequacy of both the DT and ST model, and to see which of the two does a better job in out-of-sample forecasting. Further confidence in the empirical outcomes is also obtained when the ADF test results appear robust to changes in the sample size, outliers, additional lags, and the inclusion or exclusion of deterministic components.

To illustrate the ADF test procedure, consider the test results in table 4.2. In table 4.2, two new series are analyzed, which also appear in the data appendix. The first is the market share during 103 weeks, displayed in figure 4.7, and the second is the (relative) distribution during the same weeks,

Table 4.2. *Testing for unit roots: some empirical time series*

Variable	Linear trend?	n	p	ADF($p-1$)
Market share	no	101	3	-0.983
	yes	101	3	$-3.162*$
Distribution	no	101	3	-0.457
	yes	101	3	-2.693
Prices	no	102	2	$-3.341**$
	yes	102	2	$-3.970**$
Pepper, black	no	269	2	-1.785
Pepper, white	no	269	2	-2.172
Output in China				
Agriculture	yes	35	2	-3.027
Industry	yes	35	2	$-4.341**$
Construction	yes	36	1	-2.787
Transportation	yes	35	2	$-3.543**$
Commerce	yes	36	1	-0.554
USA Industrial production				
SA (1960.3–1982.4)	yes	90	2	-1.723

Notes:
** Significant at the 5% level.
 * Significant at the 10% level.
Linear trend? means whether a linear deterministic trend is included in the auxiliary regression or not. n denotes the effective number of observations, p is the lag order of the AR(p) model where the possible $(1-L)$ component is still included, and ADF($p-1$) means t-test for ρ in the augmented Dickey–Fuller model (4.50) with $p-1$ lags of the $\Delta_1 y_t$ series. The value of $p-1$ is determined by a t-test on the last lag in the ADF regression, evaluated at the 5% significance level.

displayed in figure 4.8, both for the same fast-moving consumer good as the price series displayed in chapter 2.

Both time series in figures 4.7 and 4.8 display a trending pattern, where the trend this time has a downward slope. Notice that in principle such bounded time series cannot have a unit root. However, for part of the data it may be difficult to reject this hypothesis. Also, it may be that the unit root restriction yields better forecasts.

For the marketing variables, I find that market share has a unit root at the 5 percent level, while the evidence of the unit root seems to disappear (at least at the 10 percent level) when a deterministic trend is included. Distribution can be described by a ST model, while the corresponding price

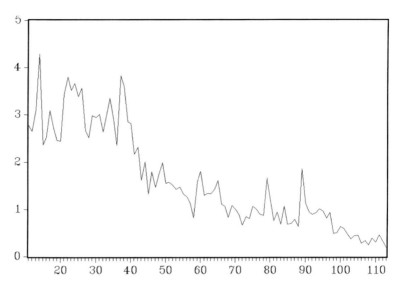

Figure 4.7 *Weekly market share of a fast moving consumer good (week 11 in 1989 to week 8 in 1991)*

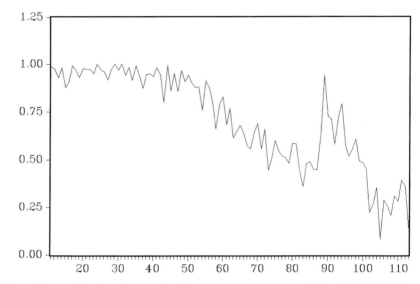

Figure 4.8 *Weekly distribution of a fast moving consumer good (week 11 in 1989 to week 8 in 1991)*

level seems stationary. Such mixed results may complicate a multivariate analysis, see also chapter 10.

As expected, both the pepper prices appear to have a unit root. The ADF models do not include a deterministic trend since their graphs show that no such trends seem present. Hence, a deterministic trend model does not seem a reasonable alternative model. The constant is included, though. Since p equals 2, the time series can be described by an ARI(1,1) model. In chapter 10, we will investigate whether perhaps the difference between the logs of the prices does not contain a unit root, that is, whether these two series have a common trend.

The five Chinese output variables yield mixed results. The data obviously show trending patterns, and hence the auxiliary ADF regressions include a constant and a trend. For the industry sector and the transportation sector, we can reject the presence of a unit root at the 5 percent level. Whether this finding is due to some aberrant events such as the Great Leap Forward, will be checked in chapter 6.

Finally, for the estimation sample 1960.3 to 1982.4 (where the last years of data are saved for the evaluation of forecasts) for industrial production in the USA, we find that there is a unit root since -1.723 is greater than the relevant critical value in table 4.1. Hence, shocks to the AR(2) model for the production variable appear to be permanent. This statistical evidence seems to correspond with the graphical impression one gets from figure 4.2.

As an example of the possible presence of two unit roots, consider the stock of motor cycles in The Netherlands (for 1948–1988) as in figure 2.2. An AR(2) model for this series (when no logs are taken) results in

$$w_t = 5.260 + 1.815 w_{t-1} \quad -0.861 w_{t-2} + \hat{\varepsilon}_t. \tag{4.51}$$
$$(2.060)\ (0.073) \qquad (0.071)$$

Clearly, the value of 2 is included in the 95 percent confidence interval for $\hat{\phi}_1$ and -1 is included in the similar interval for $\hat{\phi}_2$. As mentioned above, the proper procedure is now to consider the auxiliary regression

$$\Delta_1^2 w_t = 0.051 - 0.142 \Delta_1 w_{t-1} + \hat{\varepsilon}_t, \tag{4.52}$$
$$(0.670)\ (0.077)$$

which results in a t-ratio of -1.851. In sum, this variable seems to be I(2).

Since for an I(2) time series the rate of growth changes over time (in a random fashion), we may also wish to investigate whether the unemployment rate in Germany (seasonally adjusted) has two unit roots in its AR polynomial (see also figure 2.16). For the untransformed unemployment series, the regression (4.52) becomes

$$\Delta_1^2 w_t = 0.009 - 0.226 \Delta_1 w_{t-1} + \hat{\varepsilon}_t, \tag{4.53}$$
$$(0.016)\ (0.059)$$

for 118 effective observations. Here, $t(\hat{\rho})$ is equal to -3.834 which is significant at the 1 percent level (see the second panel of table 4.1). Hence, the unemployment series is not I(2). Next, consider the ADF regression for w_t, i.e.

$$\Delta_1 w_t = 0.038 - 0.007 w_{t-1} + 0.773 \Delta_1 w_{t-1} + \hat{\varepsilon}_t, \qquad (4.54)$$
$$\;\;\;\;\;\;(0.026)\;\;(0.005)\;\;\;\;\;\;(0.059)$$

which leads to the conclusion that this w_t series is I(1) since -0.007 is not significant.

4.3   Testing for stationarity

The test procedure for one or two unit roots in the previous section compares the ST model with the DT model. When the null hypothesis of a unit root can not be rejected, the ST model is preferred over the DT model. The reason to take the ST model as the most important model (since we design a test which should find evidence against it, and only if so, will we reject it) is that the ST model assumes permanent effects of shocks, which can be important from an economic policy point of view. There are however occasions in which we are interested in the DT hypothesis. For example, when, say, $y_t - z_t$ is stationary, we may say that y_t and z_t have the same pattern and have some common features. Although we will see in chapter 10 that most currently applied methods test whether the difference $y_t - z_t$ is an ST process, it may seem natural to take the DT model as the null hypothesis.

A test that takes stationarity as the null hypothesis is developed in Kwiatkowski *et al.* (1992) [KPSS]. It is based on the idea that, for a DT time series, the variance of the partial sum series

$$S_t = \sum_{i=1}^{t} \hat{e}_i, \qquad (4.55)$$

where the relevant $\hat{e}_t$ is obtained from the auxiliary regression

$$y_t = \hat{\tau} + \hat{\delta} t + \hat{e}_t, \qquad (4.56)$$

should somehow be relatively small, while it should be important for a ST time series. In fact, since (4.55) can be written as $S_t = S_{t-1} + e_t$, a variance of zero while not all $e_t = 0$ implies that there is no stochastic trend. To obtain a test statistic, we can consider

$$\eta = n^{-2} \sum_{t=1}^{n} S_t^2, \qquad (4.57)$$

which in the next step has to be scaled by the variance of $\hat{e}_t$. Phillips (1987) and Phillips and Perron (1988) estimate the so-called long-run variance by

$$s^2(l) = n^{-1}\sum_{t=1}^{n}\hat{e}_t^2 + 2n^{-1}\left[\sum_{j=1}^{l}w(j,l)\sum_{t=j+1}^{n}\hat{e}_t\hat{e}_{t-s}\right], \tag{4.58}$$

where the weights $w(j,l)$ can be set equal to

$$w(j,l) = 1 - j/(l+1), \tag{4.59}$$

following Newey and West (1987), although also other weights are possible. Note that (4.58) assumes that an ARMA model for the error time series $\hat{e}_t$ can be approximated by an MA(l) model. The l is usually selected as $l = n^{1/2}$, since Monte Carlo simulations show that this choice yields the most favorable results in terms of accurate rejection frequencies. When we want to allow explicitly for an AR model, we can modify the above using the method described in Leybourne and McCabe (1994).

The test statistic for the null hypothesis of stationarity versus an ST representation is then

$$\hat{\eta} = n^{-2}(s^2(l))^{-1}\sum_{t=1}^{n}S_t^2. \tag{4.60}$$

The asymptotic distribution of this test statistic is derived in KPSS, and the asymptotic critical values are calculated according to that expression. For further use, I present the critical values in the last panel of table 4.1. In the first row of that panel, I give the critical values in case (4.56) does not contain a trend. The null hypothesis of (trend) stationarity is rejected when $\hat{\eta}$ exceeds the critical value. Notice that since η can take positive values only, the test procedure based on $\hat{\eta}$ is one sided.

As an illustration, consider again the USA industrial production in the last row of table 4.2, that is, for the sample 1960.3 to 1982.4, which amounts to 90 observations. This number of observations implies that l can be set equal to 10. The stationarity test statistic is calculated for the regression which includes a deterministic trend as 0.503, which entails that the null hypothesis of stationarity can be rejected at the 1 percent significance level. Hence, both the unit root test and the KPSS test suggest that the ST model yields an accurate representation of the trend in the USA industrial production data for 1960.1–1982.4.

4.4   Forecasting

An important issue when selecting a model for the trend in economic data is the impact of this choice on the precision of out-of-sample forecasts. In this section, I will illustrate that these forecasting intervals become wider the more unit roots are assumed. Furthermore, I discuss whether point forecasts can differ across the DT and ST models.

Table 4.3. *Forecasting the level of the stock of motor cycles using models calibrated for 1948–1988 and where forecasts are generated for 1989–1993*

	Model		
	AR(2)	ARI(1,1)	I(2)
RMSPE	89.100	81.894	77.922
Square root of forecast error variance			
1989	3.980 (+)	4.260 (+)	4.331 (+)
1990	8.144	8.899	9.685 (+)
1991	12.536	14.078	16.207
1992	16.800	19.549	23.724
1993	20.703	25.162	32.122

Note:
A "+" in parentheses means that the true y_{n+h} observation lies within the 95% forecasting interval.

Forecasting intervals

Consider again the simple AR(1) model

$$y_t = \phi_1 y_{t-1} + \varepsilon_t, \tag{4.61}$$

for which is can be shown that the SPE(h) for $h = 1,2,3$ are given by

$$SPE(1) = \sigma^2,$$
$$SPE(2) = (1 + \phi_1^2)\sigma^2,$$
$$SPE(3) = (1 + \phi_1^2 + \phi_1^4)\sigma^2.$$

Clearly, when $\phi_1 = 1$, these SPEs become σ^2, $2\sigma^2$, $3\sigma^2$. Hence, SPE(2) for the random walk model exceeds that of the stationary AR(1) model. In other words, the non-stationarity of a random walk time series is reflected by the smaller precision in out-of-sample forecasting.

To illustrate this, consider again the stock of motor cycles for which we can use for forecasting the unrestricted AR(2) model, the ARI(1,1) model, and the I(2) model, where the last one is selected based on the Dickey–Fuller test. The parameters in the first two models are estimated for the sample 1948–1988, and out-of-sample forecasts are generated for 1989 to 1993, that is, $m = 5$. In the first row of table 4.3, I give the root mean squared prediction error [RMSPE] for each of these models for these five years. It appears that the I(2) model has the lowest RMSPE value. Additionally, I give the square root of the 95 percent forecasting intervals. Obviously, the more unit roots are assumed, the wider are these intervals. Furthermore, the differences seem to increase when h gets larger.

Similar results can be obtained for a comparison of the ST model and a model which includes a deterministic trend. For USA industrial production, we may consider the unrestricted AR(2) model

$$y_t = 0.184 + 0.344 \, (t/1000) + 1.506y_{t-1} - 0.553y_{t-2} + \hat{\varepsilon}_t, \qquad (4.62)$$
$$(0.102) \, (0.270) \qquad\qquad (0.090) \qquad (0.094)$$

where the parameters are estimated for the sample 1960.3 to 1982.4, and the ST model

$$\Delta_1 y_t = 0.00364 + 0.537\Delta_1 y_{t-1} + \hat{\varepsilon}_t, \qquad (4.63)$$
$$(0.00196) \, (0.090)$$

for the same sample. The h-step out-of-sample forecasts generated from both models for 1983.1–1991.4, as well as their 95 percent forecasting intervals are given in figures 4.9 and 4.10.

The point forecasts for the AR(2) model in figure 4.9 seem closer to the true observations in the out-of-sample period than the forecasts for the ARI(1,1) model in figure 4.10. Furthermore, even though the 95 percent forecasting intervals for the ARI(1,1) model are much wider, the number of observations that lie outside this interval is larger than for the AR(2) model. Hence, clearly the in-sample diagnostic results (reported in the last row of table 4.2 and in the previous two sections) on which the model should be selected do not automatically lead to the most appropriate forecasting results.

To investigate the out-of-sample forecasting performance of the ST and DT models, I collect (and construct) seasonally adjusted and unadjusted data for US industrial production for 1992.1–1995.4. The data are given in table 4.4. The data are constructed such that they match those prior to 1992.1. The seasonally unadjusted data will be used below in chapter 5. Here, I confine the analysis to the adjusted data.

The parameters in model (4.62) and (4.63) are re-estimated for the sample 1960.3–1991.4. The ADF test for (4.62) has a value of -3.001, and hence again the conclusion is that seasonally adjusted production has a unit root. The 16 h-step out-of-sample forecasts from the DT model result in a RMSPE value of 0.0197, while those forecasts from the ST model have a RMSPE value of 0.0210. The 16 one-step ahead forecasts obtain RMSPE values of 0.0078 and 0.0079, respectively. In sum, although the differences are small, the DT model appears to yield the best out-of-sample forecasts, despite the fact that the ST model would be selected using a unit root test for the within-sample data.

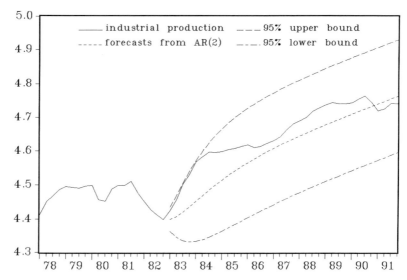

Figure 4.9 *Forecasts and 95% forecast interval from a AR(2) model for US industrial production for 1983.1–1991.4*

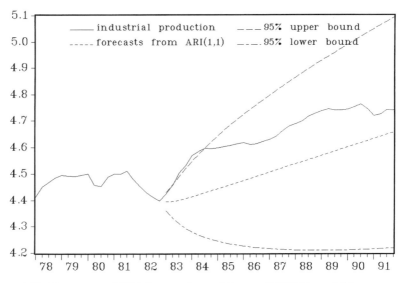

Figure 4.10 *Forecasts and 95% forecast interval from a ARI(1,1) model for US industrial production for 1983.1–1991.4*

Table 4.4. *Index of industrial production USA (1985 = 100),*
1992.1–1995.4

Year	Not seasonally adjusted				Seasonally adjusted			
	Q1	Q2	Q3	Q4	Q1	Q2	Q3	Q4
1992	112.8	114.4	116.9	116.0	113.5	114.9	115.5	117.0
1993	117.1	118.1	121.1	121.1	118.4	119.5	120.5	122.5
1994	123.2	125.2	129.3	129.3	124.6	126.6	127.6	130.1
1995	130.1	130.1	133.5	131.2	131.2	130.1	131.2	132.4

Sources: OECD Main Economic Indicators and OECD Indicators of Industrial
Activity (since 1992) and own calculations (because of change in measurement in
1992).

Do unit roots matter for point forecasts?

A natural empirical question is now which of the ST or DT models yields
the most appropriate out-of-sample forecasting results. Nelson and Plosser
(1982) investigate 14 annual USA macroeconomic time series for the presence of a unit root using the Dickey–Fuller (1979) method. They find that
only one of the 14 time series they investigate, that is, the Unemployment
Rate, is not a ST process, that there is weak evidence that Real GNP is a
DT process, and hence that most time series analyzed can be described by
a ST process. Since this seminal study, many researchers have re-analyzed
the Nelson and Plosser (1982) data set, possibly in an extended form. The
main motivation for most additional studies is that the Dickey–Fuller test
can have low power in small samples. Another drawback of this unit root
test may be that it assumes the approximate adequacy of an autoregressive
[AR] time series model. A limited selection of relevant studies contains
Schotman and Van Dijk (1991) where a Bayesian approach is considered,
Rudebusch (1992) where a small-sample correction of the original
Dickey–Fuller test is given, Lucas (1995) where outlying observations are
taken into account, and Perron (1989). As expected, the conclusion of these
studies usually is that more than one of the 14 time series can be described
using the DT model, although the results are mixed across the various
approaches.

The relative forecasting properties of the ST and DT models is studied in
Franses and Kleibergen (1996). Their evaluation method is straightforward. ST and DT models are quantified for various sample sizes and one-
step and multi-step ahead forecasts are generated for various horizons.

For the forecasting evaluation the 14 Nelson–Plosser time series are

Table 4.5. *Unit roots in the Nelson–Plosser data: do they matter for forecasting?*

| | Forecast procedure (for 36 years) | | |
Variable	One-step ahead	One-step ahead (Rolling regressions)	h-steps ahead
Real GNP	+	+	+
Nominal GNP	+	+	+
Real GNP per capita	+	−	+
Industrial production	−	−	−
Employment	−	+	+
GNP deflator	+	+	+
Consumer prices	+	−	−
Wages	+	+	+
Real wages	+	+	+
Nominal money stock	+	−	−
Velocity	+	+	+
Bond yield	+	+	+
Stock prices	+	+	+
Unemployment	−	−	−

Note:
A "+" indicates that the ST model has a smaller RMSPE than that of the DT model.
Source: Tables 1 to 3 in Franses and Kleibergen (1996).

considered, including such variables as Real GNP, Stock Prices, Real Money, and the Unemployment Rate. The original Nelson–Plosser data cover only years until 1970. In Franses and Kleibergen (1996) this data set is analyzed in its extended format (until 1988) given in Schotman and Van Dijk (1991). The number of annual observations for the various macro-economic time series now ranges from about 80 to about 120.

The orders of the AR polynomial in the DT and ST models are set equal to those displayed in Rudebusch (1992). Both models are estimated using the observations until 1952. Based on the estimated models, one-step ahead and multi-step ahead forecasts are generated for 1953–1988, resulting in 36 pairs of forecast errors to evaluate. Additionally, the one-step forecasts are generated when the parameters are re-estimated when new data are added. The results for the case of 36 forecasts are reported in table 4.5.

The results in table 4.5 lead to the conclusion that the ST model often outperforms the DT model. Only for Unemployment and Industrial

Production the DT model consistently performs better. Notice that this last result matches the visual evidence for production obtained from figures 4.9 and 4.10.

Obviously, the results in table 4.5 do not automatically imply that an ST process is the "true" underlying data generating process for the 14 time series under consideration. Neither do they imply that the ST process is the most likely model, nor that the same results will emerge for other time series variables for the USA economy or for similar variables for other economies. What the results in table 4.5 do suggest is that it pays off to evaluate the forecasting performance of the various trend models on a hold-out sample prior to generating long-run out-of-sample forecasts.

Growth curves

Meade and Islam (1995) survey and evaluate various methods to construct the out-of-sample forecasting intervals for the logistic and Gompertz models in (4.27) and (4.28). Their simulations suggest that the prediction intervals based on the approximated variance work well in practice. This method requires knowledge of the estimated variances of the parameters α, β, and γ, denoted as σ_α^2, σ_β^2, and σ_γ^2, of the error time series, σ^2, and of the covariances between the parameter estimates $\sigma_{\alpha\beta}$, $\sigma_{\alpha\gamma}$ and $\sigma_{\beta\gamma}$. The conditional variance of the one-step ahead forecast SPE(1) is then equal to

$$\sigma^2 + (\partial y_t/\partial\alpha)^2\sigma_\alpha^2 + (\partial y_t/\partial\beta)^2\sigma_\beta^2 + (\partial y_t/\partial\gamma)^2\sigma_\gamma^2 \qquad (4.64)$$
$$+ 2(\partial y_t/\partial\alpha)(\partial y_t/\partial\beta)\sigma_{\alpha\beta} + 2(\partial y_t/\partial\alpha)(\partial y_t/\partial\gamma)\sigma_{\alpha\gamma}$$
$$+ 2(\partial y_t/\partial\beta)(\partial y_t/\partial\gamma)\sigma_{\beta\gamma},$$

where for the logistic curve with (4.28) holds that

$$\partial y_t/\partial\alpha = 1/[1 + \beta\exp(-\gamma t)],$$
$$\partial y_t/\partial\beta = -\alpha\exp(-\gamma t)/[1 + \beta\exp(-\gamma t)]^2,$$
$$\partial y_t/\partial\gamma = \alpha\beta\exp(-\gamma t)/[1 + \beta\exp(-\gamma t)]^2.$$

The one-step ahead forecast from a logistic model is

$$\hat{y}_{n+1} = \hat{\alpha}/[1 + \hat{\beta}\exp(-\hat{y}(n+1))]. \qquad (4.65)$$

For the Olympic Games example, we can now calculate that for the Olympic Games in 2000 to be held in Sydney $\hat{y}_{2000}$ equals 465 million dollars. Since the coefficient covariance matrix is

$$\text{Variance}\begin{bmatrix} \hat{\alpha} \\ \hat{\beta} \\ \hat{\gamma} \end{bmatrix} = \begin{bmatrix} 474.59 & & \\ -23187.25 & 2483202 & \\ -1.85 & 173.77 & 0.01246 \end{bmatrix}, \qquad (4.66)$$

and $\hat{\sigma}^2 = 145.16$, the 90 percent forecasting interval is [431, 500] million dollars.

Conclusion

In this chapter I have reviewed a selection of methods that can help to decide on the most useful model for trending data. Theoretical and empirical research in this area is still on-going, and new developments may be expected.

For practical purposes it seems sensible to evaluate various models and to select a favorite model based on forecasting the hold-out data. In the next chapter, we will see that the analysis of trends can become more involved when the data show seasonality.

5 Seasonality

In this chapter the focus is on seasonal fluctuations in business and economic time series. The graphs and the results of some tentative auxiliary regression models in chapter 2 suggest that seasonal fluctuations can dominate variation in a detrended time series. For example, the regression results in section 2.2 indicate that for some variables more than 80 percent of the variation can be assigned to seasonal movements. A second observation from the graphs in chapter 2 is that often the seasonal patterns do not appear constant over time. These evolving patterns may emerge because the time series behavior in one or a few seasons changes, and it may also be that total seasonal variation changes as time passes by.

The typical approach to the analysis of macroeconomic time series is to assume that seasonality is some form of data contamination, which does not yield much useful information, and hence that seasonal fluctuations should be removed prior to any further time series analysis. The resulting seasonally adjusted time series can then be investigated for the presence of deterministic or stochastic trends using the methods discussed in the previous chapter. There are however several occasions in which forecasts of the seasonal fluctuations themselves are required, and hence in which the analysis of seasonally adjusted data may not be useful. For example, in marketing and tourism applications, we may expect that forecasts on possible changes in seasonality can be very useful, additional to forecasts of the long-run trend. In macroeconomics we may also wish to investigate seasonal movements in production, investment, stock-building, and consumption. The latter information may be useful to investigate an appropriate timing of issuing policy measures. Hence, in several cases it seems sensible to study seasonal patterns in business and economic variables in their own right. See Ghysels (1994), Hylleberg, (1994), and Miron (1996) for additional arguments in favor of modeling seasonality instead of removing it.

The outline of this chapter is as follows. In section 5.1, the discussion centers around typical autocorrelation patterns for seasonally observed time series. These functions are useful within the Box–Jenkins (1970) type of modeling approach. It is shown that this approach often leads to considering a double differencing filter of the time series to remove any non-stationarity. The resulting model for this differenced time series tends to be a simple moving average model, with only a few parameters to estimate. Given that such moving average parameters typically obtain values close to the unit circle, the adequacy of the double differencing filter seems questionable. Therefore, section 5.2 concerns a variety of methods to select the most appropriate differencing filter for seasonal time series, which are based on formal unit root tests. Such tests usually concern seasonal unit roots in univariate time series. Additionally, a few methods are discussed which can be applied to variables with increasing seasonal variation. The latter time series patterns often seem present in business time series as sales or expenditures. Next, in section 5.3, an overview is given of a class of models, in which the autoregressive parameters vary across the seasons. Such periodic models can be useful for forecasting seasonal variation, especially in the short-run, see, for example, Osborn and Smith (1989) and Franses (1996). Finally, section 5.4 treats miscellaneous topics as seasonal adjustment and the relation between seasonal and business cycles.

The notation in this chapter is the following. A seasonally observed time series y_t ($t = 1,2,\ldots,n$) is observed during S seasons per year, where S may take such values as 2, 4, 6, 12, or 13. Of course, all approaches can be modified to allow S to be equal to 5 (days), where years should then be replaced by weeks, but this is not pursued here. The data may have a non-zero mean μ_s for $s = 1,2,\ldots,S$. For notational convenience, but without loss of generality, it is regularly assumed that $n = SN$, where N is the number of years. In section 5.3, the focus will be on modeling y_t via S different models for $Y_{s,T}$, $s = 1,2,\ldots,S$, where $Y_{s,T}$ denotes the observation in season s in year T, $T = 1,2,\ldots,N$. Such models are called periodic models since it is then assumed that each period or season may be modeled differently. The notation for seasonal dummy variables is $D_{s,t}$, $s = 1,2,\ldots,S$. These $D_{s,t}$ variables take a value of 1 in season s and a value of 0 in other seasons. Obviously, in a regression with S seasonal dummies, there is no need to include a constant term.

The sample series used here are quarterly industrial production in the USA, quarterly consumption of non-durables in the United Kingdom, the monthly retail sales index in The Netherlands, and the four-weekly television advertising expenditures in The Netherlands, see the data appendix. In this chapter, the data are analyzed after taking natural logarithms. Of course, the data concern seasonally unadjusted time series.

Finally, the estimation results in this chapter concern models that are investigated for their empirical adequacy using diagnostic tests on residual autocorrelation and normality, as discussed in chapter 3. To save space, it will only be reported when one or more of these test statistics suggest that the model can somehow be improved. The significance level is set at 5 percent for all these occasions.

5.1   Typical features of seasonal time series

The graphs in chapter 2 indicate that, next to a trend, seasonal fluctuations in business and economic time series are a dominant source of variation and that such patterns can change over time. Similar to the methods described in chapter 3, we can consider the EACF of a time series y_t and compare it with autocorrelation functions for certain ARMA type models for seasonal time series. For non-seasonal time series, this method may work well since we usually only focus on the first few autocorrelations. For seasonal time series, however, we should also consider the correlations around S, $2S$, and so on. This leads to a potentially large set of possible AR, MA, or ARMA models that can be evaluated. See, for example, Hylleberg (1986) for some examples of ACFs for various seasonal models.

Estimated autocorrelation functions

The Box and Jenkins (1970) approach to seasonal time series modeling is given by applying various differencing filters Δ_k to y_t and investigating the EACFs of the transformed series, see, for example, Abraham and Ledolter (1983) and Granger and Newbold (1986). Usually, the differencing filters are applied until the EACF shows an easily interpretable pattern with only a few significant autocorrelations. The resulting identified ARIMA models are often called Seasonal ARIMA [SARIMA] models, since these usually contain relevant parameters at lags kS, with $k = 1,2,\dots$. Typically, we consider the EACFs of y_t, $\Delta_1 y_t$, $(\Delta_1 y_t)^c$, $\Delta_S y_t$, and $\Delta_1 \Delta_S y_t$, where $(\Delta_1 y_t)^c$ denotes the residual time series after a regression of $\Delta_1 y_t$ on S seasonal dummy variables. Note that the double differencing filter $\Delta_1 \Delta_S$ amounts to the transformation $y_t - y_{t-1} - y_{t-S} + y_{t-S-1}$. In general, it does not seem necessary to consider additional differencing filters for y_t.

In table 5.1, the five relevant EACFs are presented for the USA industrial production data. Since these are quarterly data, the EACFs are calculated for lags 1 to 12 which cover a period of three years. The relevance of the EACFs is evaluated using the 5 percent significance level, yielding an approximate interval of $\pm 2n^{-\frac{1}{2}}$, see Box and Jenkins (1970). As can be seen from the first column of table 5.1, the EACF values for y_t are all significant. However, a clear pattern to indicate the usefulness of some ARMA model cannot be observed. Taking first differences of y_t yields a somewhat more

Table 5.1. *Estimated autocorrelation functions of USA industrial production, 1960.1–1991.4*

Lags	y_t	$\Delta_1 y_t$	$(\Delta_1 y_t)^c$	$\Delta_4 y_t$	$\Delta_1 \Delta_4 y_t$
1	0.975**	0.162	0.242**	0.851**	0.535**
2	0.947**	0.140	0.196**	0.586**	0.162
3	0.918**	−0.110	−0.061	0.295**	−0.051
4	0.888**	0.300**	0.205**	0.036	−0.328**
5	0.853**	−0.268**	−0.264**	−0.126	−0.296**
6	0.821**	−0.046	−0.032	−0.220**	−0.190**
7	0.789**	−0.249**	−0.224**	−0.274**	−0.165
8	0.761**	0.120	0.008	−0.296**	−0.204**
9	0.732**	−0.257**	−0.253**	−0.262**	−0.066
10	0.705**	0.015	0.044	−0.207**	0.080
11	0.676**	−0.198**	−0.165	−0.172	0.025
12	0.649**	0.199**	0.099	−0.138	0.018

Note:
** Significant at the 5% level. The asymptotic standard error of the estimated autocorrelations is 0.089.

interpretable EACF, as can be observed from the third column of table 5.1. Only six of the 12 EACF values are significant at the 5 percent level. The significant value of 0.199 at lag 12, however, seems to suggest that further differencing may be needed. When we regress the $\Delta_1 y_t$ series on $D_{1,t}$ to $D_{4,t}$, resulting in $(\Delta_1 y_t)^c$, the EACF values appear to remain roughly similar to those of $\Delta_1 y_t$, although the values at lags 4, 8, and 12 now take smaller values. Hence, some EACF values of the uncorrected $\Delta_1 y_t$ data can be significant because of seasonally varying deterministic terms. A common transformation to get rid of seasonal patterns in quarterly series is the Δ_4 transformation. The EACF of $\Delta_4 y_t$ is presented in the last to final column of table 5.1. The first three EACF values suggest the possible usefulness of an AR model, while the significance of the EACF values at lags 6 to 10 indicate that the order of this AR model should at least be 2, see also figures 3.5 and 3.6. Finally, the last column of table 5.1 gives the EACF of $\Delta_1 \Delta_4 y_t$, which suggests the possible usefulness of an ARMA model with at least MA(1) and MA(4) components.

The EACF of UK consumption non-durables is presented in table 5.2. Similar to the results for USA industrial production, the EACF for this y_t does not die out rapidly. Furthermore, we can observe that the values at lags 4, 8, and 12 are slightly larger than those around these lags, confirming that seasonal fluctuations are quite pronounced. This is also reflected by the

Table 5.2. *Estimated autocorrelation functions of UK consumption non-durables, 1955.1–1988.4*

Lags	y_t	$\Delta_1 y_t$	$(\Delta_1 y_t)^c$	$\Delta_4 y_t$	$\Delta_1 \Delta_4 y_t$
1	0.928**	−0.463**	−0.074	0.779**	−0.164
2	0.900**	−0.014	−0.359**	0.625**	0.050
3	0.876**	−0.481**	−0.034	0.449**	0.048
4	0.891**	0.947**	0.554**	0.248**	−0.444**
5	0.823**	−0.438**	0.023	0.238**	0.236**
6	0.795**	−0.014	−0.390**	0.130	−0.118
7	0.771**	−0.471**	−0.045	0.082	0.115
8	0.788**	0.910**	0.491**	−0.014	0.023
9	0.723**	−0.421**	−0.081	−0.125	−0.251**
10	0.697**	−0.014	−0.328**	−0.133	0.122
11	0.674**	−0.464**	−0.148	−0.196**	−0.131
12	0.691**	0.877**	0.414**	−0.196**	−0.001

Note:
** Significant at the 5% level. The asymptotic standard error of the estimated autocorrelations is 0.086.

EACF of $\Delta_1 y_t$, where, for example, the estimated autocorrelation at lag 12 takes the value of 0.877. A regression of $\Delta_1 y_t$ on four seasonal dummies does not result in insignificant values at the seasonal lags, although the values decrease to a large extent. The EACF of $\Delta_4 y_t$ suggests the possible usefulness of an AR(1) model, although the significance of the values at lags 11 and 12 suggest a higher order. Finally, the EACF of $\Delta_1 \Delta_4 y_t$ only has significant values at lags 4, 5, and 9, suggesting the possibility of a simple MA model.

The usefulness of analyzing the estimated autocorrelation functions of somehow differenced time series becomes even more apparent when considering monthly time series as in table 5.3. The first 36 values of the EACF for y_t, which is the log of retail sales, in the first column of table 5.3 are all significant. Similar to the results in table 5.2, we can observe that the EACF values at lag 12 is relatively larger than at lags around this seasonal frequency. The same holds for the EACF of $\Delta_1 y_t$, even after correcting for the seasonal dummies $D_{1,t}$ to $D_{12,t}$, as can be noticed from the second and third column of table 5.3. The EACF of $\Delta_{12} y_t$ clearly indicates that even the Δ_{12} filter does not reduce the significance of autocorrelations. The final column of table 5.3 contains the EACF of $\Delta_1 \Delta_{12} y_t$. Even after differencing the data as such, there do not emerge simple recognizable patterns.

Table 5.3. *Estimated autocorrelations functions of Dutch retail sales,*
1960.05–1995.09

Lags	y_t	$\Delta_1 y_t$	$(\Delta_1 y_t)^c$	$\Delta_{12} y_t$	$\Delta_1 \Delta_{12} y_t$
1	0.980**	−0.264**	−0.556**	0.456**	−0.532**
2	0.967**	−0.238**	−0.024	0.490**	−0.121**
3	0.961**	−0.004	0.221**	0.654**	0.307**
4	0.954**	−0.256**	−0.180**	0.486**	−0.200**
5	0.954**	0.163**	0.010	0.534**	−0.011
6	0.950**	0.236**	0.160**	0.593**	0.148**
7	0.940**	0.093	−0.150**	0.492**	−0.093
8	0.929**	−0.195**	−0.025	0.492**	−0.106**
9	0.922**	−0.004	0.223**	0.607**	0.268**
10	0.912**	−0.306**	−0.256**	0.431**	−0.276**
11	0.913**	−0.098**	−0.035	0.556**	0.228**
12	0.916**	0.816**	0.453**	0.432**	−0.061
13	0.897**	−0.248**	−0.497**	0.375**	−0.290**
14	0.885**	−0.113**	0.344**	0.633**	0.408**
15	0.877**	−0.112**	−0.125**	0.446**	−0.119**
16	0.870**	−0.238**	−0.109**	0.392**	−0.189**
17	0.870**	0.218**	0.176**	0.540**	0.240**
18	0.865**	0.181**	−0.008	0.429**	−0.045
24	0.827**	0.656**	−0.007	0.300**	−0.308**
36	0.738**	0.593**	−0.125**	0.210**	−0.312**

Note:
** Significant at the 5% level. The asymptotic standard error of the estimated
autocorrelations is 0.049.

As a final example, consider the estimated ACF of the various transformed (logs of) television advertising series in table 5.4. Notice that this
series has 13 observations per year since it concerns four-weekly data, and
hence that table 5.4 includes EACF values for lags which are multiples of
13. The first column shows the EACF of y_t itself, and it is clear that many
of its values are significant. This holds true also for $\Delta_1 y_t$ and $(\Delta_1 y_t)^c$, of
which the EACF values do not suggest possibly useful ARMA structures.
On the other hand, the EACF values of $\Delta_{13} y_t$ suggest that an AR model
may be useful. The order of this model should be larger than 1 since the
EACF does not correspond to the familiar exponential decay of an AR(1)
time series as observed in chapter 3. Finally, the EACF of $\Delta_1 \Delta_{13} y_t$ yields a
relatively simple pattern, i.e., only the values at lags 1, 13, 14, and 18 are
significant.

Table 5.4. *Estimated autocorrelation functions of TV advertising expenditures, 1978.01–1994.13*

Lags	y_t	$\Delta_1 y_t$	$(\Delta_1 y_t)^c$	$\Delta_{13} y_t$	$\Delta_1 \Delta_{13} y_t$
1	0.933**	0.215**	0.039	0.663**	−0.301**
2	0.836**	−0.352**	−0.255**	0.529**	−0.111
3	0.781**	−0.418**	−0.316**	0.471**	−0.083
4	0.774**	−0.351**	−0.301**	0.466**	0.044
5	0.813**	−0.013	−0.020	0.431**	0.001
6	0.857**	0.417**	0.346**	0.393**	−0.003
7	0.848**	0.438**	0.409**	0.357**	0.036
8	0.786**	−0.008	0.024	0.299**	0.008
9	0.723**	−0.348**	−0.308**	0.233**	−0.031
10	0.700**	−0.398**	−0.288**	0.191**	−0.022
11	0.725**	−0.324**	−0.191**	0.162**	0.026
12	0.788**	0.240**	0.109	0.119	0.105
13	0.829**	0.810**	0.531**	0.004	−0.412**
14	0.773**	0.265**	0.183**	0.172**	0.312**
15	0.683**	−0.331**	−0.210**	0.125	−0.103
16	0.630**	−0.370**	−0.222**	0.146**	0.096
17	0.621**	−0.334**	−0.277**	0.103	0.008
18	0.656**	−0.025	−0.053	0.050	−0.187**
19	0.699**	0.383**	0.274**	0.127	0.003
26	0.672**	0.728**	0.399**	0.111	−0.002
39	0.500**	0.650**	0.294**	0.172**	0.034

Note:
** Significant at the 5% level. The asymptotic standard error of the estimated autocorrelations is 0.067.

The empirical results so far can be summarized as follows. The typical pattern of the estimated ACF of seasonal time series is that the EACF of the untransformed time series y_t seems hard to interpret, that the EACF of $\Delta_1 y_t$ may become more easy to handle after a regression on seasonal dummies, that the EACF of $\Delta_S y_t$ often suggests AR type patterns, and that the EACF values of the doubly transformed series can suggest parsimonious model structures.

The airline model

Easily interpretable EACF values of the doubly differenced series are reported in many empirical studies and textbooks on time series, see, for

example, Abraham and Ledolter (1983), Granger and Newbold (1986), and
Mills (1990). The first analysis of a $\Delta_1 \Delta_S$ transformed time series is given in
Box and Jenkins (1970). This analysis concerns the monthly observed time
series for airline passengers using a model like

$$\Delta_1 \Delta_S y_t = (1 + \theta_1 L)(1 + \theta_S L^S)\varepsilon_t. \quad t = S+2, S+3, \ldots, n. \tag{5.1}$$

Notice that the MA part of this model contains only two parameters. Given
its specific application in Box and Jenkins (1970), model (5.1) is often
termed the "airline model." For $S>2$, the theoretical ACF of $\Delta_1 \Delta_S y_t$ is

$$\rho_1 = (\theta_1 + \theta_1 \theta_S^2)/(1 + \theta_1^2 + \theta_S^2 + \theta_1^2 \theta_S^2) = \theta_1/(1 + \theta_1^2) \tag{5.2}$$

$$\rho_S = \theta_S/(1 + \theta_S^2) \tag{5.3}$$

$$\rho_{S-1} = \rho_{S+1} = \theta_1 \theta_S/[(1 + \theta_1^2)(1 + \theta_S^2)] \tag{5.4}$$

$$\rho_k = 0 \text{ for positive } k \neq 0, 1, S, S \pm 1. \tag{5.5}$$

In case the airline model contains an unrestricted MA polynomial with lags
at 1, S, and $S+1$ such that (5.1) contains three parameters, the expressions
in (5.2) to (5.4) differ slightly. For convenience, such an unrestricted model
will also be called an airline model.

For quarterly data, the possible usefulness of the airline model is
reflected by the empirical significance of only $\hat{\rho}_1$, $\hat{\rho}_3$, $\hat{\rho}_4$, and $\hat{\rho}_5$. Comparing
this result with the EACF values in the last two columns of tables 5.1 and
5.2 shows that (5.1) can be useful for these two example series. The estimation results (using the routines described in chapter 3) for an unrestricted
airline model for USA industrial production are

$$\Delta_1 \Delta_4 y_t = -0.0003 + \hat{\varepsilon}_t + 0.388\hat{\varepsilon}_{t-1} - 0.739\hat{\varepsilon}_{t-4} - 0.452\hat{\varepsilon}_{t-5}, \tag{5.6}$$
$$ (0.0017) \quad\quad (0.063) \quad\quad (0.060) \quad\quad (0.069)$$

where the estimated standard errors are given in parentheses. Given the loss
of five observations due to the $\Delta_1 \Delta_4$ filter, the number of effective observations equals 123. Normality appears to be rejected, and hence we should
consider the results in (5.6) with some care. On the other hand, the residual
autocorrelation checks do not suggest different lag structures, and hence
the dynamic pattern of y_t seems to be characterized by only three MA parameters and a double differencing filter.

The out-of-sample forecasts from the airline model for a quarterly time
series are

$$\hat{y}_{n+1} = y_n + y_{n-3} - y_{n-4} + \hat{\theta}_1 \hat{\varepsilon}_n + \hat{\theta}_4 \hat{\varepsilon}_{n-3} + \hat{\theta}_1 \hat{\theta}_4 \hat{\varepsilon}_{n-4} \tag{5.7}$$

$$\hat{y}_{n+2} = \hat{y}_{n+1} + y_{n-2} - y_{n-3} + \hat{\theta}_4 \hat{\varepsilon}_{n-2} + \hat{\theta}_1 \hat{\theta}_4 \hat{\varepsilon}_{n-3} \tag{5.8}$$

$$\hat{y}_{n+3} = \hat{y}_{n+2} + y_{n-1} - y_{n-2} + \hat{\theta}_4 \hat{\varepsilon}_{n-1} + \hat{\theta}_1 \hat{\theta}_4 \hat{\varepsilon}_{n-2} \tag{5.9}$$

$$\hat{y}_{n+4}=\hat{y}_{n+3}+y_n-y_{n-1}+\hat{\theta}_4\hat{\varepsilon}_n+\hat{\theta}_1\hat{\theta}_4\hat{\varepsilon}_{n-1} \tag{5.10}$$

$$\hat{y}_{n+5}=\hat{y}_{n+4}+\hat{y}_{n+1}-y_n+\hat{\theta}_1\hat{\theta}_4\hat{\varepsilon}_n \tag{5.11}$$

$$\hat{y}_{n+h}=\hat{y}_{n+h-1}+\hat{y}_{n+h-4}-\hat{y}_{n+h-5} \text{ for } h=6,7,8,\dots \tag{5.12}$$

Note that (5.12) indicates that the forecasts are a deterministic function after $h=5$.

A typical feature of many doubly differenced seasonal time series is that the EACF at lags 1 and S can take values which are close to -0.5. For example, the $\hat{\rho}_4$ in the last column of table 5.2 equals -0.444, and the $\hat{\rho}_{13}$ in the last column of table 5.4 equals -0.412. This may suggest that the $\Delta_1\Delta_S y_t$ series is overdifferenced. In fact, when the $(1-L^S)$ factor of the $\Delta_1\Delta_S$ filter is redundant, this factor will appear on the right-hand side of the airline model (5.1). In that case, the θ_S value equals -1, and given (5.3) the corresponding ρ_S equals -0.5. Similarly, when $(1-L)$ is redundant, the theoretical value of ρ_1 equals -0.5.

Additional information on the possibility that the double differencing filter may not be needed, and hence that it introduces non-invertibility of the MA polynomial, can be obtained from solving the characteristic equation $\theta(z)=0$ for the estimated parameters. To illustrate matters, consider the characteristic equation corresponding to the MA polynomial in (5.6), that is

$$(1+0.388z-0.739z^4-0.452z^5)=0. \tag{5.13}$$

The solutions to this polynomial are 0.964, $0.042\pm0.950i$, and $0.718\pm0.061i$, where $i^2=-1$. The first three roots seem close to 1 and $\pm i$, respectively. Since one can decompose the double filter $\Delta_1\Delta_4$ as

$$\begin{aligned}\Delta_1\Delta_4&=(1-L)(1-L^4)\\&=(1-L)(1-L)(1+L)(1-iL)(1+iL),\end{aligned} \tag{5.14}$$

the solutions to (5.13) suggest that the $(1-L)(1+iL)(1-iL)$ component of (5.14) appears on the right-hand side of the airline model in (5.6) as well. Hence, the $\Delta_1\Delta_4$ filter may be reduced to $\Delta_1\Delta_4/[(1-L)(1+iL)(1-iL)]=(1-L^2)$, yielding a more parsimonious data transformation for industrial production.

In sum, it appears that the selection of a differencing filter guided by an interpretable autocorrelation function may not always correspond to the most useful transformation. In other words, the filter selected on the basis of an inspection of the EACF may yield non-invertible MA polynomials. Obviously, we may expect that an inappropriate differencing filter may result in biased forecasts. For example, given certain assumptions on the starting values, Bell (1987) shows that when for the MA model

$$(1-L^4)y_t = \varepsilon_t + \theta_4\varepsilon_{t-4}, \tag{5.15}$$

$\theta_4 \to -1$, the limiting case

$$y_t = \delta_1 D_{1,t} + \delta_2 D_{2,t} + \delta_3 D_{3,t} + \delta_4 D_{4,t} + \varepsilon_t \tag{5.16}$$

emerges. This suggests that forecasts from (5.15) and (5.16) can be equal in case θ_4 is set equal to -1. However, when (5.16) is the data generating process [DGP], the estimated value of θ_4 in (5.15) will be biased downwards, see Plosser and Schwert (1977). The forecasts from (5.15) then become different from those of (5.16). This suggests that the selection of the differencing filter can be important for forecasting. Notice also that when the explicit purpose is to forecast $\Delta_4 y_t$ when (5.16) is the DGP, we can still better consider the model (5.16) instead of the inadequate model for $\Delta_4 y_t$ as in (5.15). Recently, several testing methods have become available to formally investigate the most appropriate differencing filter for y_t. These methods are based on extensions of the Dickey–Fuller method, see chapter 4. The next section reviews several such methods.

5.2   Seasonal unit roots

If a Δ_S differencing filter is required to transform y_t to stationarity, a time series is said to be seasonally integrated. The assumption of a certain differencing filter amounts to an assumption on the number of seasonal and non-seasonal unit roots in a time series. This can be seen from writing $\Delta_S = (1-L^S)$ and solving the equation

$$(1-z^S) = 0 \tag{5.18}$$

or

$$\exp(Si\phi) = 1$$

for z or ϕ. The general solution to (5.18) is $\{1, \cos(2\pi k/S) + i\sin(2\pi k/S)\}$ for $k = 1,2,\ldots$ yielding S different solutions, which all lie on the unit circle. The first solution 1 is called the non-seasonal unit root and the $S-1$ other solutions are called seasonal unit roots, see Hylleberg et al. (1990) (which will be often abbreviated as HEGY). For example, in case $S=4$, the double filter $\Delta_1\Delta_4$ assumes the presence of two non-seasonal unit roots and three seasonal unit roots -1 and $\pm i$, see also (5.14).

There are several methods to investigate whether the double filter $\Delta_1\Delta_S$ is appropriate to remove non-seasonal and seasonal stochastic trends such that the EACF of the resultant time series can be easily interpreted. Hasza and Fuller (1982) consider the model

$$y_t = \phi_1 y_{t-1} + \phi_S y_{t-S} + \phi_{S+1} y_{t-(S+1)} + u_t, \tag{5.19}$$

where u_t is some stationary and invertible ARMA time series. The null hypothesis of interest is that jointly $\phi_1 = \phi_S = -\phi_{S+1} = 1$. The alternative hypothesis is that there are no unit roots at all. Osborn *et al.* (1988) [OCSB] extend this approach by considering the auxiliary regression

$$\phi_{p-S-1}(L)\Delta_1\Delta_S y_t = \sum_{s=1}^{S} \delta_s D_{s,t} + \pi_1 \Delta_S y_{t-1} + \pi_2 \Delta_1 y_{t-S} + \varepsilon_t, \qquad (5.20)$$

where $\phi_{p-S-1}(L)$ is some polynomial in L of order $p-S-1$, with $p-S-1$ chosen such that the estimated residuals are approximately white noise. For (5.20) it holds that when $\pi_2 = 0$ the Δ_S filter is appropriate and when $\pi_1 = \pi_2 = 0$ the $\Delta_1\Delta_S$ filter is required. Since Δ_S contains the Δ_1 component, the π_1 parameter itself is not decisive. When π_1 and π_2 jointly do not equal zero, we can proceed with the unit roots test as in chapter 4. Critical values of the various t- and F-type test statistics for (5.20) are given in Osborn (1990) (and in table 5.10 to be discussed below). The OCSB method will be discussed again below, when time series with increasing seasonal variation are treated. The application in Osborn (1990) of the auxiliary regression (5.20) to several quarterly series for the UK macroeconomy results in a clear rejection of the empirical adequacy of the $\Delta_1\Delta_4$ filter. This result indicates that often the Δ_4 filter may be useful.

Testing for seasonal unit roots

When at most the Δ_S filter seems sufficient to remove one or more stochastic trends from a seasonal time series y_t, this naturally leads to a closer investigation of the empirical adequacy of the Δ_S filter and its nested filters as, for example, Δ_1, see again (5.14). Similar to testing the adequacy of the $\Delta_1\Delta_S$ filter, we may also test whether the Δ_S filter amounts to an adequate data transformation. Hylleberg *et al.* (1990) [HEGY] extend the approach in Dickey, Hasza, and Fuller (1984) by proposing a simple procedure to test for seasonal and non-seasonal unit roots in a quarterly time series, and hence to test the $(1-L^4)$ filter versus its nested variants like $(1-L)$ or $(1+L)$. The HEGY approach is based on the expansion

$$\phi_p(L) = -\pi_1 L\phi_1(L) + \pi_2 L\phi_2(L) + (\pi_3 L + \pi_4)L\phi_3(L) \\ + \phi_{p-4}^*(L)\phi_4(L), \qquad (5.21)$$

where the $\phi_i(L)$ polynomials ($i = 1,2,3,4$) are defined by

$$\phi_1(L) = (1 + L + L^2 + L^3) \qquad (5.22)$$

$$\phi_2(L) = (1 - L)(1 + L^2) = (1 - L + L^2 - L^3) \qquad (5.23)$$

$$\phi_3(L) = (1 - L^2) \qquad (5.24)$$

$$\phi_4(L) = (1 - L^4),\tag{5.25}$$

see HEGY. Suppose for simplicity that $\phi_{p-4}^*(L) = 0$, it can be seen from (5.21) that when, for example, $\pi_1 = 0$, $\phi_p(L)$ can be decomposed as $\phi_{p-1}(L)$ $(1-L)$ since all components contain $(1-L)$. When it is assumed that y_t can be described by

$$\phi_p(L)y_t = \mu_t + \varepsilon_t,$$

where μ_t can represent

$$\mu_t = \delta_0 + \sum_{s=1}^{3}\delta_s D_{s,t} + \beta t,\tag{5.26}$$

where t denotes the deterministic trend variable, then, given (5.21), the HEGY auxiliary regression to test for the presence of non-seasonal and seasonal unit roots in a quarterly series becomes

$$\phi_{p-4}^*(L)y_{4,t} = \mu_t + \pi_1 y_{1,t-1} + \pi_2 y_{2,t-1} + \pi_3 y_{3,t-2} + \pi_4 y_{3,t-1} + \varepsilon_t,\tag{5.27}$$

where

$$y_{1,t} = \phi_1(L)y_t$$
$$y_{2,t} = -\phi_2(L)y_t$$
$$y_{3,t} = -\phi_3(L)y_t$$
$$y_{4,t} = \phi_4(L)y_t,$$

with the $\phi_i(L)$ polynomials defined as in (5.22)–(5.25).

The application of OLS to (5.27) gives values for $\hat{\pi}_i$ $(i = 1,2,3,4)$, where the order of the AR polynomial $\phi_{p-4}^*(L)$ is selected such that the estimated residuals are approximately white noise. Because the π_i parameters are zero in case the corresponding roots of the AR polynomial are on the unit circle, testing the significance of the $\hat{\pi}_i$ parameters implies testing for unit roots. There are no seasonal unit roots if π_2 and π_3 (or π_4) are different from zero. If $\pi_1 = 0$, the presence of the non-seasonal unit root 1 cannot be rejected.

The t-tests for π_1 and π_2 are denoted as $t(\pi_1)$ and $t(\pi_2)$. The alternative hypotheses for the unit roots 1 and -1 are that the roots are smaller than unity in an absolute sense. This means that the $t(\pi_1)$-test and $t(\pi_2)$-test are one-sided tests similar to the standard Dickey–Fuller tests discussed in the previous chapter. The significance of π_3 and π_4 is evaluated through the joint F-test, denoted as $F(\pi_3, \pi_4)$. Additionally, one may consider F-tests for other sets of π_i parameters, see in Ghysels, Lee, and Noh (1994).

The joint null hypothesis in the HEGY test procedure for quarterly data is that the $(1-L^4)$ filter is the appropriate filter to remove unit roots. This

Table 5.5. *Critical values for the one-sided t-test for π_1 and π_2 in quarterly and monthly data*

(The DGP is $(1-L^S)y_t = \epsilon_t$, with $\epsilon_t \sim N(0,1)$, and the test equations are (5.27) and (5.28). Based on 25,000 Monte Carlo replications.)

Model	Years	S=4				S=12			
		0.01	0.025	0.05	0.10	0.01	0.025	0.05	0.10
No trend	10	−3.42	−3.06	−2.77	−2.44	−3.20	−2.91	−2.67	−2.38
	20	−3.43	−3.09	−2.81	−2.51	−3.28	−3.00	−2.76	−2.47
	30	−3.43	−3.10	−2.83	−2.53	−3.33	−3.02	−2.76	−2.48
	40	−3.41	−3.11	−2.84	−2.54	−3.40	−3.07	−2.81	−2.51
Trend	10	−4.02	−3.64	−3.34	−3.02	−3.73	−3.44	−3.19	−2.91
(only π_1)	20	−3.97	−3.66	−3.37	−3.06	−3.83	−3.54	−3.29	−3.01
	30	−3.96	−3.65	−3.40	−3.09	−3.89	−3.57	−3.32	−3.05
	40	−3.96	−3.65	−3.39	−3.10	−3.91	−3.60	−3.35	−3.08

Notes:
The auxiliary test regression contains a constant, seasonal dummies and possibly a trend. The latter case with a trend only concerns the *t*-test for π_1 since the critical values of the *t*-test for π_2 do not change with the inclusion of a trend.
Source: Franses and Hobijn (1997).

implies that the asymptotics for the various *t*- and *F*-tests are non-standard. Discussions of the relevant asymptotic distributions are given in Engle, Granger, and Hylleberg (1993) and HEGY. Similar to the standard Dickey and Fuller (1979) type tests discussed in chapter 4, these asymptotic distributions depend on the deterministic terms that are included in the auxiliary regression. Tables with critical values for the $t(\pi_1)$, $t(\pi_2)$, and $F(\pi_3,\pi_4)$-test statistics are displayed in HEGY. Some critical values for $t(\pi_1)$ are displayed in table 5.5 (under the header "$S=4$"), for a sample of 10, 20, 30, and 40 years of quarterly observations and in case where the auxiliary regression (5.27) includes a constant and three seasonal dummies and possibly a linear trend. For many practical purposes, the latter two choices for μ_t in (5.26) are the most relevant.

In HEGY it is shown that the asymptotic distribution of this $t(\pi_1)$-test is the same as that of the standard Dickey–Fuller test for a non-seasonal unit root in non-seasonal time series. Comparing the values in table 5.5 with those in table 4.1 seems to substantiate this asymptotic result, at least for 40 years of quarterly observations. In HEGY it is also shown that the $t(\pi_2)$-test has the same asymptotic distribution as that of the $t(\pi_1)$-test. This seems to hold true also for small samples, see, for example, HEGY and Franses and Hobijn (1997) for simulated critical values. Some simulated

Table 5.6. *Critical values for the joint F-test for π_3 and π_4 in quarterly and monthly data*

(The DGP is $(1-L^S)y_t = \epsilon_t$, with $\epsilon_t \sim N(0,1)$, and the test equations are (5.27) and (5.28). Based on 25,000 Monte Carlo replications.)

Model	Years	S=4				S=12			
		0.10	0.05	0.025	0.01	0.10	0.05	0.025	0.01
No trend	10	5.44	6.63	7.80	9.32	4.88	5.82	6.71	7.91
	20	5.47	6.62	7.65	8.94	5.28	6.27	7.12	8.35
	30	5.62	6.70	7.72	8.97	5.33	6.35	7.19	8.40
	40	5.52	6.57	7.57	8.79	5.45	6.35	7.36	8.40
Trend	10	5.38	6.56	7.77	9.30	4.86	5.77	6.66	7.86
	20	5.44	6.57	7.58	8.86	5.26	6.24	7.10	8.30
	30	5.59	6.66	7.67	8.91	5.33	6.35	7.18	8.39
	40	5.48	6.55	7.54	8.79	5.45	6.35	7.35	8.38

Note:
The auxiliary test regression contains a constant, seasonal dummies and possibly a trend.
Source: Franses and Hobijn (1997).

fractiles for the $F(\pi_3, \pi_4)$-test are displayed in table 5.6 (again under the header "$S=4$").

The HEGY test approach has been evaluated in the simulation exercises in Hylleberg (1995) and Ghysels, Lee, and Noh (1994). The results in the latter study indicate that the size of the tests deteriorates when the DGP is a seasonal MA series with a parameter close to the unit circle. For practical applications, it is therefore again necessary to thoroughly check the EACF of the error series of the auxiliary test regression. If this EACF does not die out at seasonal lags, one should be cautious with the interpretation of HEGY test outcomes. Furthermore, and similar to the standard Dickey–Fuller tests, the power of the tests for seasonal unit roots is not high when the DGP is close to the null hypothesis.

The HEGY tests are applied to the quarterly USA industrial production and UK consumption non-durables series. The results are reported in table 5.7. The lags in the auxiliary regression are 1,2, and 3 for the first series, and 1,4, and 5 for the second series. Hence, it seems that AR models of order 7 and 9 can be fitted to the untransformed data. For both series, we cannot reject the hypotheses that $\pi_1 = 0$ and $\pi_2 = 0$. For UK consumption non-durables we can neither reject that $\pi_3 = \pi_4 = 0$. We can conclude from these results that the Δ_4 filter is most appropriate for the latter series. For the USA

Table 5.7. *Testing for seasonal unit roots in quarterly data*

(The auxiliary regression is $\phi(L)\Delta_4 y_t = \mu_t + \pi_1 S(L)y_{t-1} + \pi_2 A(L)y_{t-1} + (\pi_3 L + \pi_4)(L^2-1)y_{t-1} + \epsilon_t$, where $S(L) = (1+L+L^2+L^3)$, $A(L) = -(1-L)(1+L^2)$, and μ_t contains four seasonal dummies and a trend.)

	Variable	
Test	USA industrial production	UK consumption non-durables
$t(\pi_1)$	-2.952	-2.703
$t(\pi_2)$	-1.751	-1.997
$F(\pi_3, \pi_4)$	12.139***	2.499
Lags	1,2,3	1,4,5
n	121	127

Notes:
*** Significant at the 1% level.
Critical values of the various tests are given in tables 5.5 and 5.6. n denotes the effective number of observations. Lags refers to the lagged $\Delta_4 y_t$ variables included in the auxiliary regression to remove residual autocorrelation. The residuals of the regression for USA industrial production do not pass the JB normality test.

industrial production series, the results in table 5.7 suggest the adequacy of the $(1-L^2)$ filter.

For monthly time series where $S = 12$, the relevant HEGY test equation is

$$\phi(L)y_{8,t} = \mu_t + \pi_1 y_{1,t-1} + \pi_2 y_{2,t-1} + \pi_3 y_{3,t-1} + \pi_4 y_{3,t-2}$$
$$+ \pi_5 y_{4,t-1} + \pi_6 y_{4,t-2} + \pi_7 y_{5,t-1} + \pi_8 y_{5,t-2}$$
$$+ \pi_9 y_{6,t-1} + \pi_{10} y_{6,t-2} + \pi_{11} y_{7,t-1} + \pi_{12} y_{7,t-2} + \varepsilon_t, \quad (5.28)$$

see Beaulieu and Miron (1993) and Franses (1991a), where

$$y_{1,t} = (1+L)(1+L^2)(1+L^4+L^8)y_t,$$

$$y_{2,t} = -(1-L)(1+L^2)(1+L^4+L^8)y_t,$$

$$y_{3,t} = -(1-L^2)(1+L^4+L^8)y_t,$$

$$y_{4,t} = -(1-L^4)(1-L\sqrt{3}+L^2)(1+L^2+L^4)y_t,$$

$$y_{5,t} = -(1-L^4)(1+L\sqrt{3}+L^2)(1+L^2+L^4)y_t,$$

$$y_{6,t} = -(1-L^4)(1-L^2+L^4)(1-L+L^2)y_t,$$

$$y_{7,t} = -(1-L^4)(1-L^2+L^4)(1+L+L^2)y_t \text{ and}$$

$$y_{8,t} = (1-L^{12})y_t.$$

Table 5.8. *Critical values for the joint F-test for various pairs of* π_j
parameters in monthly data

(The DGP is $(1 - L^{12})y_t = \epsilon_t$, with $\epsilon_t \sim N(0,1)$, and the test equation is (5.28).
Based on 25,000 Monte Carlo replications.)

Model	Years	$F(\pi_5, \pi_6)$				$F(\pi_7, \pi_8)$			
		0.10	0.05	0.025	0.01	0.10	0.05	0.025	0.01
No trend	10	4.90	5.80	6.75	7.92	4.85	5.78	6.75	7.81
	20	5.22	6.28	7.22	8.40	5.21	6.21	7.15	8.32
	30	5.46	6.37	7.26	8.42	5.31	6.29	7.28	8.59
	40	5.46	6.48	7.46	8.58	5.32	6.33	7.13	8.39
Trend	10	4.86	5.77	6.69	7.88	4.86	5.77	6.70	7.86
	20	5.21	6.26	7.20	8.38	5.22	6.18	7.14	8.31
	30	5.46	6.34	7.24	8.40	5.30	6.30	7.21	8.55
	40	5.46	6.48	7.44	8.55	5.33	6.30	7.15	8.39

Model	Years	$F(\pi_9, \pi_{10})$				$F(\pi_{11}, \pi_{12})$			
		0.10	0.05	0.025	0.01	0.10	0.05	0.025	0.01
No trend	10	4.94	5.86	6.76	7.98	4.94	5.86	6.81	7.97
	20	5.23	6.22	7.14	8.34	5.26	6.21	7.14	8.27
	30	5.39	6.36	7.35	8.55	5.36	6.31	7.19	8.43
	40	5.46	6.41	7.31	8.56	5.36	6.47	7.45	8.76
Trend	10	4.90	5.84	6.68	7.87	4.90	5.82	6.74	7.92
	20	5.21	6.20	7.11	8.30	5.23	6.20	7.08	8.29
	30	5.36	6.37	7.33	8.53	5.34	6.31	7.17	8.44
	40	5.47	6.40	7.29	8.50	5.36	6.46	7.45	8.75

Note:
The auxiliary test regression contains a constant, seasonal dummies and possibly
a trend.
Source: Franses and Hobijn (1997).

Similar to the above cases, the $y_{1,t}$ and $y_{2,t}$ variables correspond to the unit
roots $+1$ and -1. The $y_{3,t}$ variable corresponds to the seasonal unit roots
$\pm i$. For monthly time series, we can consider the t-ratios for π_1 and π_2, and
the F-tests for $\{\pi_3, \pi_4\}$, $\{\pi_5, \pi_6\}$, $\{\pi_7, \pi_8\}$, $\{\pi_9, \pi_{10}\}$, and $\{\pi_{11}, \pi_{12}\}$. Critical
values of the t-tests appear in table 5.5 and of the $F(\pi_3, \pi_4)$-test in table 5.6
(both under the header "$S = 12$"). Some critical values of F-tests for the last
four pairs of the π_i parameters are given in table 5.8.

As an application of the HEGY test to a monthly time series, consider the following results for the retail sales data, where the auxiliary regression model like (5.28) contains a constant, eleven seasonal dummies, and a linear deterministic time trend. To obtain an uncorrelated error series, we need the inclusion of lags at 1, 2, 3, 6, and 7. The $t(\pi_1)$-test obtains a value of -1.321 and the $t(\pi_2)$-test value equals -2.662. Further test results are $F(\pi_3,\pi_4) = 12.940$, $F(\pi_5,\pi_6) = 19.956$, $F(\pi_7,\pi_8) = 6.901$, $F(\pi_9,\pi_{10}) = 35.896$, and $F(\pi_{11},\pi_{12}) = 13.511$. Comparing these estimated values with the critical values in the various tables indicates that only π_1 is not significant at the 10 percent level. Given that the other test statistics are all significant, the overall conclusion seems to be that the $(1 - L)$ filter may be an appropriate transformation for this retail sales series.

Forecasting USA industrial production

To investigate whether the differencing filter selected using the HEGY method also leads to improved forecasting, consider the forecasting results for USA industrial production in table 5.9.

This table reports on the one-step ahead and multi-step ahead forecasts. The one-step ahead forecasts are based on the most recently available information, while the multi-step ahead forecasts are made at time n for $n+1$ until $n+h$. In the present example h equals 24 (and 16), that is, since the parameters in the various models are estimated for the sample 1960.1–1985.4 (1960.1–1991.4) and 24 (16) forecasts are generated for the sample 1986.1–1991.4 (1992.1–1995.4). To evaluate the second set of 16 forecasts, I use the data given in table 4.4. The first four rows of table 5.9 deal with ARMA models for the time series y_t, $\Delta_1 y_t$, $\Delta_4 y_t$, and $\Delta_1 \Delta_4 y_t$, which are the time series transformations we would consider in the Box–Jenkins approach. The forecast evaluation criterion is the RMSPE. From the first four rows we can observe that the RMSPE for one-step ahead forecasts is smallest for the AR model for the untransformed time series for both samples, while the RMSPE is substantially larger for the airline model for the first sample. In contrast, for the multi-step ahead forecasts it appears that the airline model yields the most adequate forecasts for the first sample and that the model for $\Delta_4 y_t$ performs well for the second sample. The fifth row of table 5.9 gives the RMSPE for an AR(4) model for the $\Delta_2 y_t$ transformed series, which is the transformation suggested by the HEGY tests. It is clear that for both types of forecasts, the forecasting performance does not improve very much, although the HEGY based transformation outperforms the other models on one-step ahead forecasting for the second sample. In sum, we can observe that a small number of imposed unit roots leads to better one-step ahead forecasts, while imposing a large number of unit roots

Table 5.9. *Forecasting industrial production in the USA for*
I: 1986.1–1991.4 and II: 1992.1–1995.4, when the parameters in the various
models are estimated for I: 1960.1–1985.4 and for II: 1960.1–1991.4

			RMSPE ($\times 100$)			
			1-step ahead		multi-step ahead	
	Forecasting model					
Variable[1]	Model[2]	Deterministics[3]	I	II	I	II
Box–Jenkins transformations						
y_t	AR(1–6)	c,d,t	1.334	0.846	2.961	2.056
$\Delta_1 y_t$	AR(1,4,5)	c,d	1.448	1.015	4.611	2.008
$\Delta_4 y_t$	AR(1,2)	c	1.387	0.912	4.915	1.816
$\Delta_1 \Delta_4 y_t$	MA(1,4,5)	c	3.282	0.883	2.619	5.995
Transformation indicated by HEGY test (for sample I and II)						
$\Delta_2 y_t$	AR(1–4)	c,d	2.086	0.750	5.012	2.084
Periodic models						
y_t	PAR(1,2)	c,d	0.857	0.806	8.403	7.523
$(1-\hat{\phi}_s L)y_t$	PAR(1)	c,d	0.863	0.673	3.914	1.703

Notes:
[1] The variable on the left-hand side of the regression model. Note that the
   forecasts evaluated in this table concern the untransformed time series y_t (which
   is the log of industrial production).
[2] The time series model includes lags as indicated in parentheses. "1–6" denotes
   lags 1 through 6, while "1,4,5" denotes lags 1, 4, and 5.
[3] The time series model can include a constant (c), seasonal dummies (d), and a
   trend (t).

seems best for multi-step ahead forecasting. The first result corresponds
with the findings in Franses (1991a) among others, while the latter result
corresponds with those in Clements and Hendry (1997).

Some remarks

The presence of seasonal unit roots in an autoregressive polynomial for y_t
implies that y_t contains so-called seasonal stochastic trends, which in turn
implies that the seasonal fluctuations in y_t can change over time because of
certain values of shocks ε_t. For example, consider the seasonal unit root
series

$$y_t = -y_{t-1} + \varepsilon_t, \tag{5.29}$$

which (with $y_0 = 0$) can be written as

$$y_t = (-1)^t \sum_{i=0}^{t-1} (-1)^i \varepsilon_{t-i}. \qquad (5.30)$$

This expression indicates that y_t is non-stationary since the variance of y_t is $t\sigma^2$. Additionally, the correlation between y_t as in (5.30) and $y_t = \sum_{i=0}^{t} \varepsilon_i$ is zero when $t \to \infty$. This result implies that we can evaluate π_1, π_2 (and $\pi_3 - \pi_4$) in the HEGY regression separately. Expression (5.29) implies that shocks to y_t have a permanent effect on the seasonal pattern of y_t. When (5.29) is the DGP, and the regression model

$$\Delta_1 y_t = \sum_{s=1}^{4} \delta_s D_{s,t} + u_t \qquad (5.31)$$

is considered, the estimated seasonal dummy parameters δ_s will not be constant over time, if we estimate these parameters for various subsamples (as is done in chapter 2). The reader can verify this using simulation experiments. Franses, Hylleberg, and Lee (1995) show that for example in the case where $y_t = y_{t-2} + \varepsilon_t$ is the DGP, and the regression model (5.31) is used to investigate the seasonal patterns, the asymptotic distribution of R^2 and the parameters for the seasonal dummies are not standard. In other words, we may obtain spuriously large R^2 values and seemingly significant dummy parameters in (5.31) because of neglecting seasonal unit roots.

With respect to the practical application of the HEGY test equations, it should be mentioned that such regressions are useful in case the AR order for y_t equals or exceeds S. It can also be used for smaller models, but then we should consider an additional step to the standard HEGY procedure. This is easily demonstrated by the AR(1) model $y_t = \phi_1 y_{t-1} + \varepsilon_t$. Suppose we consider $x_t = (1 + L)y_t$, which resembles the $y_{1,t}$ variable in the HEGY regression (5.27). The value of the theoretical ACF at lag 1 of this x_t series is $(\phi_1 + 1)/2$, which exceeds ϕ_1 in case $\phi_1 \in [0,1)$. Hence, in case a stationary AR(1) model is the DGP, and a standard HEGY test equation is used, we may lose power when testing for a non-seasonal unit root. In practice, we should therefore consider an additional step in case there are no seasonal unit roots, that is, a standard Dickey–Fuller test in a regression which includes seasonal dummies.

Increasing seasonal variation

The graph of four-weekly TV advertising expenditures series in chapter 2 suggests that the seasonal variation in this series increases with the trend, even after applying the log transformation. Increasing seasonal variation, which may not be removable by the natural log transformation, is typical for business economic time series as sales and expenditures, see also Chatfield and Prothero (1973) for an early example and Bowerman, Koehler, and Pack (1990) for some more recent examples. The airline model and its nested variants discussed above cannot generate such increasing seasonal patterns. More appropriate models may then be, for example

$$\Delta_1 \Delta_S y_t = \alpha_0 + \sum_{s=1}^{S-1} \alpha_s D_{s,t} + \beta_0 t + \sum_{s=1}^{S-1} \beta_s D_{s,t} t + u_t \tag{5.32}$$

$$\Delta_1 y_t = \alpha_0 + \sum_{s=1}^{S-1} \alpha_s D_{s,t} + \beta_0 t + \sum_{s=1}^{S-1} \beta_s D_{s,t} t + u_t \tag{5.33}$$

or

$$\Delta_S y_t = \alpha_0 + \sum_{s=1}^{S-1} \alpha_s D_{s,t} + \beta_0 t + \sum_{s=1}^{S-1} \beta_s D_{s,t} t + u_t, \tag{5.34}$$

where u_t is some ARMA error series. The model in (5.32) generates data with an exponential trend and with exponentially increasing seasonality. When some of the β_i parameters and/or α_i parameters are set equal to zero, we can obtain linearly increasing trends and/or seasonality.

To test for the most appropriate differencing filter, while allowing for increasing seasonal variation, we can consider an extension of the OCSB regression equation

$$\phi(L)\Delta_1 \Delta_S y_t = \mu_t + \pi_1 (1 - L^S) y_{t-1} + \pi_2 (1 - L) y_{t-S} + \varepsilon_t, \tag{5.35}$$

where μ_t can now be equal to

$$\mu_t = \alpha_0 + \sum_{s=1}^{S-1} \alpha_s D_{s,t} + \beta_0 t + \sum_{s=1}^{S-1} \beta_s D_{s,t} t. \tag{5.36}$$

In the standard OCSB case, see (5.20), the β_0 through β_{S-1} in (5.36) equal zero. Notice that (5.35) only concerns the filters $\Delta_1 \Delta_S$ and Δ_S versus Δ_1 or no filter. Similar to the OCSB method, the appropriate differencing filter for y_t can be found via testing the significance of π_1 and π_2. There are three relevant outcomes. When both π_1 and π_2 are equal to zero, the $\Delta_1 \Delta_S$ filter is selected. When they both are unequal to zero the Δ_1 or no differencing filter is needed. Finally, when only $\pi_2 = 0$, one selects the Δ_S filter.

Table 5.10 displays the critical values of the one-sided t-test for π_2 and the joint $F(\pi_1, \pi_2)$-test for monthly and four-weekly time series for 20 years of observations. In this table, the μ_t in (5.36) contains a constant and $S-1$ seasonal dummies, which is the standard OCSB case (nt,ndt). Additionally, β_0 can be unequal to zero (t,ndt) and the β_i for $i = 0, \ldots, S-1$ can be unequal to zero (t,dt).

An application of this method in case of increasing seasonal variation is

Table 5.10. *Critical values for tests for the differencing filter in time series with increasing seasonal variation*

(The DGP is $(1-L)(1-L^S)y_t = \epsilon_t$, with $\epsilon_t \sim N(0,1)$, and the test equation is (5.35) with (5.36). Based on 25,000 Monte Carlo replications. Sample size is 20 years.)

Model	S=12				S=13			
	0.01	0.025	0.05	0.10	0.01	0.025	0.05	0.10
			$t(\pi_2)$					
nt,ndt	−6.27	−5.95	−5.63	−5.30	−6.45	−6.09	−5.81	−5.47
t,ndt	−6.28	−5.95	−5.64	−5.30	−6.46	−6.10	−5.81	−5.48
t,dt	−8.50	−8.18	−7.90	−7.58	−8.76	−8.42	−8.17	−7.85
			$F(\pi_1, \pi_2)$					
nt,ndt	15.95	17.91	19.70	21.72	16.84	18.84	20.62	22.76
t,ndt	17.23	19.28	20.97	23.25	18.15	20.25	22.19	24.52
t,dt	31.97	34.45	36.87	39.91	34.00	36.63	38.93	41.86

Note:
The auxiliary regression contains (no) trend ((n)t) and (no) seasonal trends ((n)dt).
Sources: Franses and Hobijn (1997) and Franses and Koehler (1998)

given by an analysis of the four-weekly TV advertising expenditures. The key results are summarized in table 5.11 when the auxiliary regression contains a trend or a trend and seasonal trends. The first row of the table shows that in case of a single trend, the $t(\pi_2)$-test and the $F(\pi_1, \pi_2)$-test are insignificant at the 5 percent level. This suggests the possible adequacy of the Δ_{13} filter. However, when seasonal trends are included, both test statistics are significant at the 1 percent level, implying that no differencing filter is required. For illustrative purposes, an ARMA model for $\Delta_{13}y_t$ is fitted, with no seasonal trends included, and the estimation results are

$$\Delta_{13}y_t = -0.010 + 0.0003t + 0.538\Delta_{13}y_{t-1} + 0.180\Delta_{13}y_{t-6} + \hat{\epsilon}_t - 0.587\hat{\epsilon}_{t-13},$$
$$(0.014)\ (0.0001)\ (0.053)\qquad\quad (0.054)\qquad\qquad (0.060)$$

where estimated standard errors are given in parentheses. Clearly, the parameter for the deterministic trend is significant. The JB diagnostic for normality suggests that this model, which includes only five parameters for 202 effective observations, may suffer from aberrant observations.

To summarize this section on seasonal unit roots, we can conclude that there are several approaches to select an appropriate differencing filter. A common feature of these methods is the assumption of the adequacy of an

Table 5.11. *Selecting a differencing filter for a
time series with increasing seasonal variation
using the OCSB method: 4-weekly TV
advertising expenditures*

(The auxiliary regression is $\phi(L)\Delta_1\Delta_{13}y_t = \mu_t +
\pi_1(1-L^{13})y_{t-1} + \pi_2(1-L)y_{t-13} + \epsilon_t$ where μ_t includes
13 seasonal dummies, and a trend but no seasonal
trend (t,ndt), or a trend and seasonal trends (t,dt).)

Model	Lags	$t(\pi_2)$	$F(\pi_1, \pi_2)$
t, ndt	13	−4.581	33.963*
t, dt	0	−12.161***	119.181***

Notes:
*** Significant at the 1% level.
*   Significant at the 10% level.
"Lags" refers to the lagged $\Delta_1\Delta_{13}y_t$ variables included
in the auxiliary model to remove residual
autocorrelation. The residuals of both regressions do
not pass the normality test.

AR model. As an alternative method, Canova and Hansen (1995) propose
an extension of the KPSS test (see chapter 4) to seasonal time series.

Finally, in case of a set of seasonal time series, we may want to construct
a multivariate model. Such a model may contain a substantial number of
parameters, and it seems therefore desirable to investigate the presence of
common seasonal stochastic or deterministic trends and seasonal constants. In chapter 10, the seasonal cointegration model will be analyzed for
the purpose of parameter reduction.

5.3   Periodic models

The variants of the SARIMA models considered so far assume that seasonality can be modeled by including lags at (multiples of) seasonal frequency
S. This may involve a loss of observations, since a model with k lags reduces
the effective sample size with k observations. An alternative approach to
modeling seasonal time series amounts to allowing seasonal variation in the
dynamic parameters, see Tiao and Grupe (1980). This section surveys some
important concepts in the analysis of periodic AR models of order p
[PAR(p)] such as representation, estimation, testing for parameter restrictions, and unit roots. A detailed account of periodicity and stochastic

trends in economic time series, as well as a more comprehensive list of references on periodic models, can be found in Franses (1996).

A periodic autoregression [PAR] extends a non-periodic AR model by allowing the autoregressive parameters to vary with the seasons. In other words, the PAR model assumes that the observations in each of the seasons can be described using a different model. Such a property may be useful since sometimes we may expect economic agents to behave differently in different seasons. For example, technological advances throughout the years have made it possible to buy certain vegetables in almost all seasons now, while these products were available in, say, only the summer season several years ago. Hence, we may observe an increasing trend in the consumption of these vegetables in one or more seasons and no trend in the summer season. Another example is that tax measures can become effective in the first part of the year, leading to seasonal variation in inflation, which may establish that economic agents increasingly anticipate such inflation patterns. Osborn (1988), Todd (1990), and Hansen and Sargent (1993) give economic examples which concern seasonally varying utility functions and optimization schemes. In this section the focus will be on a few econometric properties of PAR time series models.

Notation and representation

Consider a univariate seasonal time series y_t which is observed for N years, that is, $t = 1,2,\ldots,n$, with $n = SN$. A periodic autoregressive model of order p [PAR(p)] can be written as

$$y_t = \mu_s + \phi_{1,s} y_{t-1} + \ldots + \phi_{p,s} y_{t-p} + \varepsilon_t, \tag{5.37}$$

or

$$\phi_{p,s}(L) y_t = \mu_s + \varepsilon_t,$$

with

$$\mu_s = \sum_{s=1}^{S} \delta_s D_{s,t}, \tag{5.38}$$

and where $\phi_{p,s}(L) = 1 - \phi_{1,s} L - \ldots - \phi_{p,s} L^p$. The $\phi_{1,s}$ through $\phi_{p,s}$ are autoregressive parameters up to order p which may vary with the season s, $s = 1,2,\ldots,S$. The ε_t is assumed to be standard white noise with constant variance σ^2, although we may also allow ε_t to have seasonal variances σ_s^2. Since some $\phi_{i,s}$ parameters ($i = 1,2,\ldots,p$) can take zero values, the order p in (5.37) is the maximum of all p_s, where p_s denotes the AR order per season s. The μ_s in (5.37) does not necessarily reflect that the mean of y_t is also seasonally varying. In fact, rewriting a PAR model for y_t with constant mean

μ, that is, $\phi_{p,s}(L)(y_t - \mu) = \varepsilon_t$ as (5.37), amounts to the restriction $\mu_s = (\phi_{p,s}(1))\mu$, and hence μ_s varies seasonally because the autoregressive parameters do so. Obviously, the number of autoregressive parameters in a PAR(p) model for a seasonal time series is S times as large as that in a non-periodic AR(p) model. This can also be understood by observing that in case $p = 1$, (5.37) can be written as the system of equations (in the notation discussed in the introduction to this chapter)

$$Y_{4,T} = \mu_4 + \phi_{1,4} Y_{3,T} + \varepsilon_{4,T}$$

$$Y_{3,T} = \mu_3 + \phi_{1,3} Y_{2,T} + \varepsilon_{3,T}$$

$$Y_{2,T} = \mu_2 + \phi_{1,2} Y_{1,T} + \varepsilon_{2,T}$$

$$Y_{1,T} = \mu_1 + \phi_{1,1} Y_{4,T-1} + \varepsilon_{1,T},$$

which indicates that four parameters are needed to describe the first order AR parameters.

Estimation and model selection

There are at least two approaches to modeling PAR(p) time series. The first is to investigate the possible usefulness of periodic time series models via checking the properties of estimated residuals from non-periodic models. The second approach is simply to estimate a PAR(p) model, where p is selected using conventional model selection criteria, and to test whether there is indeed periodic variation in the autoregressive parameters.

To test for periodicity in the estimated residuals, we may consider an LM type procedure, which starts with fitting a non-periodic AR(k) model to a time series x_t, where x_t is the appropriately differenced y_t series according to the HEGY tests, yielding residuals $\hat{v}_t$. The auxiliary regression

$$\hat{v}_t = \sum_{i=1}^{k} \eta_i x_{t-i} + \sum_{s=1}^{S} (\psi_{1,s} D_{s,t} \hat{v}_{t-1} + \ldots + \psi_{m,s} D_{s,t} \hat{v}_{t-m}) + u_t, \qquad (5.39)$$

may then be used to investigate the presence of periodicity in the estimated residuals. The F-test for $\psi_{i,s} = 0$ ($i = 1,2,\ldots,m$) can be used to test the null hypothesis of no periodic autocorrelation of order m. This F-test is denoted here as $F_{PeAC,1-m}$. Under the null hypothesis, this statistic asymptotically follows a standard F-distribution with $(Sm, n - k - Sm)$ degrees of freedom. An LM-type test for seasonal heteroskedasticity can be performed using

$$\hat{v}_t^2 = \omega_0 + \omega_1 D_{1,t} + \omega_2 D_{2,t} + \ldots + \omega_{S-1} D_{S-1,t} + \lambda_t. \qquad (5.40)$$

Under the null hypothesis of no seasonal heteroskedasticity, the F-test statistic for the significance of the ω_1, ω_2 to ω_{S-1} parameters, denoted as F_{SH}, follows a standard F-distribution. The F_{SH}-test may also be useful in case we want to consider non-periodic models with seasonal variances.

As an illustration, consider again the quarterly USA industrial production and UK non-durables consumption series. According to the HEGY test results in table 5.7, we should transform the series with the Δ_2 and the Δ_4 filter, respectively. For both transformed series, we have to fit an AR(6) model to remove serial correlation in the residuals (based on the $F_{AC,1-4}$-test). An application of the $F_{PeAC,1-1}$-test yields the values 3.077 and 2.474, respectively, and these values are significant at the 5 percent level. Additionally, the $F_{PeAC,1-2}$-test statistics obtain the 5 percent significant values of 2.596 and 2.609 indicating that the non-periodic models for both transformed series have periodic features in the estimated residuals. The F_{SH} tests for seasonal heteroskedasticity have the insignificant values of 1.836 and 2.257 for industrial production and consumption, respectively.

The second simple approach to investigate periodic variation in the AR parameters is given by estimating, for example, a PAR(p) model to y_t and to test the null hypothesis of no periodic variation. Consider the regression model

$$y_t = \sum_{s=1}^{S} \mu_s D_{s,t} + \sum_{s=1}^{S} \phi_{1,s} D_{s,t} y_{t-1} + \ldots + \sum_{s=1}^{S} \phi_{p,s} D_{s,t} y_{t-p} + \varepsilon_t. \tag{5.41}$$

Under normality of ε_t and with fixed starting values, the maximum likelihood [ML] estimates of the parameters $\phi_{i,s}$, $i=1,2,\ldots,p$ and $s=1,2,\ldots,S$ are obtained from OLS estimation of (5.41). Notice that the available sample for estimating the periodic parameters is $N=n/S$.

A next step is to test for periodic variation in the autoregressive parameters. Boswijk and Franses (1996) show that an F-test for the null hypothesis H_0: $\phi_{i,s}=\phi_i$ for $s=1,2,\ldots,S$ and $i=1,2,\ldots,p$, denoted here by F_{PAR}, has the standard $F(3p,n-(S+Sp))$-distribution in case of a PAR(p) series with S seasonal intercepts, irrespective of the presence of non-seasonal or seasonal unit roots. An important implication of this result is that (5.41) can be estimated for the y_t series itself, that is, there is no need to consider an *a priori* differenced y_t series. Hence, for practical purposes, it seems most convenient to start with estimating the model in (5.41) and then to test for periodic parameter variation. In a second step we may test for unit roots. An additional advantage is that this sequence of steps allows for the adequacy of a periodic differencing filter, that is, a differencing filter that varies with the season, see Franses (1996).

The order of a periodic autoregression is not known in practice and has to be estimated from the data. For this purpose, we can use model selection criteria such as $\text{AIC}(p)=n\log\hat{\sigma}^2+2Sp$, where $\hat{\sigma}^2$ is RSS/n, with n the effective sample size, or $\text{SIC}(p)=n\log\hat{\sigma}^2+Sp\log n$. An alternative approach is to use an F-test to decide if the model order can be set equal to p when some or all $\phi_{ps} \neq 0$, while the $\phi_{p+1,s} = 0$ for all s.

An application of these model selection criteria to the USA industrial production series yields that the PAR order is estimated as 2, while the PAR order can be set equal to 1 for consumption non-durables. The F_{SH}-test statistics obtain the values 1.418 and 1.878, respectively. Hence, model (5.41) does not need to be modified to allow for seasonal heteroskedasticity. The F_{PAR}-test statistic obtains the value 11.299 for USA production, and it equals 31.504 for UK consumption. Obviously, these two F_{PAR}-test values exceed the 1 percent significance level. Similar results hold true when the PAR model includes four deterministic trends. Hence, we can conclude that low order PAR models can be fitted to these two quarterly example series.

Testing for unit roots in PAR processes

For notational convenience, consider the simple PAR(1) for a quarterly series

$$y_t = \alpha_s y_{t-1} + \varepsilon_t. \tag{5.42}$$

It can be shown that y_t contains a unit root when

$$H_0: \prod_{s=1}^{4} \alpha_s = 1, \tag{5.43}$$

see chapter 9 below. When (5.43) holds and not all α_s are equal to 1 or -1, the y_t series is said to be periodically integrated. Imposing $\alpha_1 \alpha_2 \alpha_3 \alpha_4 = 1$ leads to the regression

$$y_t = \alpha_1 D_{1,t} y_{t-1} + \alpha_2 D_{2,t} y_{t-1} + \alpha_3 D_{3,t} y_{t-1} + (\alpha_1 \alpha_2 \alpha_3)^{-1} D_{4,t} y_{t-1} + \varepsilon_t, \tag{5.44}$$

which can be estimated by NLS. A likelihood ratio [LR] test statistic is constructed as

$$LR = n.\log (RSS_0/RSS_1), \tag{5.45}$$

where RSS_0 and RSS_1 correspond to (5.44) and to the unrestricted model, respectively. A one-sided test can be constructed as

$$LR_\tau = [\text{sign} (\hat{\alpha}_1 \hat{\alpha}_2 \hat{\alpha}_3 \hat{\alpha}_4 - 1)] LR^{\frac{1}{2}}, \tag{5.46}$$

where $\hat{\alpha}_1 \hat{\alpha}_2 \hat{\alpha}_3 \hat{\alpha}_4$ is evaluated under the alternative hypothesis. Boswijk and Franses (1996) show that the asymptotic distribution of LR_τ is the same as that of the standard Dickey–Fuller test discussed in chapter 4. Extensions to periodic models that include constants and trends are also straightforward and similar to the standard Dickey–Fuller case.

To generalize the likelihood ratio test for a unit root to higher order periodic autoregressions, consider

$$y_t = \sum_{i=1}^{p}\sum_{s=1}^{4}\phi_{i,s}D_{s,t}y_{t-i} + \sum_{s=1}^{4}\mu_s D_{s,t} + \sum_{s=1}^{4}\tau_s D_{s,t}t + \varepsilon_t, \tag{5.47}$$

which can be estimated using OLS. Denote RSS_1 as the residual sum of squares of (5.47) in case $\tau_s = 0$, and RSS_2 in the case where the four trends are included. Note that including four trends does not necessarily mean that the data show increasing seasonal variation. The following non-linear (pseudo-differenced) regression

$$y_t = \sum_{s=1}^{4}\alpha_s D_{s,t}y_{t-1} + \sum_{i=1}^{p-1}\sum_{s=1}^{4}\beta_{i,s}D_{s,t}(y_{t-1} - \alpha_{s-i}y_{t-i-1})$$

$$+ \sum_{s=1}^{4}\mu_s D_{s,t} + \sum_{s=1}^{4}\tau_s D_{s,t}t + \varepsilon_t, \tag{5.48}$$

can be estimated using NLS under the restriction $\alpha_1\alpha_2\alpha_3\alpha_4 = 1$, where $\alpha_{-k} = \alpha_{4-k}$ for all k. Denote the residual sum of squares of (5.48) for both cases as RSS_0. The relevant LR tests for a unit root are $LR_i = n\log(RSS_0/RSS_i)$. The distributions of the LR_i tests are given in Boswijk and Franses (1996). Similar to (5.46) we may construct the one-sided LR tests $LR_{1\tau}$ and $LR_{2\tau}$.

For the USA industrial production series the $LR_{1\tau}$ test obtains a value of -1.807 and the $LR_{2\tau}$ value is -2.999. For UK consumption non-durables the PAR order is 1, and the $LR_{1\tau}$ test has a value of 0.585, and the $LR_{2\tau}$ test obtains the value of -1.258. Comparing these test values with the critical values in table 4.1, it is clear that both series have a unit root. The estimated values of α_1 through α_4 in the relevant differencing filters $(1 - \hat{\alpha}_s L)$ in (5.48) are 1.004, 0.981, 1.047, and 0.969 for industrial production and 1.003, 0.932, 1.030, and 0.991 for consumption non-durables.

When the hypothesis of $\alpha_1\alpha_2\alpha_3\alpha_4 = 1$ cannot be rejected, the next step is to investigate the hypotheses

$$H_0: \alpha_s = 1 \quad \text{for } s = 1,2,3 \tag{5.49}$$

$$H_0: \alpha_s = -1 \quad \text{for } s = 1,2,3, \tag{5.50}$$

which, given $\alpha_1\alpha_2\alpha_3\alpha_4 = 1$, imply that either $\alpha_4 = 1$ or $\alpha_4 = -1$. The first H_0 reduces the periodic differencing filter $(1 - \alpha_s L)$ to $(1 - L)$, while the second H_0 reduces it to the $(1 + L)$ differencing filter. In case the H_0 in (5.49) cannot be rejected, the PAR(p) series contains a non-seasonal unit root. Boswijk and Franses (1996) show that, conditional on the restriction $\alpha_1\alpha_2\alpha_3\alpha_4 = 1$, the likelihood ratio test statistics for the hypotheses (5.49) and (5.50) have asymptotic $\chi^2(3)$ distributions under the null hypothesis. The relevant F-test statistics for the $(1-L)$ filter are 17.939 and 31.617 for production and consumption, respectively. Since these are both significant at the 1 percent level, and given the obvious inadequacy of the $(1+L)$ filter, we can conclude that both time series need periodic differencing filters to remove a single stochastic trend, that is, both variables are periodically integrated.

Periodic integration in comparison with seasonal integration

Based on the EACF in table 5.2, we may want to describe the UK consumption non-durables series by an airline type of model. In fact, a simple model for this variable is estimated to be

$$\Delta_1\Delta_4 y_t = \hat{\varepsilon}_t - 0.632\hat{\varepsilon}_{t-4}. \tag{5.51}$$
$$(0.069)$$

To investigate the connection of this model with the PAR of order 1 with a unit root, consider again the expression

$$y_t = \alpha_s y_{t-1} + \varepsilon_t \quad \text{with } \alpha_1\alpha_2\alpha_3\alpha_4 = 1. \tag{5.52}$$

Backward substitution yields

$$y_t = y_{t-4} + \varepsilon_t + \alpha_s\varepsilon_{t-1} + \alpha_s\alpha_{s-1}\varepsilon_{t-2} + \alpha_s\alpha_{s-1}\alpha_{s-2}\varepsilon_{t-3}, \tag{5.53}$$

which shows that $\Delta_4 y_t$ is a periodic moving average model of order 3 and that $\Delta_4 y_t$ is stationary, see also Osborn *et al.* (1988). This expression seems to suggest that the Δ_4 filter can be used to remove the non-stationarity from y_t. However, it is clear that the assumption of four unit roots via the Δ_4 filter should amount to overdifferencing since (5.52) can only contain a single unit root because it includes only one lag of y_t. Taking first differences of (5.53) yields

$$\Delta_1\Delta_4 y_t = \varepsilon_t + (\alpha_s - 1)\varepsilon_{t-1} + \alpha_{s-1}(\alpha_s - 1)\varepsilon_{t-2} + \alpha_{s-1}\alpha_{s-2}(\alpha_s - 1)\varepsilon_{t-3}$$
$$- \alpha_{s-1}\alpha_{s-2}\alpha_{s-3}\varepsilon_{t-4}. \tag{5.54}$$

When the α_s are unequal but very close to unity, the $\alpha_s - 1$ values can become quite small, and (5.54) can be approximated by $\Delta_1\Delta_4 y_t = \varepsilon_t - \eta_s\varepsilon_{t-4}$. When such a series is analyzed in a non-periodic manner, one in fact considers a model as in (5.51).

Finally, to highlight a specific property of the forecast error variances from periodic models, consider the SPEs that correspond to the model in (5.52), that is

$$SPE(1) = \sigma^2$$
$$SPE(2) = [\alpha_2^2 + 1]\sigma^2$$
$$SPE(3) = [\alpha_2^2\alpha_3^2 + \alpha_3^2 + 1]\sigma^2$$
$$SPE(4) = [\alpha_2^2\alpha_3^2\alpha_4^2 + \alpha_3^2\alpha_4^2 + \alpha_4^2 + 1]\sigma^2,$$

where the forecasts are made at time $n = 4N$. Comparing these expressions with those of $y_t = y_{t-1} + \varepsilon_t$, which are σ^2, $2\sigma^2$, $3\sigma^2$, and $4\sigma^2$, it is clear that a periodic time series allows forecast intervals to vary with the seasons. To illustrate that periodic models can be useful for forecasting, consider again table 5.9. In the last two rows of this table, the RMSPEs are reported of a PAR(2) model for USA industrial production. The numbers in the last row correspond with a PAR(2) model with the imposed restriction $\alpha_1\alpha_2\alpha_3\alpha_4 = 1$. It is clear that the periodically integrated models generally outperform the non-periodic models for the one-step and multi-step ahead forecasts.

5.4   Miscellaneous topics

The results in the previous two sections show that the Box–Jenkins approach to modeling seasonal time series can be refined by formal tests for the presence of seasonal and non-seasonal unit roots, and by allowing for seasonal variation in the parameters. A possible drawback of these two approaches is that it may require additional modeling skills from the practitioner. Naturally, this raises the issue whether modeling seasonality instead of removing is worth the effort anyway. In this section, I therefore take a brief look at seasonal adjustment methods.

Seasonal adjustment

The assumption underlying seasonal adjustment methods is that seasonality is a data contamination that can be removed from the data in order to facilitate the analysis of, for example, trends and business cycles. The first and simplest approach to seasonal adjustment [SA] amounts to a regression of the time series on deterministic sine and cosine functions. This method is only useful when the seasonal fluctuations are constant. The second and more realistic approach assumes that seasonal fluctuations can be filtered out using a sequence of moving average filters. This approach is followed in the well-known Census X-11 method. The third so-called model-dependent approach (which will not be treated here) considers the construction of ARIMA type time series models for the various unobserved components including the seasonal component. For detailed accounts of the various methods, see Bell and Hillmer (1984), Hylleberg (1986), and several papers in Hylleberg (1992).

The main idea of seasonal adjustment is that a seasonally observed time series y_t can be decomposed into two unobserved components

$$y_t = y_t^{ns} + y_t^s, \tag{5.55}$$

where y_t^{ns} denotes the non-seasonal component containing trend, cycles, and irregularity, and where y_t^s denotes the seasonal component. Since the two components have to be estimated from the data, it is more appropriate to use the notation $\hat{y}_t^{ns}$ and $\hat{y}_t^s$. Of course, in case the seasonal fluctuations are multiplicative, (5.55) should be replaced by $y_t = y_t^{ns} y_t^s$.

In case the trend and seasonal fluctuations are evolving over time, we use certain moving average filters to remove trend and seasonality. In many practical occasions, such moving average filters are linear, symmetric, and centered around the current observation. Defining the forward shift operator F by $F = L^{-1}$, and hence $F^k y_t = y_{t+k}$, such a linear moving average filter is given by

$$C_m(L,F) = c_0 + \sum_{i=1}^{m} c_i (L^i + F^i), \tag{5.56}$$

where $c_0, c_1, \ldots, c_m$ are the weights. An example is the $C_1(L,F)$ filter with $c_0 = 1/2$ and $c_1 = -(1/4)$, which equals $-(1/4)(L^2 - 2L + 1)F$ since $FL = 1$. This filter concerns two non-seasonal unit roots because $(L^2 - 2L + 1) = (1 - L)^2$. In general, $C_m(1,1) = c_0 + 2\sum_{i=1}^{m} c_i = 0$ in the case where we remove an evolving or stochastic trend. For the standard $(1 - L)$ filter, $c_0 = 1$ and $c_1 = -1$ for the L part of (5.56) only.

For a seasonal time series, we may consider the $C_1(L,F)$ filter with $c_0 = 1/2$ and $c_1 = 1/4$, since in that case $C_1(L,F)$ corresponds to $(1/4)(L^2 + 2L + 1) = (1/4)(1 + L)^2$. Notice that this filter imposes 2(!) seasonal unit roots -1 on the transformed time series. In general, $c_0 + 2\sum_{i=1}^{m} c_i = 1$ in the case where we remove an evolving seasonal pattern. Details of the use of linear moving average filters are given in Grether and Nerlove (1970).

The Census X–11 seasonal adjustment method is often applied in practice. Early references to this approach include Shiskin and Eisenpress (1957) and Shiskin, Young, and Musgrave (1967). An extensive documentation of this method is given in Hylleberg (1986). Apart from the treatment of holiday, trading-day, and calendar effects, the additive version of the Census X–11 method involves two main actions. The first is the sequential application of moving average filters as in (5.56). The second action is the removal of aberrant observations in each round of moving average filtering and the replacement of such influential observations by weighted data points. Both actions involve decisions made by the practitioner, which can vary with the time series at hand. The outlier weighting part makes the overall procedure an intrinsically non-linear method in the sense that, for example, such data weights depend on the choice of moving average filters. A recent discussion of the non-linearity aspects of Census X–11 is given in Ghysels, Granger, and Siklos (1996). Laroque (1977) shows that a linearized version of the Census X–11 filter for quarterly data approximately contains the component $(1 + L + L^2 + L^3)^2 = (1 + L)^2(1-iL)^2(1 + iL)^2$. This corresponds with six roots on the unit circle, that is, two times -1, two times $-i$, and two times $+i$. The results in section 5.2 suggest that for economic time series the maximum number of seasonal unit roots appears to be equal to three, that is, the filter $(1 + L + L^2 + L^3)$ is usually more than sufficient to remove evolving seasonal patterns from the time series. Hence, the application of linear moving average filters as in (5.56) and also the Census X–11 filter may yield non-invertible MA models for the seasonally adjusted time series.

Finally, in order to seasonally adjust observations at a certain time t, for example, with a filter like (5.56), we need the observations over the sample $y_{t-m}, \dots, y_{t+m}$. Since such observations are not available at the beginning and at the end of a sample, we need to obtain earlier data and forecasts in order to seasonally adjust the y_t series for all observations. A simple approach is now to estimate seasonal ARIMA models for the y_t series, and to generate $\hat{y}_{-(m-1)}, \dots, \hat{y}_0$, $\hat{y}_{n+1}, \dots, \hat{y}_{n+m}$, when the sample contains n observations. Notice, however, that seasonally adjusted series therefore have to be updated every time new observations on y_t become available.

An important requirement for SA data is that the non-seasonal unit root and/or long-memory properties of the original time series are preserved in the SA series. This seems relevant in the case of business cycle analysis. However, in, for example, Jaeger and Kunst (1990) it is shown that shocks to seasonally adjusted time series are more persistent. Furthermore, Ghysels and Perron (1993) show that for a stationary time series a linear two-sided moving average filter biases unit root tests toward non-rejection. These results may provide a motivation to consider econometric time series models that explicitly incorporate a description of seasonal variation.

6   Aberrant observations

For many economic time series one or more observations on the same variable can be strikingly different from the other observations. An illustrative example is given by the May 1968 uproar in France, which caused such important variables as industrial production to have a suddenly much lower value than we could have expected given its earlier general pattern. As another example, we may consider the stock market crash on Monday, October 19, 1987 as an extraordinary event, which in a sense does not correspond to the bulk of the data.

Aberrant time series data, or outliers, can be most easily defined in terms of a descriptive model. For example, suppose that a time series y_t is generated by the AR(1) model

$$y_t = \phi_1 y_{t-1} + \varepsilon_t, \quad t = 1,2,\ldots,n, \tag{6.1}$$

where ε_t is assumed to be drawn from a standard normal distribution $N(0,1)$, y_0 is set equal to 100 and $|\phi_1| < 1$. We can now expect that it is highly unlikely that the observation at $t = 20$ is equal to 1,000. Suppose however, that the data on y_t are recorded by a statistical agency, and that, when downloading these numbers, somehow a mistake is made and y_{20} erroneously becomes 1,005 instead of the true value of 105, say. In that case, we observe a new variable y_t^* which is y_t as in (6.1) with one value changed. For this y_t^* variable, we can easily conclude that observation y_{20}^* does not correspond to the general pattern of y_t^*. In fact, for most data points it approximately holds that $y_t^* = \phi_1 y_{t-1}^*$, while for y_{20}^* this is clearly not the case. Hence, y_{20}^* can be called an outlier. Since there are various types of outliers or even sequences of outliers, I use the more general phrase of aberrant observations instead of outliers in the sequel.

The above example already shows that it can be important to account for outliers when modeling and forecasting economic time series. In fact, neglecting such aberrant observations can have at least three major effects. The first is that when the y_t^* data (with the outlier at $t = 20$) are used to esti-

128

mate ϕ_1, we may expect that this $\hat{\phi}_1$ can be quite different from the true ϕ_1. Below, it will be illustrated that for the so-called additive outlier [AO], see Fox (1972) for a discussion of terminology, the $\hat{\phi}_1$ will be biased toward zero, while for a so-called level shift (where the mean of the series changes) this $\hat{\phi}_1$ is biased toward 1. Hence, when we aim to forecast y_{n+1}, and we use $\hat{\phi}_1$ from a model such as (6.1), while neglecting outliers, we can expect some forecasting bias. The second major effect of neglecting aberrant data, especially those which are close to the forecasting origin, that is, observation n, is that forecasts can be very inaccurate. For example, suppose that the above y_t^* series ends at $t = 20$, and we wish to forecast y_{21}^*. In that case, the value of 1,005 for y_{20}^* will have a dramatic effect on this forecast. The third major effect is that when an AR model as in (6.1) is estimated for the y_t^* data, we may expect that the $\hat{\sigma}^2$ for these contaminated data is much larger than the true σ^2. This, in turn, implies that the corresponding forecasting intervals will be much too wide.

There are different and sometimes conflicting views on how to treat such aberrant data when modeling and forecasting economic variables. One approach assumes that there is (almost) no *a priori* knowledge about the observation(s) that could possibly be aberrant. For the statistical analysis of a time series, we may then assume that apparently irregular data are generated by a distribution that is different from most other data points. For example, we can assume that most returns on the Dow Jones index are normally distributed with mean 0 and variance ω, while for only a few it holds that the data seem to have been generated by a normal distribution with variance ν with ν being much larger than ω or with a mean unequal to zero. Notice that this touches upon the important assumption of standard time series analysis where it is usual to assume that all data are generated from the same process (see also the stationarity concept in chapter 4).

An alternative and somewhat simpler approach is to replace the normality assumption of the error process as in (6.1) by the assumption of, for example, a Student-t distribution. This distribution has fatter tails than the normal distribution, and hence may generate more extreme values of ε_t once in a while, so that the corresponding y_t data can take larger values. Yet another approach, which focuses more on estimating ϕ_1 in (6.1), concerns replacing OLS estimation methods by methods that consider the median instead of the mean, see Denby and Martin (1979) and Bustos and Yohai (1986). Although these above approaches incorporate the possibility to examine particular observations with respect to their possible influence, see, for example, Lucas (1996), in general these methods focus on reducing the impact of aberrant data on estimation and forecasting without paying specific attention to the influential observations themselves.

In this book, I adopt the contrasting view that outliers, or sets of these aberrant data in the form of breaking trends or level shifts, somehow convey important information which we would want to exploit explicitly for forecasting or for taking into account prior to forecasting. Additionally, it is assumed that the practitioner has some *a priori* knowledge about the likely location and relevance of such data, or that some recursive technique is used indicating such patterns. For example, for the radio advertising expenditures data in figure 2.9, it is known that the obvious level shift in the beginning of the sample is caused by an expansion of radio broadcasting minutes by 60 percent. Such an external cause is often called an intervention, see Box and Tiao (1975).

From a modeling and forecasting point of view it is important to have knowledge of the location of outliers. For example, a one-time promotion (like "buy three for the price of two") in week j can generate a large increase in sales in week j, maybe a little decrease in week $j + 1$, and then its effect may fade out. Removal of this observation would not make it possible to study the effect of promotion on sales. See Leone (1987) for an approach that explicitly allows for outliers and level shifts to study the possible long-run impact of promotional activities. In this chapter, I include (models for) aberrant data within the class of ARMA type time series models. Again, all these models are regression based. In general, it seems sensible to include as much information as possible on aberrant data in our model, so that we can decide on their impact on modeling and forecasting in a next step.

The outline of this chapter is as follows. In section 6.1, I give some models that allow us to describe several forms of aberrant data and to understand how these may emerge in economic variables. Such models can be useful to test their impact, as well as to exploit their description in a forecasting model. A brief discussion of formal tests appears in section 6.2. In both sections, I assume that the time series is stationary in the sense that there are no unit roots in the AR component of the ARMA model. Since aberrant data can have an impact on the decision whether a time series is stationary or not, I will discuss the issue of unit root testing in the presence of aberrant data in section 6.3.

6.1   Modeling aberrant observations

In practice, the possible presence of aberrant observations is often indicated by a large value of the JB normality test see (3.103), suggesting rejection of the null hypothesis of a normal distribution for the estimated residuals. In case of such non-normality, we may consider including descriptions of different types of aberrant data in the time series model. In this section, I will review some of these descriptions. Additionally, I will illustrate how various forms of irregular data affect parameter estimates in case these data are neglected and how non-normality is reflected through the resultant residuals. I start with the single additive and innovation outliers. Next, I proceed with models for sets of aberrant data, that is, permanent and transient level shifts and changing trends.

Additive Outlier [AO]

An additive outlier can be viewed as an observation which is the genuine data point plus or minus some value. This latter value can be caused by a recording error, as for example is the case when the number of unemployed should be 100, and a computer breakdown at the registration office causes that we can only register the first 50. The "added" value can also be caused by misinterpreting sudden news flashes, which can cause a stock market to take unexpectedly large values, while such news may appear not important (and hence having no effect) in the next period. In other words, the data point is then aberrant because of some cause outside the intrinsic economic environment that generates the time series data at hand. Needless to say it is unlikely that such additive outliers are predictable.

Since the additive outlier can be viewed as a measurement error, one approach to describe it is given by

$$y_t = x_t + \omega I_t[t = \tau], \tag{6.2}$$

where $I_t[.]$ is an indicator dummy variable observed for $t = 1,2,\ldots,n$, that is, the I_t in (6.2) takes a value of 1 when $t = \tau$ and a value zero otherwise. The time series x_t is the uncontaminated but unobserved time series, while y_t corresponds to the observed variable. The size of the outlier is denoted by ω. Notice that in practice, the value of τ can be unknown, and also that the value of ω can be stochastic.

Suppose that x_t is generated by an AR(1) model with some parameter ϕ_1. In case we do not observe x_t but y_t as in (6.2), then we can expect that at time τ there is an AO of size ω which appears on the left-hand side of the AR(1) model, while at time $\tau + 1$, this AO observation moves toward the right-hand side of the model in the y_{t-1} part. In other words, when we make a scatter plot of y_t versus y_{t-1}, an AO looks like two irregular data points. In figure 6.1, I give such a scatter plot for a simulated time series with $n = 100$, $\phi_1 = 0.8$, $\omega = 10$, and $\tau = 50$. Clearly, we can observe the two data points (y_t, y_{t-1}) which do not seem to correspond to the general pattern of observations.

As is obvious from figure 6.1, an AO is reflected in two pairs of (y_t, y_{t-1}) in case of an AR(1) time series x_t. Hence, neglecting such an AO while estimating the parameter in an AR(1) model for y_t using OLS results in two large estimated residuals. In fact, since y_τ is an extraordinary data point, its

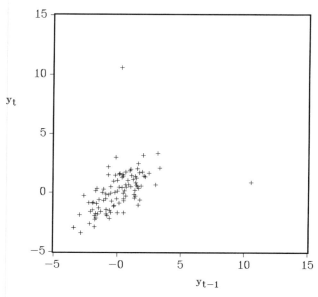

Figure 6.1 *Effect of a single additive outlier on regression of y_t on y_{t-1}*

forecast $\hat{y}_\tau$ given $y_{\tau-1}$ and some $\hat{\phi}_1$ can be quite different from the true y_τ value. Additionally, y_τ itself is a biased predictor variable for $y_{\tau+1}$. In sum, when an AO in an AR(1) series is neglected, we find two large errors, that is $\hat{\varepsilon}_\tau$ and $\hat{\varepsilon}_{\tau+1}$. This is illustrated by the graphs in Figure 6.2 which shows the same simulated time series as before, the fit from an AR(1) model (based on OLS estimates), and the estimated residual series. Clearly, there are two large residuals, which will imply large values of the normality test statistic.

Given that there are two observations for an AR(1) series that do not correspond with the cloud of (y_t, y_{t-1}) points, as visualized in figure 6.1, we may expect that neglecting AOs can have a severe impact on the OLS estimate of ϕ_1. This impact of neglecting AOs on $\hat{\phi}_1$ is illustrated through four simulated examples in table 6.1.

It is clear from this table that when ω in (6.2) increases, the difference between $\phi_1 - \hat{\phi}_1$ becomes large and positive. Lucas (1996) shows that for the data generating process with

$$x_t = \phi_1 x_{t-1} + \varepsilon_t \qquad (6.3)$$

$$y_t = x_t + \omega \delta_t, \quad \omega > 0 \qquad (6.4)$$

$$\delta_t = -1 \text{ with probability } \pi/2 \qquad (6.5)$$
$$ = 0 \quad \text{with probability } 1 - \pi$$
$$ = 1 \quad \text{with probability } \pi/2,$$

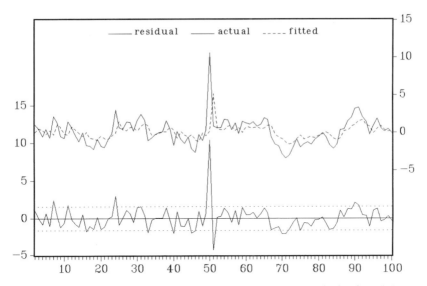

Figure 6.2 *Effect of neglecting a single additive outlier on residuals of AR(1) model*

which is more general than that used in table 6.1, it holds that

$$\text{plim } \hat{\phi}_1 = \phi_1/[1 + \pi\omega^2/\sigma_x^2] \tag{6.6}$$

in case the AOs generated by the δ_t process are neglected. In other words, the estimate of ϕ_1 deviates toward zero for larger values of π and/or ω. Also, we can observe from table 6.1 that AOs yield large values of skewness and kurtosis, and hence significant results for the JB test for normality. Furthermore, we observe that the estimated standard error for the $\hat{\phi}_1$ parameter increases with increasing ω.

A typical example of one or more additive outliers is provided by the inflation rate in Argentina, 1970.1–1989.4, when it is measured here as $y_t = (w_t - w_{t-1})/w_{t-1}$, where w_t is the price level, see also figure 2.11. The inflation rate in 1989.3 is about 600 percent, while its average value before that date is much smaller. In figure 6.3, I give the scatter plot of this y_t versus y_{t-1}, and it is evident that there is at least one outlying observation and that the pattern in figure 6.3 looks like that in figure 6.1.

Since the outlier is close to the last observation of the available data, the inflation in Argentina series can serve as an illustration of how outliers affect forecasts. See Ledolter (1989) for more formal expressions of bias in forecasts due to neglecting AOs. The first step is to estimate a model for y_t. According to LM tests for residual autocorrelation, we need

Table 6.1. *Simulated effect of a single additive outlier on inference from an AR(1) model*

ω	$\hat{\phi}_1$		SK	K	JB
0	0.791	(0.062)	-0.062	2.558	0.867
5	0.705	(0.072)	0.179	4.907	15.527
10	0.519	(0.087)	1.534	16.136	750.589
20	0.215	(0.099)	4.657	39.579	5877.10

Notes:
The generating process is $y_t = x_t + \omega I_t[t = \tau]$, with $x_t = 0.8x_{t-1} + \epsilon_t$, where the ϵ_t are drawn from $N(0,1)$, $x_1 = 0$, $n = 100$ and $\tau = 50$. For each choice of ω, I use the same ϵ_t process. $\hat{\phi}_1$ denotes the estimate of ϕ_1 in the regression of y_t on y_{t-1}, with the estimated standard error in parentheses. SK is the skewness of the residuals, $SK = \hat{m}_3 / \hat{m}_2^{\frac{3}{2}}$, K the measure for kurtosis defined by $\hat{m}_4 / \hat{m}_2^2$, where $\hat{m}_j = (n)^{-1} \sum_{t=1}^{n} \hat{\epsilon}_t^j$, where $\hat{\epsilon}_t$ are the estimated residuals and n is the number of effective observations. JB is the $\chi^2(2)$ test for normality.

to estimate an AR(3) model for this y_t. The corresponding estimation results however indicate that the roots of the AR polynomial are the reciprocals of 1.179 and ± 0.750, that is, two of these solutions suggest that the AR(3) model is not stable because these are outside the unit circle. This implies that forecasts from this model will explode. Note that this example already shows that AOs can affect model selection and the stability of the model. An alternative and reasonably adequate model for y_t appears to be

$$y_t = 0.253 + 0.379 y_{t-1} + \hat{\epsilon}_t, \quad t = 1970.3,\ldots,1989.4, \quad (6.7)$$
$$(0.084)\ (0.106)$$

where standard errors are given in parentheses. The JB test for this AR(1) model has a value of 3910.67, which is highly significant compared to fractiles from the $\chi^2(2)$ distribution. If I consider an AR(1) model for the same data while deleting the last four observations, I get

$$y_t = 0.103 + 0.673 y_{t-1} + \hat{\epsilon}_t, \quad t = 1970.3,\ldots,1988.4, \quad (6.8)$$
$$(0.033)\ (0.086)$$

for which the JB statistic equals 11.897. This value indicates that the error process $\hat{\epsilon}_t$ still is not normal, although its value has reduced considerably compared to that for (6.7). As expected, given the simulations in table 6.1, the $\hat{\phi}_1$ in (6.8) exceeds that of the contaminated model (6.7).

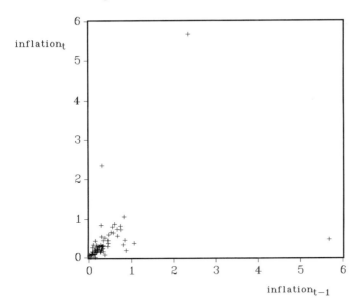

Figure 6.3 *Inflation$_t$ versus inflation$_{t-1}$ for Argentina, 1970.1–1989.4*

Also, the estimated standard error is smaller. In table 6.2, I give the fore-casts of y_t in 1990 and 1991, when these forecasts are generated from (6.7) and (6.8).

The forecasts in this table (under the headers: "Model (6.7)" and "Model (6.8)") and the corresponding standard errors show that we can obtain quite different patterns depending on whether the estimation sample con-tains AOs or not. Comparing the multi-step ahead forecasts with the real-ized inflation data in 1990.1–1991.4, we observe that both models perform poorly for 1990.1 and 1990.2 since inflation takes exceptionally large values, that (6.7) performs best for 1990.3, but that (6.8) is to be preferred for 1990.4–1991.4. The results in this table also show that forecasts for more than six steps ahead are not very precise. In section 6.2, I will return to this inflation series to test for an AO.

Innovation outlier [IO]

A second important type of outlier is the so-called innovation outlier [IO], where now the outlier occurs in the driving noise process. For an ARMA(p,q) process, an IO can be described by

$$\phi_p(L)y_t = \theta_q(L) (\varepsilon_t + \omega I_t[t = \tau]), \tag{6.9}$$

Table 6.2. *Forecasting inflation in Argentina, 1990.1–1991.4*

		Model (6.7)		Model (6.8)		Model (6.18)	
Quarter	Realization	Forecast	SE	Forecast	SE	Forecast	SE
1990.1	8.532	0.429	0.642	0.318	0.229	0.385	0.176
1990.2	1.090	0.416	0.686	0.317	0.230	0.343	0.199
1990.3	0.458	0.411	0.692	0.317	0.231	0.321	0.204
1990.4	0.307	0.409	0.693	0.316	0.231	0.310	0.206
1991.1	0.388	0.408	0.693	0.316	0.231	0.304	0.206
1991.2	0.248	0.408	0.693	0.316	0.231	0.301	0.206
1991.3	0.072	0.407	0.693	0.315	0.231	0.300	0.206
1991.4	0.035	0.407	0.693	0.315	0.231	0.298	0.206

Notes:
The realized inflation observations for 1990.1–1991.4 are obtained from the International Financial Statistics. Model (6.7) is the AR(1) model for 1970.1–1989.4, while neglecting possible AOs. Model (6.8) is the AR(1) model for 1970.1–1988.4, where possible AOs are deleted from the sample by deleting the entire last year. Model (6.18) is an AR(1) model for 1970.1–1989.4 with the inclusion of a description for the two AOs in the model.

where now the indicator time series $I_t[.]$ is added to the error (or innovation) process. For illustration, consider the AR(1) time series with an IO at time τ,

$$y_t = \phi_1 y_{t-1} + \varepsilon_t + \omega I_t[t = \tau]. \tag{6.10}$$

This expression shows that for most observations the predicted value of y_t is $\phi_1 y_{t-1}$. For y_τ, however, and in case the IO is neglected, the predictor $\phi_1 y_{\tau-1}$ makes a mistake of value $\varepsilon_\tau + \omega$. In contrast to the AO model, the predictor for $y_{\tau+1}$, that is, $\phi_1 y_\tau$, has no bias. Hence, in a scatter plot of y_t versus y_{t-1}, we would observe only the single aberrant combination $(y_\tau, y_{\tau-1})$, while all other combinations lie close to the regression line.

Since all observations subsequent to τ obey the AR(1) model, we can expect that the corresponding pairs of y_t, y_{t-1} (with $t > \tau$) lie on the regression line with slope ϕ_1. When ω is very large, the graph in figure 6.4 suggests that neglecting an IO leads to a biased estimate of the possible intercept (if this is added to (6.10)), and that $\hat{\phi}_1$ may show virtually no bias. Obviously, when y_t is a growth rate, and we are interested in the average growth rate, it is important to take care of IOs. When such an IO is neglected for an AR(1) series, we will have only a single extraordinarily

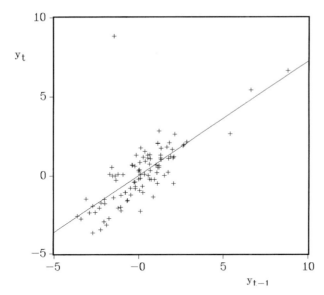

Figure 6.4 *Effect of a single innovation outlier on regression of y_t on y_{t-1}*

large estimated residual, due to the fact that $\hat{\phi}_1 y_{\tau-1}$ is a biased predictor for y_τ. This effect is visualized in figure 6.5 for a simulated AR(1) time series with $\omega = 10$, $\tau = 50$, and $\phi_1 = 0.8$. Hence, an isolated IO can be recognized by a single large estimated residual.

Notice that for an AR(1) series when there are two IOs at τ and $\tau+1$, with weights ω and $-\phi_1\omega$, respectively, it is impossible to disentangle these from a single AO. Given that the IO is governed by a drawing from the error process, that is, at time τ the error is $\varepsilon_t + \omega$, we can say that it corresponds more to the series itself than an AO does. Additionally, equation (6.10) already shows that a large shock at time τ has a longer lasting effect (through ϕ_1) on sequential observations than an AO does. This difference between an AO and an IO is highlighted for two simulated series in figure 6.6, where the ε_t series and $\omega = 20$ is the same for both realizations. The value of ϕ_1 is set at 0.8 and of τ at 50.

These two graphs clearly show that an AO results in one large y_t value, while the IO generates a sequence of large observations. Since ϕ_1 is 0.8, the effect of the IO at time τ eventually dies out at a rate of $(0.8)^j$, $j=1,2,\ldots$. Notice that when $\phi_1 = 1$, the effect of the IO never dies out, see also figure 3.1. Hence, for a time series with $\phi_1 = 0.9$ and sometimes large IOs, it may be difficult to detect that ϕ_1 is not equal to 1, see, for example, Hendry and Neale (1990).

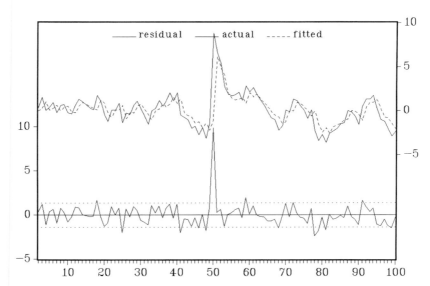

Figure 6.5 *Effect of neglecting a single innovation outlier on residuals of AR(1) model*

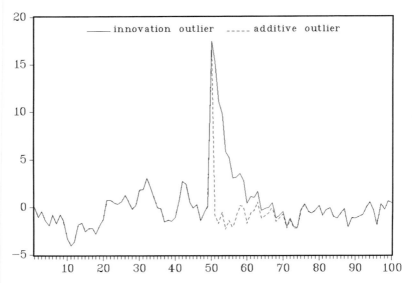

Figure 6.6 *The effect of an AO and an IO on identically generated AR(1) series*

Table 6.3. *Simulated effect of a single innovation outlier on inference from an AR(1) model*

ω	$\hat{\phi}_1$		SK	K	JB
0	0.791	(0.062)	−0.062	2.558	0.867
5	0.708	(0.072)	0.512	4.754	17.003
10	0.674	(0.075)	3.139	23.341	1869.23
20	0.702	(0.072)	6.922	61.611	14960.7

Notes:
The generating process is $y_t = 0.8y_{t-1} + \epsilon_t + \omega I_t[t=\tau]$ where the ϵ_t are the same as those in table 6.1, $y_1 = 0$, $n = 100$ and $\tau = 50$. For each choice of ω, I use the same ϵ_t process. $\hat{\phi}_1$ denotes the estimate of ϕ_1 in the regression of y_t on y_{t-1}, with the estimated standard error in parentheses. SK is the skewness of the residuals, SK $= \hat{m}_3/\hat{m}_2^{\frac{3}{2}}$, K the measure for kurtosis defined by $\hat{m}_4/\hat{m}_2^2$, where $\hat{m}_j = (n)^{-1}\sum_{t=1}^{n}\hat{\epsilon}_t^j$, where $\hat{\epsilon}_t$ are the estimated residuals and n is the number of effective observations. JB is the $\chi^2(2)$ test for normality.

To illustrate the effects of neglecting an IO on parameter estimation, I repeat the exercise as in table 6.1, and report the results in table 6.3. From the column with $\hat{\phi}_1$ it can be observed that indeed this estimate is not much affected. Furthermore, the last three columns of this table show that the estimated residuals will again have excess skewness and kurtosis.

Permanent level shift [PLS]

When ϕ_1 in (6.10) equals 1, it is clear that an IO at time τ can result in a permanent change in the level of a time series. An alternative description of such a level shift in case of an AR(1) model, which does not require that $\phi_1 = 1$, is given by the model

$$y_t = \phi_1 y_{t-1} + \delta I_t[t<\tau] + \delta\omega I_t[t\geq\tau] + \varepsilon_t, \tag{6.11}$$

where the mean of y_t shifts from $\delta/(1-\phi_1)$ in the first part of the sample to $\delta\omega/(1-\phi_1)$ in the second part. Hence, starting with observation y_τ, the level of the time series shifts permanently. Figure 6.7 displays some illustrative graphs of time series generated by

$$y_t = \phi_1 y_{t-1} + \omega I_t[t\geq\tau] + \varepsilon_t, \tag{6.12}$$

where ε_t is standard white noise, τ equals 51, and ω takes values of 0, 1, 2, and 3. The value of ϕ_1 is set at 0.8, and that of y_1 at 0.

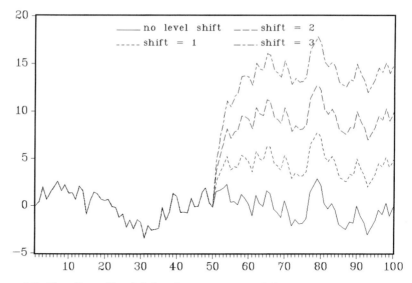

Figure 6.7 *The effect of level shifts of size ω on an AR(1) time series*

For larger values of ω, figure 6.7 indicates that the corresponding series seems to display an upward trend. Hence, it can be difficult to select between the stochastic or deterministic trend models in chapter 4 and a PLS model as in (6.12). Perron (1989) shows that the larger ω in (6.12), the more $\hat{\phi}_1$ approaches 1 when the level shift is neglected. In other words, it will not be easy to reject that $\phi_1 = 1$ when there is a permanent level shift. This conjecture seems confirmed by the estimated ACF for the same four simulated time series in table 6.4. When ω increases, we observe that $\hat{\rho}_i$ take increasingly larger values. This suggests in a sense that there is much more memory in a time series with a level shift, which is obviously due to the fact that the level shift is permanent. In turn, neglecting such a level shift can lead to inappropriate forecasts because $\hat{\phi}_1$ is inadequately estimated. In section 6.3, I will return to the issue of testing for unit roots in the presence of level shifts.

In practice, such permanent level shifts usually have some reason that can be known from the outset. Obviously, we may view a PLS as a set of AOs in a sequence, and hence for practical purposes we may interpret a level shift as a persistent change of the measurement system. Otherwise, we may think of a change in the environment. For example, during the first 11 years of the four-weekly radio advertising expenditures, as given in figure 6.8, we can observe a clear shift in the level.

Table 6.4. *Simulated effect of neglecting a single level shift on the autocorrelation function*

ω	$\hat{\rho}_1$	$\hat{\rho}_2$	$\hat{\rho}_3$	$\hat{\rho}_4$	$\hat{\rho}_5$	$\hat{\rho}_{10}$
0	0.790	0.621	0.518	0.416	0.304	0.256
1	0.901	0.820	0.767	0.696	0.629	0.564
2	0.960	0.924	0.894	0.852	0.813	0.703
3	0.974	0.948	0.923	0.890	0.857	0.733

Notes:
The generating process is $y_t = 0.8y_{t-1} + \epsilon_t + \omega I_t[t \geq \tau]$, where the ϵ_t are the same as those in table 6.1, $y_1 = 0$, $n = 100$ and $\tau = 51$. For each choice of ω, the same ϵ_t drawings are used.

This shift in level is caused by the fact that in 1982.01, the broadcasting time on the radio increased by 60 percent, and hence the radio advertising expenditures increased as well. Whether this 60 percent increase has led to a similar increase in spending is a question we can answer using models such as (6.11), see section 6.2 below.

The level shift model that can describe patterns which are in between the PLS model and a set of IOs and AOs, and which may have some interpretation in a business or economic context, is the so-called Transient Level Shift [TLS] model. For a simple white noise series, the model is written as

$$y_t = \delta I_t[t < \tau] + \omega I_t[t = \tau] + \omega \lambda I_t[t = \tau+1] + \omega \lambda^2 I_t[t = \tau+2] + \ldots + \varepsilon_t$$

$$= \delta I_t[t < \tau] + \sum_{i=0}^{k} \omega \lambda^i I_t[t = \tau+i] + \varepsilon_t, \quad \text{with } |\lambda| < 1. \tag{6.13}$$

Until τ, the mean of the series is δ. At time τ, the series gets an impulse ω, which fades out slowly, depending on the value of λ. The value of k can be very large, although in practice we usually set k at some smaller value which depends on the specific application. The parameters in (6.13) can be estimated using non-linear least squares because the model structure imposes parameter restrictions for large values of k. This TLS model is particularly useful if we want to estimate λ, that is, the rate at which the shock ω dies out. For example, the TLS model is used in Leone (1987) to study the impact of promotional activity ω at time τ on sales y_t, and in Box and Tiao (1975) to study the possibly permanent impact of a measure to reduce the CO_2 output in Los Angeles.

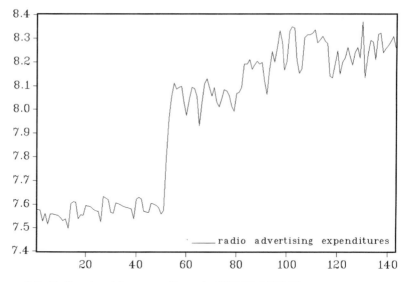

Figure 6.8 *Radio advertising expenditures in 1978.01–1988.13*

Changing trend [CT]

A final useful model to characterize (sets of) aberrant data in economic time series allows for the presence of a changing deterministic trend. It may occur that a certain event changes the structure of a business or economic situation such that the trend before that event has diverged toward a different trend. For example, the Great Leap Forward in China during 1958–1962 has changed the structure of the Chinese economy quite dramatically, and hence it may be that this event has an effect on the trends in the various sector outputs, depicted in figure 2.1. In figure 6.9, I give the output of the transportation sector again. It is clear from this figure that the trend in this sector has changed since around 1960.

A simple regression model that allows for a changing trend [CT] is given by

$$y_t = \nu t + \omega I_t[t \geq \tau]t + \varepsilon_t, \tag{6.14}$$

where the trend is ν until time τ and $\nu + \omega$ from τ onwards. Usually, in practice we should enlarge (6.14) to include additional regressors in order to make a more useful model. For example, when y_1 is unequal to zero, we should include an intercept term in (6.14), as well as a dummy variable which takes values of 1 from τ onwards. This is because the changing trend assumes another starting value for y_t, which we could find when

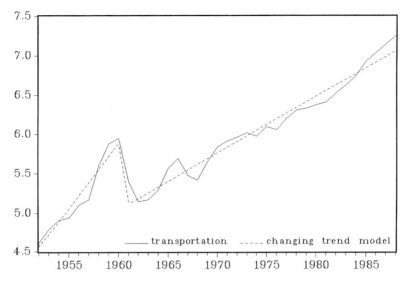

Figure 6.9 *Breaking trend in the output of the transportation sector in China*

extrapolating y_t backwards to time $t = 1$. Additionally, it is unlikely that a trend changes instantaneously. Hence, it may be wise to allow for a gradual change by including dummy variables around τ and thereafter, depending on how many lags of y_t are needed to describe the dynamic patterns. An enlarged version of (6.14) for a white noise series may then look like

$$y_t = \mu + \nu t + \omega I_t[t \geq \tau]t + \lambda_1 I_t[t = \tau] + \lambda_2 I_t[t \geq \tau] + \varepsilon_t. \tag{6.15}$$

The estimation results for (6.15) for output in another sector in China, that is, the industrial sector (which bears similarities with the transportation sector in figure 6.9) are

$$y_t = 4.374 + 0.216t - 0.115I_t[t \geq 1960]t$$
$$+ 0.711I_t[t = 1960] + 0.305I_t[t \geq 1960], \tag{6.16}$$

where I assume that the effect of the Great Leap Forward reaches its peak in 1960. Notice that (6.16) does not include standard errors since the estimated error process is found not to be white noise. From this regression, we can observe that the trend reduces from a 21.6 percent growth to a 10.1 percent per year after 1960. Furthermore, notice that the estimate of λ_2 is positive. This is caused by the fact that extrapolation of y_t toward y_1 for data after 1960 implies that the corresponding estimated y_1 exceeds the true starting value.

In this section I have discussed several models to describe various types of aberrant data. Obviously, these descriptive devices can be combined into a model that allows for AOs, IOs, CTs, and PLSs. Needless to say, the specification of such a model becomes increasingly difficult the more aberrant data there are. In the context of AR models we may not expect many problems with parameter estimation. For MA models however we may face some estimation problems because single-observation dummy variables in regression models force the corresponding residuals to be equal to zero, while the estimation routine may try to fit non-zero values. Finally, once the above models are specified, straightforward extrapolation methods as in chapter 3 can be used to generate forecasts and forecast error variances.

6.2   Testing for aberrant observations

With *a priori* knowledge of specific events and approximate dates which may yield aberrant observations (as I will assume below), it is not difficult to examine their relevance for a model that will be used for forecasting. We can simply extend our model with additional regressors, such as the dummy variables in the previous section, that can accommodate for the various possible patterns. Standard tests for significance can then be used to decide which regressors are potentially important for forecasting. The empirical analysis however becomes more complicated when we do not have an *a priori* idea of important dates. In that case, a first and natural check is a test for normality of the estimated residuals. If these are not normal, we may have encountered aberrant data points. A useful next step is then to have a closer look at these residuals to examine whether some of these take values which are more than, say, four times the standard error. For normal time series this is highly unlikely to happen. Additionally, if such large residuals appear isolated, we may have IOs or a level shift. If these come in clusters, we may have encountered AOs. Abstaining from any knowledge of specific events, we can use the statistical methods proposed in Abraham and Yatawara (1988), Tsay (1988), Chen and Liu (1993), among others. With these methods, we can search over all possible dates τ for the presence of some type of aberrant data. In a sense, these techniques provide overall diagnostic checks for model adequacy. Notice that, because of this searching, which leads to sequences of decision rules based on for example the 5 percent significance level, the various test statistics may not be distributed as χ^2 or standard normal.

In this section, I continue with a description of empirical methods to decide on the presence and type of aberrant data, while assuming knowledge of the (approximate) value of τ. I assume that the data are stationary, in the sense that they do not have a unit root. If we are uncertain about this, we should first use the methods in section 6.3, before turning to those in this section.

Additive and innovation outliers

As shown in section 6.1, an innovation outlier results in one estimated error with an exceptionally large value. A simple test for an IO is now given by including the single-observation dummy variable $I_t[t = \tau]$ and testing the significance of the corresponding parameter.

To illustrate the analysis of AOs, consider again the example series on the inflation rate in Argentina. The scatter plot in figure 2.12 conveys that the observations in 1989.2, 1989.3, and 1989.4 seem extraordinarily large. If these data are explicitly incorporated in the AR(1) model, the resultant model is

$$y_t = 0.103 + 0.673y_{t-1} + 2.040I_t[t = 1989.2] + 3.991I_t[t = 1989.3]$$
$$(0.032)\ (0.085) \quad (0.170) \quad (0.244)$$

$$- 3.455I_t[t = 1989.4] + \hat{\varepsilon}_t. \quad t = 1970.3, \ldots, 1989.4 \quad (6.17)$$
$$(0.488)$$

The pattern of the parameters for the dummy variables seems to correspond with an AO of size ω_1 at 1989.2 with an effect of $\phi_1\omega_1$ at 1989.3, which is followed by a new AO of value ω_2 in 1989.3, with an effect of $\phi_1\omega_2$ in 1989.4. This pattern of the dummies yields the opportunity to impose a parameter restriction. After estimating the parameters with NLS, I get

$$y_t = 0.143 + 0.520y_{t-1} + 2.046I_t[t = 1989.2]$$
$$(0.030)\ (0.067) \quad (0.177)$$

$$+ 4.468\ (I_t[t = 1989.3] - 0.520I_t[t = 1989.4]) + \hat{\varepsilon}_t. \quad (6.18)$$
$$(0.177) \quad (0.067)$$

Forecasts from this model of inflation for 1990.1 through 1991.4 are also given in table 6.2. These forecasts seem similar to those of the model for the sample which excludes 1989 in (6.8), although the forecast intervals for (6.18) are less wide. Additionally, the RMSPE of these eight forecasts from (6.18) is clearly smaller than that for (6.8), where the forecast for 1990.4 is exceptionally good for model (6.18). Hence, inflation in Argentina has two large AOs (1989.2 and 1989.3), with the second being more than twice as large as the first. Including these AOs in a forecasting model yields out-of-sample forecasts with smaller forecast intervals.

Level shifts

An empirical illustration of the treatment of a (possible) level shift is given by an analysis of the first part of the radio advertising expenditures series, see figure 6.8. The expansion of broadcasting minutes was effectuated in 1982.01. However, since this change must have been known beforehand, and given that contracts may have been settled earlier than this date, I set τ equal to 1981.13. Neglecting this obvious mean shift results in

$$y_t = 0.180 + 0.978 y_{t-1} + \hat{\varepsilon}_t, \tag{6.19}$$
$$(0.133)\ (0.017)$$

for 142 effective observations. Notice that the estimate for ϕ_1 is very close to 1. In fact, the Dickey–Fuller test gives the insignificant value of -1.321. The $F_{AC,1-1}$ and $F_{AC,1-13}$ diagnostics (see chapter 3) do not indicate misspecification, but the JB test for normality with a value of 23.511 does. Adding a level shift dummy variable for all observations after and including 1981.13, as well as single dummy variables for 1982.01, 1982.02 (to accommodate for outliers and possibly higher order AR effects), and additional lags for the same reason, and reducing the initial model by excluding all insignificant terms, I finally obtain

$$y_t = 2.306 + 0.552 y_{t-1} + 0.144 y_{t-13} + 0.193 I_t[t \ge 1981.13] + \hat{\varepsilon}_t. \tag{6.20}$$
$$(0.314)\ (0.056)\qquad (0.032)\qquad (0.026)$$

The JB test now obtains a value of 4.911, which is not significant at the 5 percent level. This estimated model shows that the 60 percent increase in broadcasting time leads to only an 8.4 percent increase in advertising spending. Notice that (6.20) now also includes the y_{t-13} variable, which was not found necessary for (6.19).

To illustrate the analysis of a time series for which there may be AOs, as well as IOs and level shifts, consider the price series depicted in figure 2.14. As it seems, this series suffers from several types of aberrant data points. It is likely that these shifts in the relative price can be caused by promotions by the company or its competitors, by the introduction of new product variations with higher prices, or just by the management decision to set lower prices. The EACF suggests that an AR(2) model may be useful to describe this y_t series (where I do not take logs). The ADF Fuller regression, which includes a constant and $\Delta_1 y_{t-1}$, results in an ADF test value of -3.341. Hence, y_t does not seem to have a unit root at the 5 percent level. As the JB test for normality has a value of 223.072, the AR(2) model clearly suffers from outliers. Particularly large residuals are found around the observations in week 45 of 1989, and the weeks 5, 19, 20, 21, and 27 of 1990. After week 27, the level of the series seems to have undergone a persistent change. Including the relevant dummy variables, and deleting the insignificant ones, results in a final simplified model for y_t

$$y_t = 62.729 + 0.320 y_{t-1} + 0.111 y_{t-2} + 9.858 I_t[t = 1989.45]$$
$$(7.622) \ (0.064) \quad (0.061) \quad (1.438)$$

$$+ 10.559 I_t[t = 1990.05] + 4.694 I_t[t = 1990.19]$$
$$(1.435) \quad\quad\quad (1.435)$$

$$+ 5.630 I_t[t = 1990.20] - 2.696 I_t[t = 1990.21]$$
$$(1.463) \quad\quad\quad (1.495)$$

$$- 10.468 I_t[t = 1990.27] - 1.968 I_t[t \geq 1990.27] + \hat{\varepsilon}_t. \quad\quad (6.21)$$
$$(0.145) \quad\quad\quad (0.423)$$

For this model, the JB test obtains the insignificant value of 4.567. Finally, the ADF test value equals -8.270 for (6.21), and hence y_t certainly seems stationary after taking care of an apparent level shift.

Some remarks on testing and modeling

For some of the examples above, it seems straightforward how to proceed. In many practical occasions, however, this is much more complicated. It may be quite difficult, as was shown above, to distinguish a level shift model from a unit root model with an IO. Hence, it often seems wise to test for unit roots first using the methods described in the next section. If we find a unit root, we can impose it, and proceed with the techniques in this section. Notice however that overdifferencing a stationary AR(1) time series with a single IO may result in a series that seems to have an AO since the weight ω of the IO will appear as $-\omega$ in the next period. Additionally, an inspection of the EACF may then suggest that an MA type of model is needed. Hence, quite some skill and experience is needed to come up with a sound model that takes account of unit roots, appropriate model order, and all possible aberrant data features.

When a time series is encountered which seems to have many aberrant data, it may be possible that a univariate linear time series model such as an ARMA model may not yield a good description of the data. For example, non-linear time series data can be characterized by regular regime switches (as will be shown in chapter 8), and a linear model for these data may result in many large residuals. Furthermore, outliers may reflect the fact that a multivariate time series model (such as those discussed in chapter 9) or an AR model with exogenous variables may be more appropriate.

6.3   Irregular data and unit roots

As indicated in the previous two sections, it may be the case that it is not easy to decide whether a time series has a unit root or not in case there are permanent or transitory level shifts, sets of AOs, or changing deterministic trends, see, for example, Maddala and Kim (1996) for a recent survey. For example, neglecting level shifts or breaking trends leads to spurious unit roots, see Perron (1989, 1990), and neglected AOs lead to a spurious finding of stationarity, see, for example, Franses and Haldrup (1994). Given that knowledge of the presence of unit roots is important for forecasting, forecasting intervals, and for multivariate modeling, it seems sensible to start any analysis with an examination of unit roots while allowing for possible aberrant observations. Again, I assume that the break date is (approximately) known. If not, we can use the rolling sample or recursive methods in, for example, Banerjee *et al.* (1992), or the minimum DF test approach in, for example, Zivot and Andrews (1992), and Perron and Vogelsang (1992). Alternatively, we may rely on the outlier robust tests for unit roots propagated in Lucas (1995, 1996), where alternative assumptions for the error process are considered as well as estimation methods alternative to OLS. In the first part of this section I focus on non-seasonal time series. Next, I briefly discuss seasonal time series.

Non-seasonal series, additive outliers

The results in section 6.1, especially in (6.6), indicate that the estimate of ϕ_1 is downward biased in case of a neglected AO. Hence, even when the true parameter is 1, the $\hat{\phi}_1$ will be below 1 when there are neglected AOs. In other words, under the null hypothesis we find a unit root in the case where the data are contaminated by one or more AOs less often. Some intuition behind this result can be visualized. For example, in Figure 6.10, I depict a scatter plot of $\Delta_1 y_t$ versus y_{t-1}, where data are generated from a random walk model and where there are three large AOs (with $\omega = 20$).

Due to these AOs, it is evident that the regression line obtains a negative slope, while it should have a slope equal to zero. Hence, the ρ parameter in the Dickey–Fuller regression becomes large and negative. Depending on the number of observations and the variance of the ε_t process, this may lead to a significant $t(\hat{\rho})$-test value. In other words, the asymptotic distribution of the ADF (or DF) test becomes more skewed to the left when there are neglected additive outliers. In table 6.5, I give some empirical fractiles of the $t(\rho)$ test when the data are generated according to (6.3)–(6.5). Clearly, the critical values shift to the left. Franses and Haldrup (1994) recommend to

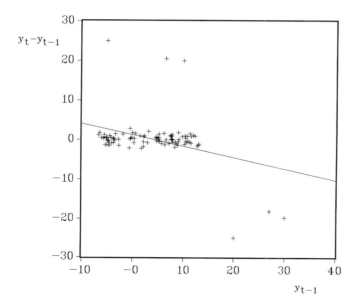

Figure 6.10 *The effect of neglecting AOs on the Dickey–Fuller test*

follow the strategy in Chen and Liu (1993) to detect AOs, and to apply the DF test to an auxiliary regression which includes dummy variables for the detected AOs. It can be shown that the DF test based on this enlarged regression asymptotically follows the DF distribution tabulated in table 4.1. For the inflation rate in Argentina, however, for which $\hat{\phi}_1$ in (6.18) equals 0.520, however, there are no changes in the decision that this series is stationary.

Non-seasonal series, level shifts

In contrast to AOs, (permanent) level shifts do not cause the DF test to reject the null hypothesis often enough, that is, we find too many spurious unit roots when such a shift is not incorporated in the model for a stationary time series. Perron (1989, 1990) shows that the larger the shift is, that is, the larger is ω in (6.12), the more $\hat{\phi}_1$ in an AR(1) model is biased toward unity. If we wish to allow for such a possible level shift, we should include it in the DF regression like

$$\Delta_1 y_t = \rho y_{t-1} + \omega I_t[t \geq \tau] + \lambda_1 I_t[t = \tau] + \lambda_2 I_t[t = \tau + 1] + \varepsilon_t, \qquad (6.22)$$

where the dummy variables at τ and $\tau + 1$ ensure that there is a gradual shift, see Perron and Vogelsang (1992). When $\lambda = \tau/n$, that is, λ measures the

Table 6.5. *Empirical fractiles of the Dickey–Fuller test*

(DGP is $y_t = y_{t-1} + \epsilon_t$, with $\epsilon_t \sim N(0,1)$ and $z_t = y_t + \theta \delta_t$ with δ_t is $+1$ or -1 with probability π and 0 otherwise. Test regression is $\Delta_1 z_t = \rho z_{t-1} + u_t$, and test is $t(\rho)$. Sample size is 100 and number of replications is 10,000.)

π	θ	Nominal size			Empirical size at 0.05
		0.01	0.05	0.10	
0		-2.60	-1.95	-1.61	0.05
0.05	3	-3.65	-2.75	-2.32	0.18
	4	-4.38	-3.26	-2.74	0.26
	5	-4.89	-3.72	-3.13	0.33
0.10	3	-4.17	-3.37	-2.85	0.27
	4	-5.13	-4.00	-3.40	0.39
	5	-6.01	-4.77	-4.11	0.49

Source: Table 1 in Franses and Haldrup (1994).

location of the level shift in the sample, Perron (1990) shows that the asymptotic distribution of $t(\rho)$ depends on λ only.

In the first panel of table 6.6, I give some critical values of this unit root test for various values of λ. Comparing these with those in table 4.1, we observe that the critical values based on regression (6.22) shift to the left. Intuitively, this is because we include information in the regression model which favors the alternative hypothesis, and hence we should find, say, extra-large negative values for $t(\hat{\rho})$ to be able to reject the null hypothesis of a unit root.

A useful time series model for the first eleven years of radio advertising data is given in (6.20). The ADF value corresponding to this regression is -6.481. Comparing this value with the critical values in table 6.6 shows that this series does not have a unit root. Note however that if we were to neglect the level shift in 1982.01, we would decide that this series has a unit root, see (6.19).

Non-seasonal series, changing trends

If additional to a level shift there is a changing trend, we may expect even more difficulty in detecting stationarity using a standard unit root test. Hence, in that case it seems sensible to test the null hypothesis of a unit root in a regression that allows for a PLS and a CT, as for example

$$\Delta_1 y_t = \rho y_{t-1} + \mu + \nu t + \omega I_t[t \geq \tau]t + \lambda_1 I_t[t = \tau] + \lambda_2 I_t[t \geq \tau] + \varepsilon_t. \quad (6.23)$$

Table 6.6. *Asymptotic critical values of Dickey–Fuller t-test in the presence of level shifts and breaking trends at a known date*

					λ				
Size	0.1	0.2	0.3	0.4	0.5	0.6	0.7	0.8	0.9
Level shift									
0.01	−3.67	−3.80	−3.88	−3.92	−3.90	−3.92	−3.88	−3.80	−3.67
0.05	−3.10	−3.23	−3.30	−3.35	−3.34	−3.35	−3.30	−3.23	−3.10
0.10	−2.78	−2.92	−2.99	−3.05	−3.04	−3.05	−2.99	−2.92	−2.78
Breaking trend									
0.01	−4.38	−4.65	−4.78	−4.81	−4.90	−4.88	−4.75	−4.70	−4.41
0.05	−3.75	−3.99	−4.17	−4.22	−4.24	−4.24	−4.18	−4.04	−3.80
0.10	−3.45	−3.66	−3.87	−3.95	−3.96	−3.95	−3.86	−3.69	−3.46

Notes:
$\lambda = \tau/n$, where τ is the observation for which there is a shift. The test regression for the level shift is given in (6.22) and the test regression for the breaking trend in (6.23).
Sources: Perron (1990, table 4) and Perron (1989, table VI.B), respectively.

Perron (1989) derives the asymptotic distribution of $t(\hat{\rho})$, and again it turns out that this distribution only depends on $\lambda = \tau/n$. In the second panel of table 6.6, I give some asymptotic critical values for the $t(\hat{\rho})$ test for regression models such as (6.23). Given that this regression includes yet another set of regressors that favor the alternative hypothesis, it is no surprise that the critical values shift even further to the left as compared to the level shift model.

For the output in the Chinese transportation sector, depicted in figure 2.1, I obtain a value of -7.113 for $t(\rho)$ in a model as (6.23) with $\tau = 1960$, which also has $\Delta_1 y_{t-1}$ as an additional regressor. When I do not include the additional deterministic variables $I_t[t \geq \tau]t$, $I_t[t = \tau]$ and $I_t[t \geq \tau]$ as in (6.23), this t-test has a value of -3.540, which is marginally significant at the 5 percent level. In other words, when including deterministics that correspond to the Great Leap Forward, the evidence against a unit root becomes much more convincing.

It should be mentioned here that the asymptotic critical values of the $t(\rho)$-test are different in case the location of the break λ is unknown. For example, for model (6.23), Zivot and Andrews (1992) show that the 5 percent critical value for the minimum value of $t(\rho)$, which is now calculated for all possible break points, is -5.08. For practical purposes where sometimes no precise information on the break date is available, we may use the following rule of thumb (for the 5 percent significance level). If

Table 6.7. *Asymptotic critical values of HEGY test statistics in the presence of seasonal level shifts at known break date*

					λ				
Size	0.1	0.2	0.3	0.4	0.5	0.6	0.7	0.8	0.9
					$t(\pi_2)$				
0.01	−3.68	−3.81	−3.87	−3.92	−3.94	−3.95	−3.90	−3.83	−3.67
0.05	−3.08	−3.22	−3.29	−3.34	−3.35	−3.35	−3.31	−3.22	−3.34
0.10	−2.77	−2.91	−2.99	−3.04	−3.05	−3.04	−3.00	−2.91	−3.77
					$F(\pi_3,\pi_4)$				
0.10	6.37	7.02	7.52	7.80	7.93	7.87	7.56	7.01	6.35
0.05	7.47	8.20	8.74	9.07	9.16	9.11	8.81	8.25	7.50
0.01	9.88	10.80	11.38	11.74	11.68	11.72	11.35	10.84	9.86

Note:
$\lambda = \tau/n$, where τ is the observation for which there is a shift.
Source: Franses and Vogelsang (1998).

a unit root test value is below -5.08, we can safely conclude that there is no unit root. If this value is above -3.75, there is a unit root. Any value in between can be viewed as corresponding to a possibly inconclusive region.

Seasonal time series and seasonal level shifts

Similar to the above arguments of the effects of level shifts on tests for unit roots in a non-seasonal time series, we may expect that level shifts in one or more seasons have an effect on tests for seasonal unit roots. Since such seasonal unit roots amounts to ever widening forecasting intervals for out-of-sample forecasts as well, it is also important to examine seasonal unit roots while allowing for possible seasonal mean shifts. Simulation results in Paap, Franses, and Hoek, (1997) show that neglecting seasonal mean shifts leads to substantial forecasting errors. Franses and Vogelsang (1998) propose to enlarge the HEGY regression model in (5.27) by including dummy variables for the mean shifts. For the case of no additional lags, this model for quarterly data is

$$\Delta_4 y_t = \sum_{s=1}^{4} \delta_s D_{s,t} + \sum_{s=1}^{4} \delta_s^* D_{s,t} I[t \geq \tau] \qquad (6.24)$$

$$+ \sum_{j=1}^{4} \kappa_j I_t[t = \tau - 1 + j] + \pi_1 (1 + L + L^2 + L^3) y_{t-1}$$
$$+ \pi_2 (-1 + L - L^2 + L^3) y_{t-1} + (\pi_3 L + \pi_4)(1 - L^2) y_{t-1} + \varepsilon_t,$$

where the four κ_j parameters in this regression are needed to allow for four possible mean shifts from τ onwards. Franses and Vogelsang (1998) show that the asymptotic distributions of the t-tests for π_1 and π_2 and the joint F-test for π_3 and π_4 only depend on λ. Since the distribution of $t(\pi_1)$ is the same as that of $t(\rho)$, table 6.7 only reports some critical values for the $t(\pi_2)$ and $F(\pi_3,\pi_4)$ test.

When these critical values are compared with those in tables 5.5 and 5.6 it is clear that the critical values of $t(\pi_2)$ shift to the left, while those of the $F(\pi_3,\pi_4)$ shift to the right. Notice that the values in table 6.7 can also be used in case (6.24) contains a single non-breaking deterministic trend variable since the regressors in the auxiliary regression models are orthogonal.

An illustration of testing for seasonal unit roots in the presence of seasonal mean shifts is provided by the USA industrial production. In chapter 5, we saw that the standard HEGY method results in a seasonal unit root -1. Hence, we need the Δ_2 filter to transform this series to stationarity. When we assume that mean shifts may have occurred in or around 1979/1980 because of the second oil crisis, we can set τ in (6.25) for example at 1980.1. The HEGY regression needs two lags of $\Delta_4 y_t$ at $t-1$ and $t-2$, and hence we include single observation dummy variables for all observations in 1980 and in 1981.1 and 1981.2. The $t(\pi_2)$ test obtains a value of -4.811 and the $F(\pi_3,\pi_4)$ test now obtains a value of 16.736. Comparing these with the critical values in table 6.7 indicates that there is no evidence for a seasonal unit root anymore. Hence, the seasonal unit root -1 disappears once we allow for seasonal mean shifts right after the second major oil crisis in 1979.4.

A second example of changing seasonality that may be due to deterministic mean shifts is given by the second part of the radio advertising data. I do not consider the first five years of data because these contain the level shift already discussed above. A graph of the relevant data is given in figure 6.11.

Clearly, seasonality has changed roughly halfway through the sample, jointly with a change in the direction of the trend. Closer inspection shows that this change occurs after October 1989, and that this is the month in which a new commercial channel started in The Netherlands. When this structural break is neglected, and the OCSB test procedure in (5.35) is applied, where the included deterministics are 13 seasonal dummies and a trend, the $t(\pi_2)$ test obtains a value of -5.330 and the joint $F(\pi_1,\pi_2)$ test has a value of 33.000. Comparing these values with the critical values in table 5.13 (in the row with "t,ndt"), we find that this radio series may need the Δ_{13} filter become stationary. Hence, when the obvious break is neglected, there seem to be 13 unit roots in the data. On the other hand, when the OCSB test regression in (5.23) is enlarged with 13 seasonal mean shift variables which start at $\tau = 1989.11$ (which contains most of October

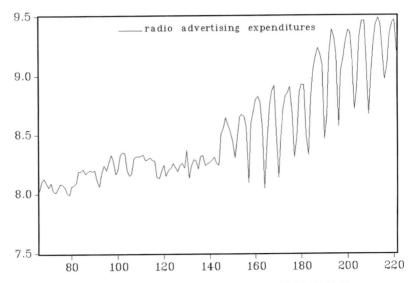

Figure 6.11 *Changing seasonality in radio advertising, 1983.01–1994.13*

1989), and with a new deterministic trend starting at the same date, the $t(\pi_2)$ test obtains a value of -11.984 and $F(\pi_1,\pi_2)$ a value of 102.56. The simulated 5 percent critical values (using Gauss programs) for these two tests in case of seasonal level shifts and a changing trend are -6.86 and 27.74, respectively. Hence, when we allow for seasonal mean shifts and a changing trend, the seasonal unit roots in this radio series disappear.

Conclusion

In this chapter I have assumed that a practitioner is somehow interested in describing a few aberrant observations in a time series before generating out-of-sample forecasts. Usually this interest is motivated by prior knowledge of some specific events. However, if such information is not available, the material in this chapter can still be useful as a general check for model adequacy. When many observations are aberrant, we may want to reconsider the model, since it may be a sign of misspecification. It may be, for example, that a multivariate model or a non-linear model can describe and forecast the data more accurately. On the other hand, we can try to exploit the occurrence of sequences of outliers by modeling these clusters of aberrant data. The analysis of these clusters is the focus of the so-called ARCH models, which will be considered in the next chapter.

7   Conditional heteroskedasticity

For many economic time series one may expect that additive and innovation outliers do not occur too frequently. The main exception, however, concerns financial time series. Since such data reflect the result of trading amongst buyers and sellers at, for example, stock markets, various sources of news and other exogenous economic events may have an impact on the time series pattern of asset prices. Given that news can lead to various interpretations, and also given that specific economic events like an oil crisis can last for some time, we often observe that large positive and large negative observations in financial time series tend to appear in clusters.

One possible approach to take account of sets of outliers may now be to use the methods described in the previous chapter to remove the impact of these aberrant data in order to have a clearer view on the pattern of the underlying time series. However, in empirical finance we tend to be less interested in the level of the asset price or stock market index since it is widely assumed that such time series can be best described as random walks. Therefore, another approach is to exploit the fact that outliers emerge in clusters by trying to construct a time series model for the outliers themselves. Since a sequence of outliers can be considered to reflect a more volatile period, such a time series model can eventually be used to forecast volatility. In other words, due to these sets of aberrant data, the variance of financial time series varies over time and hence the forecasting intervals for the levels should also vary. The intuition is that in volatile periods there is more uncertainty about the next observation than there is in less volatile periods, and hence in volatile periods the forecasting intervals will be larger.

In this chapter, I discuss a few time series models for the type of time-varying variance that is regularly observed for financial time series. The common property of these models is that they allow the squares of the level series (after removal of autocorrelation) to have autocorrelation patterns that are similar to those of, for example, standard ARMA time series. For most models it applies that they consist of two linear equations, that is, one for the level and one for the conditional variance of the time series.

The outline of this chapter is as follows. In section 7.1, I review some aspects of the so-called Autoregressive Conditional Heteroskedasticity [ARCH] model. The ARCH model was initially proposed in Engle (1982). Since then, there have appeared hundreds (if not thousands) of studies with refinements and modifications to the basic ARCH model and also with empirical applications to exchange rates, stock markets, interest rates, individual stocks, and many other types of assets. For more complete surveys of ARCH type models, the interested reader is referred to Bollerslev, Engle, and Nelson (1994), the papers summarized in Engle (1995), and the excellent surveys in Bera and Higgins (1993), Bollerslev, Chou, and Kroner (1992), and Pagan (1996). In section 7.2, I discuss specification, estimation, evaluation, and forecasting matters. In section 7.3, I conclude this chapter by reviewing a selective set of empirically useful extensions to the basic ARCH model. Illustrations are provided by analyzing our monthly black and white pepper prices and the weekly observed Dow-Jones index, of which the data are given in the data appendix.

7.1   Models for conditional heteroskedasticity

This section concerns a description of some typical properties of time series data that are generated by an ARCH model. Next, the Generalized ARCH [GARCH] model is reviewed since this model is very often used in practice.

Typical properties of data generated by an ARCH model

Consider the information set Y_{t-1}, which contains all information on the variable y_t until time $t-1$. Next, consider a time series y_t, which can be described by the set of equations

$$y_t | Y_{t-1} = (h_t)^{\frac{1}{2}} \eta_t, \tag{7.1}$$

$$\eta_t \sim NID(0,1), \tag{7.2}$$

$$h_t = \alpha_0 + \alpha_1 y_{t-1}^2, \quad \alpha_0 > 0, \, 0 < \alpha_1 < 1, \tag{7.3}$$

where (7.1) describes the behavior of y_t conditional on Y_{t-1}, and where *NID* means normal and identically distributed. For the moment it is assumed that y_t is uncorrelated with elements of Y_{t-1}. However, in practice, the y_t series may equal $[\phi_p(L)/\theta_q(L)]x_t$, where x_t is the truly observed time series. Usually, x_t is the return on a financial asset, that is, $x_t = \log(z_t) - \log(z_{t-1})$, with z_t the level series.

Because h_t depends on the one-period lagged y_{t-1}^2, the y_t series is said to be ARCH of order 1. The expression in (7.3) indicates that the conditional variance of y_t is time varying. Note that it does not contain an additional error term. Finally, (7.2) assumes that all η_t observations have the same distributional properties.

To analyze the properties of ARCH type data, it is convenient to write (7.1)–(7.3) as

$$y_t|Y_{t-1} = \eta_t(\alpha_0 + \alpha_1 y_{t-1}^2)^{\frac{1}{2}}, \tag{7.4}$$

$$\eta_t \sim NID(0,1). \tag{7.5}$$

Since $E(\eta_t) = 0$, where E denotes expectation, it is easy to see from (7.1) that the unconditional expectation of y_t equals

$$E(y_t) = E(E(y_t|Y_{t-1})) = E((h_t)^{\frac{1}{2}}E\eta_t) = 0.$$

For the conditional variance of y_t we already have from (7.3) that

$$E(y_t^2|Y_{t-1}) = h_t = \alpha_0 + \alpha_1 y_{t-1}^2.$$

Using (7.4), we derive that the unconditional variance of y_t equals

$$E(y_t^2) = E(E(y_t^2|Y_{t-1})) = E(h_t) = \alpha_0 + \alpha_1 E(y_{t-1}^2). \tag{7.6}$$

This expression shows that y_t^2 mimics an AR(1) process with parameter α_1, that is, the squared time series shows autocorrelation. For a strict white noise series ε_t as defined in chapter 3, this is obviously not the case. Since, y_t may be the residual series of an ARMA model for x_t, this indicates a key difference between ARCH and no ARCH time series. With $0 < \alpha_1 < 1$, we can solve (7.6) as

$$E(y_t^2) = \alpha_0/(1-\alpha_1). \tag{7.7}$$

The expression in (7.3) shows that large (small) absolute values of y_t are expected to be followed by large (small) absolute values, even while

$$E(y_t y_{t-h}) = E(E(y_t y_{t-h})|Y_{t-1}) = E(y_{t-h}E(y_t|Y_{t-1})) = 0, \tag{7.8}$$

that is, the y_t series is uncorrelated. Hence, an ARCH(1) model can describe a time series with sequences of data points that look like outliers, where the fact that these outliers appear in clusters is caused by the variance equation and not by relevant autocorrelations in the level time series.

To illustrate some of the data properties of ARCH models, I simulate five series from the AR(1)–ARCH(1) data generating process

$$x_t = \phi_1 x_{t-1} + \eta_t[\alpha_0 + \alpha_1(x_{t-1} - \phi_1 x_{t-2})^2]^{\frac{1}{2}}, \quad t = 3,4,\dots,200, \tag{7.9}$$

where ϕ_1 is set equal to 0.5, η_t is $NID(0,1)$, and $x_1 = 0$, $x_2 = 0$. Table 7.1 reports the EACF of x_t with varying values of α_1, and the EACF of $\hat{y}_t^2$,

Table 7.1. *Estimated autocorrelation functions for some simulated*
AR(1)–ARCH(1) processes

	EACF of x_t			EACF of $\hat{y}_t^2$		
α_1	$\hat{\rho}_1$	$\hat{\rho}_2$	$\hat{\rho}_3$	$\hat{\rho}_1$	$\hat{\rho}_2$	$\hat{\rho}_3$
0	0.563**	0.300**	0.121	0.053	−0.033	0.059
0.2	0.559**	0.277**	0.093	0.149**	−0.004	0.089
0.5	0.559**	0.258**	0.070	0.232**	0.060	0.105
1.0	0.550**	0.245**	0.039	0.415**	0.213**	0.099
2.0	0.274**	0.110	−0.115	0.290**	0.117	0.014

Notes:
** Significant at the 5% level (when $n^{-\frac{1}{2}}$ is taken as the standard error of the
estimated residuals).
Data generating process is $x_t = \phi_1 x_{t-1} + \eta_t (\alpha_0 + \alpha_1(x_{t-1} - \phi_1 x_{t-2})^2)^{\frac{1}{2}}$, with x_1 and x_2
set equal to zero, $\alpha_0 = 1$, $\phi_1 = 0.5$ and $n = 200$, and where for each of the simulated
time series, the η_t are the same 200 drawings from a standard normal distribution.
$\hat{y}_t^2$ denotes the squared estimated residuals of regressing x_t on a constant and x_{t-1}.

where $\hat{y}_t$ is the estimated error process of the regression of x_t on a constant
and x_{t-1}. It is clear from the entries in this table that $\hat{\rho}_1$ of x_t has about the
same value for all α_1 except when α_1 exceeds 1. Furthermore, the $\hat{\rho}_1$ of $\hat{y}_t^2$ is
significant when α_1 is unequal to zero. When α_1 exceeds 1, the $\hat{\rho}_1$ of $\hat{y}_t^2$
becomes smaller. In the sequel, I assume that $\alpha_1 < 1$ and I do not focus on
values of α_1 that exceed 1. It should be mentioned, though, that for $\alpha_1 = 1$
the x_t^2 series does not show similar properties as in the case of an AR(1)
model for x_t with $\phi_1 = 1$. The intuition is that the random η_t process in (7.2)
establishes that x_t itself will not explode. For technical details on the stationarity properties of ARCH series, the reader is referred to Nelson (1990).

To visualize the presence of sequences of outliers for ARCH time series,
consider the (connected) scatter plots of y_t versus y_{t-1}, when the data are
generated as (7.1)–(7.3) with $\alpha_0 = 1$, with $\alpha_1 = 0.6$ in figure 7.1, and with
$\alpha_1 = 1.0$ in figure 7.2.

The sequence of outliers is clear when we observe the set of observations
in the lower left corner in both figures. For larger α_1 as in figure 7.2, such a
pattern becomes more obvious. Additionally, these graphs show that the
data indeed have a tendency to return to the cloud of data points in the
middle of the graph.

In figure 7.3, I give the same connected scatter plot as in the previous two
graphs for the weekly Dow-Jones index. This real-life time series appears to
mimic the patterns in figures 7.1 and 7.2. The obvious sequence of outliers

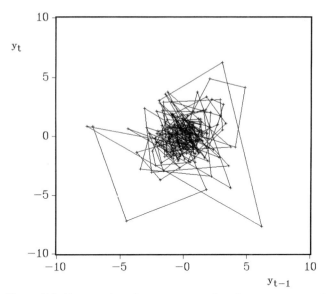

Figure 7.1 *Scatter plot of* y_t *versus* y_{t-1} *when data are generated according to (7.1)–(7.3) with* $\alpha_1 = 0.6$

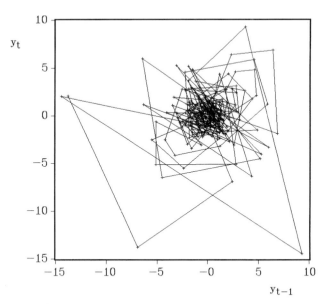

Figure 7.2 *Scatter plot of* y_t *versus* y_{t-1} *when data are generated according to (7.1)–(7.3) with* $\alpha_1 = 1.0$

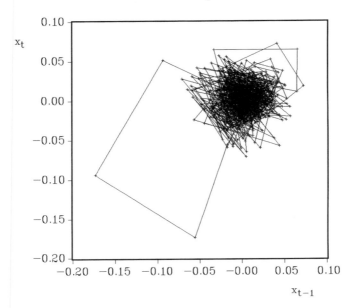

Figure 7.3 *Scatter plot of x_t versus x_{t-1} for returns on the Dow-Jones index*

that is known to be related to the 1987 stock market crash is clearly visible in the lower left corner.

Additional to relevant autocorrelation in the y_t^2 series, the sequences of aberrant data in financial time series lead to excess kurtosis. Again, the ARCH(1) model can be used to illustrate that ARCH models can describe data with such kurtosis. The fourth moment of y_t, when it is generated by the simple ARCH(1) model in (7.1)–(7.3), is given by

$$E(y_t^4) = E(E(y_t^4 | Y_{t-1})) = E(h_t^2(E\eta_t^4)) \qquad (7.10)$$
$$= 3E(\alpha_0^2 + 2\alpha_0\alpha_1 y_{t-1}^2 + \alpha_1^2 y_{t-1}^4)$$
$$= 3\alpha_0^2 + 6\alpha_0\alpha_1(\alpha_0/(1-\alpha_1)) + 3\alpha_1^2 E(y_{t-1}^4),$$

where I make use of (7.7), and it is implicitly assumed that $0 < \alpha_1 < 1$. Under the additional assumption that $0 < \alpha_1 < (1/3)^{\frac{1}{2}}$, repeated substitution leads to

$$E(y_t^4) = [3\alpha_0^2(1+\alpha_1)]/[(1-\alpha_1)(1-3\alpha_1^2)].$$

When $\alpha_1 = 0$ and $\alpha_0 = 1$, that is, in case y_t is a standard normal distributed variable, the kurtosis defined by $E(y_t^4)/(E(y_t^2))^2$ equals 3. For $0 < \alpha_1 < 1$, the kurtosis exceeds 3, which can be seen from

$$E(y_t^4)/(E(y_t^2)^2) = \{[3\alpha_0^2(1+\alpha_1)]/[(1-\alpha_1)(1-3\alpha_1^2)]\}/\{\alpha_0/(1-\alpha_1)\}^2$$
$$= 3 + (6\alpha_1^2/(1-3\alpha_1^2)).$$

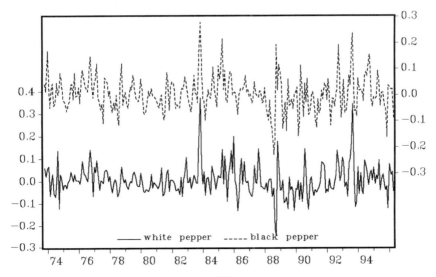

Figure 7.4 *First differences of the logs of black and white pepper prices*

Only when $0 < \alpha_1 < (1/3)^{\frac{1}{2}}$, this kurtosis is finite. Notice that since $E(\eta_t^3) = 0$, the skewness of an ARCH(1) time series equals zero. Hence, the basic ARCH process is symmetric, in the sense that positive and negative outliers emerge equally in the data.

To illustrate the above results on the kurtosis and skewness for some empirical series, consider again the two monthly observed pepper prices and the weekly observed Dow-Jones index. In figure 7.4, I give the first differences of the logs of the black and white pepper prices.

From these graphs, we can observe that there are periods where the two prices fluctuate heavily (see, e.g., around 1988 and 1993), and also that these patterns seem roughly similar. Furthermore, there seems to be more large price increases than there are large negative price changes. Hence, the pepper price series seem to have positive skewness. As another example, if we look again at the graph of the returns on the Dow-Jones index in figure 2.15, we observe that this series displays more negative than positive spikes, which in turn implies negative skewness. Most importantly, for these three series it holds that there are (sets of) aberrant data which may generate significant autocorrelation in the squared time series y_t^2 and also that y_t itself may have excess kurtosis and possibly significant skewness.

These conjectures seem to be confirmed by the results in table 7.2, where the first three estimated autocorrelations of the return series x_t and three statistics concerning normality of $\hat{y}_t$ are given, as well as the EACF of $\hat{y}_t^2$, where $\hat{y}_t$ are the residuals from an AR(p) regression for x_t.

Table 7.2. *Estimated autocorrelation functions, skewness, and kurtosis for three demeaned and/or prewhitened sample series*

Series			
EACF of x_t:	$\hat{\rho}_1$	$\hat{\rho}_2$	$\hat{\rho}_3$
Dow-Jones index	0.027	−0.019	0.047
White Pepper	0.302**	−0.005	−0.032
Black Pepper	0.338**	0.024	0.012
Normality of $\hat{y}_t^2$:	SK	K	JB
Dow-Jones index	−0.944**	9.443**	1444.23**
White Pepper	0.968**	7.046**	225.527**
Black Pepper	0.540**	4.470**	37.011**
EACF of $\hat{y}_t^2$:	$\hat{\rho}_1$	$\hat{\rho}_2$	$\hat{\rho}_3$
Dow-Jones index	0.292**	0.090**	0.019
White Pepper	0.268**	0.127**	0.016
Black Pepper	0.136**	0.194**	0.010

Notes:
** Significant at the 5% level (when $n^{-\frac{1}{2}}$ is taken as the standard deviation of the estimated residuals).
The x_t series is the return series, that is, $x_t = \log(z_t) - \log(z_{t-1})$, where z_t is the level of the Dow-Jones index or the price levels of black and white pepper. For the Dow-Jones series, the AR model is of order 0, while for the pepper prices, an AR (1) model is fitted. The estimated residuals are denoted as $\hat{y}_t$. For the Dow-Jones series, the effective number of observations is 769. For the pepper prices, this number is 270 for the EACF of x_t, and 269 for the EACF of $\hat{y}_t^2$ and for the normality of $\hat{y}_t$. SK is the estimated skewness of the residuals, $\text{SK} = \hat{m}_3/\hat{m}_2^{1\frac{1}{2}}$, and K is the estimated kurtosis defined by $\hat{m}_4/\hat{m}_2^2$, where $\hat{m}_j = (n)^{-1}\Sigma_{t=1}^{n}\hat{y}^j$, where n is the number of effective observations. JB is the $\chi^2(2)$ test for normality. Skewness differs significantly from zero if $n\text{SK}^2/6$ exceeds the 5% critical value of the $\chi^2(1)$ distribution. Similarly, the kurtosis is significantly different from 3 if $n(\text{K}-3)^2/24$ exceeds the same critical value.

The first panel of table 7.2 shows that no relevant autocorrelation exists for the Dow-Jones index, which seems to confirm that the level of this series follows a random walk (possibly with drift). For the two pepper prices, their returns have substantial first order autocorrelation, which can be removed by fitting an AR(1) model to these series. In the next panel of table 7.2, I give the estimated skewness, kurtosis, and JB normality test statistic. Clearly, all three series display non-normality since all three test statistics are highly significant. As expected, given the visual evidence in figures 2.15

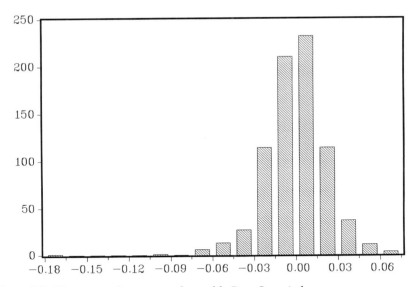

Figure 7.5 *Histogram of returns on the weekly Dow-Jones index*

and 7.4, the Dow-Jones index shows negative skewness, while the pepper prices have positive skewness. Hence, more outliers with negative values are found for the Dow-Jones index and more positive-valued outliers are found for the pepper prices. This can also be observed from the histograms of the $\hat{y}_t$ for the Dow-Jones index in figure 7.5 and the (log) price of white pepper in figure 7.6.

Finally, the third panel of table 7.2 shows for all three series that the squared residuals have substantial autocorrelation at the first two lags. Hence, abstaining from excess skewness for a moment, the current three sample series may be described by AR(p)–ARCH(q) models, for example, by

$$x_t - \mu - \phi_1 x_{t-1} - \ldots - \phi_p x_{t-p} = y_{t-1} = (h_t)^{\frac{1}{2}} \eta_t \qquad (7.11)$$

$$\eta_t \sim NID(0,1), \qquad (7.12)$$

$$h_t = \alpha_0 + \alpha_1 y_{t-1}^2 + \alpha_2 y_{t-2}^2 + \ldots + \alpha_q y_{t-q}^2, \qquad (7.13)$$

with $\alpha_0 > 0$, $\alpha_i \geq 0$ $(i=1,2,\ldots,q)$, and $\phi_p(1) > 0$ and $\Sigma_{i=1}^{q} \alpha_i < 1$. The results in table 7.2 suggest that q may equal 1 or 2 as only the first two estimated auto-correlations of $\hat{y}_t^2$ are significant. See Bollerslev (1988) for some general expressions for the theoretical ACFs of y_t^2 when y_t is an ARCH series.

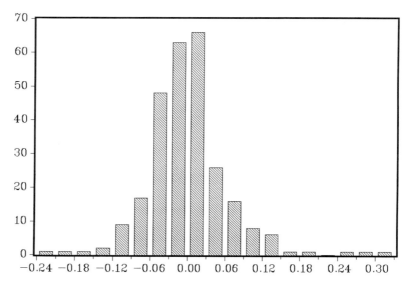

Figure 7.6 *Histogram of the estimated residuals from an AR(1) regression for the first differences of logged white pepper prices*

GARCH

For many financial time series, it appears that the value of q in (7.13) takes an inconveniently large value so that we have to estimate many parameters. Additionally, it can be inconvenient to impose the restrictions $\alpha_i \geq 0$ for all i in (7.13). It can therefore be useful to approximate the qth order polynomial in (7.13) by a rational polynomial of order (p,q), similar to the standard ARMA models for y_t series. This was first proposed in Bollerslev (1986), which results in the so-called Generalized ARCH [GARCH] model. The GARCH model replaces (7.13) by

$$h_t = \alpha_0 + \alpha_1 y_{t-1}^2 + \ldots + \alpha_q y_{t-q}^2 + \beta_1 h_{t-1} + \ldots + \beta_p h_{t-p}, \qquad (7.14)$$

that is, the GARCH(p,q) equation, where α_0, $\alpha_1, \ldots, \alpha_q$ and $\beta_1, \ldots, \beta_p$ exceed 0 and $\Sigma_{j=1}^{q} \alpha_j + \Sigma_{i=1}^{p} \beta_i < 1$. In practice, the value of q in (7.14) is much smaller than that in (7.13). In fact, it is typically found that the GARCH(1,1) model yields an adequate description of many financial time series data, see, for example, Bollerslev, Chou, and Kroner (1992). Again, we can derive explicit expressions for the kurtosis and the autocorrelations of an y_t series generated by (7.11)–(7.13) showing that a GARCH(p,q) model can describe time series with sequences of large positive and large negative observations. The autocorrelation function of y_t^2 can now simply be found by applying the techniques in chapter 3 to a re-arranged version of (7.14), see Bollerslev (1988). For example, the GARCH(1,1) equation

$$h_t = \alpha_0 + \alpha_1 y_{t-1}^2 + \beta_1 h_{t-1} \tag{7.15}$$

can be read as

$$y_t^2 | Y_{t-1} = \alpha_0 + (\alpha_1 + \beta_1) y_{t-1}^2 + v_t - \beta_1 v_{t-1}, \tag{7.16}$$

where $v_t = y_t^2 | Y_{t-1} - h_t$. Since the v_t series can be shown to be uncorrelated with its own past, equation (7.16) indicates that the GARCH(1,1) model implies that the ACF of y_t^2 looks like that of an ARMA(1,1) model. Notice that when $\alpha_1 = 0$, the β_1 parameter in (7.16) is not identified. Hence, for any GARCH(p,q) process, the value of q should at least be equal to 1.

The Integrated GARCH(1,1) [IGARCH(1,1)] model emerges when $\alpha_1 + \beta_1 = 1$ in (7.15). In this case, the AR parameter for y_{t-1} in (7.16) equals 1, and hence shocks have a persistent effect. As argued above, the persistence of shocks in case of GARCH models for y_t^2 is not the same as that for AR models for y_t. Nelson (1990) gives the details of how the effect of shocks translates into stationarity properties of a GARCH time series.

7.2   Specification and forecasting

In this section I review some aspects of specifying symmetric GARCH models in practice, and their use for forecasting.

Testing

Prior to parameter estimation, it is sound practice to test for the possible presence of (G)ARCH in an empirical time series. A simple LM test for ARCH of order q is given by n times the coefficient of determination R^2 of the auxiliary regression

$$\hat{y}_t^2 = \omega_0 + \omega_1 \hat{y}_{t-1}^2 + \omega_2 \hat{y}_{t-2}^2 + \ldots + \omega_q \hat{y}_{t-q}^2 + \kappa_t, \tag{7.17}$$

where $\hat{y}_t^2$ are the squared residuals of the ARMA filtered x_t time series. Under the null hypothesis of no ARCH, this LM test for ARCH(q) has an asymptotic $\chi^2(q)$ distribution. Lee (1991) shows that (7.17) can also be used to test the no ARCH hypothesis versus a GARCH(p,q) process (with $p \leq q$). The F-version of this LM test, to be denoted as $F_{ARCH,1-q}$ follows an $F(q,k)$ distribution, where k is the number of effective observations minus the number of regressors.

For the returns on the weekly Dow-Jones index, for which no ARMA model is needed to whiten x_t, the $F_{ARCH,1-1}$ statistic obtains a value of 74.625 and the $F_{ARCH,1-10}$ statistic has a value of 8.394, both of which are significant at the 1 percent level. For white pepper prices we obtain for the residuals of an estimated AR(1) model that $F_{ARCH,1-1} = 20.677$ and $F_{ARCH,1-12} = 1.782$, where q is set to 12 because the pepper prices are observed monthly. For the black pepper prices, we obtain $F_{ARCH,1-1} = 5.027$ and $F_{ARCH,1-12} = 1.515$. These test results suggest that there is evidence that q is much larger than 1 for the Dow-Jones index (which in turn suggests that a GARCH(1,1) can be useful), while for the pepper prices q may be set equal to 1 (or at least to a small value) as the $F_{ARCH,1-12}$ statistics are not significant at the 5 percent level.

The test for ARCH may also be used as a general test for misspecification of an ARMA model for some series. Indeed, two sequential additive outliers may suggest that there is ARCH. As an example, consider again the Argentinean inflation series analyzed in chapter 6. When an AR(1) model is fitted to all data, so that the AOs at the end of the sample are included, the $F_{ARCH,1-1}$ test obtains a value of 9.759, which is significant at the 1 percent level.

Estimation

Typically, given the NID assumption of η_t, we use the maximum likelihood [ML] method to estimate the parameters in the two equations of an ARMA-GARCH model. Details of this method are given in Bollerslev (1986), Bera and Higgins (1993) among others. Given appropriate choices for the starting values, the number of iterations can usually be kept at a moderate level.

For an AR(0)-GARCH(1,1) model for the returns on the Dow-Jones index, I obtain the following estimation results (using the Eviews 2.0 package):

$$\hat{y}_t = x_t - 0.00241 = (\hat{h}_t)^{\frac{1}{2}}\hat{\eta}_t, \text{ and} \qquad (7.18)$$
$$\quad (0.00072)$$

$$\hat{h}_t = 0.0000520 + 0.164\hat{y}_{t-1}^2 + 0.727\hat{h}_{t-1}, \qquad (7.19)$$
$$\quad (0.0000135)\ (0.017) \qquad (0.043)$$

where estimated standard errors are given in parentheses. For (7.19) it holds that $\hat{\alpha}_1$ and $\hat{\beta}_1$ both exceed 0, that $\hat{\alpha}_0$ exceeds 0, and that $\hat{\alpha}_1 + \hat{\beta}_1 = 0.891 < 1$.

In table 7.3, I report the parameter estimates for the ARCH(1), ARCH(2), and the GARCH(1,1) models for the first differences of logged pepper prices, where the x_t series can be described by an AR(1) model. In other words, I estimate the parameters in

$$x_t - \delta - \phi_1 x_{t-1} = y_t = (h_t)^{\frac{1}{2}}\eta_t, \qquad (7.20)$$

Table 7.3. *Parameter estimates of AR(1)–GARCH (p,q) models for first differences of logged black and white pepper prices*

Model	Parameter estimates				AIC	SIC
	ϕ_1	α_1	α_2	β_1		
Black pepper						
$p=0, q=1$	0.282	0.226			−5.463	−5.410
	(0.048)	(0.073)				
$p=0, q=2$	0.321	0.180	0.139		−5.459	−5.392
	(0.067)	(0.072)	(0.072)			
$p=1, q=1$	0.357	0.161		0.670	−5.460	−5.393
	(0.057)	(0.047)		(0.120)		
White pepper						
$p=0, q=1$	0.282	0.294			−5.454	−5.400
	(0.067)	(0.063)				
$p=0, q=2$	0.312	0.266	0.226		−5.448	−5.381
	(0.067)	(0.061)	(0.076)			
$p=1, q=1$	0.305	0.285		0.404	−5.448	−5.381
	(0.076)	(0.065)		(0.135)		

Note:
The AR(1)–GARCH (p,q) model is given in (7.20)–(7.22). AIC and SIC denote the Akaike and Schwarz model selection criteria using the residual sum of squares, where the relevant residuals are $\hat{\eta}_t$.

$$\eta_t \sim NID(0,1), \tag{7.21}$$

$$h_t = \alpha_0 + \alpha_1 y_{t-1}^2 + \alpha_2 y_{t-2}^2 + \beta_1 h_{t-1}, \tag{7.22}$$

where α_2 and β_1 can be zero. Given the relevance of the α_j ($j=1,2$) and β_1 parameters in table 7.3, all three models seem to fit the data well.

Lumsdaine (1995) shows that standard Likelihood Ratio and Wald tests can be used to test hypotheses on the parameters in GARCH models. Additionally, it is shown that t-tests for, for example, α_1 and β_1 in (7.22), can be evaluated using the standard normal distribution, provided that we consider a large enough sample. Furthermore, when the normality assumption in, for example, (7.21), does not hold, it appears that in finite samples the test statistics have distorted size, in the sense that the null hypothesis is rejected too often. Hence, before interpreting various parameter estimates, we should evaluate the properties of the estimated GARCH model.

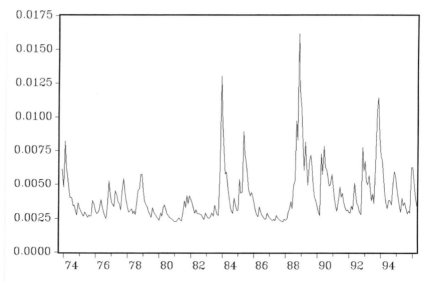

Figure 7.7 *Estimated conditional variance from a GARCH(1,1) model for the first differences of logged black pepper prices*

Evaluation and model selection

Once the parameters in AR-GARCH models are estimated, we can obtain estimates of the conditional variance time series h_t. By construction, this $\hat{h}_t$ series should take larger values in more volatile periods. In figure 7.7, I give the $\hat{h}_t$ series for the AR(1)–GARCH(1,1) model for black pepper prices. The graph in this figure shows that the effect of shocks does not die out very quickly, which is not unexpected given the $\hat{\alpha}_1 + \hat{\beta}_1$ value of 0.831 (see table 7.3).

The estimated h_t series can also be used to scale the y_t series and to test whether the GARCH model has effectively removed autocorrelation in the squared series and whether the estimated residuals $\hat{\eta}_t$ do not display excess kurtosis. A simple test statistic constructed from the estimated autocorrelations of the squared residuals $\hat{\eta}_t^2 = \hat{y}_t^2/\hat{h}_t$, is the Ljung–Box test given by

$$\text{LB}(m) = n(n+2)\sum_{k=1}^{m}(n-k)^{-1}r_k(\hat{\eta}_t^2), \tag{7.23}$$

where the $r_k(\hat{\eta}_t^2)$ denotes the estimated kth order autocorrelation of $\hat{\eta}_t^2$. Under the null hypothesis of no autocorrelation in the squares of the residuals, $\text{LB}(m)$ test values should be evaluated against the $\chi^2(m-p-q)$ distribution, see McLeod and Li (1983). For the AR(1)–GARCH(1,1) models for black and white pepper, this test (with $m = 12$) obtains the insignificant values 5.88 and 3.71, respectively. Hence, some of the GARCH models in table 7.3 seem to have effectively removed the autocorrelation in the squared time series.

A second diagnostic concerns the approximate normality of $\hat{\eta}_t = \hat{y}_t / (\hat{h}_t)^{\frac{1}{2}}$. The JB test for these residuals obtains a value of 15.95 for black pepper and a value of 51.48 for white pepper. Hence, although the GARCH models seem to describe a large part of the non-normality, which is substantiated by the fact that these JB test values are much lower than the JB values reported in table 7.2, the residuals $\hat{\eta}_t$ still display non-normality. Among other causes, this may be due to aberrant data that cannot be explained by the GARCH model.

In case there are two or more rival AR-GARCH models, Sin and White (1996) recommend to use the AIC and SIC model selection criteria to make a final decision. These criteria are calculated for the estimated residuals $\hat{\eta}_t$. In the last two columns of table 7.3, I give the estimated AIC and SIC values for the three models for the two pepper prices. It appears that in both cases, the ARCH(1) model is preferred.

Forecasting

One of the motivations to consider GARCH type models is that such models allow to forecast conditional volatility. For example, with a GARCH(1,1) model, we can generate one-step ahead forecasts for h_t (at time n) as

$$\hat{h}_{n+1} = \hat{\alpha}_0 + \hat{\alpha}_1 \hat{y}_n^2 + \hat{\beta}_1 \hat{h}_n. \tag{7.24}$$

To compare the out-of-sample forecasting performance of various rival GARCH models, we may use

$$v_{n+1} = (x_{n+1} - \bar{x})^2 \tag{7.25}$$

as a measure of the true, but unobserved, volatility, where $\bar{x}$ is some average of an *a priori* selected long range of past returns, see Day and Lewis (1992) and Pagan and Schwert (1990).

As an illustration, consider the forecasting results in table 7.4, which are obtained from Franses and Van Dijk (1996). GARCH (1,1) models are fitted to four years of weekly returns on stock market indices for Germany (DAX), The Netherlands (EOE), Spain (MAD), Italy (MIL), and Sweden (VEC), where data are available for 1986 to 1994. In a next step, one-step ahead forecasts are generated for all weeks in the next year, where the true observations y_{n+h} are used when forecasting y_{n+h+1}, $h = 0,1,2....$ Next, the sample is shifted one year, and the exercise is repeated. This results in

Table 7.4. *Out-of-sample forecasting performance of random walk (RW), GARCH, and QGARCH models for the volatility of some weekly observed European stock market indices*

		Forecast period				
Index	Model	1990	1991	1992	1993	1994
DAX	RW	3.566	0.585	0.230	1.013	3.219
	GARCH	4.395	3.359	1.520	1.775	2.854
	QGARCH	3.146	3.322	1.425	0.877	2.780
EOE	RW	1.146	0.148	0.090	0.633	0.983
	GARCH	1.305	1.050	0.848	0.767	0.928
	QGARCH	1.497	1.076	0.707	0.552	1.006
MAD	RW	1.112	1.062	0.859	1.214	5.021
	GARCH	3.249	1.118	2.717	2.076	2.423
	QGARCH	3.298	1.085	1.839	1.008	1.962
MIL	RW	1.173	1.664	6.736	19.851	10.803
	GARCH	1.130	2.358	3.351	8.895	8.444
	QGARCH	1.083	1.943	2.349	6.047	8.479
VEC	RW	2.483	1.104	2.554	1.621	3.103
	GARCH	3.027	2.396	3.040	6.607	3.098
	QGARCH	3.462	2.978	2.279	5.357	3.200

Notes:
The indices concern the stock markets in Germany (DAX), The Netherlands (EOE), Spain (MAD), Italy (MIL), and Sweden (VEC). The cells are the median squared errors of forecasted volatility.
Source: Table IV in Franses and Van Dijk (1996).

forecast errors for 1990 until 1994. In table 7.4, I report the median squared errors in order to give less weight to extremely irregular observations. In the first two rows for each stock market, the forecasts of the GARCH (1,1) model are compared with those of the random walk model, which generates forecasts using (7.25) as $\hat{v}_{n+h+1} = v_{n+h}$. The results in table 7.4 show that it is only for 1994 that we seem to do better with a GARCH model for all five stock markets. Furthermore, for the Italian stock market index, the GARCH model outperforms the random walk model in four of the five cases. However, in 17 of the total number of 25 cases, the random walk model beats the GARCH model.

7.3   Various extensions

The number of extensions to the basic (G)ARCH model is very large. The reader is referred to the surveys mentioned earlier for more complete overviews. When the GARCH model is viewed as an ARMA type model for the squared residuals (or squared time series), it can be extended or modified toward allowing for long memory (Fractional GARCH), for seasonality (Seasonal or Periodic GARCH), and for the non-negativeness of the variances (Exponential GARCH), to mention just a few. Also, we may allow for an additional error process in the GARCH model, as is (approximately) done in the so-called stochastic volatility model, see Taylor (1986), *inter alia*. Often considered extensions of the basic GARCH model these are motivated by the empirical observation that the estimated residuals $\hat{\eta}_t$ display non-normality. This may be caused by some extreme outliers which cannot be described by the GARCH model. In that case we may modify the AR-GARCH set of equations by assuming that $\eta_t \sim t(\kappa)$, where $t(.)$ denotes the Student-t distribution with κ degrees of freedom, see, for example, Bollerslev (1987). We may also wish to use the techniques in the previous chapter to reduce the effects of these outliers.

If irregular data points are not equally distributed in the sense that positive and negative outliers do not occur about equally frequently, the $\hat{\eta}_t$ series will display excess skewness. For example, stock markets tend to crash with larger decreases in returns than the increases that they experience in a boom. We can now assume that these larger crashes are AOs and that these should be removed from the time series. Alternatively, we may allow for the possibility that negative and positive returns somehow follow different regimes or have a different impact on the returns series itself. An example of a model that accounts for the latter is the so-called GARCH-M model introduced in Engle, Lilien, and Robins (1987). A simple example of this model is

$$x_t - \mu - \delta(h_t)^{\frac{1}{2}} = y_t = (h_t)^{\frac{1}{2}}\eta_t, \tag{7.26}$$

$$\eta_t \sim NID(0,1), \tag{7.27}$$

$$h_t = \alpha_0 + \alpha_1 y_{t-1}^2 + \beta_1 h_{t-1}. \tag{7.28}$$

When the parameters in this model are estimated for the weekly Dow-Jones index we get that $\hat{\mu} = -0.0035$ (0.0040) and $\hat{\delta} = 0.317$ (0.206). Hence, the previously significant growth rate in the Dow-Jones index in (7.18) seems to be offset by the δ, which is however only significant at the 12 percent level. Since δ is positive, these estimation results show that returns are positively correlated with large volatility.

Another example of a GARCH type model that allows for different treatment of positive and negative shocks is the so-called Threshold ARCH [TARCH] model, proposed in Glosten, Jagannathan, and Runkle (1992) and Rabemananjara and Zakoian (1993). The conditional variance equation of this model is

$$h_t = \alpha_0 + \alpha_1 y_{t-1}^2 + \delta I_{t-1}[y_{t-1} < 0] y_{t-1}^2 + \beta_1 h_{t-1}, \tag{7.29}$$

where I_{t-1} is an indicator dummy variable that takes a value of 1 when y_{t-1} is negative, and a value of 0 when $y_{t-1} \geq 0$. When $\delta > 0$, negative shocks have a larger impact on volatility h_t than do positive shocks. When the parameters in (7.29) are estimated for the weekly Dow-Jones index (again using Eviews 2.0 routines), the estimation results are

$$\hat{h}_t = 0.000123 + 0.042 \hat{y}_{t-1}^2 + 0.418 I_{t-1}[\hat{y}_{t-1} < 0] \hat{y}_{t-1}^2 + 0.492 \hat{h}_{t-1}. \tag{7.30}$$
$$\quad\;\; (0.000024)\;\; (0.037) \qquad (0.070) \qquad\qquad\quad (0.075)$$

Comparing these results with those in (7.19) for the GARCH(1,1) model, it is clear that the β_1 parameter obtains a much lower value in (7.30) and also that the α_1 parameter is now insignificant. Since $\hat{\delta}$ in (7.30) is very relevant, negative shocks to the Dow-Jones index play quite an important role.

The practical experience with forecasting stock market volatility in, for example, Franses and Van Dijk (1996) shows that the TARCH model often looses from the simple GARCH(1,1) model. However, in that study it is found that an alternative to TARCH, which can cope with similarly skewed time series, can yield much better forecasts. This model is the Quadratic GARCH [QGARCH] model, proposed and analyzed in Engle and Ng (1993), see also Sentana (1995). The QGARCH(1,1) equation is

$$h_t = \alpha_0 + \alpha_1 (y_{t-1} - \delta)^2 + \beta_1 h_{t-1}, \tag{7.31}$$

where again a positive δ indicates that negative shocks have more impact on the conditional variance. The third row for each of the five stock market variables in table 7.4 contains the median squared forecasting errors for the QGARCH model. Clearly, in 17 of the 25 cases the QGARCH model outperforms the linear GARCH model, and it also beats the random walk more frequently.

Conclusion

In this chapter, I have reviewed a few time series models that can be used to describe and forecast financial time series. Typical features of these financial data are excess kurtosis and significant autocorrelation in the squared returns. There is still much current research that focuses on the relative merits of these univariate models for forecasting and inference on conditional variance. Additionally, various multivariate GARCH models have been proposed.

The Threshold and Quadratic ARCH models in section 7.3 indicated that it may be useful to allow some observations to be described by a different model. The switch between different models is then established when the observations pass a certain threshold. Such switching regime models are in fact non-linear models. In the next chapter, the focus will be on some specific non-linear models. Notice that these models can also be useful in case the diagnostic test for ARCH suggests the presence of conditional heteroskedasticity. This test can not only take significant values in case of a small number of neglected AOs, ARCH may also seem present because of neglected non-linearity. In practice, this means that it may be useful to apply diagnostic tests for non-linearity together with tests for ARCH prior to analyzing possibly complicated GARCH models.

8 Non-linearity

The final typical feature of some business and economic time series that is treated in this book is non-linearity. Similar to the features such as trend and seasonality (discussed in chapters 4 and 5), it is difficult to define non-linearity otherwise than in the context of a model. Loosely speaking, however, an economic time series may be said to be non-linear when large shocks have a different impact than small shocks in the sense that the impact of a shock is not proportional to its size. Additionally, non-linearity can imply that the impact of shocks depends on whether they are positive or negative. As an example, consider again the quarterly seasonally adjusted USA industrial production index in figure 2.3. For this series we can observe that there is a general upward trend, which once in a while seems to be hampered by large downward shifts, which display a substantial negative trend. This relative decrease in industrial output during recessions seems larger in absolute sense than the average increase in output during expansions. We may now say that USA industrial production is asymmetric over the business cycle, see, for example, Neftçi (1984), and that negative shocks have a larger impact in an absolute sense than do have positive shocks. Notice that some of the empirical results in the previous chapter for the Dow-Jones index show that similar findings can hold for financial series. For example, large negative shocks on stock markets do occur more frequently than similarly sized positive shocks.

As an illustrative graph of possible non-linearity, consider the scatter plot in figure 8.1 of y_t versus y_{t-1}, where y_t is the seasonally adjusted quarterly German unemployment. From this graph we can observe that this series displays cyclical behavior around points that shift over time. When these shifts are endogenous, i.e., caused by past observations on y_t themselves, this can be viewed as a typical feature of non-linear time series. In contrast, note that for a linear AR(1) series with mean μ, the time series data are all grouped around the constant μ.

Once the linear model is dismissed in favor of some form of a non-linear

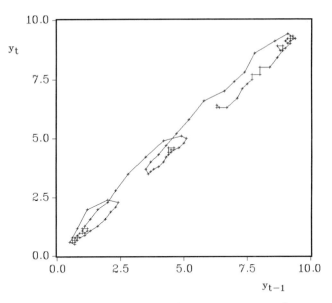

Figure 8.1 *Scatter plot of unemployment versus unemployment one period lagged*

model, it is clear that there is a wealth of possible non-linear structures that can be used to describe and forecast economic time series. In this chapter, I cannot give a survey of all non-linear time series models that can possibly be useful in practice, and therefore I limit the focus on the essentials of a few models which recently have been used in several practical occasions. Specifically, these models allow for various forms of regime switching behavior. In section 8.1, I mainly discuss Smooth Transition AR [STAR] and Artificial Neural Network [ANN] models. Additionally, I mention a few models that serve to highlight typical properties of certain non-linear models. One of these properties is that some non-linear models can generate time series that look like ARCH data. In section 8.2, I review some specification and evaluation issues. Since this research area attracts much current attention and hence not all approaches are generally agreed upon, this review is necessarily limited. For some more extensive surveys, the interested reader is referred to Granger and Teräsvirta (1993), Teräsvirta, Tjøstheim, and Granger (1994), De Gooijer and Kumar (1992), and Tong (1990). The empirical examples in this chapter concern the two aforementioned USA industrial production and German unemployment rate time series, where the first is transformed using logs while the second is left untransformed.

8.1   Some models and their properties

This section deals with a few non-linear models, the application of which has been disseminated through various empirical studies. These models are the STAR and ANN models. Next, I briefly discuss simple examples of the so-called bilinear model, random coefficient model, and the Markov regime-switching model. To save notation, I usually consider only first order AR type models. Extensions to higher order models are however not necessarily straightforward, while extensions to MA structures are even more complicated.

Smooth transition autoregression [STAR]

Consider the following model for a time series y_t, i.e.,

$$y_t = \delta + \phi_1 y_{t-1} + F(y_{t-d})(\psi + \lambda y_{t-1}) + \varepsilon_t, \tag{8.1}$$

where $F(y_{t-d})$ is some function of the so-called transition variable y_{t-d}. Model (8.1) assumes that y_t can be described by a linear AR(1) model with parameters δ and ϕ_1, while on some occasions, that is, when $F(y_{t-d})$ takes non-zero values, y_t can be described by this AR(1) model added to a possibly non-linear component $F(y_{t-d})(\psi + \lambda y_{t-1})$. Obviously, we can also interpret $\psi F(y_{t-d})$ and $\lambda F(y_{t-d})y_{t-1}$ as components that render the intercept and the first order autoregressive parameter to be time varying. As such, (8.1) belongs to the class of so-called state-dependent models, see Priestley (1988). The transition function $F(.)$ is usually chosen such that its realizations lie within the $[0,1]$ interval. Hence, an alternative interpretation of (8.1) is that when $F(.)=0$, y_t can be described by the AR(1) model $\delta + \phi_1 y_{t-1}$, when $F(.)=1$, the AR(1) model with parameters $\delta + \psi$ and $\phi_1 + \lambda$ is useful, and when $F(.)$ takes values in between 0 and 1, y_t can be described by a weighted sum of these two individually linear AR models. This suggests an alternative representation of (8.1), that is

$$y_t = (1 - F(y_{t-d}))(\delta_1 + \alpha_1 y_{t-1}) + F(y_{t-d})(\delta_2 + \alpha_2 y_{t-1}) + \varepsilon_t. \tag{8.2}$$

Notice that (8.2) indicates that when, for example, α_1 equals 1 (or even exceeds 1), the effects of shocks ε_t to the y_t series may still be only transitory. In other words, the stationarity of y_t given (8.2) depends on α_1, α_2 and on the specific form of the $F(y_{t-d})$ function. Testing for (some form of) stationarity of the y_t series generated as (8.2) is a complicated issue. For convenience, I assume that y_t corresponds to a suitably differenced variable.

Typical choices for the $F(y_{t-d})$ transition function, which are often used in practice, are (*i*) the exponential function

$$F(y_{t-d}) = 1 - \exp(-\gamma(y_{t-d} - c)^2), \quad \gamma > 0 \tag{8.3}$$

which leads to the so-called ESTAR model, (*ii*) the logistic function

$$F(y_{t-d}) = [1 + \exp(-\gamma(y_{t-d} - c))]^{-1}, \quad \gamma > 0 \tag{8.4}$$

which results in the LSTAR model, and (*iii*) the function

$$F(y_{t-d}) = 0 \quad \text{for } y_{t-d} \leq c \tag{8.5}$$

$$F(y_{t-d}) = 1 \quad \text{for } y_{t-d} > c \tag{8.6}$$

which gives the Threshold AR [TAR] model, see Tong (1983) and Tsay (1989). The c parameter is called the threshold parameter. Notice that the AR model is a special case of the LSTAR model in case $\gamma = \infty$. The ESTAR model assumes a symmetric response of y_t to positive and negative values of $y_{t-d} - c$. The TAR model assumes that the shift in regimes is abrupt. For practical purposes, it may therefore sometimes be useful to consider the LSTAR model instead of the ESTAR or TAR models since it allows for smooth changes and an asymmetric response to shocks, see Teräsvirta and Anderson (1992) and Granger and Teräsvirta (1993). Applications to the analysis of business cycles in various industrial production series can also be found in these two studies.

Generalizations of the LSTAR model in (8.2) with (8.4) amount to the inclusion of more lags of y_t, which results in, for example

$$y_t = (1 - F(y_{t-d}))(\delta_1 + \alpha_{1,p_1}(L)y_t) + F(y_{t-d})(\delta_2 + \alpha_{2,p_2}(L)y_t) + \varepsilon_t, \tag{8.7}$$

with

$$\alpha_{i,p_i}(L) = \alpha_{i,1}L + \alpha_{i,2}L^2 + \ldots + \alpha_{i,p_i}L^{p_i}, \tag{8.8}$$

$i = 1,2$, where p_1 may differ from p_2. Additionally, we may wish to extend $F(y_{t-d})$ by allowing for more lags or for certain functions of lagged y_t. Notice however that (8.7) with (8.8) can result in a large number of parameters to be estimated.

Point forecasts for y_{n+h} can be easily generated from STAR models. For example, in case $d = 1$, and $p_1 = p_2 = 1$, the one-step ahead forecast from (8.7)–(8.8) for y_{n+1} can be found as

$$\hat{y}_{n+1} = (1 - \hat{F}(y_n))(\hat{\delta}_1 + \hat{\alpha}_1 y_n) + \hat{F}(y_n)(\hat{\delta}_2 + \hat{\alpha}_2 y_n). \tag{8.9}$$

Based on the values of y_n, $\hat{c}$ and $\hat{\gamma}$, such a forecast can for example also be used to indicate whether $\hat{y}_{n+1}$ corresponds to a recession (if this would correspond with, say, $F(.) < 0.5$) or to an expansion (for $F(.) \geq 0.5$). A discussion of the non-trivial construction of forecasting intervals for these point forecasts is given in De Gooijer and Kumar (1992) and Tong (1990), among others.

Artificial Neural Network [ANN]

There are various forms of the widely applied artificial neural network model [ANN]. Its origin can be found in the neurological sciences, where external pulses are filtered through hidden layers such that the initial signals can be properly analyzed by brain cells. Recent surveys that focus on the use of ANNs for pattern recognition are contained in Bishop (1995) and Ripley (1994). In most economic applications where the number of observations can be quite small, the ANN model appears in simplified versions which usually contain only one hidden layer, see, for example, Kuan and Liu (1995), Kuan and White (1994), and Swanson and White (1995).

In a form similar to (8.1), that is, for a time series with only first order AR dynamics, the ANN with a single hidden layer and a linear component is written as

$$y_t = \delta + \phi_1 y_{t-1} + \sum_{j=1}^{q} \beta_j G(\psi_j + \lambda_j y_{t-1}) + \varepsilon_t, \tag{8.10}$$

where q is the number of hidden layer cells. Notice that, in contrast to the STAR model, this ANN only renders the intercept parameter to be time varying. The $G(.)$ function is usually set equal to the logistic function similar to (8.4), that is

$$G(\psi_j + \lambda_j y_{t-1}) = [1 + \exp(-(\psi_j + \lambda_j y_{t-1}))]^{-1}, \tag{8.11}$$

which is now called the logistic activation function since the non-linear part of the ANN model becomes "active" when the argument $(\psi_j + \lambda_j y_{t-1})$ is relevant enough. Similar to the LSTAR model, the ANN model can describe regime switches in economic time series, at least when these are confined to the intercepts.

The expression in (8.10), together with the flexibility of (8.11), shows that when q takes a large enough value, the ANN model can approximate any function f in $y_t = f(y_{t-1}) + \varepsilon_t$ arbitrarily close, see Kuan and White (1994) for a proof. Hence, with large enough q, the R^2 of regression (8.10) will approach 1 quite easily. Since (8.10) sums a set of logistic functions of the data, it is difficult to assign interpretations to the values of the parameters in the $G(.)$ functions. In section 8.2 below, I will briefly discuss the issue of model selection and interpretation for the possibly heavily parameterized ANN models.

Some other non-linear models

Before turning to empirical specification issues, I present some alternative non-linear models that can also be useful in practice. For some of these models it may be more easy to analyze the properties of time series generated by such models because of the availability of explicit expressions for the variance, kurtosis, and other functions.

The bilinear model, initially proposed in Granger and Andersen (1978), is a non-linear model that considers lagged errors multiplied by lagged time series realizations as regressors. A simple but illustrative example is given by

$$y_t = \beta \varepsilon_{t-1} y_{t-2} + \varepsilon_t. \tag{8.12}$$

Since $E(y_t) = 0$, it holds that

$$E(y_t y_{t-1}) = E(\beta \varepsilon_{t-1} y_{t-2} y_{t-1} + \varepsilon_t y_{t-1}) = 0 \tag{8.13}$$

$$E(y_t y_{t-2}) = E(\beta \varepsilon_{t-1} y_{t-2} y_{t-2} + \varepsilon_t y_{t-2}) = 0 \tag{8.14}$$

$$= \beta E(y_{t-2}^2) E(\varepsilon_{t-1}) = 0, \text{ and}$$

$$E(y_t y_{t-k}) = 0, \tag{8.15}$$

and hence that y_t is uncorrelated with its own past. However, the one-step ahead forecast of y_t can be generated by

$$\hat{y}_{n+1} = \beta \hat{\varepsilon}_n y_{n-1}, \tag{8.16}$$

where $\hat{\varepsilon}_n$ is the estimated residual at time n.

To understand the properties of this specific non-linear model, we can calculate the autocorrelation structure of certain functions of y_t. Under the condition that $\beta^2 \sigma^2 < 1$, we find for the variance of y_t

$$E(y_t^2) = E(\beta \varepsilon_{t-1} y_{t-2} + \varepsilon_t)(\beta \varepsilon_{t-1} y_{t-2} + \varepsilon_t) \tag{8.17}$$

$$= E(\beta^2 \varepsilon_{t-1}^2 y_{t-2}^2 + 2\beta \varepsilon_t \varepsilon_{t-1} y_{t-2} + \varepsilon_t^2)$$

$$= \sigma^2 / (1 - \beta^2 \sigma^2).$$

Additionally, it is easy to derive that $E(y_t^3) = 0$ and (under the condition that $3\beta^4 \sigma^4 < 1$) that

$$E(y_t^4) = 3\sigma^4 (1 + \beta^2 \sigma^2) / [(1 - \beta^2 \sigma^2)(1 - 3\beta^4 \sigma^4)]. \tag{8.18}$$

These two expressions show that when $\alpha_0 = \sigma^2$ and $\alpha_1 = \beta^2 \sigma^2$ in (7.3), the ARCH model of order 1 and this bilinear model have the same first four moments. In other words, the bilinear model in (8.12) with two parameters (β and σ) can also describe ARCH type patterns. This is confirmed by the autocovariance function of the squares of y_t, which takes non-zero values, see Granger and Andersen (1978). The reader may verify this using simulated data. Notice, however, that in contrast to the simple ARCH(1) model in (7.3) the bilinear model can generate non-zero forecasts for y_{n+1} as in

(8.16). This suggests that particular non-linear time series models can be useful to describe and forecast the squares and the levels of financial data, see also Weiss (1986) and Bera and Higgins (1993).

A non-linear model that is closely related to the bilinear model is the random coefficient model. A simple example is

$$y_t = \alpha_t y_{t-1} + \varepsilon_t, \text{ with} \tag{8.19}$$

$$\alpha_t \sim N(\alpha, \tau^2). \tag{8.20}$$

Tsay (1987) and Bera and Higgins (1993) show that such models can describe the same phenomena as GARCH models. Recently, stochastic coefficient models have gained interest since it also allows a unit root to become stochastic, that is, α in (8.20) can be 1. Granger and Swanson (1997) and McCabe and Tremayne (1995) consider various versions of the resultant stochastic unit root models.

A simple version of the so-called Exponential AR model [EAR], proposed in Haggan and Ozaki (1981), can be represented as

$$y_t = \phi_t y_{t-1} + \varepsilon_t, \tag{8.21}$$

with, for example

$$\phi_t = \alpha + \beta \exp(-\gamma y_{t-1}^2). \tag{8.22}$$

Notice that this EAR model bears similarities with the ESTAR model above. All these expressions show that it is not difficult to propose many different non-linear time series models, and therefore that model selection may not be a straightforward exercise.

So far, all these non-linear models assume that regime switches are caused by certain past values of y_t itself. Hence, regime switches are assumed to be endogenous. Alternatively, we may assume that such shifts are exogenous and perhaps caused by such external effects as wars and oil crises. For example, the shifts in figure 8.1 may also be caused by shocks of the latter type. An example of a time series model that assumes such exogenous effects, but at the same time does not assume *a priori* knowledge of the location of shifts, is the Markov switching-regime model, see Hamilton (1989, 1990). A simple example of this model is given by

$$y_t = \mu_0 + \phi_0 y_{t-1} + \nu_{0,t} \quad \text{if } s_t = 0 \tag{8.23}$$

$$y_t = \mu_1 + \phi_1 y_{t-1} + \nu_{1,t} \quad \text{if } s_t = 1, \tag{8.24}$$

where s_t is a Markov state variable which is governed by

$$P(s_t = 1 | s_{t-1} = 1) = p \tag{8.25}$$

$$P(s_t = 0 | s_{t-1} = 1) = 1 - p \tag{8.26}$$

$$P(s_t = 0 | s_{t-1} = 0) = q \tag{8.27}$$

$$P(s_t = 1 | s_{t-1} = 0) = 1 - q. \tag{8.28}$$

When state 0 is a recession, (8.27) implies that the probability of staying in a recession is q. The probability of staying in an expansion is p. Again, using (8.23) and (8.24) it is easy to generate one-step ahead forecasts for y_{n+1} given estimates of the various parameters and given a forecasted value of s_{n+1}. Additionally, we can quantify the probability that the forecasted value is in a recession or not.

To summarize, the limited survey of possibly useful non-linear time series models in this section already indicates that there are many options. This large number means that the practitioner usually will have to face many more specification decisions than in the linear case. In the next section, I will discuss a few aspects of an empirical strategy. It should be stressed that several aspects are not yet well understood and therefore much current research is dedicated to solving several issues.

8.2 Empirical specification strategy

For many non-linear models there are no simple explicit forms for the auto-correlation function of either y_t, y_t^2, or other transformations. Hence, an empirical specification strategy for non-linear time series models is much more difficult than for linear or ARCH models. In this section, I consider some useful rules for STAR models that are currently applied in practical applications. Alternative rules for other models, as well as portmanteau tests for non-linearity, can be found in the relevant literature.

Testing for non-linearity

A useful first step is to test whether non-linear functions of lagged regressor variables contribute significantly to the fit (after correction for a linear AR part). Although there are various tests for non-linearity that can deal with many non-linear variants, Monte Carlo simulation results show that tests for STAR type non-linearity have substantial power against various forms of non-linearity, see for example Teräsvirta, Lin, and Granger (1993). The test for STAR properties is based on the auxiliary regression

$$y_t = \beta_0 + \beta_1 y_{t-1} + \ldots + \beta_p y_{t-p} \tag{8.29}$$

$$+ \sum_{j=1}^{p} \beta_{2j} y_{t-j} y_{t-d} + \sum_{j=1}^{p} \beta_{3j} y_{t-j} y_{t-d}^2 + \sum_{j=1}^{p} \beta_{4j} y_{t-j} y_{t-d}^3 + \eta_t,$$

for some value of d, see Teräsvirta (1994) and Teräsvirta and Anderson (1992). The F-test values for the significance of the regressors added to the

Table 8.1. *Testing for STAR type non-
linearity in German unemployment and in
USA industrial production (both seasonally
adjusted)*

d	Unemployment	Industrial production
1	5.364**	1.669
2	6.365**	1.817*
3	5.196**	1.245
4	4.189**	1.087

Notes:
**Significant at the 5% level.
* Significant at the 10% level.
The test regression in given in (8.29). For both
time series the linear AR order can be set equal
to 1.

linear AR regressions can be used to test the null hypothesis of no STAR
non-linearity (i.e., all β_{ij} parameters are equal to zero, $i = 2,3,4$).
Additionally, we can obtain a first impression of the d value by looking at
the relative value of the F-test statistics, that is, the d for which the corresponding p-value is smallest may be selected.

In table 8.1, I report the test results for (seasonally adjusted) German
unemployment and USA industrial production. The null hypothesis of
linearity is rejected convincingly for unemployment, but only marginally
for industrial production.

Estimation

The next step is to estimate the parameters in the LSTAR model. Usually,
simple NLS routines result in stable parameter estimates after several itera-
tion steps. When estimating parameters, it may be useful first to fix γ and c
at some values, estimate the other parameters using OLS, and, secondly, to
stepwise allow γ and c to get estimated using NLS. Given uncertainty about
the most appropriate value of d, I estimate LSTAR models for each value
and report the estimation results for the two sample series that correspond
to the largest R^2 of the non-linear regression model. For the first differences
of seasonally adjusted unemployment in Germany (not in logs), I find that
the order of the linear component in (8.29) equals 1, and that d can best be
set at 1. The estimated LSTAR model is

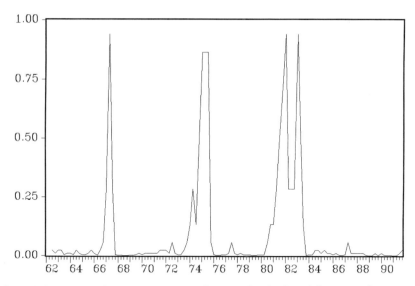

Figure 8.2 *Estimated LSTAR transition function for the first differences of seasonally adjusted unemployment in Germany*

$$\Delta_1 y_t = (1 - \hat{F}(\Delta_1 y_{t-1}))(-0.040 + 0.454\Delta_1 y_{t-1}) \tag{8.30}$$
$$(0.061) \ (0.261)$$

$$+ \hat{F}(\Delta_1 y_{t-1})(1.901 - 1.840\Delta_1 y_{t-1}) + \hat{\varepsilon}_t, \text{ with}$$
$$(1.664) \ (2.111)$$

$$\hat{F}(\Delta_1 y_{t-1}) = [1 + \exp(-9.231 \ (\Delta_1 y_{t-1} - 0.500))]^{-1}, \tag{8.31}$$
$$(5.800) \qquad\qquad (0.149)$$

where estimated standard errors are given in parentheses. Because of (8.31) and also given that the data have mean 0.05 and standard deviation 0.26, if $\Delta_1 y_{t-1}$ exceeds 0.500, $\hat{F}(.)$ takes values close to 1, which in this case of unemployment implies a recession. In figure 8.2, I give the graph of (8.31) versus time in quarters, and figure 8.3 displays $\hat{F}(\Delta_1 y_{t-1})$ versus $\Delta_1 y_{t-1}$. From figure 8.2, we can clearly notice the recession periods, and from figure 8.3, we can see that transition between recessions and expansions for this unemployment series is reasonably smooth, although there are not many data points for which $\Delta_1 y_{t-1}$ exceeds 0.5.

Suppose it is assumed that a recession quarter for this unemployment series corresponds with a value of $\hat{F}(\Delta_1 y_{t-1})$ that exceeds 0.5, we can calculate the quarters which correspond with peaks and troughs in conventional business cycle analysis. These dates are presented in the first two columns of table 8.2

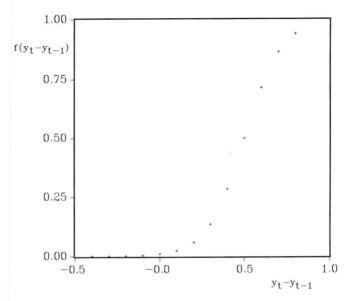

Figure 8.3 *Scatter plot of $F(\Delta_1 y_{t-1})$ versus $\Delta_1 y_{t-1}$ for the first differences of seasonally adjusted unemployment in Germany*

It can be seen from this table (and also from the graph in chapter 2) that there may have been three recessions in Germany (at least based on quarterly data), which here are defined as periods with significant increases in unemployment.

To evaluate the out-of-sample forecasting performance of the LSTAR model in (8.30)–(8.31), as compared to the linear AR model (which appears to be an AR(1)), I use observations on German unemployment for 1992.1–1996.4. Due to a change in measurement, the data after 1994.1 are not those that are published officially, but are constructed such that they match those prior to 1994.1. The data are displayed in table 8.3.

One-step ahead forecasts from (8.30)–(8.31) and from an AR(1) model are generated for 1992.1–1996.4. The mean squared prediction error (for 20 forecasts) of the linear model equals 0.0417, while that of the LSTAR model equals 0.0589. Hence, for this variable, the LSTAR model seems to fit the within-sample data well, but it does not outperform a linear AR(1) model in terms of one-step ahead forecasting.

As mentioned above, the LSTAR model assumes that regime shifts can be predicted using (functions of) lagged realizations of the variable itself. In order to compare the estimation results in (8.30)–(8.31) with a model that assumes that the timing of shifts is exogenous (although still unknown), I

Table 8.2. *Business cycle peaks and troughs according to LSTAR and Markov switching models for German unemployment*

LSTAR		Markov-switching	
Peak	Trough	Peak	Trough
1974.3	1975.3	1966.1	1967.2
1981.2	1982.1	1973.2	1975.2
1983.1	1983.2	1980.1	1983.2

Notes:
For the LSTAR model, a recession is defined when the estimated $F(\Delta_1 y_{t-1})$ takes a value that exceeds 0.5. For the Markov switching model a recession corresponds with $\hat{s}_t < 0.5$. A peak is defined as the last observation before a recession. A trough is the last quarter of a recession. A recession should at least last for two quarters.

Table 8.3. *Quarterly unemployment in Germany, 1992.1–1996.4*

Year	Not seasonally adjusted				Seasonally adjusted			
	Q1	Q2	Q3	Q4	Q1	Q2	Q3	Q4
1992	6.7	6.3	6.6	7.0	6.2	6.5	6.7	7.2
1993	8.1	7.8	8.4	8.8	7.6	8.0	8.5	9.0
1994	9.7	9.1	9.1	8.9	9.2	9.3	9.2	9.1
1995	9.6	8.8	9.0	9.2	8.9	9.0	9.2	9.4
1996	10.6	9.8	9.9	10.1	9.9	9.9	10.1	10.5

Sources: OECD Main Economic Indicators (1992–1993) and own calculations for 1994–1996 (because of change of measurement).

present estimation results for a simple Markov switching model. Details are provided in Franses and Paap (1998). For the first differenced unemployment series, Franses and Paap (1998) obtain

$$\text{Recession:} \quad \Delta_1 y_t = 0.385 + 0.504 \Delta_1 y_{t-1} + \nu_{0,t}, \quad \sigma_0^2 = 0.037 \quad (8.32)$$
$$\phantom{\text{Recession:} \quad} (0.071) \ (0.100)$$

$$\text{Expansion:} \quad \Delta_1 y_t = -0.062 + 0.504 \Delta_1 y_{t-1} + \nu_{1,t}, \quad \sigma_1^2 = 0.013 \quad (8.33)$$
$$\phantom{\text{Expansion:} \quad} (0.025) \ (0.100)$$

with

$$P(\hat{s}_t = 0 | \hat{s}_{t-1} = 0) = 0.871 \ (0.020) \tag{8.34}$$

$$P(\hat{s}_t = 1 | \hat{s}_{t-1} = 1) = 0.966 \ (0.067). \tag{8.35}$$

As expected, the probability of staying in a recession is smaller than staying in an expansion. The peaks and troughs found from this model are given in the last two columns of table 8.2. For some recessions these dates appear to differ several quarters from those of the LSTAR model.

For the quarterly seasonally adjusted industrial production in the USA, the NLS routine (in Eviews 2.0) yields the following parameter estimates (where the R^2 indicates $d = 4$)

$$\Delta_1 y_t = (1 - \hat{F}(\Delta_1 y_{t-4}))(0.004 + 1.019\Delta_1 y_{t-1}) \tag{8.36}$$
$$\quad\quad (0.006) \ (0.156)$$

$$+ \hat{F}(\Delta_1 y_{t-4})(0.005 + 0.410\Delta_1 y_{t-1}) + \hat{\varepsilon}_t, \text{ with}$$
$$\quad\quad (0.002) \ (0.099)$$

$$\hat{F}(\Delta_1 y_{t-4}) = [1 + \exp(-196.11(\Delta_1 y_{t-4} + 0.018))]^{-1}. \tag{8.37}$$
$$\quad\quad (319.27) \quad\quad\quad (0.011)$$

The estimation results for the transition variable show that regime shifts occur very abruptly. The graphs of $\hat{F}(\Delta_1 y_{t-4})$ versus time and versus $\Delta_1 y_{t-4}$ are given in figures 8.4 and 8.5, respectively. For this industrial production series, a recession observation at time t corresponds with values of $\Delta_1 y_{t-4}$ which are below -0.018.

An adequate linear model for the growth rates of seasonally adjusted production for 1960.1–1991.4 is an AR(2) model. Using the data in table 4.4, we can compare the one-step ahead forecasting performance of the LSTAR model in (8.36)–(8.37) with this linear AR(2) model. The non-linear model obtains a mean squared prediction error (over 16 forecasts and multiplied by 10^5) of 5.486, while the linear model has a value of 6.193. Hence, in this case it appears that the non-linear model outperforms the linear model in terms of one-step ahead forecasting.

Evaluation

To evaluate the within-sample performance of non-linear time series models we may use the Ljung-Box test for residual autocorrelation, although simulation studies suggest that the χ^2 asymptotic distribution may not be valid, see Eitrheim and Teräsvirta (1996). We can also consider the McLeod and Li test for autocorrelation in the squared residuals (see chapter 7), the standard JB normality test, and the test for ARCH also outlined in the previous chapter.

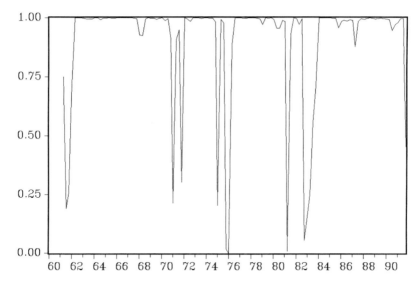

Figure 8.4 *Estimated LSTAR transition function for the first differences of seasonally adjusted US industrial production*

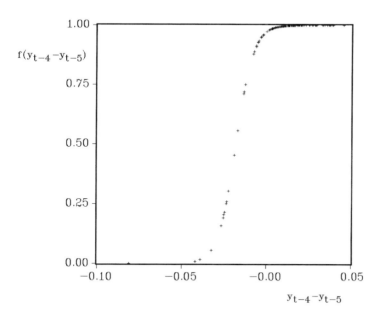

Figure 8.5 *Scatter plot of $F(\Delta_1 y_{t-4})$ versus $\Delta_1 y_{t-4}$ for the first differences of seasonally adjusted US industrial production*

If there is a final decision to be made between some adequate models, most practitioners use the Akaike or Schwarz type model selection criteria, see chapter 3. Given that non-linear models can have many parameters, the Schwarz criterion seems the most useful, see, for example, Sin and White (1996). To illustrate its use, consider the ANN model

$$y_t = \sum_{s=1}^{4} \delta_s D_{s,t} + \delta_0 t + \phi_1 y_{t-1} + \phi_2 y_{t-2} + \phi_3 y_{t-3} + \phi_4 y_{t-4} \tag{8.38}$$

$$+ \sum_{j=1}^{q} \beta_j G[\sum_{s=1}^{4} \delta_{sj} D_{s,t} + \delta_{0j} t + \phi_{1j} y_{t-1} + \phi_{2j} y_{t-2} + \phi_{3j} y_{t-3} + \phi_{4j} y_{t-4}] + \varepsilon_t,$$

of which the $10q + 9$ parameters are estimated for seasonally unadjusted German unemployment. Since the data are unadjusted and not differenced, model (8.38) includes seasonal dummies and a trend. The estimation method is outlined in Franses and Draisma (1997), who use sequences of Gauss optimization routines to estimate the parameters. The data are scaled between 0 and 1 for computational convenience. The SIC values for $q = 0$ (the linear model), 1, 2, and 3 are equal to -756.3, -790.8, -809.5, and -789.0, respectively, and hence the linear model seems rejected in favor of the ANN with two hidden layer cells.

With 29 parameters, the fit of this ANN model for seasonally unadjusted unemployment must be very close to 1. Furthermore, given this large number of parameters, it may be difficult to assign interpretations to their estimated values. An alternative and very simple approach to evaluate an ANN is proposed in Franses and Draisma (1997) and it amounts to checking the relative contribution of the hidden layer component. In the case of German unemployment, this component equals $\Sigma_{j=1}^{2} \hat{\beta}_j \hat{G}(.)$. In figure 8.6, I depict the contribution of this neural component, and also the contribution of the linear component, which obviously is $\hat{y}_t - \Sigma_{j=1}^{2} \hat{\beta}_j \hat{G}(.)$, see (8.38).

The estimated non-linear part of (8.38) displays substantial seasonality. Additionally, given the differences between the fit of the linear component and the time series itself, it is clear that the non-linear component amounts to an important contribution to the overall fit. Because the data are seasonal, we can consider the output of the hidden layer per quarter, which parallels the analysis of seasonal data using periodic models in section 5.3. For this unemployment series it appears that the largest increases in unemployment (exceeding values of 0.8 after seasonal adjustment) occurs in quarters 1 and 4. Hence, it may be that the relative contribution of the non-linear part in (8.38) also displays seasonality. This conjecture seems to be corroborated by the four graphs of the neural component for each of the four quarters in figure 8.7, where these correspond with observations in quarter s in year T, $T = 1, 2, \ldots, N$.

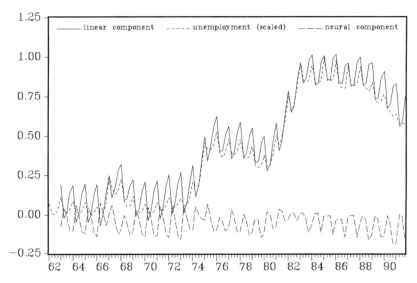

Figure 8.6 *Fit of linear and neural component in ANN for seasonally unadjusted unemployment Germany*

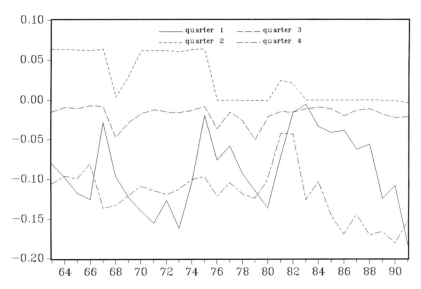

Figure 8.7 *Contribution of the neural component in an ANN for seasonally unadjusted unemployment Germany in each of the four quarters*

The contribution of the hidden layer is about equal to zero in quarter 3, it becomes zero in quarter 2 after 1975, and takes large non-zero values in quarters 1 and 4.

A useful tool to evaluate non-linear time series models is to use a hold-out sample and to compare out-of-sample forecasting performance. Results for LSTAR models above and in Granger and Teräsvirta (1993) and for ANNs in Swanson and White (1995), Kuan and Liu (1994), and Gençay (1996), indicate that these non-linear models can sometimes out-perform linear models in out-of-sample forecasting of macroeconomic and financial time series. Using simulations and empirical examples, Franses and Van Homelen (1998) show that ANNs are not misled by the presence of ARCH in financial time series. In fact, if there is some form of non-linearity in the data other than ARCH, ANNs are found to yield accurate predictions of the sign of exchange rate returns.

Conclusion

Theoretical and empirical research in the area of non-linear time series models for forecasting business and economic data is rapidly developing. At the time of writing of this book, some of the yet unsolved issues concern formal model selection methods across different types of models (i.e., LSTAR versus ANN), the evaluation of the persistence of shocks, extensions to multivariate models, and the construction of explicit expressions for forecasting intervals, to name just a few.

This chapter concludes the discussion of forecasting models for single univariate time series. For practical purposes, it may seem sensible to follow the sequence of the last five chapters when constructing a forecasting model. First, we may best decide on the type of trend, then on how to describe seasonality. The second stage concerns outliers, ARCH, and non-linearity. Preferably, we should treat all these features simultaneously, although this is probably easier said than done. It may be, however, that some of these features are caused by the impact of another time series variable. In that case, we may wish to analyze more than a single time series at the same time. The next two chapters will deal with such multivariate time series models.

9   Multivariate time series

Univariate time series models, as discussed in the previous chapters, can be very useful for out-of-sample forecasting and for descriptive analysis. It may however be that the empirical specification of such univariate models is hampered by many outliers and structural shifts, which in turn all may be attributed to one or more other variables than the y_t variable considered. For example, the change in the trend of USA industrial production around 1979 (see figure 2.3) may be caused by the increase in the oil price around that period. Additionally, this oil price variable may be responsible for the large negative growth in production around 1974/1975, which seems to correspond to a set of outliers (although the results in the previous chapter suggest that these observations may also reflect non-linearity). In other words, a useful descriptive model for USA industrial production can include an oil price variable. When production is denoted as y_t and the price of oil as x_t, we may thus wish to consider

$$y_t = \beta x_t + [\theta_q(L)/\phi_p(L)]\varepsilon_t, \tag{9.1}$$

where β measures the effect of x_t on y_t at time t. It may now be that the estimated residuals $\hat{\varepsilon}_t$ from (9.1) do not show typical outlier or structural break patterns. Hence, including only a single extra variable can substantially reduce the number of parameters since no additional descriptive measures for outliers and breaks are needed.

A model like (9.1) introduces new problems. The first is that it is unknown whether the oil price x_t has to be included as is done in (9.1), or that it enters the model with a time lag, that is, whether x_{t-i} for some $i=1,2,\ldots,k$ should be included. This time lag will also depend on the sampling interval of the data. When the data are observed daily, we may consider including x_{t-i}, but when the data are only observed each quarter, then x_t may do. We can only base our decisions on the available data, as economic theory usually provides no guidelines on dynamics.

An additional problem with models as (9.1) is that maybe not only y_t is somehow explained by x_t, but also x_t somehow depends on current and/or past y_t. For USA industrial production, we may reasonably assume that the oil price affects production and not the other way round. For the three marketing variables (see the data appendix) concerning market share, distribution, and price this is however unclear. When distribution is low, market shares cannot be large. In turn, with increasing market shares, we may want to increase distribution. Advertising (not in our data set) can increase market share, but it seems useless to increase advertising for a fast-moving consumer product when the product is not widely available. Finally, prices will vary because of promotional activities when a marketeer observes a decreasing market share, and lower prices may increase sales.

When we want to take all possible relations between variables into account, it seems sensible to construct a model for a vector of time series instead of constructing models like (9.1) for all individual series. In case we also do not know *a priori* which variable is affecting which, or in other words, when it is uncertain which variables are exogenous and which are endogenous, it seems useful to start with the construction of a general time series model for a vector time series.

Another motivation for starting with an unrestricted multiple time series model instead of a static regression like $y_t = \alpha x_t + u_t$, is given by the fact that such static models may lead to spurious inference. A simple illustration is given by the following example. Suppose that sales y_t and the advertising expenditures x_t (both in terms of money) are generated by the following set of equations

$$y_t = \rho y_{t-1} + \varepsilon_t, \quad |\rho| < 1 \tag{9.2}$$

$$x_t = \beta y_{t-1} + \psi_t, \tag{9.3}$$

where ε_t and ψ_t are mutually independent white noise variables with variances σ_ε^2 and σ_ψ^2, which are also independent of past realizations of x_t and y_t. On average, advertising expenditures are thus set at a proportion β of previous sales. Clearly, and unfortunately, advertising does not generate extra sales since the equation for y_t does not include x_t, x_{t-1}, and so on. This feature of advertising is however not detected when we consider the static model

$$y_t = \alpha x_t + u_t. \tag{9.4}$$

The variance of x_t, denoted as $\gamma_0(x_t)$, is

$$\gamma_0(x_t) = E[(\beta y_{t-1} + \psi_t)(\beta y_{t-1} + \psi_t)] \tag{9.5}$$
$$= \beta^2 \gamma_0(y_t) + \sigma_\psi^2$$
$$= \beta^2 \sigma_\varepsilon^2 / (1 - \rho^2) + \sigma_\psi^2.$$

The covariance of y_t with x_t is

$$\gamma_0(y_t, x_t) = E[(\rho y_{t-1} + \varepsilon_t)(\beta y_{t-1} + \psi_t)] \tag{9.6}$$
$$= \rho\beta\gamma_0(y_t)$$
$$= \rho\beta\sigma_\varepsilon^2/(1-\rho^2).$$

In other words, in theory the OLS value of α can be found to be equal to

$$\hat\alpha = \gamma_0(y_t, x_t)/\gamma_0(x_t) \tag{9.7}$$
$$= \beta\rho/[\beta^2 + (1-\rho^2)\sigma_\psi^2/\sigma_\varepsilon^2].$$

As an example, when the variances of the error terms equal 1, $\beta=1$ and $\rho=0.6$, α equals about 0.37. In other words, advertising can seem to have an effect on sales, while (9.2) states it has not. Furthermore, this spurious effect can easily be shown not to disappear when y_t is regressed on x_{t-i} ($i=1,2,\ldots,k$) instead. The solution to this problem is simple. If, given y_t and x_t, we consider the multivariate regression model

$$y_t = \phi_1 y_{t-1} + \phi_2 x_{t-1} + \psi_{1,t}, \tag{9.8}$$

$$x_t = \phi_3 y_{t-1} + \phi_4 x_{t-1} + \psi_{2,t}, \tag{9.9}$$

where $(\psi_{1,t}, \psi_{2,t})'$ is a (2×1) variable with mean zero and a covariance matrix Σ, we find that ϕ_2 and ϕ_4 are zero. The model in (9.8)–(9.9) is called a vector autoregression of order 1 [VAR(1)] since it includes on the right-hand side only y_t and x_t variables with one time lag.

We may also wish to allow for possible simultaneous effects of x_t on y_t and vice versa. In that case we can consider

$$y_t = \pi_1 y_{t-1} + \pi_2 x_t + \psi_{1,t}, \tag{9.10}$$

$$x_t = \pi_3 y_t + \pi_4 x_{t-1} + \psi_{2,t}, \tag{9.11}$$

instead of (9.8)–(9.9), that is, a model with simultaneous effects π_2 and π_3. In vector notation, this so-called dynamic simultaneous model can be written as

$$\begin{bmatrix} 1 & -\pi_2 \\ -\pi_3 & 1 \end{bmatrix} \begin{bmatrix} y_t \\ x_t \end{bmatrix} = \begin{bmatrix} \pi_1 & 0 \\ 0 & \pi_4 \end{bmatrix} \begin{bmatrix} y_{t-1} \\ x_{t-1} \end{bmatrix} + \begin{bmatrix} \psi_{1,t} \\ \psi_{2,t} \end{bmatrix}. \tag{9.12}$$

Multiplying both sides with the inverse of the matrix on the left-hand side gives

$$\begin{bmatrix} y_t \\ x_t \end{bmatrix} = (1 - \pi_2\pi_3)^{-1} \begin{bmatrix} 1 & \pi_2 \\ \pi_3 & 1 \end{bmatrix} \begin{bmatrix} \pi_1 & 0 \\ 0 & \pi_4 \end{bmatrix} \begin{bmatrix} y_{t-1} \\ x_{t-1} \end{bmatrix} + (1 - \pi_2\pi_3) \begin{bmatrix} 1 & \pi_2 \\ \pi_3 & 1 \end{bmatrix} \begin{bmatrix} \psi_{1,t} \\ \psi_{2,t} \end{bmatrix}$$

$$= (1 - \pi_2\pi_3)^{-1} \begin{bmatrix} \pi_1 & \pi_2\pi_4 \\ \pi_1\pi_3 & \pi_4 \end{bmatrix} \begin{bmatrix} y_{t-1} \\ x_{t-1} \end{bmatrix} + \begin{bmatrix} \psi_{1,t}^* \\ \psi_{2,t}^* \end{bmatrix}, \tag{9.13}$$

where the (2×1) vector series ψ_t^* has mean zero and covariance matrix Σ^*. This expression shows that (9.12) can be written as a VAR(1) like (9.8)–(9.9). For this example, it also holds that the $\phi_i(i=1,2,3,4)$ parameters in this VAR(1) model lead to unique estimates of the $\pi_i(i=1,2,3,4)$ in the simultaneous equations model in (9.10)–(9.11). Notice that even when, for example, $\pi_3=0$, the resultant vector series is a VAR(1) (with one parameter restriction). In fact, any simultaneous equation model with one or more lagged endogenous variables leads to a VAR model, see Zellner and Palm (1974) and see also Sims (1980), who uses this observation as an argument in favor of the use of VAR time series models for so-called structural macroeconomic analysis.

In this chapter I discuss some linear models for multivariate time series and some of their representations in section 9.1. For practical purposes, the VAR model is often the most useful (particularly for analyzing stochastic trends), and hence I consider only the VAR model when discussing empirical modeling strategies, forecasting, and other issues in sections 9.2 and 9.3. For illustrative purposes, I use the five-variate annually observed time series for sectoral production in China, and the weekly observed trivariate series with market share, distribution, and prices.

For extensive and more theoretical treatments of multivariate time series models, the reader should consult Hannan (1970), Fuller (1976), Lütkepohl (1991) and Hamilton (1994).

9.1   Representations

Consider m time series denoted as $y_{1,t}$, $y_{2,t}$ to $y_{m,t}$, and m individually white noise series $\varepsilon_{1,t}$ to $\varepsilon_{m,t}$, when these are stacked in the $(m \times 1)$ vector series Y_t and e_t as

$$
Y_t = \begin{bmatrix} y_{1,t} \\ y_{2,t} \\ \vdots \\ y_{m,t} \end{bmatrix} \text{ and } e_t = \begin{bmatrix} \varepsilon_{1,t} \\ \varepsilon_{2,t} \\ \vdots \\ \varepsilon_{m,t} \end{bmatrix}, \tag{9.14}
$$

with $e_t \sim N(0,\Sigma)$, where Σ not necessarily equals $\sigma^2 I_m$ or $\mathrm{diag}(\sigma_1^2, \sigma_2^2, \ldots, \sigma_m^2)$, where diag denotes an $(m \times m)$ diagonal matrix with elements σ_1^2 to σ_m^2, and where I_m is the $(m \times m)$ identity matrix. This means that the individual $\varepsilon_{i,t}$ series are uncorrelated with their own past and with the past of the other $\varepsilon_{j,t}$ variables $(i \neq j)$, but that there can be contemporaneous correlation between the error series.

Vector autoregressive moving average [VARMA] model

Analogous to the ARMA model for a univariate series, we can consider a vector ARMA model of order (p,q), which is written as

$$
\begin{bmatrix} y_{1,t} \\ y_{2,t} \\ \vdots \\ y_{m,t} \end{bmatrix} = \begin{bmatrix} \phi_{11,1} & \cdots & \phi_{1m,1} \\ \phi_{21,1} & \cdots & \phi_{2m,1} \\ \vdots & & \vdots \\ \phi_{m1,1} & \cdots & \phi_{mm,1} \end{bmatrix} \begin{bmatrix} y_{1,t-1} \\ y_{2,t-1} \\ \vdots \\ y_{m,t-1} \end{bmatrix} + \ldots + \begin{bmatrix} \phi_{11,p} & \cdots & \phi_{1m,p} \\ \phi_{21,p} & \cdots & \phi_{2m,p} \\ \vdots & & \vdots \\ \phi_{m1,p} & \cdots & \phi_{mm,p} \end{bmatrix} \begin{bmatrix} y_{1,t-p} \\ y_{2,t-p} \\ \vdots \\ y_{m,t-p} \end{bmatrix}
$$

$$
+ \begin{bmatrix} \mu_1 \\ \mu_2 \\ \vdots \\ \mu_m \end{bmatrix} + \begin{bmatrix} \varepsilon_{1,t} \\ \varepsilon_{2,t} \\ \vdots \\ \varepsilon_{m,t} \end{bmatrix} + \begin{bmatrix} \theta_{11,1} & \cdots & \theta_{1m,1} \\ \theta_{21,1} & \cdots & \theta_{2m,1} \\ \vdots & & \vdots \\ \theta_{m1,1} & \cdots & \theta_{mm,1} \end{bmatrix} \begin{bmatrix} \varepsilon_{1,t-1} \\ \varepsilon_{2,t-1} \\ \vdots \\ \varepsilon_{m,t-1} \end{bmatrix}
$$

$$
+ \ldots + \begin{bmatrix} \theta_{11,q} & \cdots & \theta_{1m,q} \\ \theta_{21,q} & \cdots & \theta_{2m,q} \\ \vdots & & \vdots \\ \theta_{m1,q} & \cdots & \theta_{mm,q} \end{bmatrix} \begin{bmatrix} \varepsilon_{1,t-q} \\ \varepsilon_{2,t-q} \\ \vdots \\ \varepsilon_{m,t-q} \end{bmatrix} \tag{9.15}
$$

Additional to the elements of μ and Σ, the VARMA(p,q) model contains $m^2(p+q)$ unknown parameters. For 4 time series with $p=1$ and $q=1$, this already amounts to 32 parameters. To save notation, the VARMA(p,q) model can be abbreviated as

$$
Y_t = \mu + \Phi_1 Y_{t-1} + \ldots + \Phi_p Y_{t-p} + e_t + \Theta_1 e_{t-1} + \ldots + \Theta_q e_{t-q}, \tag{9.16}
$$

or

$$
\Phi_p(L) Y_t = \mu + \Theta_q(L) e_t, \tag{9.17}
$$

with

$$
\Phi_p(L) = I_m - \Phi_1 L - \ldots - \Phi_p L^p \quad \text{and} \tag{9.18}
$$

$$
\Theta_q(L) = I_m + \Theta_1 L + \ldots + \Theta_q L^q. \tag{9.19}
$$

In practice, the general VARMA(p,q) model often is inconvenient. One reason for this is that parameters may not be identified. For example, consider the following simple VMA(1) model

$$
\begin{bmatrix} y_{1,t} \\ y_{2,t} \end{bmatrix} = \begin{bmatrix} \varepsilon_{1,t} \\ \varepsilon_{2,t} \end{bmatrix} + \begin{bmatrix} 0 & \pi \\ 0 & 0 \end{bmatrix} \begin{bmatrix} \varepsilon_{1,t-1} \\ \varepsilon_{2,t-1} \end{bmatrix} \tag{9.20}
$$

and compare it with the VAR(1) model

$$\begin{bmatrix} y_{1,t} \\ y_{2,t} \end{bmatrix} = \begin{bmatrix} 0 & \pi \\ 0 & 0 \end{bmatrix} \begin{bmatrix} y_{1,t-1} \\ y_{2,t-1} \end{bmatrix} + \begin{bmatrix} \varepsilon_{1,t} \\ \varepsilon_{2,t} \end{bmatrix}. \tag{9.21}$$

Both models can be found using different restrictions on the parameters in a VARMA(1,1) model, although they imply the same relationship between $y_{1,t}$ and $y_{2,t}$, see also Hannan (1970). A second problem with a VARMA model is that empirical specification is not easy and also that estimation of the parameters can be complicated when p and q get large. Finally, and similar to the univariate case, the model is not particularly useful to analyze common stochastic trends and cointegration. Since the latter issue is very important for modeling and forecasting, it seems sensible to stick to the VAR(p) model in many empirical occasions.

Stationarity of a vector autoregression

Similar to the univariate AR case, we can investigate the presence of unit roots in the VAR(p) model. We then again consider the characteristic equation of the autoregressive polynomial, which, in case of matrices with polynomials in L as in the vector model, amounts to considering

$$|\Phi_p(z)| = 0, \tag{9.22}$$

where $|.|$ denotes the determinant of a matrix. The VAR(p) model is said to be stable (or the corresponding vector Y_t series is stationary) if all solutions to (9.22) lie outside the unit circle. When one or more solutions to (9.22) lie on the unit circle, the VAR(p) model contains unit roots.

As an example, consider the VAR(1) model for a bivariate time series

$$\begin{bmatrix} y_{1,t} \\ y_{2,t} \end{bmatrix} = \begin{bmatrix} \phi_{11} & \phi_{12} \\ \phi_{21} & \phi_{22} \end{bmatrix} \begin{bmatrix} y_{1,t-1} \\ y_{2,t-1} \end{bmatrix} + \begin{bmatrix} \varepsilon_{1,t} \\ \varepsilon_{2,t} \end{bmatrix}, \tag{9.23}$$

where the additional index 1 in (9.15) is dropped to save notation. For this VAR(1) we have

$$\Phi_1(z) = \begin{bmatrix} 1 - \phi_{11}z & -\phi_{12}z \\ -\phi_{21}z & 1 - \phi_{22}z \end{bmatrix}, \tag{9.24}$$

and hence the characteristic equation equals

$$\begin{aligned} |\Phi_1(z)| &= (1 - \phi_{11}z)(1 - \phi_{22}z) - \phi_{21}\phi_{12}z^2 \\ &= 1 - (\phi_{11} + \phi_{22})z + (\phi_{11}\phi_{22} - \phi_{21}\phi_{12})z^2 \\ &= (1 - \nu_1 z)(1 - \nu_2 z) = 0, \end{aligned} \tag{9.25}$$

where ν_1 and ν_2 are functions of the form $\nu_j = a_j + b_j i$, where a_j and b_j are functions of the parameters ϕ_{11}, ϕ_{12}, ϕ_{21}, ϕ_{22} and the complex number i is defined by $i^2 = -1$. When the parameter restriction

$$(\phi_{11}+\phi_{22})-(\phi_{11}\phi_{22}-\phi_{21}\phi_{12})=1 \tag{9.26}$$

holds, such that either ν_1 or ν_2 lies on the unit circle, we can rewrite (9.25) as

$$|\Phi_1(z)|=(1-z)(1-(\phi_{11}\phi_{22}-\phi_{21}\phi_{12})z), \tag{9.27}$$

and the VAR(1) model contains a single unit root.

As a second illustrative example, consider again the periodic AR(1) model for a univariate quarterly time series y_t as in (5.42), that is

$$y_t=\alpha_s y_{t-1}+\varepsilon_t. \tag{9.28}$$

Since α_s implies that the autoregressive parameter varies with the quarter s, $s=1,2,3,4$, the PAR(1) model assumes that there is a different model for different seasons. When the observations in season s are denoted as $Y_{s,T}$, where T is an index for the years, and also when the error process ε_t is correspondingly stacked into $\varepsilon_{s,T}$, the PAR(1) assumes that $Y_{s,T}=\alpha_s Y_{s-1,T}+\varepsilon_{s,T}$ for $s=2,3,4$ and $Y_{1,T}=\alpha_1 Y_{4,T-1}+\varepsilon_{1,T}$ for $s=1$. This (4×1) system of equations can be summarized as a dynamic simultaneous model (or VAR(1) model) like

$$\begin{bmatrix} 1 & 0 & 0 & -\alpha_1 L \\ -\alpha_2 & 1 & 0 & 0 \\ 0 & -\alpha_3 & 1 & 0 \\ 0 & 0 & -\alpha_4 & 1 \end{bmatrix}\begin{bmatrix} Y_{1,T} \\ Y_{2,T} \\ Y_{3,T} \\ Y_{4,T} \end{bmatrix}=\begin{bmatrix} \varepsilon_{1,T} \\ \varepsilon_{2,T} \\ \varepsilon_{3,T} \\ \varepsilon_{4,T} \end{bmatrix}, \tag{9.29}$$

since $LY_{4,T}=Y_{4,T-1}$, that is, L operates on the years, not on the seasons. It is easy to derive that the characteristic equation for this PAR(1) model is

$$|\Phi_1(z)|=(1-\alpha_1\alpha_2\alpha_3\alpha_4 z)=0. \tag{9.30}$$

In other words, when $\alpha_1\alpha_2\alpha_3\alpha_4=1$, the VAR(1) has a unit root and hence the PAR(1) model with this restriction implies that y_t has a stochastic trend (as was already mentioned in (5.43)).

It is difficult to test hypotheses on the values of, for example, $\hat{\nu}_1$ and $\hat{\nu}_2$ in (9.25) in order to examine the presence of unit roots. In the next chapter, I will discuss methods (based on cointegration techniques) which are more useful. To obtain a preliminary and tentative impression of stationarity, we can of course, similar to the univariate AR(p) case where we look at the sum of the ϕ_i parameters $(i=1,2,\dots,p)$, calculate the eigenvalues of $\Phi_1+\Phi_2+\dots+\Phi_p$ to see if these are close to unity. When they are, there may be unit roots in the vector AR model.

Implied univariate time series models

There are various ways to represent a multivariate time series model for Y_t. Two of these are the implied univariate ARMA models and the so-called transfer function models for the individual elements of Y_t. Consider again the VAR(p) model for a zero mean time series Y_t, that is

$$\Phi_p(L)Y_t = e_t, \tag{9.31}$$

for which it is assumed that there are only roots on or outside the unit circle. One of the possible representations of this model is suggested by the equality

$$\Phi_p(z)^{-1} = |\Phi_p(z)|^{-1}\Phi_p^*(z), \tag{9.32}$$

where $\Phi_p^*(z)$ is the so-called adjoint matrix containing the cofactors (see for an example equation (9.35) below). These cofactors are the determinants of $(m-1)\times(m-1)$ matrices. Each of the matrix elements can contain the terms 1, z, z^2 up to z^p. Hence, the cells of this adjoint matrix can contain polynomials of maximum order $(m-1)p$. When we rewrite (9.32) as

$$|\Phi_p(z)|\Phi_p(z)^{-1} = \Phi_p^*(z), \tag{9.33}$$

the VAR(p) model in (9.31) can be written as

$$|\Phi_p(L)|Y_t = \Phi_p^*(L)e_t. \tag{9.34}$$

Since $|\Phi_p(z)|$ contains terms up to z^{mp}, the resultant univariate models for $y_{1,t}$ to $y_{m,t}$ are ARMA models with maximum order $(mp, (m-1)p)$. Often, the order is much lower because common factors in the AR and MA polynomials cancel out. As an example, for a VAR(2) model for 5 time series the implied univariate models are ARMA of maximum order (10,8). Clearly, in practice however, we seldom find that such highly parameterized ARMA models are required to fit the data, see also chapter 3. When e_t in (9.34) is replaced by a VMA(q) model, the implied univariate ARMA models are of maximum order $(mp, (m-1)p+q)$. Finally, note that because each row of (9.34) is multiplied with the same determinant, the AR(mp) polynomials are equal for the m variables $y_{i,t}$.

The expression in (9.34) shows that a dynamic simultaneous model, which was shown to be equivalent to a VAR, implies that the univariate time series can be described by univariate ARMA models, see Zellner and Palm (1974). This means that simultaneous models, which are often claimed to be based on economic theory, can correspond quite well with univariate ARMA models, which are often based on the desire to have a simple descriptive model to forecast economic data.

As an illustration of (9.34), consider the VAR(1) model for $(y_{1,t}, y_{2,t})'$ as in (9.23) with $|\Phi_1(z)|$ as in (9.25) and with the following adjoint matrix (containing the cofactors)

$$\Phi_1^*(z) = \begin{bmatrix} 1 - \phi_{22}z & \phi_{12}z \\ \phi_{21}z & 1 - \phi_{11}z \end{bmatrix}. \tag{9.35}$$

The implied univariate ARMA(2,1) models for $y_{1,t}$ and $y_{2,t}$ are

$$y_{1,t} = (\phi_{11} + \phi_{22})y_{1,t-1} + (\phi_{21}\phi_{12} - \phi_{11}\phi_{22})y_{1,t-2} \tag{9.36}$$
$$+ \varepsilon_{1,t} - \phi_{22}\varepsilon_{1,t-1} + \phi_{12}\varepsilon_{2,t-1},$$

$$y_{2,t} = (\phi_{11} + \phi_{22})y_{2,t-1} + (\phi_{21}\phi_{12} - \phi_{11}\phi_{22})y_{2,t-2} \tag{9.37}$$
$$+ \varepsilon_{2,t} - \phi_{11}\varepsilon_{2,t-1} + \phi_{21}\varepsilon_{1,t-1}.$$

When the unit root restriction in (9.27) holds, the two models are ARIMA(1,1,1). In other words, one unit root in a bivariate VAR model leads to a unit root in each of the univariate models. In this case, it seems that these two univariate models have the unit root in common. The phenomenon of such a common unit root is called cointegration. In the next chapter, I will discuss this empirically relevant concept in more detail.

Transfer function models

A second possibility to represent a VARMA(p,q) model, or a VMA(q) model, is implied by the equality

$$\Theta_q(z)^{-1} = |\Theta_q(z)|^{-1}\Theta_q^*(z), \tag{9.38}$$

where $\Theta_q^*(z)$ is the adjoint matrix containing the cofactors of $\Theta_q(z)$. The VARMA(p,q) model can now be rewritten as

$$\Theta_q^*(L)\Phi_p(L)Y_t = |\Theta_q(L)|e_t. \tag{9.39}$$

As an illustration, consider the VMA(1) model for a bivariate series, that is

$$\begin{bmatrix} y_{1,t} \\ y_{2,t} \end{bmatrix} = \begin{bmatrix} 1 + \theta_{11}z & \theta_{12}z \\ \theta_{21}z & 1 + \theta_{22}z \end{bmatrix} \begin{bmatrix} \varepsilon_{1,t} \\ \varepsilon_{2,t} \end{bmatrix}. \tag{9.40}$$

For the $\Theta_1(z)$ matrix holds

$$|\Theta_1(z)| = 1 + (\theta_{11} + \theta_{22})z + (\theta_{11}\theta_{22} - \theta_{21}\theta_{12})z^2 \tag{9.41}$$

and

$$\Theta_1^*(z) = \begin{bmatrix} 1 + \theta_{22}z & -\theta_{12}z \\ -\theta_{21}z & 1 + \theta_{11}z \end{bmatrix}. \tag{9.42}$$

This implies that the univariate series can now be described by

$$y_{1,t} = -\theta_{22} y_{1,t-1} + \theta_{12} y_{2,t-1} + \varepsilon_{1,t} + (\theta_{11} + \theta_{22})\varepsilon_{1,t-1}$$
$$+ (\theta_{11}\theta_{22} - \theta_{21}\theta_{12})\varepsilon_{1,t-2} \qquad (9.43)$$

$$y_{2,t} = -\theta_{11} y_{2,t-1} + \theta_{21} y_{1,t-1} + \varepsilon_{2,t} + (\theta_{11} + \theta_{22})\varepsilon_{2,t-1}$$
$$+ (\theta_{11}\theta_{22} - \theta_{21}\theta_{12})\varepsilon_{2,t-2}. \qquad (9.44)$$

Sometimes, these single equation models are called ARMAX models. This is because they include autoregressive terms [AR], lags of explanatory variables [X] and MA terms. Notice that these ARMAX models include the error terms corresponding to only one variable, which is in contrast to the implied univariate models in (9.36)–(9.37). Amongst others, Bierens (1987) gives a specification strategy, and Franses (1991b) applies it to a set of marketing data.

When the multivariate model would be a simultaneous model, like in (9.10) and (9.11), with a VMA(1) error term, then the data can be described by

$$\begin{bmatrix} 1 - \gamma_1 z & -\alpha \\ -\beta & 1 - \gamma_2 z \end{bmatrix} \begin{bmatrix} y_{1,t} \\ y_{2,t} \end{bmatrix} = \begin{bmatrix} 1 + \theta_{11}z & \theta_{12}z \\ \theta_{21}z & 1 + \theta_{22}z \end{bmatrix} \begin{bmatrix} \varepsilon_{1,t} \\ \varepsilon_{2,t} \end{bmatrix}. \qquad (9.45)$$

The corresponding implied univariate ARMAX type models then also include current $y_{1,t}$ and $y_{2,t}$ variables. In sum, even though a vector Y_t series can be described by a VARMA(p,q) model, we can also describe the component series by univariate time series models or by ARMAX models. It should be mentioned that in practice, we sometimes use an alternative representation of an ARMAX model, which is then called a transfer function model. A simple example of such a model is

$$y_{1,t} = [\omega_w(L)/v_v(L)]y_{2,t} + [\theta_q(L)/\phi_p(L)]\varepsilon_{1,t}, \qquad (9.46)$$

see, for example, Box and Jenkins (1970) and Mills (1990), where $\omega_w(L)$ and $v_v(L)$ are polynomials in L of orders w and v. Notice that when $y_{2,t}$ is replaced by a zero–one dummy variable, this transfer function model looks very much like some of the models for additive or innovative outliers discussed in chapter 6.

This section has shown that there are many links between multivariate VARMA models, univariate time series models, simultaneous equation models with lagged variables, ARMAX models, and transfer function models. When we have a set of m time series and are willing to link these series explicitly in a multivariate model, it generally seems most easy in practice to start with a VAR, see also Hendry (1995). In the sequel to this chapter, I therefore continue with an analysis of the VAR(p) model.

9.2   Empirical model building

Similar to the univariate AR models, the construction of VAR models involves several specification steps. First, we need to specify an initial value of p, next, we should estimate the parameters, and then, investigate the properties of the estimated residuals. If there is more than one option, we need to select between several values of p to find a somehow optimal model. Finally, we may use the estimated VAR(p) model for various purposes. These purposes will be dealt with in the next section. In the current section, I review some guidelines for empirical specification.

In principle, we can derive explicit expressions for the autocorrelation function of VAR(p) processes. These would then be multivariate versions of the ACFs for the AR(p) model given in chapter 3. For practical purposes, however, the ACFs for VAR(p) models are not very straightforward to interpret. In fact, we get expressions for autocorrelation functions of the individual series and also for all cross-equation correlations. When m is large, this can amount to a large set of statistics, which should all be investigated simultaneously. In practice, we therefore usually fit a set of VAR models with orders 1, 2,..., K, for some value of K, and then evaluate whether one or more of these models fit the data well.

Estimation

The parameters in a VAR(p) model can be estimated using OLS per equation. For example, for the bivariate VAR(1) model in (9.23), we can estimate the ϕ_{ij} parameters by applying OLS to

$$y_{1,t} = \phi_{11}y_{1,t-1} + \phi_{12}y_{2,t-1} + \varepsilon_{1,t}, \tag{9.47}$$

and to

$$y_{2,t} = \phi_{21}y_{1,t-1} + \phi_{22}y_{2,t-1} + \varepsilon_{2,t}, \tag{9.48}$$

separately. This gives consistent and efficient estimates. Even though the residual series $\varepsilon_{1,t}$ and $\varepsilon_{2,t}$ may be contemporaneously correlated, which in other circumstances would lead to the use of the seemingly unrelated regression [SUR] technique, the fact that both regression models contain the same right-hand side variables renders that OLS per equation is the same as SUR, see Zellner (1962) and Lütkepohl (1991).

When the parameters in a VAR(p) model are estimated, it may be that some of these seem insignificant. At this stage, however, it is not sensible to try to set these parameters equal to zero. The main reason is that when the component series $y_{1,t}$ to $y_{m,t}$ of Y_t have stochastic trends, the t-ratios of the various parameters in a VAR(p) model will not be distributed as standard normal. To examine stationarity of Y_t, we consider the solutions to $|\Phi(1)| = 0$, which amounts to investigating the rank of the matrix $I_m - \Sigma_{i=1}^{p} \Phi_i$. Testing for this rank is usually called cointegration testing, and some methods will be outlined in the next chapter.

When we are confident from the outset that the m time series are all stationary, we can of course set insignificant parameters equal to zero. It should be stressed, though, that we should use SUR in that case, since with certain parameter restrictions the m equations may not contain the same right-hand side regressors anymore.

Order selection

Suppose we estimate the parameters of several VAR models, where the orders range from 1 to K. We may now examine the estimated residuals of each of these models. However, a more commonly applied procedure (which is slightly different from the selection procedure in the univariate case), is first to choose some order p, and, next, to examine the properties of the corresponding estimated residuals. Useful model selection criteria are the multivariate extensions of the Akaike and Schwarz information criteria, given by

$$\text{AIC} = \log|\hat{\Sigma}_p| + 2m^2 p/n, \qquad p = 1, 2, \ldots, K \qquad (9.49)$$

$$\text{SIC} = \log|\hat{\Sigma}_p| + (\log n)m^2 p/n, \quad p = 1, 2, \ldots, K \qquad (9.50)$$

respectively, where $|\hat{\Sigma}_p|$ denotes the determinant of the residual covariance matrix for the VAR(p) model and n is the number of effective observations, see Lütkepohl (1991). Paulsen (1984) shows that these criteria perform well, even when the Y_t vector series contains unit roots.

As an illustration, consider the five-sectoral production series in China again. A VAR(p) model for this five-variate series (all in logs) involves the estimation of $25p$ parameters. Given that there is only a limited number of available annual data, K is set equal to 3. The model selection results for the effective sample 1955–1988 are summarized in the first panel of table 9.1.

The SIC obtains its smallest value for $p = 1$, while the AIC is smallest for $p = 3$. The VAR(3) model contains 75 parameters, which seems quite a lot for $5 \times 34 = 170$ observations. With the diagnostic checks to be discussed below, I find that the estimated residuals of the VAR(1) model display significant autocorrelation. Hence, it seems best to opt for $p = 2$, also since the estimated residuals do not suggest misspecification.

For the trivariate marketing series (which are not logged), we have more effective observations per equation, that is, 103, and hence K is set equal

Table 9.1. *VAR order selection for a (5×1) vector series containing sectoral output in China and for a (3×1) vector series containing market share, distribution and prices*

(The *m* equations of the VAR models contain intercepts but no deterministic trends.)

			Model selection criteria	
p	$\log|\hat{\Sigma}_p|$	m^2p	AIC	SIC
Sectoral output in China ($m=5$)				
1	−27.955	25	−26.484	−<u>25.362</u>
2	−29.435	50	−26.494	−24.249
3	−31.487	75	−<u>27.075</u>	−23.930
Marketing variables ($m=3$)				
1	−4.982	9	−4.807	−<u>4.577</u>
2	−5.159	18	−4.809	−4.349
3	−5.391	27	−<u>4.867</u>	−4.176
4	−5.474	36	−4.775	−3.854
5	−5.536	45	−4.662	−3.511

Notes:
The models for the Chinese data (in logs) are estimated for the sample 1955–1988. The VAR models for the marketing data (not in logs) are estimated using 103 weekly data, running from week 11 to 113. The data that are available before week 11 (see the Data Appendix) are used as starting values. $\log|\hat{\Sigma}_p|$ denotes the log of the determinant of the estimated residual covariance matrix for a VAR of order p (containing m^2p unknown parameters). The AIC and SIC are defined in (9.49) and (9.50). The underlined values are smallest per criterion.

to 5. The values of the model selection criteria appear in the second panel of table 9.1. Again, the criteria point toward different models. The SIC suggests a VAR model of order 1, while the AIC favors a VAR(3) model. Since the parameters of several variables at $t-3$ seem significant (implementing t-ratios as if the data were stationary), I will continue to use the VAR(3) model for these market share (m_t), distribution (d_t), and price (p_t) data. The estimation results for the VAR(3) model, where $Y_t=(m_t,d_t,p_t)'$, are

$$Y_t = \hat{\mu} + \hat{\Phi}_1 Y_{t-1} + \hat{\Phi}_2 Y_{t-2} + \hat{\Phi}_3 Y_{t-3} + \hat{e}_t, \tag{9.51}$$

with

$$\hat{\Phi}_1 = \begin{bmatrix} 0.510^* & 0.076 & -0.020 \\ (0.111) & (0.488) & (0.018) \\ 0.005 & 0.478^* & -0.003 \\ (0.025) & (0.109) & (0.004) \\ -0.196 & 5.582^* & -0.429^* \\ (0.670) & (2.936) & (0.108) \end{bmatrix} \quad \hat{\Phi}_2 = \begin{bmatrix} 0.097 & 0.216 & 0.009 \\ (0.122) & (0.536) & (0.019) \\ 0.027 & 0.142 & -0.003 \\ (0.027) & (0.120) & (0.004) \\ -0.688 & 2.971 & 0.080 \\ (0.731) & (3.228) & (0.116) \end{bmatrix}$$

$$\hat{\Phi}_3 = \begin{bmatrix} 0.268^* & 0.175 & 0.002 \\ (0.109) & (0.503) & (0.017) \\ 0.001 & 0.240^* & 0.008^* \\ (0.024) & (0.113) & (0.004) \\ 0.298 & -3.145 & 0.099 \\ (0.654) & (3.025) & (0.103) \end{bmatrix} \quad \hat{\mu} = \begin{bmatrix} 0.848 \\ (1.954) \\ -0.190 \\ (0.438) \\ 39.945 \\ (11.757) \end{bmatrix}$$

where the estimated standard errors are given in parentheses. In case the data would be stationary, and hence the VAR (3) model would not have unit roots, the parameters indicated with an asterisk would be considered significant at the 5% level. These estimation results can be viewed as representative for many empirical unrestricted VAR models, that is, a substantial amount of the autoregressive parameters does not seem very relevant. Hence, it is worthwhile to see if the VAR(3) model for these marketing data can somehow be reduced.

As a tentative indication of the possible presence of unit roots in an empirical VAR model, we can check whether the eigenvalues of $\hat{\Phi}_1 + \hat{\Phi}_2 + \ldots + \hat{\Phi}_p$ are close to unity. For the VAR(2) model for the Chinese data, we find that these five eigenvalues are estimated as -0.093, $0.537 \pm 0.236i$ and $0.953 \pm 0.055i$. The last two eigenvalues are close to the unit circle. For the marketing data in model (9.51), the three estimated eigenvalues equal 0.988, 0.826, and 0.529, indicating that there may be one or perhaps two unit roots in this VAR model. A formal test for the number of unit roots will be discussed in chapter 10.

Diagnostic testing

The investigation of the properties of the estimated residuals from a VAR(p) model is not a simple exercise. This is caused by the fact that we may wish to see whether all the individual $\hat{\varepsilon}_{i,t}$ series ($i = 1,2,\ldots,m$) seem approximately white noise, but also whether there are no systematic patterns across current $\hat{\varepsilon}_{i,t}$ and lagged $\hat{\varepsilon}_{j,t}$, for any $i \neq j$, which lead to modifications of the VAR model. Additionally, a practical problem with diagnostic checks for these properties is that it is often unclear in which direction the model should be modified, see also Tiao and Box (1981). In fact, one may need to add regressor variables to only a few of the m equations and not to all. Such new regressor variables may also differ across the equations, which implies that an alternative and perhaps more adequate model is not a VAR model anymore.

To obtain insights into the autocorrelation properties of the estimated residuals, in order to examine whether the model is really dramatically mis-specified, we can of course consider the multivariate extensions of the port-manteau and LM tests for serial correlation, see Hosking (1980) and Poskitt and Tremayne (1982). A practical problem with these system tests is that a large number of estimated autocorrelations and cross-equation correlations is considered, and that many of these are required to be signif-icant in order to make the overall test statistic significant. Put differently, the power of these tests may not be very large.

On the other hand, we may also consider the estimated autocorrelations of the residual series $\hat{\varepsilon}_{i,t}$ and some cross-equation correlations, that is, we can consider matrices like

$$r_k(\hat{e}_t) = \begin{bmatrix} r(\hat{\varepsilon}_{1,t}, \hat{\varepsilon}_{1,t-k}) & .. & r(\hat{\varepsilon}_{1,t}, \hat{\varepsilon}_{m,t-k}) \\ \vdots & & \vdots \\ r(\hat{\varepsilon}_{m,t}, \hat{\varepsilon}_{1,t-k}) & .. & r(\hat{\varepsilon}_{m,t}, \hat{\varepsilon}_{m,t-k}) \end{bmatrix} \tag{9.52}$$

The theoretical standard deviations of these correlations are not equal to $n^{-\frac{1}{2}}$, as shown in Lütkepohl (1991, chapter 4). In fact, when we use $2n^{-\frac{1}{2}}$ as the supposedly 95 percent confidence interval, the true significance level is smaller than 5 percent. An additional problem with the interpretation of the individual correlations in (9.52) is that it is unclear how many of these values should be significant to justify modification of the tentative model.

As an illustration of (9.52), consider this matrix for $k = 1$ and $k = 2$ for the VAR(3) model for the three marketing series, that is,

$$r_1(\hat{e}_t) = \begin{bmatrix} -0.225^* & -0.181 & -0.041 \\ -0.192 & -0.255^* & -0.090 \\ 0.104 & -0.010 & -0.109 \end{bmatrix}, \quad \text{and} \tag{9.53}$$

$$r_2(\hat{e}_t) = \begin{bmatrix} -0.106 & -0.081 & 0.072 \\ 0.019 & -0.060 & -0.098 \\ -0.068 & 0.061 & 0.050 \end{bmatrix}. \tag{9.54}$$

With 103 observations and assuming normality, the 95 percent confidence interval would be at most ± 0.198. This means that only two correlations are significant at the 5 percent level, which in turn suggests that the VAR(3) model seems reasonably adequate. Note that a VAR(4) model requires nine additional parameters to be estimated in the hope that these two correlations would become irrelevant.

Additional diagnostic tests for a VAR(p) model can concern parameter stability, normality, outliers, ARCH, and non-linearity. Tests for the first two features are given in Lütkepohl (1991). Empirical details of these statistics can be found in Ooms (1994). Multivariate tests for ARCH and non-linearity are still under development.

9.3   Use of VAR models

Once we have selected an appropriate order p for the VAR model, such that a VAR($p-1$) is misspecified and a VAR($p+1$) contains too many redundant parameters, and we have estimated the parameters, we can use the resultant empirical model for various purposes. Two of these are out-of-sample forecasting and so-called structural analysis. The latter analysis can include the investigation of exogeneity and causality properties of certain variables and of impulse response functions and forecast error variance decompositions. Under the assumption that a VAR model has not yet been simplified by setting parameters equal to zero, I will briefly treat each of these issues in this section. Some of the theoretical illustrations involve the bivariate VAR(1) model as in (9.23).

Forecasting

Similar to the univariate AR model, forecasts from a VAR(p) model amount to simple extrapolation schemes. Consider the simple VAR(1) model

$$Y_t = \Phi_1 Y_{t-1} + e_t. \tag{9.55}$$

The one-step ahead forecast at time n is given by

$$\hat{Y}_{n+1} = \Phi_1 Y_n, \tag{9.56}$$

and hence the h-step ahead forecast equals

$$\hat{Y}_{n+h} = \Phi_1^h Y_n. \tag{9.57}$$

For a VAR(p) model, we have

$$\hat{Y}_{n+h} = \Phi_1 \hat{Y}_{n+h-1} + \ldots + \Phi_h Y_n + \ldots + \Phi_p Y_{n+h-p}, \tag{9.58}$$

where $\hat{Y}_{n+h-1}, \ldots, \hat{Y}_{n+1}$ are forecasted using similar schemes, and where $\hat{Y}_j = Y_j$ for $j = 1, 2, \ldots, n$. In practice, we need to substitute the estimated parameter matrices for the Φ_i, $i = 1, 2, \ldots, p$.

The theoretical one-step ahead forecast error for a VAR(1) model equals e_{n+1} since (9.56) lacks this term. The two-step ahead forecast from a VAR(1) model is

$$\hat{Y}_{n+2} = \Phi_1^2 Y_n, \tag{9.59}$$

while the true observation at time $n+2$ is

$$Y_{n+2} = \Phi_1 Y_{n+1} + e_{n+2} = \Phi_1^2 Y_n + e_{n+2} + \Phi_1 e_{n+1}. \tag{9.60}$$

The $(m \times m)$ forecast error covariance matrix for two steps ahead equals

$$\text{SPE}_2 = \Sigma + \Phi_1' \Sigma \Phi_1. \tag{9.61}$$

With the normality assumption, we can derive simple expressions for forecast intervals for the individual time series by considering the diagonal values of the estimated SPE_h matrices. Since the forecast errors for $y_{i,t}$ are also affected by the forecasts for the other $m-1$ $y_{j,t}$ variables, we may consider the determinant or the trace of the SPE_h matrices in order to compare rival empirical models.

Clements and Hendry (1993) evaluate this measure and conclude that it is not invariant to data transformations as first differencing. These authors show that a model that is best for forecasting the levels of a time series is not necessarily the best for forecasting its growth rates. Instead, they propose a measure which is invariant to such data transformations which is the determinant of the general forecast error second moment matrix.

As an example of an evaluation of the forecasting performance, consider the comparison of one-step ahead forecasts for each of the three variables, market share, distribution, and price, from the VAR(3) model and from univariate AR(p) models. (Notice that I do not evaluate system forecasts here). For this purpose, I re-estimate the parameters in (9.51) for the first 103–26 observations, and I generate one-step ahead forecasts for the last 26 weeks. The univariate AR models appear to be of order 3, 5, and 1 for m_t, d_t, and p_t, respectively, when I use the methods outlined in chapter 3 to reach this decision. The mean squared prediction errors for m_t, d_t, and p_t from the VAR(3) model are 0.119, 0.023, and 4.256, and from the univariate models are 0.078, 0.026, and 5.022, respectively. Hence, for market share a univariate model yields better forecasts, while for distribution and price, the multivariate VAR(3) is better.

Exogeneity and causality

Sometimes it may be useful to know (for economic theory considerations, but also for forecasting) whether a variable is exogenous to key parameters in the model. Loosely speaking, this means that we can then limit attention to a smaller set of equations. In other words, imposing exogeneity can imply a reduction of the number of parameters and also an improved precision in forecasting. For example, consider the bivariate VAR(1) model again, that is

$$
\begin{bmatrix} y_{1,t} \\ y_{2,t} \end{bmatrix} = \begin{bmatrix} \phi_{11} & \phi_{12} \\ \phi_{21} & \phi_{22} \end{bmatrix} \begin{bmatrix} y_{1,t-1} \\ y_{2,t-1} \end{bmatrix} + \begin{bmatrix} \varepsilon_{1,t} \\ \varepsilon_{2,t} \end{bmatrix}, \tag{9.62}
$$

with e_t distributed with mean zero and covariance matrix Σ. When $\phi_{21} = 0$ and $\Sigma = \operatorname{diag}(\sigma_1^2, \sigma_2^2)$, the $y_{2,t}$ variable is said to be strictly exogenous, see Engle, Hendry, and Richard (1983) for more exogeneity concepts and test procedures. Notice that in this case, (9.62) reduces to a simple recursive system with the advantage that in order to construct a forecasting model for $y_{1,t}$, we can simply consider the first equation of (9.62).

The concept of Granger causality, put forward in Granger (1969), bears similarities with the concept of exogeneity in the sense that it allows us to draw inference on the dynamic impact of one variable on another. Such inference can be given an economically meaningful interpretation. This concept of causality draws upon the concept of forecastability. For example, for a bivariate series, the variable $y_{2,t}$ is said to be Granger-non-causal for $y_{1,t}$ if

$$
E(y_{1,t} | Y_{1,t-1}, y_{2,t-1}) = E(y_{1,t} | Y_{1,t-1}), \tag{9.63}
$$

that is, the past of $y_{2,t}$ does not help in forecasting $y_{1,t}$. For the bivariate model (9.62), Granger non-causality of $y_{2,t}$ implies that $\phi_{12} = 0$.

Impulse response functions

When we forecast out of sample using the expressions in (9.55)–(9.58), we substitute known and forecasted values of Y_t into the forecasting schemes. As such, it is not easy to see what the dynamic effects are of the error process e_t. To this end, we calculate the so-called impulse response function. Suppose Y_t can be described by

$$
Y_t = \Phi_1 Y_{t-1} + e_t, \quad e_t \sim (0, \operatorname{diag}[\sigma_1^2, \ldots, \sigma_m^2]), \tag{9.64}
$$

and suppose there is an interest in the effect of the shocks from the first variable. We can calculate

$$
X_0 = e_0^* = (\sigma_1 \ 0 \ 0 \ldots 0) \tag{9.65}
$$

$$
X_1 = \Phi_1 e_0^*
$$

$$
X_2 = \Phi_1^2 e_0^*
$$

$$
\vdots
$$

$$
X_h = \Phi_1^h e_0^*. \tag{9.66}
$$

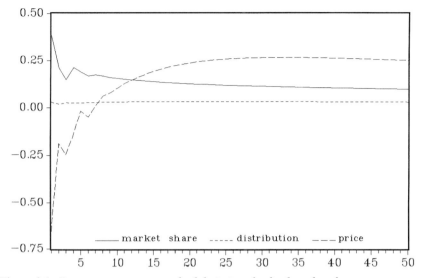

Figure 9.1 *Responses to a one standard deviation shock of market share*

The resulting m trajectories, that is, the m elements of the X_t vector series, $t = 0, 1, 2, \ldots, h$ are called the impulse response functions. When e_t has covariance matrix Σ with relevant off-diagonal elements, e_0^* in (9.65) is replaced by Pe_0^*, where P is defined by $\Sigma = PP$, and P is a lower triangular matrix. Notice that when the components of Y_t are arranged differently, we have a different P matrix. This implies that the m series contained in X_t can become different across different arrangements of Y_t.

The long-run impulse response matrix for a VAR(p) model can be calculated as

$$\Psi_\infty = (I_m - \Phi_1 - \ldots - \Phi_p)^{-1}. \tag{9.67}$$

For the empirical VAR(3) model for our marketing series, where Y_t is arranged as (m_t, d_t, p_t), this matrix is estimated as

$$\hat{\Psi}_\infty = \begin{bmatrix} 49.96 & 152.37 & -0.37 \\ 13.34 & 49.57 & -0.05 \\ 109.32 & 456.15 & 2.37 \end{bmatrix}, \tag{9.68}$$

for which we can conclude for example that prices have a negative long-run effect on market share and distribution, while market share and distribution have a positive impact on all variables.

These long-run impact results are illustrated by the estimated impulse response functions for the three variables based on a VAR(3) model in figures 9.1 to 9.3.

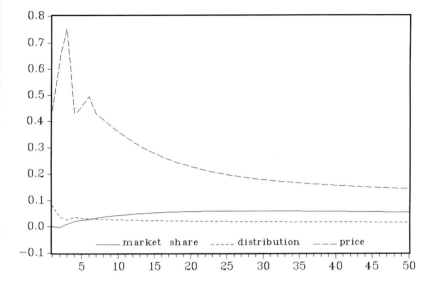

Figure 9.2 *Responses to a one standard deviation shock of distribution*

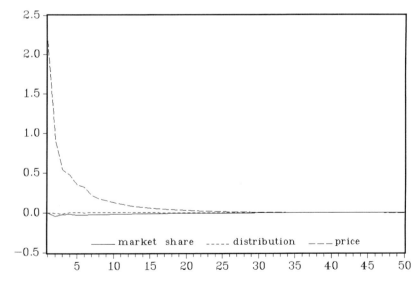

Figure 9.3 *Responses to a one standard deviation shock of price*

Table 9.2. *Variance decomposition for VAR(3) model for the trivariate marketing series containing market share, distribution and price for $_h$-step ahead forecasts*

(The cells contain the percentage of the variance of the forecast errors that can be attributed to the variance in each of the three variables.)

h	Market share			Distribution			Price		
	m_t	d_t	p_t	m_t	d_t	p_t	m_t	d_t	p_t
1	100.00	0.00	0.00	12.26	87.74	0.00	8.01	3.62	88.37
2	99.02	0.00	0.98	13.54	85.98	0.48	6.96	9.05	83.99
3	98.85	0.05	1.10	18.23	80.15	1.75	6.91	15.50	77.60
4	98.80	0.20	1.01	20.45	77.89	1.66	6.78	16.91	76.30
5	98.47	0.38	1.15	22.49	76.00	1.51	6.51	18.74	74.74
10	96.98	1.75	1.26	32.57	66.38	1.06	6.00	25.68	68.32
15	95.30	3.54	1.17	40.17	59.01	0.82	6.98	28.73	64.29
20	93.65	5.30	1.05	45.81	53.53	0.66	8.95	30.06	60.99
25	92.17	6.58	0.95	50.00	49.44	0.56	11.35	30.57	58.08
30	90.89	8.24	0.87	53.15	46.36	0.48	13.81	30.68	55.51
35	89.81	9.39	0.80	55.57	44.00	0.43	16.15	30.61	53.24
40	88.90	10.35	0.75	57.46	42.15	0.39	18.29	30.46	51.24
45	88.13	11.16	0.70	58.96	40.67	0.36	20.23	30.29	49.48
50	87.49	11.85	0.67	60.18	39.48	0.34	21.96	30.12	47.93

Notes:
The numbers (per variable and horizon h) are rounded to two decimal places, and hence the sum may not be exactly equal to 100.00. For example, for $h=4$, 98.80% of the forecast error variance of market share can be attributed to variation in market share itself, while only 20.45% and 6.78% can be attributed to the same variable for distribution and price, respectively.

The most obvious feature of these graphs is that, even after 50 periods, some of the effects of shocks do not become zero. Because of this large persistence of the shocks, there may be unit roots in this VAR model.

Variance decomposition

A final structural application of VAR models is that we can investigate which part of the forecast error variance is caused by which variable. Consider again the bivariate model in (9.60) with its corresponding two-step ahead forecast errors

$$\begin{bmatrix} \varepsilon_{1,t+2} \\ \varepsilon_{2,t+2} \end{bmatrix} + \begin{bmatrix} \phi_{11} & \phi_{12} \\ \phi_{21} & \phi_{22} \end{bmatrix} \begin{bmatrix} \varepsilon_{1,t+1} \\ \varepsilon_{2,t+1} \end{bmatrix}. \tag{9.69}$$

For the first variable, and assuming that $\Sigma = \mathrm{diag}(\sigma_1^2, \sigma_2^2)$, the forecast error variance equals

$$\sigma_1^2(1 + \sigma_{11}^2) + \sigma_{12}^2 \sigma_2^2. \tag{9.70}$$

The first part of (9.70) can be seen to be due to the own error variance, while the $\sigma_{12}^2 \sigma_2^2$ part is due to the second variable. Expressed as percentages, we can thus examine the relative importance of the error variance of variable $y_{i,t}$ for forecasting $y_{j,t}$.

As an illustration, consider the decomposed error variances for the VAR(3) model for the marketing data in table 9.2.

The first (left-hand side) panel shows that forecast errors in market share are mainly due to uncertainty in market share itself. The second panel for distribution shows that these errors also become increasingly due to market share. This can be interpreted as that market share and distribution are very much related. Finally, the third panel shows that forecast errors in price are mainly due to price itself, although the other two variables are important as well.

Conclusion

In this chapter, I have reviewed some concepts in multivariate time series analysis. The key assumption underlying most of the previous discussion is that the data are stationary. For several business and economic time series, however, this assumption does not hold. It is therefore important to carefully analyze trend properties in multivariate systems. In the next chapter, I will focus on methods for such an analysis. A side effect of these methods is also that it allows us to reduce the number of parameters.

10 Common features

When univariate business and economic time series have one or more of the features discussed in chapters 4 to 8, that is, trends, seasonality, outliers, ARCH, or non-linearity, multivariate models for sets of these series can contain many unknown parameters. One of the purposes of this chapter is to discuss methods that are useful to reduce the number of parameters. Such reduction may increase efficiency of parameter estimates since redundant factors can be removed. Also, common features can be exploited for improved forecasting. In fact, when x_t and y_t have a trend, while $x_t - y_t$ has not, we may need only to model the trend in y_t in order to forecast x_t. Given that many economic time series are somehow related, common features can also be relevant from an economic point of view. For example, economic theory predicts that consumption and income should somehow have similar trends since in equilibrium these two quantities should be approximately equal.

As most recent developments focus on common trends and seasonality, I restrict the attention in this chapter mainly to these two features, although the major focus in this chapter will be on investigating the presence of common stochastic trends (also called cointegration). Since the appearance of Engle and Granger (1987), the issue of cointegration has attracted an enormous amount of attention. An important reason for this attention, additional to that of striving for parameter reduction, of using the appropriate statistical evaluation techniques, and of the opportunity for modeling trending economic variables which obey equilibrium relations, is that cointegration allows us to solve the problem of spurious regressions. In fact, when two time series variables are independently generated as

$$y_{1,t} = y_{1,t-1} + \varepsilon_{1,t}$$

$$y_{2,t} = y_{2,t-1} + \varepsilon_{2,t},$$

that is, as independent random walks, and we consider the static regression

$$y_{1,t} = \beta y_{2,t} + u_t,$$

the estimated β parameter will seem significant with a large absolute t-ratio and also the R^2 of this regression will be close to unity, see Granger and Newbold (1974) for simulation evidence and Phillips (1986) for a formal statistical treatment. Apparently, if account is not properly taken of stochastic trends, we tend to find spurious results. Cointegration analysis is now very useful.

In this chapter I consider cointegration in VAR models in section 10.2. Before that, I introduce some concepts and notation in section 10.1, where the analysis is restricted to a bivariate VAR(1) model. I limit attention to simple representations of cointegrated models. For a review of alternative representations, the reader can consult, for example, Hylleberg and Mizon (1989b). To save space, I will highlight only three often applied cointegration methods. These are the methods proposed in Engle and Granger (1987), Johansen (1991), and Boswijk (1994). It should be mentioned that the content of this chapter lacks much technical detail. The interested reader can find more rigorous treatments of cointegration in Banerjee *et al.* (1993), Hendry (1995), Johansen (1995), and Boswijk (1998). Finally, in section 10.3, I review some approaches to examine common seasonality and other features.

10.1   Some preliminaries for a bivariate time series

This section concerns the concept of common trends and its companion concept of cointegration. This chapter uses the three weekly observed series on market share, distribution and prices, the five Chinese production series, and the monthly pepper prices for illustration. Most technical issues are illustrated for a bivariate VAR(1) model.

Representation

Consider two time series $y_{1,t}$ and $y_{2,t}$, and assume that these can be described by the following bivariate model, which is (at first sight) slightly different from the standard VAR(1) model in chapter, that is,

$$y_{1,t} + \delta y_{2,t} = v_t, \qquad v_t = \mu_1^* + \rho_1 v_{t-1} + \varepsilon_{1,t}^*, \qquad 0 \leq \rho_1 \leq 1 \qquad (10.1)$$

$$y_{1,t} + \eta y_{2,t} = w_t, \qquad w_t = \mu_2^* + \rho_2 w_{t-1} + \varepsilon_{2,t}^*, \qquad 0 \leq \rho_2 \leq 1 \qquad (10.2)$$

where $\delta \neq \eta$. The latter restriction prevents δ and η from being equal to zero at the same time, although either δ or η may be equal to zero. The μ_1^* and μ_2^* are intercept terms, and it is assumed that $\varepsilon_{1,t}^*$ and $\varepsilon_{2,t}^*$ are standard white noise error processes, which are mutually independent at all lags. The two equations (10.1)–(10.2) reflect that two distinct linear combinations of $y_{1,t}$ and $y_{2,t}$ can be described by AR(1) models. The two equations will be written in a VAR(1) model later, but for the moment we stick to (10.1) and (10.2).

The interpretation of the two linear combinations depends on the values of ρ_1 and ρ_2. In this bivariate case, there are three relevant cases, each of which implies a different interpretation of (10.1) and/or (10.2). The first is that $\rho_1 = \rho_2 = 1$, which implies that any linear combination of $y_{1,t}$ and $y_{2,t}$ is a random walk variable (possibly with drift if μ_1^* or μ_2^* is unequal to zero). In turn, this implies that $y_{1,t}$ and $y_{2,t}$ are I (1) variables and hence are non-stationary themselves. In this first case, $y_{1,t}$ and $y_{2,t}$ individually have a stochastic trend since $\rho_1 = \rho_2 = 1$, but they do not have such a trend in common since no linear combination of $y_{1,t}$ and $y_{2,t}$ is stationary. These variables are now said not to be cointegrated.

The second case is that both $0 \leq \rho_i < 1$ for $i = 1, 2$. This implies that any linear combination of $y_{1,t}$ and $y_{2,t}$ is a stationary AR(1) process, and hence that $y_{1,t}$ and $y_{2,t}$ themselves are stationary variables. The individual series do not need to be differenced in order to obtain stationary time series.

The third and often quite interesting case is when $\rho_1 = 1$ and $0 \leq \rho_2 < 1$ (or when $\rho_2 = 1$ and $0 \leq \rho_1 < 1$). There is then one linear combination between $y_{1,t}$ and $y_{2,t}$ which is a stationary AR(1) process, while the other combination is a random walk (with drift). This implies that, although both $y_{1,t}$ and $y_{2,t}$ individually are I(1) time series, which can be seen by suitably subtracting (10.1) from (10.2), there is one linear combination which is stationary. In this case, the two time series are said to be cointegrated, see Engle and Granger (1987). When there is such a stationary relationship between $y_{1,t}$ and $y_{2,t}$, which individually have a stochastic trend, cointegration among $y_{1,t}$ and $y_{2,t}$ implies that these series also have a common stochastic trend (as will become clear below).

To illustrate matters, I give graphs of generated series in case $\delta = 0$, $\eta = -1$, $\mu_1^* = \mu_2^* = 0.5$, $\rho_1 = 1$ and $\rho_2 = 0.9$ in Figure 10.1. The graphs in this figure clearly show that both $y_{1,t}$ and $y_{2,t}$ are trending, but that the linear combination $y_{1,t} - y_{2,t}$ does not have a trend. In other words, $y_{1,t}$ and $y_{2,t}$ appear to have the stochastic trend (since only $\rho_1 = 1$) in common.

The model framework in (10.1)–(10.2) immediately suggests a simple method to test for cointegration between two variables, which is put forward in Engle and Granger (1987). It amounts to estimating δ or η in (10.1) or (10.2), and then testing whether either ρ_1 or ρ_2 is equal to 1 using the ADF regression outlined in chapter 4. More formally, we first perform the regression

$$y_{1,t} = \hat{\psi} + \hat{\lambda} y_{2,t} + \hat{u}_t, \tag{10.3}$$

then consider the auxiliary test regression

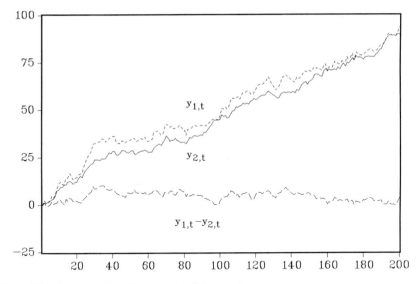

Figure 10.1 *Two simulated cointegrated time series*

$$\Delta_1 \hat{u}_t = \pi + \rho \hat{u}_{t-1} + \theta_1 \Delta_1 \hat{u}_{t-1} + \ldots + \theta_p \Delta_1 \hat{u}_{t-p} + v_t, \qquad (10.4)$$

and evaluate the t-test for the significance of ρ. When $\rho = 0$, $\hat{u}_t$ has a unit root and $y_{1,t} - \hat{\psi} - \hat{\lambda} y_{2,t}$ is a non-stationary time series. In that case, (10.3) does not reflect a stationary cointegration relationship. When $\rho < 0$, that is, when the $t(\hat{\rho})$ value is significantly negative, $y_{1,t}$ and $y_{2,t}$ are cointegrated. Notice that (10.1) and (10.2) imply that $p = 0$ in (10.4). In practice, the value of p can be selected using diagnostic tests or the AIC or SIC. Some critical values of this t-test for ρ are given in table 10.1 in case of m variables, with $m = 2, 3, 4$, and 5.

Asymptotic theory for the Engle–Granger method is presented in Phillips and Ouliaris (1990). Comparing the critical values in table 10.1 with those in table 4.1 for $m = 1$, it can be seen that the ADF critical values shift to the left in case of more than one variable. For small sample sizes, we can use the critical values tabulated in MacKinnon (1991). Finally, it should be mentioned that we may also evaluate a regression of $y_{2,t}$ on $y_{1,t}$ using the similar method. When the R^2 of these regressions is very close to 1, it may not matter much which variable is regressed on the other. When this is not the case, it becomes relevant which variable is chosen to be the regressand, see Ng and Perron (1997).

As an illustration of the Engle–Granger method, consider the bivariate pepper price series. The graphs of these series in figure 2.17 suggest a

Table 10.1. *Asymptotic critical values for the
Engle and Granger (1987) method*

(The test regression is (10.4) where the variable of
interest is $\hat{u}_t$, with $\hat{u}_t$ is the estimated residual series
from the regression of $y_{1,t}$ on $y_{2,t}$ to $y_{m,t}$, where both
regressions may include a constant and/or a trend.)

Number of variables	Significance level		
m	0.01	0.05	0.10
Regressions contain a constant			
2	− 3.96	− 3.37	− 3.07
3	− 4.31	− 3.77	− 3.45
4	− 4.73	− 4.11	− 3.83
5	− 5.07	− 4.45	− 4.16
Regressions contain a constant and a trend			
2	− 4.36	− 3.80	− 3.52
3	− 4.65	− 4.16	− 3.84
4	− 5.04	− 4.49	− 4.20
5	− 5.58	− 5.03	− 4.73

Source: Phillips and Ouliaris (1990).

common pattern, that is, perhaps a linear combination is stationary. I
analyze $y_{1,t} = \log$ (white pepper price) and $y_{2,t} = \log$ (black pepper price) for
the sample 1973.10–1992.12, and leave 1993.01–1996.04 for forecast
evaluation as an exercise for the reader. The first regression result is

$$y_{1,t} = 0.288 + 1.000 y_{2,t}, \quad R^2 = 0.921 \qquad (10.5)$$
$$(0.146) \ (0.019)$$

where the estimated standard errors are given in parentheses. Since the
series have a unit root, the t-ratios for the parameters in (10.5) cannot be
compared with the standard normal tables. The ADF test result for the $\hat{u}_t$
from (10.5), where p can be set equal to 0, is − 3.829. Comparing this with
the 5 percent critical value of − 3.37 in table 10.1 shows that $y_{1,t} - 1.000 y_{2,t}$
seems a stationary variable. The reversed regression results in

$$y_{2,t} = 0.332 + 0.921 y_{1,t}, \quad R^2 = 0.921 \qquad (10.6)$$
$$(0.140) \ (0.018)$$

with an ADF value of − 3.932 for $p = 0$. Combining (10.6) with (10.5) we
can be reasonably confident that the difference between the logs of the two

pepper prices is stationary, while they individually have the stochastic trend feature.

The Engle–Granger method is useful when we analyse two time series, but it may become less useful for more than two time series. The number of possible cointegration relations increases with the number of time series, and this implies an increasing ambiguity in determining the empirical validity of models like (10.1) and (10.2). This suggests that multivariate methods may be more useful.

Vector autoregressive representation

The expressions in (10.1)–(10.2) can be summarized as

$$
\begin{bmatrix} 1 & \delta \\ 1 & \eta \end{bmatrix} \begin{bmatrix} y_{1,t} \\ y_{2,t} \end{bmatrix} = \begin{bmatrix} \mu_1^* \\ \mu_2^* \end{bmatrix} + \begin{bmatrix} \rho_1 & \delta\rho_1 \\ \rho_2 & \eta\rho_2 \end{bmatrix} \begin{bmatrix} y_{1,t-1} \\ y_{2,t-1} \end{bmatrix} + \begin{bmatrix} \varepsilon_{1,t}^* \\ \varepsilon_{2,t}^* \end{bmatrix}. \tag{10.7}
$$

Multiplying both sides of (10.7) with the inverse of the left-hand side matrix and subtracting the one period lagged Y_{t-1} from both sides gives

$$
\Delta_1 Y_t = \mu + \Pi Y_{t-1} + e_t \tag{10.8}
$$

with $e_t = (\varepsilon_{1,t}, \varepsilon_{2,t})$, where the two $\varepsilon_{1,t}$ and $\varepsilon_{2,t}$ series are functions of $\varepsilon_{1,t}^*$, $\varepsilon_{2,t}^*$ and η and δ, and with

$$
\mu = \begin{bmatrix} (\eta\mu_1^* - \delta\mu_2^*)/(\eta - \delta) \\ (\mu_2^* - \mu_1^*)/(\eta - \delta) \end{bmatrix} \text{ and} \tag{10.9}
$$

$$
\Pi = \begin{bmatrix} (\eta\rho_1 - \delta\rho_2 - \eta + \delta)/(\eta - \delta) & \eta\delta(\rho_1 - \rho_2)/(\eta - \delta) \\ (\rho_2 - \rho_1)/(\eta - \delta) & (\eta\rho_2 - \delta\rho_1 - \eta + \delta)/(\eta - \delta) \end{bmatrix}. \tag{10.10}
$$

When $0 \leq \rho_i < 1$ for $i = 1,2$ (and given that not η and δ both equal 0), the Π matrix in (10.10) has full rank 2. On the other hand, when $\rho_1 = \rho_2 = 1$, it can easily be observed that all elements of Π have value zero, and hence that the rank of Π is equal to 0.

The interesting intermediate case is now the cointegration case. For example, when $\rho_1 = 1$ and $0 \leq \rho_2 < 1$, the Π matrix can be written as

$$
\Pi = \alpha\beta', \tag{10.11}
$$

with

$$
\alpha = \begin{bmatrix} \delta(1 - \rho_2)/(\eta - \delta) \\ -(1 - \rho_2)/(\eta - \delta) \end{bmatrix} \text{ and } \beta = \begin{bmatrix} 1 \\ \eta \end{bmatrix}. \tag{10.12}
$$

The (2×2) matrix Π equals the outer product of two (2×1) matrices. This leads to a reduction from 4 to 3 parameters in Π. In general, cointegration reduces the number of parameters in a VAR model. Notice however that the decomposition in (10.12) is not unique, and that we can find other non-linear parameter restrictions on Π which also correspond with cointegration. In this cointegration case, the characteristic polynomial of the VAR(1) model in (10.8), that is, $|I_m - (\Pi + I_m)z| = 0$, can be shown to yield one solution on the unit circle. The implied univariate models for $y_{1,t}$ and $y_{2,t}$ are ARIMA(1,1,1). Hence, both series have a unit root, while the vector series only has a single unit root. In other words, when $y_{1,t}$ and $y_{2,t}$ are co-integrated, they have a common unit root, that is, a common stochastic trend.

The parameter vector β in (10.11) is said to contain the cointegration parameters, that is, the parameters that indicate an equilibrium relation between $y_{1,t}$ and $y_{2,t}$. In this bivariate example, the equilibrium (or long-run) relation is $y_{1,t} + \eta y_{2,t}$. The (2×1) parameter matrix α in (10.11) contains the two so-called adjustment parameters. These α_1 and α_2, say, reflect the speed of adjustment toward equilibrium, which is most easily seen from writing the two equations in (10.8) with (10.11) as

$$\Delta_1 y_{1,t} = \mu_1 + \alpha_1(y_{1,t-1} + \eta y_{2,t-1}) + \varepsilon_{1,t} \tag{10.13}$$

$$\Delta_1 y_{2,t} = \mu_2 + \alpha_2(y_{1,t-1} + \eta y_{2,t-1}) + \varepsilon_{2,t}, \tag{10.14}$$

where each equation is called an error correction model [ECM]. Together, this system is called a vector error correction model [VECM].

Impact of the constant μ

With the cointegration restriction that $\rho_1 = 1$ and $0 \leq \rho_2 < 1$, the VAR(1) model in (10.8) can be written as

$$\Delta_1 Y_t = \mu + \alpha \beta' Y_{t-1} + e_t. \tag{10.15}$$

In Johansen (1995, p. 40) it is shown that this model can be solved as

$$Y_t = Y_0^* + C\mu t + C\sum_{i=1}^{t} e_i + X_t, \tag{10.16}$$

where X_t is a stationary bivariate time series, and where C is defined by

$$C = \beta_\perp(\alpha_\perp' \beta_\perp)^{-1}\alpha_\perp', \tag{10.17}$$

and $\alpha_\perp$ and $\beta_\perp$ are defined by

$$\alpha_\perp'\alpha = 0 \quad \text{and} \quad \beta_\perp'\beta = 0. \tag{10.18}$$

When $m = 1$, $C = 1$, and equation (10.16) becomes (4.12) for a univariate random walk with drift series. Notice that in our bivariate example $\alpha_\perp$ and $\beta_\perp$ are both (2×1) matrices.

The X_t series is a stationary series. The (2×1) vector series $\sum_{i=1}^{t} e_i$ in (10.16) contains the accumulated sums of the error series $\varepsilon_{1,t}$ and $\varepsilon_{2,t}$. Since cointegration amongst two time series implies the presence of a common trend, (10.16) suggests that $z_t = \alpha_\perp' \sum_{i=1}^{t} e_i$ is the common trend, see Johansen (1995). Notice that in our bivariate cointegrated example, with one common stochastic trend, z_t is a univariate time series. Multiplying both sides of (10.16) with $\alpha_\perp'$ results in

$$\alpha_\perp' Y_t = \alpha_\perp' Y_0^* + \alpha_\perp' \mu t + \alpha_\perp' \sum_{i=1}^{t} e_i + \alpha_\perp' X_t, \tag{10.19}$$

and hence $\alpha_\perp' Y_t$ has a stochastic trend component. For our bivariate example in (10.1)–(10.2), and given (10.12), it is easy to see that

$$\alpha_\perp' Y_t = (1 \; \delta) \begin{bmatrix} y_{1,t} \\ y_{2,t} \end{bmatrix} = y_{1,t} + \delta y_{2,t} = v_t, \tag{10.20}$$

where v_t is defined in (10.1). With $\rho_1 = 1$, the v_t series is a random walk with drift indeed. Equation (10.19) shows that $\alpha_\perp' Y_t$ has a deterministic trend component $\alpha_\perp' \mu t$, where in our example the parameter $\alpha_\perp' \mu$ equals

$$\begin{aligned} \alpha_\perp' \mu &= (\eta - \delta)^{-1} [(\eta \mu_1^* - \delta \mu_2^*) + \delta(-\mu_1^* + \delta \mu_2^*)] \\ &= \mu_1^*. \end{aligned} \tag{10.21}$$

Hence, when $\alpha_\perp' \mu = 0$, that is, when $\mu_1^* = 0$, the common stochastic trend in $y_{1,t}$ and $y_{2,t}$ does not have a deterministic trend component. In case $\mu_1^* = 0$ in (10.1), while $\rho_1 = 1$ and $0 \leq \rho_2 < 1$, the ECM equations in (10.13) and (10.14) become

$$\Delta_1 y_{1,t} = \alpha_1 [-\mu_2^*/(1 - \rho_2) + y_{1,t-1} + \eta y_{2,t-1}] + \varepsilon_{1,t} \tag{10.22}$$

$$\Delta_1 y_{2,t} = \alpha_2 [-\mu_2^*/(1 - \rho_2) + y_{1,t-1} + \eta y_{2,t-1}] + \varepsilon_{2,t}. \tag{10.23}$$

The constant terms in the equilibrium relations are restricted to be equal. These two equations show that the error correction variable $y_{1,t} + \eta y_{2,t}$ has mean $\mu_2^*/(1 - \rho_2)$, and this could already be seen from (10.2). If we were to generate data from (10.22) and (10.23), we would observe that $y_{1,t}$ and $y_{2,t}$ display random walk behavior, although there does not seem to be a clear trend in the data.

In sum, there are three relevant cases concerning the intercept terms for a cointegrated bivariate system based on (10.1)–(10.2). The first is that both μ_1^* and μ_2^* are equal to zero. The second is that the intercepts are both unrestricted, that is, the common stochastic trend has a deterministic trend component. The third case is the case where the intercept terms are restricted such that the underlying common stochastic trend does not display a trending pattern and hence neither do the individual time series.

When the v_t and w_t series in (10.1) and (10.2) are generated by

$$v_t = \mu_1^* + \tau_1^* t + \rho_1 v_{t-1} + \varepsilon_{1,t}^*, \qquad 0 \leq \rho_1 \leq 1 \tag{10.24}$$

$$w_t = \mu_2^* + \tau_2^* t + \rho_2 w_{t-1} + \varepsilon_{2,t}^*, \qquad 0 \leq \rho_2 \leq 1, \tag{10.25}$$

the common stochastic trend displays quadratic trend behavior when the τ_1^* and τ_2^* parameters are unequal to zero. When the data do not have quadratic trend-like properties, we may want to restrict the parameters τ_1^* and τ_2^* to zero. In that case, the term $[-\tau_2^*/(1-\rho_2)]t$ should enter the expression in parentheses in equations (10.22) and (10.23). I will return to these five cases concerning intercepts and trends when reviewing the cointegration test statistics based on VAR models.

10.2   Common trends and cointegration

Consider again the VAR(p) model

$$Y_t = \mu + \Phi_1 Y_{t-1} + \Phi_2 Y_{t-2} + \ldots + \Phi_p Y_{t-p} + e_t, \tag{10.26}$$

for an $(m \times 1)$ time series Y_t, containing $y_{1,t}$ through $y_{m,t}$. Similar to (10.8), it is convenient to write (10.26) in error correction format, that is

$$\Delta_1 Y_t = \mu + \Gamma_1 \Delta_1 Y_{t-1} + \ldots + \Gamma_{p-1} \Delta_1 Y_{t-p+1} + \Pi Y_{t-p} + e_t, \tag{10.27}$$

where

$$\Gamma_i = (\Phi_1 + \Phi_2 + \ldots + \Phi_i) - I_m, \text{ for } i = 1,2,\ldots,p-1, \tag{10.28}$$

$$\Pi = \Phi_1 + \Phi_2 + \ldots + \Phi_p - I_m, \tag{10.29}$$

where Π contains the information on possible cointegrating relations between the m elements of Y_t. Notice that when $\Sigma_{i=1}^p \Phi_p$ has eigenvalues close to unity, as we investigated for two examples in the previous chapter, Π has eigenvalues close to 0. The latter implies that the matrix Π is close to rank deficiency, and hence there may be cointegration. A statistical method is now needed to investigate whether the rank of Π differs from zero or from m. An elegant approach is proposed in Johansen (1988), see also Johansen (1991, 1995). The Johansen method essentially amounts to a multivariate extension of the univariate ADF method, which can also be seen from (10.27). In fact, for the VAR(p) model with autoregressive polynomial $\Phi_p(L)$, one can write

$$\Phi_p(L) = -\Pi L^p - \Gamma_{p-1}(L)(1-L), \tag{10.30}$$

where Π is defined in (10.29) and where $\Gamma_{p-1}(L)$ is a $(p-1)$th order matrix polynomial. With $m=1$, (10.30) forms the basis for the univariate ADF model.

In the VAR model in (10.27), there are three interesting cases. First, the matrix Π can be the zero-matrix, which implies that the rank of Π equals 0. Second, the matrix Π can have full rank m. Third, matrix Π has rank deficiency, that is, $0 < \text{rank}\Pi < m$, and it can be decomposed as $\Pi = \alpha\beta'$, where α and β are $(m \times r)$ parameter matrices. In the bivariate example above we had $m = 2$ and $r = 1$. The matrix β contains the r cointegrating relations, while the matrix α contains the adjustment parameters. Again, these α and β matrices are not unique, so it is more accurate to say that the columns of β span the space with cointegration vectors. When there are r cointegration relations, there are $m - r$ common stochastic trends, see Engle and Granger (1987) and Johansen (1991).

The Johansen maximum likelihood cointegration testing method aims to test the rank of the matrix Π in (10.27) using the reduced rank regression technique based on canonical correlations. The idea for using this technique (for a bivariate example) is that we want to find a particular linear combination $y_{1,t} + \eta y_{2,t}$ which has the largest partial correlation with any linear combination of the stationary variables $\Delta_1 y_{1,t}$ and $\Delta_1 y_{2,t}$. This amounts to the following computations for the case where the intercepts in the m equations are unrestricted. First, we regress $\Delta_1 Y_t$ and Y_{t-p} on a constant and the lagged $\Delta_1 Y_{t-1}$ through $\Delta_1 Y_{t-p+1}$ variables. This results in $(m \times 1)$ vectors of residuals r_{0t} and r_{1t} and the $(m \times m)$ residual product matrices

$$S_{ij} = (1/n)\sum_{t=1}^{n} r_{it} r_{jt}', \quad \text{for } i,j = 0,1 \tag{10.31}$$

respectively. When we wish to restrict the constants, that is, we wish not to allow for deterministic trend-like patterns, see (10.22)–(10.23), we should also regress a unity vector on the $\Delta_1 Y_{t-1}$ to $\Delta_1 Y_{t-p+1}$ variables. Adding these covariances to the rows and columns of (10.21) results in S_{ij} matrices of dimension $(m+1) \times (m+1)$. In the next two cases concerning possible quadratic trends, see (10.24)–(10.25), we should perform similar calculations with either a trend variable on the right-hand side or on the left-hand side of the auxiliary regressions. The next step is to solve the eigenvalue problem

$$|\lambda S_{11} - S_{10}S_{00}^{-1}S_{01}| = 0 \tag{10.32}$$

which gives the eigenvalues $\hat{\lambda}_1 \geq \ldots \geq \hat{\lambda}_m$ and the corresponding eigenvectors $\hat{\beta}_1$ through $\hat{\beta}_m$. A test for the rank of Π can now be performed by testing how many eigenvalues λ_i equal unity. The first test statistic for the resulting number of cointegration relations proposed in Johansen (1988) is the so-called *Trace* test statistic

$$Trace = -n \sum_{i=r+1}^{m} \log(1 - \hat{\lambda}_i). \tag{10.33}$$

The null hypothesis for this *Trace* test is that there are at most r cointegration relations. We begin with testing whether there is no cointegration ($r=0$) versus at most 1 such relation. If this is rejected, we test whether there is at most one cointegration relation versus two. When finally the null hypothesis of at most $r=m-1$ cointegration relations is rejected, we find that the Y_t vector series is stationary. Often we obtain that the null hypothesis of at most $r-1$ cointegrating relations is rejected, while the hypothesis of at most r such relations is not. Another useful test is given by testing the significance of the estimated eigenvalues themselves, or

$$\lambda_{max} = -n\log(1 - \hat{\lambda}_r), \tag{10.34}$$

which can be used to test the null hypothesis of $r-1$ against r cointegration relations. Similar to the univariate ADF test for unit roots, critical values for the *Trace* and λ_{max} tests have to be simulated. Asymptotic distributions of the test statistics are summarized in Johansen (1995). Critical values are given in Johansen (1995), Boswijk (1998), and Osterwald-Lenum (1992). Some of these critical values are given in table 10.2. Since the Johansen method is very often used in practice, I provide critical values for all five cases concerning constants and trends.

To illustrate the practical implementation of the Johansen method, consider the five Chinese production series, where $y_{1,t}$ to $y_{5,t}$ concern the logged output in agriculture, industry, construction, transportation, and commerce, respectively. In the previous chapter we found that a VAR(2) model with intercepts describes these data well. Since the individual series clearly show trending patterns (see figure 2.1), it seems most appropriate to consider the case with unrestricted constants (case II in table 10.2) to allow for one or more common stochastic trends with deterministic trend components. The estimates of the eigenvalues and of the two test statistics are given in table 10.3.

The individual estimates of the eigenvalues do not seem large enough to make the λ_{max} test find more than one cointegration relation, that is, only 36.834 is significant at the 5 percent level. Using the *Trace* tests, however, we find that the null hypotheses of 0 versus 1 (1 percent significance), 1 versus 2 (5 percent) and 2 versus 3 (10 percent) seem to be rejected. Hence, the trace tests suggest that there may be three cointegrating relations among the five sectoral output series. The estimates of the relevant parameters are

$$\hat{\beta}' = \begin{bmatrix} \hat{\beta}_1' \\ \hat{\beta}_2' \\ \hat{\beta}_3' \end{bmatrix} = \begin{bmatrix} 0.547 & -0.120 & -0.781 & 1.000 & -0.273 \\ -0.618 & 0.506 & -0.370 & -0.894 & 1.000 \\ 1.000 & 0.045 & -0.189 & -0.099 & -0.230 \end{bmatrix}. \tag{10.35}$$

Table 10.2. *Asymptotic critical values for the Johansen cointegration method*

	Trace test statistic				λ_{max} test statistic			
$m-r$	0.20	0.10	0.05	0.01	0.20	0.10	0.05	0.01
I The regression model contains no constants and no deterministic trends								
1	1.82	2.86	3.84	6.51	1.82	2.86	3.84	6.51
2	8.45	10.47	12.53	16.31	7.58	9.52	11.44	15.69
3	18.83	21.63	24.31	29.75	13.31	15.59	17.89	22.99
4	33.16	36.58	39.89	45.58	18.97	21.58	23.80	28.82
5	51.13	55.44	59.46	66.52	24.83	27.62	30.04	35.17
II The regression model contains constants but no deterministic trends, while the data display linear trending patterns (the parameters for the intercepts are unrestricted)								
1	4.82	6.50	8.18	11.65	4.82	6.50	8.18	11.65
2	13.21	15.66	17.95	23.52	10.77	12.91	14.90	19.19
3	25.39	28.71	31.52	37.22	16.51	18.90	21.07	25.75
4	41.65	45.23	48.28	55.43	22.16	24.78	27.14	32.14
5	61.75	66.49	70.60	78.87	28.09	30.84	33.32	38.78
III The regression model contains constants but no deterministic trends, while the data do not display linear trending patterns (the parameters for the intercepts are restricted)								
1	5.91	7.52	9.24	12.97	5.91	7.52	9.24	12.97
2	15.25	17.85	19.96	24.60	11.54	13.75	15.67	20.20
3	28.75	32.00	34.91	41.07	17.40	19.77	22.00	26.81
4	45.65	49.65	53.12	60.16	22.95	25.56	28.14	33.24
5	66.91	71.86	76.07	84.45	28.76	31.66	34.40	39.79
IV The regression model contains constants and deterministic trends, while the data display quadratic trending patterns (the parameters for the trends are unrestricted)								
1	7.78	9.66	11.55	15.78	7.78	9.66	11.55	15.78
2	18.30	20.87	23.37	28.80	13.76	15.99	18.04	22.41
3	32.60	36.03	39.04	45.37	19.42	22.06	23.97	28.65
4	50.49	54.79	58.57	65.73	25.28	27.76	30.31	35.60
5	72.48	77.77	82.18	90.83	30.89	33.96	36.65	42.05
V The regression model contains constants and deterministic trends, while the data have linear trends but no quadratic trending patterns (the parameters for the trends are restricted)								
1	8.65	10.49	12.25	16.26	8.65	10.49	12.25	16.26
2	20.19	22.76	25.32	30.45	14.70	16.85	18.96	23.65
3	35.56	39.06	42.44	48.45	20.45	23.11	25.54	30.34
4	54.80	59.14	62.99	70.05	26.30	29.12	31.46	36.65
5	77.83	83.20	87.31	96.58	31.72	34.75	37.52	42.36

Notes:
The statistics are given in (10.33) and (10.34). m denotes the number of time series in Y_t, r is the number of cointegration relationships.
Sources: Osterwald-Lenum (1992), Johansen (1995) and Boswijk (1998).

Table 10.3. *Testing for cointegration among the five Chinese production indices (in logs) based on a VAR(2) model with unrestricted constants (case II in table 10.2)*

λ	λ_{max}	Trace
0.651	36.834**	85.359***
0.431	19.723	48.525**
0.370	16.166	28.802*
0.234	9.312	12.636
0.091	3.324	3.324

Notes:
The number of effective observations n is 35 (1954–1988).
*** Significant at the 1% level.
** Significant at the 5% level.
* Significant at the 10% level.

In Figure 10.2, I give the graphs for $\ddot{\beta}_1' Y_t$ (CO1) to $\ddot{\beta}_3' Y_t$ (CO3), and it seems that these three series are not trending and do not display random walk like patterns.

The visual evidence in this figure 10.2 is confirmed by the estimated ACFs of the three cointegrating relations CO1 to CO3, which are given in columns 2 to 4 of table 10.4. The estimated ACF of CO1 looks very much like that of a white noise series, while the other two EACFs display only a few large absolute autocorrelations. Hence, the three cointegration relations found using the Johansen method seem stationary indeed.

For the marketing data, the $y_{1,t}$ to $y_{3,t}$ series concern the data on market shares, distribution, and prices (not in logs) for weeks 11 to 113. The data prior to week 11 are used as starting values, so we have 103 effective observations. In the previous chapter we found that a VAR(3) model describes the three level series most adequately. The Johansen method, based on a VAR(3) model with unrestricted constants, results in $\hat{\lambda}_1 = 0.153$, $\hat{\lambda}_2 = 0.058$, and $\hat{\lambda}_3 = 0.001$. This gives λ_{max} test statistics with values 17.079, 6.100, and 0.103 and *Trace* test statistics with values 23.282, 6.203, and 0.103, respectively. Comparing these values with the relevant critical values

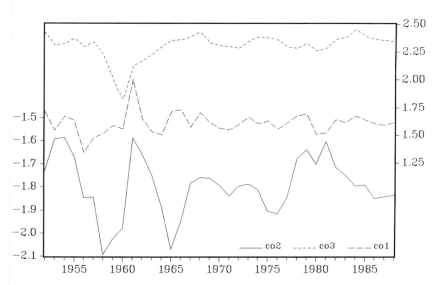

Figure 10.2 *Three cointegration relations between the five Chinese production series*

(case II) in table 10.2 shows that only the λ_{max} value of 17.079 is significant at the 20 percent level. Hence, there is only weak evidence of cointegration among our three marketing variables. After rescaling, the cointegration relation can be written as

$$market\ share_t = 6.215 distribution_t - 0.323 price_t. \tag{10.36}$$

This equilibrium relation implies that, in the long run, market share and distribution are correlated positively, and that market share and prices have negative correlation. The graphs of the impulse response functions in the previous chapter suggested similar inference. This CO1 relation (as well as two other graphs to be explained below) is given in figure 10.3 and it seems to be stationary indeed.

The estimated autocorrelation function of this CO1 variable for the marketing series in the fifth column of table 10.4 has only two large autocorrelations, and hence the visual evidence in figure 10.3 that (10.36) amounts to a stable relationship seems confirmed.

The VAR(3) model for the three marketing series m_t, d_t, and p_t can now be written in VECM format including the variables $\Delta_1 z_{t-1}$, $\Delta_1 z_{t-2}$ for $z = m,d,p$ and $m_t - 6.215 d_t + 0.323 p_t$, which is the cointegrating variable. Since all these variables do not have a unit root, standard t-tests can now be used to delete insignificant variables in order to retain only the relevant ones in the final simplified VECM. The parameters in this

Table 10.4. *Estimated autocorrelation functions of linear combinations of the five Chinese production series and the three marketing series*

	Cointegration relations				Stochastic trends			
	China			Marketing	China		Marketing	
Lag	CO1	CO2	CO3	CO1	ST2	ST1	ST2	ST1
1	0.088	0.596*	0.718*	0.375*	0.916*	0.908*	0.696*	0.914*
2	−0.177	0.104	0.419*	0.196*	0.807*	0.829*	0.585*	0.880*
3	−0.177	−0.358*	0.196	0.140	0.698*	0.758*	0.590*	0.860*
4	−0.062	−0.435*	−0.008	0.034	0.580*	0.682*	0.514*	0.830*
5	−0.194	−0.281	−0.144	0.157	0.461*	0.604*	0.459*	0.804*
6	−0.021	−0.002	−0.178	0.077	0.343*	0.534*	0.334*	0.753*
7	0.270	0.152	−0.223	0.071	0.238	0.465*	0.239*	0.728*
8	−0.125	0.151	−0.236	0.060	0.152	0.394*	0.256*	0.702*
9	−0.078	0.076	−0.077	0.118	0.087	0.320*	0.180	0.679*
10	−0.116	−0.001	−0.005	0.007	0.025	0.244	0.135	0.653*

Notes:
CO denotes the estimated cointegration relation, and ST denotes the estimated common stochastic trend.
* Significant at the 5% significance level when $\pm 2n^{-\frac{1}{2}}$ is taken as the 95% confidence interval, with $n = 37$ (1952–1988) for the Chinese data and $n = 103$ for the marketing data.

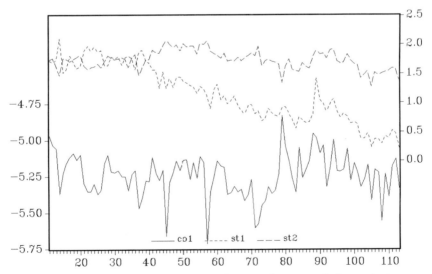

Figure 10.3 *One cointegration relation and two stochastic trends for marketing data*

final model should then be estimated using SUR. The estimation results are

$$
\begin{bmatrix}
\begin{matrix} 1+0.448L+0.408L^2 \\ (0.084) \quad (0.083) \end{matrix} & 0 & 0 \\[1em]
0 & \begin{matrix} 1+0.480L+0.323L^2 \\ (0.092) \quad (0.092) \end{matrix} & 0 \\[1em]
0 & \begin{matrix} -5.856L-8.069L^2 \\ (2.503) \quad (2.597) \end{matrix} & \begin{matrix} 1+0.565L+0.393L^2 \\ (0.094) \quad (0.104) \end{matrix}
\end{bmatrix}
\begin{bmatrix} \Delta_1 m_t \\ \Delta_1 d_t \\ \Delta_1 p_t \end{bmatrix}
$$

$$(10.37)$$

$$
=\begin{bmatrix} -0.045 \\ (0.039) \\ -0.565 \\ (0.293) \\ 32.254 \\ (9.861) \end{bmatrix}
+\begin{bmatrix} 0 \\ \\ 0.017 \\ (0.009) \\ -0.992 \\ (0.304) \end{bmatrix}
(m_{t-3}-6.215d_{t-3}+0.323p_{t-3})+
\begin{bmatrix} \hat{\varepsilon}_{1,t} \\ \\ \hat{\varepsilon}_{2,t} \\ \\ \hat{\varepsilon}_{3,t} \end{bmatrix},
$$

where standard errors are given in parentheses. The unrestricted VAR(3) model with 27 parameters can thus be simplified to a VECM with only 15 parameters. It is clear that error correction only occurs for distribution and prices, that is, deviations from the equilibrium relation in (10.36) have an effect on future distribution and prices. Additionally, since market share seems to be explained only by past market share, this variable is called weakly exogenous, see Johansen (1992) and Boswijk (1998).

Testing hypotheses

Sometimes economic theory or other motivations suggest that the cointegration relations have a specific form. For example, in the case of the pepper prices the only reasonable cointegrating relationship between these substitution goods is governed by the $(1,-1)$ restriction. Hence, in case cointegrating relations are found, we may wish to test hypotheses on these cointegrating vectors. To test for linear restrictions on the cointegrating vectors in β, it is useful to define the $(m \times r)$ matrix H, which reduces β to the $(r \times r)$ parameter matrix φ, or $\beta = H\varphi$. For example, for the Chinese data, where the output in the construction, transportation, and commerce sectors seem to display similar patterns (see Figure 2.1) and the agricultural output grows with about half the growth rate, we can test whether the cointegrating space of three cointegrating vectors (as found in table 10.3) can be spanned by

$$H = \begin{bmatrix} 1 & 0 & 0 \\ 0 & 0 & 0 \\ -0.5 & 1 & 0 \\ 0 & -1 & 1 \\ 0 & 0 & -1 \end{bmatrix}. \tag{10.38}$$

To test these parameter restrictions, we compare the estimated eigenvalues $\hat{\xi}_i$, $i=1,\ldots,r$, from

$$|\xi H' S_{11} H - H' S_{10} S_{00}^{-1} S_{01} H| = 0 \tag{10.39}$$

with the $\hat{\lambda}_i$ from (10.32), $i=1,\ldots,r$, via the test statistic

$$Q = n \sum_{i=1}^{r} \log\{(1-\hat{\xi}_i)/(1-\hat{\lambda}_i)\}, \tag{10.40}$$

see Johansen (1995). Under the null hypothesis, and conditional on the correct value of r, the test statistic Q asymptotically follows the $\chi^2(r(m-q))$ distribution. Notice that the matrix H can also contain unit vectors. In that case we investigate whether one or more of the univariate time series variables are stationary, and as such we can circumvent the problem of prior testing for unit roots in univariate time series.

Imposing the restrictions in (10.38) on the three cointegrating relations for the Chinese data (using the Matlab package) results in $\hat{\xi}_1 = 0.582$, $\hat{\xi}_2 = 0.368$, and $\hat{\xi}_3 = 0.307$. The Q statistic obtains a value of 13.323, which should be evaluated against the fractiles of the $\chi^2(6)$ distribution. The relevant 5 percent critical value is then 12.6, while that at 2.5 percent is equal to 14.4. Hence, the restrictions in (10.38) seem to amount to plausible restrictions and these imply that in the long run the agricultural sector in China will be outgrown by the other sectors.

Stochastic trends

When there are r cointegration relations among m variables, there are $m-r$ common stochastic trends in the system. Stock and Watson (1989) exploit this feature to propose an alternative method to investigate cointegration by testing for the number of stochastic trends. For some empirical purposes it is useful not only to obtain estimates of the cointegration relations, but also to obtain insight into the driving non-stationary forces. For example, Veenstra and Franses (1997) show that a set of ocean dry bulk freight rates seem to be cointegrated with cointegrating rank $m-1$, but that this

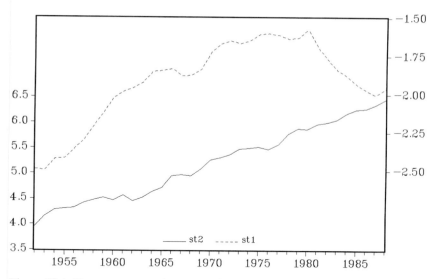

Figure 10.4 *Two common stochastic trends in the five Chinese production series*

overwhelming long-run correspondence between the freight rates cannot be exploited for forecasting since the driving common stochastic trend dominates the variation in the data.

As expected, there are several methods to estimate the stochastic trends, but I limit attention to the method proposed in Gonzalo and Granger (1995), which explicitly exploits the duality of cointegration and stochastic trends, see also Johansen (1995). The canonical correlation method, used to find those combinations of the elements of Y_t which have maximum partial correlation with the stationary variables, can also be reversed to find those combinations which have minimum correlation. Gonzalo and Granger (1995) show that the relevant eigenvalue problem then becomes

$$|\lambda S_{00} - S_{01} S_{11}^{-1} S_{10}| = 0, \tag{10.41}$$

which is the dual version of (10.32), and where the S_{ij} matrices are defined by (10.31). The solutions to (10.41) are the same eigenvalues $\hat{\lambda}_1$ to $\hat{\lambda}_m$ as before, but now we obtain eigenvectors $\hat{w}_1, \ldots, \hat{w}_m$, which are different from those of the cointegration approach. Gonzalo and Granger (1995) show/ that in case of r cointegration relations, stochastic trend variables can be constructed as $\hat{w}_{r+1}' Y_t$ to $\hat{w}_m' Y_t$.

An application of this method to the five Chinese production series with $r = 3$ gives that

$$\hat{w}_4' = [-0.285, 1.000, -0.085, -0.677, -0.493]$$

$$\hat{w}_5' = [\quad 0.356, \ 1.000, \ -0.357, \ -0.649, \quad 0.508].$$

Graphs of $\hat{w}_4' \, Y_t$ and $\hat{w}_5' \, Y_t$ (labelled as ST2 and ST1) are given in figure 10.4.

Both variables appear to be trending. The estimated ACFs in table 10.4, columns 6 and 7, show that shocks are persistent since the ACF values do not die out rapidly. The same applies to the three marketing series, for which I find two common stochastic trends, which are depicted in figure 10.3 as ST1 and ST2. Their estimated autocorrelations appear in the last two columns of table 10.4, and again these support the earlier test results that there is only one cointegration relation between market share, distribution, and prices.

Testing for cointegration in a conditional ECM

The third and final method to test for cointegration, discussed here, is the method proposed in Boswijk (1994). This method is useful in case we have a system of variables but there is a major interest in a single equation. For example, in a system relating money, income, and prices, we may be interested only in the money equation. The method makes use of the fact that cointegration implies error correction. Hence, a test for the significance of error correction variables can be used to examine if there is cointegration. A second aspect of this method is the assumption that the variables $y_{2,t}$ through $y_{m,t}$ are so-called weakly exogenous for the cointegration parameters of interest, see Engle, Hendry, and Richard (1983) for a discussion of various exogeneity concepts.

Consider again the bivariate ECM in (10.13)–(10.14). Johansen (1992) shows that if $\alpha_1 = 0$, the $y_{1,t}$ process is weakly exogenous for η. If this holds true, we can perform cointegration analysis in a conditional ECM [CECM] for $y_{2,t}$. In our bivariate example, the restriction $\alpha_1 = 0$ implies that $\delta = 0$, that is, that (10.1) reduces to $y_{1,t} = \mu_1^* + y_{1,t-1} + \varepsilon_{1,t}^*$, and that the CECM for $y_{2,t}$ can be written as

$$\Delta_1 y_{2,t} = \mu_2 + \alpha_2 y_{1,t-1} + \psi y_{2,t-1} + \nu \Delta_1 y_{1,t} + \varepsilon_{2,t}, \tag{10.42}$$

where $\psi = \alpha_2 \eta$, see Boswijk (1994) for details. The parameters in this model can be estimated using OLS, and the significance of the error correction variable can be evaluated using a joint Wald test for $\alpha_2 = 0$ and $\psi = 0$. Asymptotic theory for this Wald test is provided in Boswijk (1994). Critical values are given in table 10.5.

When the null hypothesis of no cointegration (i.e., no error correction) is rejected, we can apply NLS to estimate η. A test for the weak exogeneity of $y_{1,t}$ can be performed by regressing $\Delta_1 y_{1,t}$ on the estimated error correction term obtained in the first round, and on lagged $\Delta_1 y_{1,t}$ and $\Delta_1 y_{2,t}$ variables,

Table 10.5. *Asymptotic critical values for the cointegration test based on a conditional error correction model*

Number of variables	Significance level			
m	0.20	0.10	0.05	0.01
Regression contains no constant and no trend				
2	4.73	6.35	7.95	11.83
3	7.37	9.40	11.37	15.87
4	9.89	12.12	14.31	18.78
5	12.28	14.79	17.13	21.51
Regression contains a constant				
2	7.52	9.54	11.41	15.22
3	9.94	12.22	14.38	18.68
4	12.38	14.93	17.18	21.43
5	14.83	17.38	19.69	24.63
Regression contains a constant and a trend				
2	10.16	12.32	14.28	18.53
3	12.49	14.91	17.20	21.62
4	14.84	17.57	19.81	24.65
5	17.08	19.96	22.47	27.52

Source: Boswijk (1994).

and testing the significance of this error correction variable. Conditional on the presence of cointegration, the relevant test statistic asymptotically follows the χ^2 distribution. The same applies to tests for the values of α_2 and η in (10.42).

As an example of this CECM method, consider again the white ($y_{1,t}$) and black ($y_{2,t}$) pepper prices. One can obtain the following estimation results for the sample ending in 1992.12

$$\Delta_1 y_{2,t} = 0.072 - 0.106 y_{2,t-1} + 0.093 y_{1,t-1} \qquad (10.43)$$
$$(0.060) \ (0.029) \qquad (0.027)$$

$$+ 0.186 \Delta_1 y_{2,t-1} + 0.486 \Delta_1 y_{1,t} + \hat{\varepsilon}_t.$$
$$(0.060) \qquad (0.062)$$

The Wald test statistic value of 13.773 is significant at the 1 percent level (since the relevant critical value is 11.41). The estimate of η obtained using NLS is 0.877 with standard deviation 0.072. Since the value of 1 is included in the 5 percent confidence interval for η, we can set it equal to 1. The final CECM is then given by

$$\Delta_1 y_{2,t} = 0.072 - 0.093(y_{2,t-1} - y_{1,t-1}) + 0.180 \Delta_1 y_{2,t-1} \qquad (10.44)$$
$$\quad\ (0.060)\ (0.028) \qquad\qquad\qquad\qquad (0.060)$$

$$+ 0.491 \Delta_1 y_{1,t} + \hat{\varepsilon}_t,$$
$$(0.062)$$

for which the adjustment parameter obtains a t-ratio of -3.368. For the first differences of the white pepper series, we need to include $\Delta_1 y_{2,t}$ with lags of 1 and 3 and $\Delta_1 y_{1,t}$ with lags at 1 and 2. Adding the error correction variable $y_{2,t-1} - y_{1,t-1}$ to this model yields an estimated parameter value of -0.047 with standard deviation of 0.030. This suggests that the white pepper price may be weakly exogenous for η.

Some further practical issues

The empirical power and size of the above discussed tests for cointegration have been studied in many simulation studies. Generally, we find that the tests become over-sized and that their power becomes low in cases where we consider large systems, that is, when m gets large relative to the sample size. In practice it is therefore recommended to keep m small, say 4 or 5, and to use large enough samples covering large spans of time. Additionally, graphs of the estimated elements of β can be informative by indicating which linear combinations possess trend or random walk behavior.

When sets of variables are cointegrated, their out-of-sample forecasts are tied together as well, see Engle and Yoo (1987). This is particularly useful when we aim to forecast many observations out of sample. Simulation results in Lin and Tsay (1996) show that when the correct rank r is imposed on Π in de rewritten VAR in (10.27), the forecasts are better than when no such cointegration restrictions are imposed. Hence, for out-of-sample forecasting it is relevant to take account of cointegration. Explicit expressions of forecast intervals for cointegrated series are given in Reimers (1995), and measures to evaluate point forecasts are given in Clements and Hendry (1995). Point forecasts for cointegrated series can simply be found using the expressions in chapter 9, when imposing the non-linear restrictions that correspond to cointegration. Tests for Granger causality in cointegrated systems are derived in Lütkepohl and Reimers (1992).

To illustrate the possible usefulness of VECM models for out-of-sample forecasting, consider forecasting the growth rates of sectoral output in China for 1981–1988, where empirical models are constructed for 1952–1980. The graphs in figure 2.1 suggest a possible structural break

Table 10.6. *Forecasting growth rates of sectoral output in China for 1981–1988, using univariate and multivariate (cointegrated) models for 1952–1980*

Sector	\<div\>Models\</div\> A 1-step	A h-step	B 1-step	B h-step	C 1-step	C h-step
Agriculture	2.145	4.178	2.145	4.178	2.721	4.354
Industry	2.408	2.827	4.934	2.564	2.667	4.966
Construction	5.618	5.618	7.557	8.726	6.244	16.529
Transportation	3.613	4.018	0.925	6.919	0.822	10.738
Commerce	9.192	8.037	7.382	11.430	6.755	12.903

Note:
The cells contain the mean squared prediction errors ($\times 100$). Model A is a univariate AR model of order 1, 2, 0, 2, 2, for the sectors Agriculture to Commerce, respectively. Model B is a VAR(1) for the growth rates, and model C is a VECM of order 2, i.e., it contains growth rates at lag 1 and error correcting variables at lag 2.

around 1980 for some series, but in order to have enough observations to use for forecast evaluation I consider the selected samples. In table 10.6, I report the mean squared prediction errors of univariate AR models, a VAR(1) for the growth rates and a VECM. It appears that generally the univariate models outperform the multivariate models. It is only for the sectors transportation and commerce, that I find the VECM to outperform the other models for one-step ahead forecasting, whilst for agriculture and industry the VAR(1) for growth rates is better for h-step ahead forecasting.

Testing for cointegration among seasonal time series will be discussed in the next section. Many economic time series data, however, do not only display trends and seasonality, but also one of the other features such as outliers, ARCH, and non-linearity. Using simulation experiments, Lee and Tse (1996) examine the effects of ARCH, and find that these appear to be not too substantial when the ARCH parameters are not too large. With simulations and theoretical arguments, Franses and Haldrup (1994) show that the inclination is to find spurious cointegration when there are neglected additive outliers. Therefore, Franses and Lucas (1998) propose to use outlier robust estimation techniques to reduce the effect of aberrant data points. Finally, it may be that the data can be described by a non-linear error correction model such as, for example

$$\Delta_1 y_{1,t} = \mu + (\alpha_1 F(z_{t-1})) z_{t-1} + \varepsilon_{1,t}, \tag{10.45}$$

where $z_t = y_{1,t} - y_{2,t}$ reflects a cointegration relation, and the $F(.)$ function is defined in (8.3)–(8.6), see Balke and Fomby (1997) *inter alia*. Using simulations, Van Dijk and Franses (1998) show that the cointegration parameter can be estimated using the above linear methods with great precision.

10.3   Common seasonality and other features

In the previous section the focus was on investigating common trends across economic variables. These trends concern the non-seasonal unit root, that is, the individual time series need to be differenced using the $(1-L)$ filter to yield stationary and invertible univariate ARMA models. In a sense, cointegrated series then have this unit root in common. In this section, I will discuss methods that can be used to investigate such a common root in cases where the data also show substantial seasonality. Next, I briefly discuss approaches to investigating the presence of other common features across economic time series such as seasonality, ARCH, and non-linearity. This last discussion is necessarily quite sketchy since much current research is dedicated to designing appropriate methods.

Common non-seasonal stochastic trends in seasonal time series

If seasonally unadjusted data are available, it is most sensible to use these data when investigating common long-run non-seasonal trends. The main reason is that it can be shown that most seasonal adjustment methods have an effect on the trend behavior of individual series and hence may affect cointegration analysis. For example, simulation and empirical results in Franses (1996) and Lee and Siklos (1997) show that seasonal adjustment can lead to less cointegration, while the empirical results in Ermini and Chang (1996) show that adjustment can also lead to spurious cointegration.

Suppose we have two quarterly observed time series $y_{1,t}$ and $y_{2,t}$, each of which has a unit root 1, and we aim to test whether $y_{1,t} + \eta y_{2,t}$ does not have this unit root. When the seasonal fluctuations in each series can be described by seasonal dummies, and the data do not have seasonal unit roots, we can simply replace the intercept vector μ in (10.26) by

$$\mu_0 + \mu_1 (D_{1,t} - D_{4,t}) + \mu_2 (D_{2,t} - D_{4,t}) + \mu_3 (D_{3,t} - D_{4,t}), \tag{10.46}$$

see Johansen (1995, p. 84). The asymptotic theory for the tests reviewed in the previous section can now be applied, and hence we can use the critical values given in the various tables.

When the individual time series have seasonal unit roots, and we are not specifically interested in common seasonal unit roots (for which the relevant methods will be discussed below), we can transform the univariate series accordingly and again use the above methods. For example, suppose $y_{1,t}$ has seasonal unit root -1 and $y_{2,t}$ has roots $\pm i$, while they both also have the unit root 1, that is, we should transform $y_{1,t}$ using the $(1-L^2)$ filter and $y_{2,t}$ using $(1-L)(1+L^2)$, then we can investigate a common unit root 1 by applying the cointegration methods to $y^*_{1,t}=(1+L)y_{1,t}$ and $y^*_{2,t}=(1+L^2)y_{2,t}$.

Finally, when the individual time series are periodically integrated, or otherwise have periodic AR dynamics with unit roots, we may consider the so-called periodic cointegration model, see Birchenhall et al. (1989) and Boswijk and Franses (1995). The first equation of a simple version of this model looks like

$$\Delta_4 y_{1,t} = \mu_s + \alpha_s(y_{1,t-4} - \beta_s y_{2,t-4}) + \varepsilon_t, \tag{10.47}$$

where the index s to μ, α, and β indicates that the parameters can take values that differ across the seasons. Time-varying adjustment to equilibrium errors, which is reflected through α_s, can be caused by time-varying adjustment costs, while time-varying long-run equilibria (β_s) may be seen as reflecting seasonally varying preferences, see also Franses (1996).

Common seasonal stochastic trends

In case two or more seasonally observed time series have seasonal unit roots, we may be interested in testing for common seasonal unit roots, that is, in testing for seasonal cointegration. If these series have such roots in common, they will have common changing seasonal patterns. Engle et al. (1993) [EGHL] propose a method to examine the presence of seasonal and non-seasonal cointegration relations at the same time. Suppose that two time series $y_{1,t}$ and $y_{2,t}$ are to be differenced using the Δ_4 filter. When $y_{1,t}$ and $y_{2,t}$ have a common non-seasonal unit root, then the series u_t defined by

$$u_t = (1+L+L^2+L^3)y_{1,t} - \alpha_1(1+L+L^2+L^3)y_{2,t} \tag{10.48}$$

does not need the $(1-L)$ filter to become stationary. Seasonal cointegration at the biannual frequency π, corresponding to unit root -1, implies that

$$v_t = (1-L+L^2-L^3)y_{1,t} - \alpha_2(1-L+L^2-L^3)y_{2,t} \tag{10.49}$$

does not need the $(1+L)$ differencing filter. Finally, seasonal cointegration at the annual frequency $\pi/2$, corresponding to the unit roots $\pm i$, means that

$$w_t = (1-L^2)y_{1,t} - \alpha_3(1-L^2)y_{2,t} - \alpha_4(1-L^2)y_{1,t-1} \\ - \alpha_5(1-L^2)y_{2,t-1} \tag{10.50}$$

does not have the unit roots $\pm i$. In case all three u_t, v_t, and w_t series do not have the relevant unit roots, the first equation of a simple version of a seasonal cointegration model is

$$\Delta_4 y_{1,t} = \gamma_1 u_{t-1} + \gamma_2 v_{t-1} + \gamma_3 w_{t-2} + \gamma_4 w_{t-3} + \varepsilon_{1,t}, \tag{10.51}$$

where γ_1 to γ_4 are error correction parameters.

The test method proposed in EGHL is a two-step method, similar to the Engle–Granger approach to non-seasonal time series. The first step involves the estimation of the α_1 through α_5 parameters in (10.48), (10.49), and (10.50) using single equation regressions, where such regressions may include a constant, seasonal dummies, and a deterministic trend if necessary, followed by a test for the absence of a unit root in $\hat{u}_t$, $\hat{v}_t$, and $\hat{w}_t$. The second step is to replace the u_t, v_t, and w_t variables in (10.51) by their estimated versions, and to test the significance of the adjustment parameters γ_j. The latter step involves standard normal asymptotics for the t-values of the γ_j parameters, while the first step involves (extensions of the) asymptotics given in Phillips and Ouliaris (1990). For example, to test for a common unit root 1, we test $\rho = 0$ in the auxiliary regression

$$(1 - L)\hat{u}_t = \rho \hat{u}_{t-1} + \sum_{i=1}^{k} \lambda_i (1 - L)\hat{u}_{t-i} + \varepsilon_t. \tag{10.52}$$

The critical values for the t-test for ρ are given in table 10.1. To test for a common unit root -1, one tests $\rho = 0$ in

$$(1 + L)\hat{v}_t = -\rho \hat{v}_{t-1} + \sum_{i=1}^{k} \lambda_i (1 + L)\hat{v}_{t-i} + \varepsilon_t, \tag{10.53}$$

where again we can use the critical values in table 10.1. The test for common $(1 + L^2)$ unit roots is somewhat more complicated, and we should consult EGHL for details on asymptotics and critical values.

The presence of seasonal cointegration in a multivariate time series Y_t can also be analyzed using an extension of the Johansen approach. This approach is developed in Lee (1992), Lee and Siklos (1995), and notably in Johansen and Schaumburg (1997); see also Kunst (1993) for a useful outline of its practical implementation. It amounts to testing the ranks of matrices that correspond to variables which are transformed using the filters to remove the roots 1, -1 or $\pm i$. More precise, consider the $(m \times 1)$ vector process Y_t, and assume that it can be described by the VAR(p) process

$$Y_t = \Theta D_t + \Phi_1 Y_{t-1} + \ldots + \Phi_p Y_{t-p} + e_t, \tag{10.54}$$

where D_t is the (4×1) vector process $D_t = (D_{1,t}, D_{2,t}, D_{3,t}, D_{4,t})'$ containing the seasonal dummies, and where Θ is an $(m \times 4)$ parameter matrix. Similar to the Johansen approach and conditional on the assumption that $p > 4$, model (10.54) can be rewritten as

$$\Delta_4 Y_t = \Theta D_t + \Pi_1 Y_{1,t-1} + \Pi_2 Y_{2,t-1} + \Pi_3 Y_{3,t-2} + \Pi_4 Y_{3,t-1} \tag{10.55}$$
$$+ \Gamma_1 \Delta_4 Y_{t-1} + \ldots + \Gamma_{p-4} \Delta_4 Y_{t-(p-4)} + e_t,$$

where

$$Y_{1,t} = (1 + L + L^2 + L^3) Y_t$$
$$Y_{2,t} = (1 - L + L^2 - L^3) Y_t$$
$$Y_{3,t} = (1 - L^2) Y_t.$$

Obviously, (10.55) is a multivariate extension of the univariate HEGY model in chapter 5. The ranks of the matrices Π_1, Π_2, Π_3, and Π_4 determine the number of cointegration relations at a certain frequency. Similar to the Johansen approach, one can now construct residual processes from regressions of $\Delta_4 Y_t$ and the $Y_{1,t-1}$, $Y_{2,t-1}$, $Y_{3,t-2}$, and $Y_{3,t-1}$ on lagged $\Delta_4 Y_t$ time series and deterministics, and construct the relevant moment matrices as in (10.32). Solving four eigenvalue problems results in sets of estimated eigenvalues which can be checked for their significance using the *Trace*-test statistic. Critical values of the various test statistics are given in Lee (1992) and Lee and Siklos (1995). Applications of this method can be found in these studies, and in Kunst (1993), Ermini and Chang (1996), and Reimers (1997). The latter study also shows through simulations that imposing the correct cointegration rank can improve out-of-sample forecasting. Finally, Franses and Kunst (1997) discuss the impact of seasonal constants on seasonal cointegration analysis.

Common deterministic seasonality

Seasonal cointegration analysis can be used to investigate common seasonal stochastic trends. If such trends exist, the number of parameters in VAR models can largely be reduced. If the data do not have such seasonal stochastic trends but only seasonal deterministics, we may be interested in reducing the number of parameters by examining possible common deterministic seasonality. Engle and Hylleberg (1996) propose a general approach to testing for common seasonality, which extends the approaches proposed in Engle and Kozicki (1993) and Vahid and Engle (1993). They construct the variables $w_{1,t}$ to $w_{k,t}$, which capture the seasonal fluctuations using functions of sines and cosines, and which can be summarized in the vector W_t, and they add $\Gamma' W_t$ to the right-hand side of a VAR model and investigate whether Γ has a reduced rank using canonical correlation techniques.

In case of simple (nonseasonal) lag structures of the VAR model, we may also consider imposing cross-equation parameter restrictions. For example, for the last five years of data on the TV and radio advertising expenditures ($y_{1,t}$ and $y_{2,t}$, respectively), I find the following two useful models

$$y_{1,t} = \tau_1 t + \sum_{s=1}^{13} \alpha_{1,s} D_{s,t} + \phi_1 y_{1,t-1} + \varepsilon_{1,t}, \quad \text{and} \tag{10.56}$$

$$y_{2,t} = \tau_2 t + \sum_{s=1}^{13} \alpha_{2,s} D_{s,t} + \phi_2 y_{2,t-1} + \varepsilon_{2,t}, \tag{10.57}$$

where ϕ_1 is estimated as 0.362 with standard error 0.119 and ϕ_2 as 0.562 with error 0.114 (for 65 effective observations). These two series would have their deterministic seasonality in common when $\alpha_{1,s} = \psi \alpha_{2,s}$ for some nonzero value of ψ. This common feature amounts to 12 parameter restrictions, and can be seen to substantially decrease the number of parameters. Joint estimation of (10.56)–(10.57) gives that the determinant of the residual covariance matrix $|\hat{\Sigma}^u|$ is 3.421E−05. Imposing the restrictions results in $|\hat{\Sigma}^r| = 5.192E-05$ for the restricted model. The value of the Likelihood Ratio test, see Lütkepohl (1991), calculated as $n(\log|\hat{\Sigma}^r| - \log|\hat{\Sigma}^u|)$, obtains a value of 27.117. This statistic is significant at the 1 percent but not at the 0.5 percent level, when compared with the $\chi^2(12)$ distribution. Imposing the restriction yields the presumably common deterministic seasonal pattern, as it is depicted in figure 10.5. Clearly, the common seasonal pattern is approximately equal to an average of the estimated $\alpha_{1,s}$ and $\alpha_{2,s}$ from (10.56) and (10.57).

Common ARCH and non-linearity

When we aim to link two or more financial time series, each with substantial GARCH patterns, we may want to consider multivariate GARCH models. For many practical applications, however, these models contain too many parameters, see Bollerslev and Engle (1993), *inter alia*. In that case, we can consider models that allow a reduction of parameters by constructing variables which contain the ARCH feature and by investigating whether the data have one or more of these factors in common, see, for example, Engle, Ng, and Rothschild (1990). Such a multivariate factor GARCH model can then also be used to investigate common persistence of shocks, see Bollerslev and Engle (1993).

As a simple preliminary modeling device, we may also investigate certain linear combinations of the variables to investigate common ARCH. In fact, when $y_{1,t}$ and $y_{2,t}$ have ARCH, but $y_{1,t} - \kappa y_{2,t}$ does not, we can exploit this for forecasting since only one ARCH model needs to be estimated.

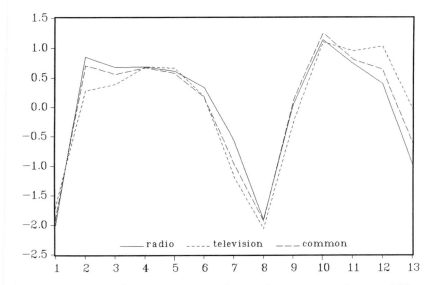

Figure 10.5 *Common deterministic seasonality in advertising expenditures or TV and radio*

Denoting $y_{1,t}$ as the log of the price of white pepper, and $y_{2,t}$ as that of black pepper, cointegration analysis shows that $x_t = y_{1,t} - y_{2,t}$ is a stationary variable. To study possible common ARCH, I fit an AR(1)–GARCH(1,1) model to this variable, which for the estimation sample 1973.11–1996.04 results in

$$\hat{y}_t = x_t - 0.029 - 0.910x_{t-1} = (\hat{h}_t)^{\frac{1}{2}} \hat{\eta}_t, \text{ and} \qquad (10.58)$$
$$\quad\quad (0.008) \ (0.022)$$

$$\hat{h}_t = 0.00005 + 0.101\hat{y}_{t-1}^2 + 0.894\hat{h}_{t-1}. \qquad (10.59)$$
$$\quad (0.00004) \ (0.020) \quad\quad (0.024)$$

Black and white pepper prices do not seem to have common ARCH since the parameters in (10.59) appear to be significant at the 1 percent level.

Finally, Anderson and Vahid (1998) extend the methods in Vahid and Engle (1993) by using the canonical correlation principle to investigate common non-linearity. The idea is to construct variables $z_{1,t}$ to $z_{g,t}$ which capture the non-linear features of the data, and to investigate whether the matrix Γ in $\Gamma' Z_t$, with $Z_t = (z_{1,t},...,z_{g,t})$ has reduced rank.

At present, the research area concerning common features in multivariate models is in rapid development. To what extent these methods appear useful is yet to be established in empirical and simulation studies.

Data appendix

(also available via http://www.cs.few.eur.nl/few/people/franses)

Table DA.1. *Real national income in China per sector (1952 = 100)*

Year	Agriculture	Industry	Construction	Transport	Commerce
1952	100.0	100.0	100.0	100.0	100.0
1953	101.6	133.6	138.1	120.0	133.0
1954	103.3	159.1	133.3	136.0	136.4
1955	111.5	169.1	152.4	140.0	137.5
1956	116.5	219.1	261.9	164.0	146.6
1957	120.1	244.5	242.9	176.0	146.6
1958	120.3	383.5	367.0	270.8	155.9
1959	100.6	501.5	388.6	356.5	170.3
1960	83.6	541.4	394.0	383.6	164.1
1961	84.7	315.9	129.5	221.1	130.1
1962	88.7	267.4	161.9	171.5	117.7
1963	98.9	300.7	205.1	176.0	120.8
1964	111.9	374.9	259.0	198.6	123.9
1965	122.9	477.7	286.0	261.7	128.0
1966	131.9	598.5	313.0	297.8	155.9
1967	134.2	504.3	296.8	239.2	164.1
1968	131.6	458.6	237.5	225.6	151.8
1969	132.2	622.3	323.8	284.3	179.6
1970	139.8	863.0	421.0	343.0	199.2
1971	142.0	979.0	468.3	370.8	201.2
1972	140.5	1043.5	452.5	389.3	208.0
1973	153.1	1134.3	457.8	412.5	224.5
1974	159.2	1128.9	484.1	394.0	220.6
1975	162.3	1297.3	542.0	444.9	220.6
1976	159.1	1249.2	568.3	426.4	214.8
1977	155.1	1434.0	578.8	491.3	242.0
1978	161.2	1679.1	573.5	546.9	296.4
1979	171.5	1814.7	584.1	560.8	316.8
1980	168.4	2012.7	757.7	584.0	318.8
1981	180.4	2046.8	770.0	607.2	379.4
1982	201.6	2170.1	806.9	681.3	397.5
1983	218.7	2383.7	954.3	755.5	449.1
1984	247.0	2738.8	1056.7	852.8	499.5
1985	253.7	3275.2	1310.6	1024.3	593.7
1986	261.4	3590.6	1540.0	1140.2	636.3
1987	273.2	4058.8	1744.8	1269.9	715.0
1988	279.4	4765.0	1884.0	1413.6	760.8

Source: Chow (1993).

Table DA.2. *Index of industrial production USA (1985 = 100), 1960.1–1991.4*

Year	Not seasonally adjusted				Seasonally adjusted			
	Q_1	Q_2	Q_3	Q_4	Q_1	Q_2	Q_3	Q_4
1960	40.2	39.8	38.5	38.0	40.5	40.0	39.0	38.1
1961	37.1	39.2	39.8	41.6	37.6	39.0	40.3	41.7
1962	41.8	43.0	42.6	43.4	42.3	42.7	43.1	43.5
1963	43.9	45.7	44.9	46.4	44.3	45.5	45.8	46.5
1964	46.7	48.6	48.1	49.6	47.1	48.3	49.1	49.8
1965	51.4	53.2	52.9	54.9	51.7	52.9	54.0	55.1
1966	56.2	58.1	57.6	59.2	56.7	57.8	58.7	59.3
1967	58.4	59.0	58.4	60.7	59.0	58.7	59.2	60.7
1968	61.5	63.1	62.5	64.2	61.6	62.4	62.9	63.9
1969	64.9	66.1	65.8	65.9	65.1	65.4	66.2	65.8
1970	63.8	64.5	63.4	62.1	64.2	63.8	63.6	62.2
1971	63.1	64.7	64.1	65.6	63.4	64.0	64.2	65.7
1972	67.8	70.7	70.7	73.2	68.3	69.9	70.7	73.4
1973	74.4	76.7	77.1	77.0	74.9	75.9	77.1	77.3
1974	74.8	76.9	76.2	72.9	75.4	76.0	76.1	73.2
1975	66.8	67.7	69.3	70.4	67.5	67.0	69.0	70.9
1976	72.4	75.1	75.5	76.5	73.0	74.2	75.3	76.9
1977	77.9	81.3	82.0	82.2	78.6	80.6	81.7	82.5
1978	81.7	86.5	87.5	88.6	82.5	85.8	87.2	88.9
1979	88.8	90.0	89.7	89.5	89.6	89.4	89.2	89.7
1980	89.3	86.6	86.6	88.7	90.0	86.3	85.9	89.0
1981	89.2	90.2	91.8	87.8	90.0	90.0	91.0	88.1
1982	85.1	83.9	83.4	81.1	85.8	83.8	82.4	81.3
1983	82.8	86.4	91.4	92.5	83.5	86.3	90.3	92.9
1984	95.5	98.1	100.4	98.7	96.4	97.9	99.2	99.0
1985	98.4	99.8	101.5	100.4	99.3	99.8	100.2	100.8
1986	100.2	100.7	102.2	101.3	101.3	100.5	100.8	101.8
1987	101.5	103.8	107.3	107.2	102.6	103.7	105.9	107.7
1988	107.6	110.0	113.5	112.6	108.7	109.9	111.9	113.1
1989	113.6	114.5	115.6	114.3	114.1	114.9	114.5	114.5
1990	114.3	115.5	118.3	114.5	114.7	115.9	117.1	114.9
1991	111.4	112.4	116.0	113.9	112.0	112.7	114.6	114.4

Source: OECD Main Economic Indicators.

Table DA.3. *Consumption of non-durables in the UK (in 1985 prices), 1955.1–1988.4.*

Year	Q1	Q2	Q3	Q4
1955	24030	25620	26209	27167
1956	24620	25972	26285	27659
1957	24780	26519	26803	28200
1958	25476	26846	27302	28601
1959	26025	27998	28258	29828
1960	27346	29174	29375	30603
1961	28168	29884	30165	31260
1962	28629	30614	30717	32054
1963	29364	31783	32532	33392
1964	30599	32528	33200	34258
1965	31111	32946	33846	34845
1966	32013	34055	34244	35084
1967	32227	34343	35301	36546
1968	33902	34838	35874	37315
1969	33742	35401	36147	38067
1970	34149	36176	37485	39047
1971	34783	37042	38008	40132
1972	36466	38680	39976	42273
1973	39131	40780	41852	43684
1974	38729	40427	41576	43886
1975	39131	40394	40956	42959
1976	38714	40062	41152	43460
1977	38695	39780	40923	44093
1978	40777	41778	43160	45897
1979	41947	44061	44378	47237
1980	43315	43396	44843	46835
1981	42833	43548	44637	47107
1982	42552	43526	45039	47940
1983	43740	45007	46667	49325
1984	44878	46234	47055	50318
1985	46354	47260	48883	52605
1986	48527	50237	51592	55152
1987	50451	52294	54633	58802
1988	53990	55477	57850	61978

Source: See Osborn (1990).

Table DA.4. *Four-weekly television and radio advertising expenditures (in real terms) in The Netherlands, 1978.01–1994.13.*

Year	Period	Radio	TV	Year	Period	Radio	TV
1978	1	1954.000	14000.01	1981	1	2044.127	14729.23
	2	1952.712	13304.53		2	2060.236	15000.55
	3	1859.740	13342.78		3	2046.263	15225.50
	4	1922.206	13571.98		4	1940.478	14055.87
	5	1836.898	13163.29		5	1935.932	14360.42
	6	1918.038	13479.05		6	1930.474	14115.46
	7	1919.126	12253.93		7	2008.903	12832.75
	8	1911.453	11619.49		8	2000.316	10627.29
	9	1908.437	12669.32		9	1992.851	12255.26
	10	1888.647	13287.85		10	1969.757	14107.90
	11	1865.246	13556.10		11	1919.527	14472.11
	12	1880.011	13451.22		12	1948.506	14638.02
	13	1804.861	13097.94		13	2425.902	16650.08
1979	1	2006.536	14729.32	1982	1	2870.684	13569.14
	2	2023.253	14817.76		2	3153.138	15020.49
	3	2017.668	14165.38		3	3334.419	14617.02
	4	1879.907	13969.46		4	3248.988	14181.70
	5	1912.606	13954.70		5	3278.923	13840.73
	6	1907.327	13850.66		6	3287.909	14255.57
	7	1989.573	12835.24		7	3063.263	12035.01
	8	1984.542	11592.87		8	2906.914	10873.61
	9	1976.360	12531.84		9	3127.502	12714.41
	10	1958.725	13793.11		10	3276.122	14449.58
	11	1943.197	15879.66		11	3263.614	14978.30
	12	1940.182	14157.02		12	3153.240	14766.04
	13	1854.530	12896.00		13	2782.426	12747.83
1980	1	2067.844	14217.56	1983	1	3069.802	15352.06
	2	2053.649	14937.18		2	3329.561	15732.00
	3	2040.385	14928.15		3	3398.982	16163.56
	4	1932.026	13776.98		4	3274.235	15718.74
	5	1924.534	14171.88		5	3155.168	15331.35
	6	2012.672	14721.06		6	3271.719	15872.48
	7	2004.084	13192.90		7	3073.174	12573.10
	8	1996.419	11521.42		8	3012.860	10750.47
	9	1982.995	12544.22		9	3121.140	12821.88
	10	1976.250	14347.83		10	3247.138	15769.25
	11	1967.046	13860.99		11	3228.017	16208.99
	12	1961.626	14115.52		12	3166.246	16128.68
	13	1880.368	13037.27		13	3020.475	14892.97

Table DA.4. (*cont.*)

Year	Period	Radio	TV	Year	Period	Radio	TV
1984	1	2958.286	14757.48	1987	1	3409.888	19051.74
	2	3188.612	16087.08		2	3602.703	21166.07
	3	3207.876	16868.57		3	3809.414	23430.87
	4	3279.751	16483.99		4	3461.443	23467.52
	5	3607.579	16492.00		5	3643.482	23960.24
	6	3610.494	15927.41		6	3705.541	22389.83
	7	3676.147	12740.04		7	3868.027	17514.73
	8	3531.811	9829.552		8	3717.150	12536.12
	9	3601.024	12005.11		9	3594.429	16408.82
	10	3651.437	15869.29		10	3794.364	23919.42
	11	3610.997	16192.64		11	3868.965	25184.15
	12	3636.841	16120.92		12	3705.909	26247.13
	13	3364.173	14468.46		13	4312.270	29103.95
1985	1	3177.644	13878.46	1988	1	3410.860	22004.04
	2	3531.842	16167.66		2	3761.494	24009.31
	3	3804.418	16778.12		3	3987.513	26029.91
	4	3638.506	16299.34		4	3961.209	26994.60
	5	3865.402	16911.40		5	3681.251	26503.60
	6	4154.599	17687.04		6	4094.450	25999.18
	7	3961.976	13769.16		7	4113.840	19215.78
	8	3519.764	10155.72		8	3787.635	14300.15
	9	3644.326	12667.59		9	3848.695	19486.53
	10	4146.022	17230.11		10	3900.287	26496.60
	11	4227.524	18251.95		11	3969.105	28958.24
	12	4207.747	18009.70		12	4059.031	29248.67
	13	3661.427	16247.06		13	3864.175	25935.58
1986	1	3473.572	15373.73	1989	1	3798.679	22060.86
	2	3542.515	17072.48		2	4946.334	24227.82
	3	4038.959	18628.86		3	5213.351	25594.85
	4	4089.100	19098.00		4	5657.749	30556.87
	5	4086.277	19161.56		5	5310.414	27832.59
	6	4112.008	18669.99		6	5062.537	28369.77
	7	4166.447	13982.87		7	4653.414	20106.21
	8	3949.806	10408.76		8	4037.962	15718.28
	9	3999.770	13750.24		9	4701.577	19850.16
	10	4054.710	19417.79		10	5712.334	26865.18
	11	3974.692	20207.49		11	5818.143	29235.12
	12	3936.313	20616.06		12	5699.307	37090.08
	13	34330.705	18029.41		13	5214.291	28041.23

Table DA.4. (*cont.*)

Year	Period	Radio	TV	Year	Period	Radio	TV
1990	1	3271.991	22189.82	1993	1	5261.234	38898.44
	2	5411.910	29221.99		2	8448.782	51812.65
	3	5955.867	35368.12		3	9465.003	53135.52
	4	6612.504	42179.22		4	10825.85	67737.80
	5	6770.600	47126.13		5	11884.62	67012.32
	6	6497.780	40073.16		6	11626.70	61443.43
	7	5107.394	26860.86		7	9083.898	43477.15
	8	3117.954	24289.96		8	6077.397	32500.71
	9	4612.984	34280.68		9	7370.473	45675.73
	10	6281.770	47586.47		10	11206.28	66699.40
	11	7094.817	51779.06		11	12847.58	81210.05
	12	7437.177	59074.53		12	12817.62	81689.08
	13	5013.224	47163.04		13	9454.016	62041.97
1991	1	3420.346	24317.47	1994	1	5823.944	43626.96
	2	4810.777	36260.37		2	7903.428	58484.43
	3	6134.229	46166.96		3	10701.77	69915.03
	4	6814.156	50765.07		4	12498.27	80583.06
	5	7016.528	53825.68		5	13190.94	84609.62
	6	7358.709	50194.55		6	12479.42	72220.41
	7	5833.066	32176.42		7	9743.129	60043.57
	8	4057.990	18805.09		8	7834.605	42633.34
	9	4796.882	30292.34		9	8857.575	56161.75
	10	7035.168	56285.24		10	11493.41	80624.65
	11	7512.396	66922.84		11	12668.12	89987.83
	12	7476.459	73532.83		12	12905.41	96333.06
	13	4913.888	51018.66		13	9938.024	75003.95
1992	1	4139.389	33675.51				
	2	6611.526	50366.55				
	3	8490.380	57669.81				
	4	9427.797	58822.11				
	5	10233.60	61073.05				
	6	9770.812	61595.21				
	7	8872.624	40790.53				
	8	4742.900	26313.30				
	9	5801.792	31789.12				
	10	9667.316	58594.46				
	11	11891.22	65916.41				
	12	11179.82	71409.87				
	13	9660.101	71546.54				

Source: Bureau of Budget Control, The Netherlands. Thanks to Arlette van Dits-huizen, Jeanine Kippers and Cassander Jupijn for their help with collecting these data.

Table DA.5. *Retail sales index, The Netherlands*

Year	M1	M2	M3	M4	M5	M6	M7	M8	M9	M10	M11	M12
1960					14	13	15	13	13	15	15	16
1961	14	12	15	15	15	14	16	14	15	15	16	18
1962	15	13	16	16	17	17	17	15	16	17	18	20
1963	17	14	17	18	19	17	19	18	17	20	21	22
1964	19	17	19	19	22	19	22	18	20	23	22	25
1965	21	18	21	23	23	21	25	20	23	25	25	30
1966	23	19	23	25	25	24	25	22	24	25	27	29
1967	24	20	25	25	26	26	25	24	26	26	29	31
1968	26	23	27	27	29	26	27	26	26	29	32	34
1969	27	25	30	30	33	29	30	29	30	34	34	37
1970	33	27	32	33	36	33	35	31	33	40	38	44
1971	34	30	36	38	39	37	38	34	38	42	42	46
1972	37	35	43	40	42	43	40	39	43	45	47	51
1973	42	39	46	45	49	49	44	45	46	51	54	58
1974	47	43	51	51	56	52	52	52	52	58	60	61
1975	54	49	57	57	63	57	57	56	60	67	64	74
1976	60	54	62	67	67	66	64	61	71	69	70	80
1977	67	59	71	73	72	78	72	69	74	76	77	81
1978	76	65	82	77	80	81	72	74	80	80	82	81
1979	76	67	87	80	85	83	73	77	76	85	86	83
1980	86	73	82	82	88	80	77	77	78	87	82	84
1981	86	72	81	85	86	82	82	73	78	89	78	86
1982	82	73	83	86	85	84	82	75	82	89	86	98
1983	77	72	83	83	83	85	82	78	86	85	86	98
1984	77	73	83	81	84	87	79	81	83	87	89	95
1985	78	71	83	84	89	84	82	86	81	91	92	95
1986	82	72	83	84	93	83	84	85	87	92	88	100
1987	86	75	82	91	92	88	90	84	87	98	88	105
1988	81	76	88	92	88	90	89	85	91	93	93	109
1989	82	78	94	91	96	98	91	91	97	97	100	112
1990	88	83	101	97	103	103	95	98	102	104	107	119
1991	96	87	105	101	108	106	103	104	100	112	111	119
1992	101	95	100	107	112	106	109	101	107	116	105	128
1993	98	90	106	110	111	112	114	102	111	113	109	129
1994	97	92	110	110	109	114	109	104	114	111	111	131
1995	98	93	111	107	114	116	107	106	115			

Source: Central Bureau of Statistics. Thanks to Margot de Steur for her help with collecting the data.

Table DA.6.1. *Average monthly European spot price of black pepper (fair average quality) 1973.10–1996.04 in US dollars per million tons*

Year	M1	M2	M3	M4	M5	M6
1974	1102.310	1150.810	1093.490	1117.740	1168.450	1117.740
1975	1283.090	1250.020	1210.340	1135.380	1084.680	1060.420
1976	1250.020	1210.340	1267.660	1402.140	1485.920	1534.420
1977	2149.510	2290.600	2591.980	2575.000	2493.430	2350.130
1978	2425.090	2325.880	2175.960	2120.850	1999.590	1999.590
1979	1849.680	1790.150	1699.770	1699.770	1750.470	1774.720
1980	1999.590	2023.840	1900.390	1750.470	1649.060	1600.560
1981	1589.530	1525.600	1450.640	1424.190	1424.190	1329.390
1982	1373.480	1439.620	1450.640	1375.690	1324.980	1261.040
1983	1419.780	1384.500	1320.570	1234.590	1215.000	1310.000
1984	2125.000	2087.000	1895.000	1840.000	1874.000	1863.000
1985	2270.000	2411.000	2652.000	3294.000	3360.000	3686.000
1986	4336.000	4382.000	4326.000	4009.000	4000.000	4070.000
1987	4857.000	4865.000	4711.000	4640.000	4877.000	4902.000
1988	4809.990	4570.991	4249.992	3849.992	3774.992	3357.493
1989	2992.992	3108.073	2729.099	2524.951	2457.490	2136.277
1990	1969.000	2025.000	1726.000	1579.000	1768.000	1766.000
1991	1508.000	1525.000	1502.000	1374.000	1212.000	1198.000
1992	1126.000	1200.000	1193.000	1058.000	1043.000	1026.000
1993	1116.667	1187.500	1100.000	1040.000	1027.500	1112.500
1994	1497.000	1521.667	1550.000	1575.000	1537.500	1650.000
1995	2425.000	2388.000	2375.000	2600.000	2742.000	2625.000
1996	2200.000	2244.000	2294.000	2100.000		

Table DA.6.1. (*cont.*)

Year	M7	M8	M9	M10	M11	M12
1973				884.050	919.329	930.350
1974	1084.680	1135.380	1137.590	1135.380	1234.590	1300.730
1975	1102.310	1150.810	1126.560	1225.770	1216.950	1214.750
1976	1567.490	1585.120	1717.400	2001.800	2085.570	2059.120
1977	2275.170	2034.870	2175.960	2290.600	2400.840	2389.810
1978	1849.680	1640.240	1699.770	1924.640	1849.680	1829.840
1979	1924.640	1999.590	1975.340	1940.070	1889.360	1880.540
1980	1624.810	1609.380	1649.060	1640.240	1640.240	1620.400
1981	1199.320	1179.470	1285.300	1349.230	1265.450	1298.520
1982	1199.320	1219.160	1250.020	1274.270	1364.660	1424.190
1983	1319.000	1319.000	1279.000	1481.000	1956.000	2165.000
1984	1836.000	1894.000	2105.000	2159.000	2131.000	2029.000
1985	3593.000	3482.000	3615.000	3963.000	4328.000	4309.000
1986	4200.000	4278.000	4435.000	4772.000	4812.000	4908.000
1987	4884.000	4833.000	4902.990	4962.990	4803.990	4678.991
1988	2945.644	2342.045	1994.046	2420.445	2464.281	2763.050
1989	2271.640	2175.000	2100.000	2068.421	1955.000	1950.000
1990	1621.000	1692.000	1634.000	1750.000	1620.000	1515.000
1991	1107.000	1052.000	1069.000	1050.000	1098.000	1150.000
1992	980.000	976.000	1000.000	1210.000	1264.000	1150.000
1993	1153.571	1350.000	1721.667	1616.250	1525.000	1403.333
1994	1800.000	1933.000	2219.000	2606.000	2563.000	2433.000
1995	2644.000	2667.000	2542.000	2431.000	2063.000	2136.000

Source: Man-Products Rotterdam, Research Department (thanks to Bram Buis).

Table DA.6.2. *Average monthly European spot price of white pepper (fair average quality) 1973.10–1994.07 in US dollars per million tons*

Year	M1	M2	M3	M4	M5	M6
1974	1629.220	1737.240	1629.220	1620.400	1671.110	1578.510
1975	1503.550	1477.100	1452.850	1406.550	1402.140	1410.960
1976	1569.690	1552.060	1587.330	1737.240	1794.560	1845.270
1977	2450.000	2550.000	2800.000	2900.000	2790.000	2800.000
1978	3250.000	3175.000	3015.000	3000.000	3025.000	3000.000
1979	2825.000	2770.000	2675.000	2640.000	2640.000	2625.000
1980	2800.000	2775.000	2650.000	2525.000	2435.000	2340.000
1981	2110.000	2040.000	2000.000	2010.000	2135.000	2000.000
1982	1980.000	1980.000	1955.000	1875.000	1800.000	1740.000
1983	1790.000	1780.000	1810.000	1750.000	1732.000	1778.000
1984	3225.000	3365.000	3157.000	3190.000	3247.000	3166.000
1985	3325.000	3386.000	3442.000	3960.000	3910.000	4364.000
1986	6522.000	6550.000	6418.000	5620.000	5256.000	5523.000
1987	6226.000	5871.000	5475.000	5327.000	5705.000	5671.000
1988	6100.000	6050.000	5750.000	5745.000	5800.000	5850.000
1989	4054.000	3900.000	3915.000	3550.000	3242.000	3014.285
1990	2043.000	1964.000	1969.000	1811.000	1794.000	1635.000
1991	1613.000	1553.000	1452.000	1394.000	1325.000	1276.000
1992	1421.000	1353.000	1366.000	1327.000	1280.000	1232.000
1993	1775.000	1925.000	1875.000	1862.500	1737.500	1881.250
1994	2995.000	2825.000	2925.000	2800.000	2637.500	2887.500
1995	3633.000	3588.000	3675.000	3708.000	4067.000	3900.000
1996	3560.000	3663.000	3813.000	3640.000		

Table DA.6.2. (*cont.*)

Year	M7	M8	M9	M10	M11	M12
1973				1419.780	1503.550	1536.620
1974	1470.480	1470.480	1684.330	1490.330	1536.620	1560.870
1975	1470.480	1503.550	1503.550	1552.060	1560.870	1565.280
1976	1869.520	1869.520	2021.640	2321.470	2455.950	2299.420
1977	2800.000	2775.000	2900.000	3050.000	3175.000	3175.000
1978	2800.000	2650.000	2600.000	2770.000	2815.000	2800.000
1979	2710.000	2825.000	2875.000	2825.000	2760.000	2700.000
1980	2235.000	2180.000	2250.000	2185.000	2175.000	2150.000
1981	1890.000	1875.000	1950.000	2050.000	1960.000	1970.000
1982	1640.000	1670.000	1560.000	1570.000	1620.000	1800.000
1983	1797.000	1780.000	1765.000	2109.000	3053.000	3266.000
1984	2983.000	3188.000	3315.000	3374.000	3252.000	3246.000
1985	4491.000	4096.000	4200.000	4515.000	5170.000	5352.000
1986	6102.000	6019.000	6557.000	6554.000	6508.000	6513.000
1987	5608.000	6459.000	6887.000	6716.000	6538.000	6326.000
1988	5450.000	5269.000	4228.563	3295.000	3924.885	4225.000
1989	2656.250	2702.174	2595.000	2529.761	2416.666	2116.250
1990	1621.000	1869.000	1945.000	1798.000	1582.000	1584.000
1991	1243.000	1241.000	1350.000	1460.000	1560.000	1478.000
1992	1230.000	1262.000	1444.000	1558.000	1558.000	1600.000
1993	2084.286	2475.000	3483.333	3475.000	3090.000	2816.667
1994	3100.000	3225.000	3169.000	3263.000	3413.000	3425.000
1995	3925.000	4042.000	3983.000	3825.000	3733.000	3300.000

Source: Man-Products Rotterdam, Research Department (thanks to Bram Buis).

Table DA.7. *Stock of motor cycles (two wheels) in The Netherlands (×1000), observed per year: 1946–1993.*

Year	Stock	Year	Stock	Year	Stock	Year	Stock	Year	Stock	Year	Stock
1946	60	1954	130	1962	163	1970	72	1978	92	1986	127
1947	72	1955	146	1963	156	1971	66	1979	98	1987	131
1948	74	1956	162	1964	150	1972	60	1980	103	1988	135
1949	82	1957	169	1965	140	1973	60	1981	114	1989	145
1950	95	1958	173	1966	129	1974	64	1982	122	1990	162
1951	106	1959	176	1967	113	1975	68	1983	125	1991	191
1952	115	1960	173	1968	98	1976	72	1984	127	1992	250
1953	118	1961	170	1969	84	1977	80	1985	128	1993	290

Source: Central Bureau of Statistics.

Table DA.8. *Consumer Price Index, Argentina (1969.4 = 1.00)*

Year	Q1	Q2	Q3	Q4
1970	1.01	1.06	1.13	1.24
1971	1.33	1.45	1.64	1.77
1972	2.24	2.58	2.92	3.20
1973	4.26	4.89	4.94	5.15
1974	5.19	5.57	6.00	6.92
1975	8.22	10.57	19.53	28.56
1976	45.68	85.61	101.12	131.67
1977	171.96	209.93	267.05	355.82
1978	466.84	606.61	744.00	950.91
1979	1255.96	1560.66	1999.51	2367.83
1980	2805.64	3328.89	3818.90	4469.26
1981	5115.07	6297.67	8125.88	9952.58
1982	12659.68	14482.68	20789.88	30153.65
1983	43626.30	59885.82	91200.11	151820.8
1984	238465.0	394707.2	688803.6	1196314
1985	2180880	4484544	6170733	6608855
1986	7194400	8140463	9834494	11798442
1987	14267856	16727634	22297936	32220516
1988	41661128	64616412	116430000	155770000
1989	203130000	679960000	4537300000	6611700000

Source: International Financial Statistics (IMF) and De Ruyter van Steveninck (1996, appendix 9.1, pp.183–185).

Table DA.9. *Weekly market share, distribution and price of fast-moving consumer good (week 11 in 1989 to week 8 in 1991)*

Week	M	D	P	Week	M	D	P
11	2.773095	0.988	105.7446	63	1.327673	0.614	110.8524
12	2.649770	0.976	107.1440	64	1.424432	0.651	110.9615
13	3.107882	0.930	105.3347	65	1.607368	0.681	110.2102
14	4.284698	0.982	108.7157	66	1.107423	0.633	111.5401
15	2.363902	0.880	109.8849	67	1.067061	0.575	110.2171
16	2.530638	0.912	108.6362	68	0.834407	0.558	112.0979
17	3.096574	0.993	107.6659	69	1.080793	0.644	112.1995
18	2.712191	0.967	107.8318	70	1.009126	0.691	111.2881
19	2.456093	0.933	108.8490	71	0.888115	0.555	115.4739
20	2.450454	0.979	109.0642	72	0.667928	0.661	117.6488
21	3.432728	0.974	109.7082	73	0.848601	0.445	110.4827
22	3.802064	0.974	109.6577	74	0.809124	0.508	111.3019
23	3.517860	0.951	110.1243	75	1.065586	0.601	110.3829
24	3.667301	1.002	109.6380	76	0.996859	0.545	110.4077
25	3.386811	0.973	111.2937	77	0.898302	0.522	109.8936
26	3.566823	0.962	110.0189	78	0.871133	0.511	107.4925
27	2.672740	0.919	108.3243	79	1.657459	0.481	96.87312
28	2.520749	0.974	108.8500	80	1.237604	0.587	104.2167
29	2.985924	1.002	110.1109	81	0.761215	0.585	107.5994
30	2.942807	0.971	109.7797	82	0.944055	0.447	106.7747
31	3.004516	1.002	109.9321	83	0.685749	0.359	107.6608
32	2.637400	0.943	110.6811	84	1.070876	0.481	102.8868
33	2.991693	0.985	110.3865	85	0.689266	0.489	108.1952
34	3.352742	0.917	109.8845	86	0.702236	0.450	106.2919
35	2.888543	0.993	110.5550	87	0.791255	0.448	104.8745
36	2.356711	0.942	110.7433	88	0.634785	0.629	105.2315
37	3.826921	0.874	109.9506	89	1.854670	0.945	108.1005
38	3.604217	0.948	110.6622	90	1.128983	0.726	108.1344
39	2.854224	0.951	110.7483	91	0.947981	0.715	107.4729
40	2.809520	0.936	110.7279	92	0.890232	0.580	110.5551
41	2.170119	0.984	110.3961	93	0.928090	0.729	110.6059
42	2.314014	0.945	111.3022	94	1.009030	0.792	108.0279
43	1.618860	0.801	111.6536	95	0.955351	0.574	108.1546
44	2.009417	0.996	112.7955	96	0.817439	0.516	107.4958
45	1.321735	0.860	121.0602	97	0.929761	0.555	107.6180
46	1.798532	0.954	114.3316	98	0.490921	0.609	107.3281
47	1.467150	0.858	112.1764	99	0.497373	0.493	109.2267
48	1.739139	0.968	111.9120	100	0.634862	0.486	106.3676
49	1.988144	0.911	111.3051	101	0.596763	0.450	107.0693
50	1.554886	0.945	111.9401	102	0.486861	0.222	104.9389
51	1.580275	0.905	111.0169	103	0.370364	0.269	105.1217

Table DA.9. (*cont.*)

Week	M	D	P	Week	M	D	P
52	1.511920	0.879	113.3566	104	0.442591	0.354	104.6538
53	1.419592	0.883	111.4493	105	0.452372	0.082	104.0938
54	1.472885	0.758	111.0158	106	0.281125	0.289	104.5382
55	1.329193	0.916	111.6139	107	0.338190	0.256	104.1523
56	1.258603	0.874	111.7877	108	0.248307	0.207	109.8333
57	1.128232	0.795	121.4340	109	0.387469	0.309	105.1434
58	0.818452	0.662	112.9864	110	0.306534	0.281	107.9035
59	1.583273	0.792	111.0651	111	0.454702	0.392	105.5276
60	1.806577	0.831	109.0553	112	0.323122	0.361	104.3665
61	1.295540	0.683	108.5117	113	0.198953	0.142	104.4973
62	1.342100	0.769	110.1749				

Note:
These data are not in logs. Thanks to Willem Verbeke for making available these data series. The observations in week 6 are 2.740407, 0.905, 105.9539, in week 7 3.008390, 0.900, 106.2491, in week 8 2.203097, 0.988, 107.1034, in week 9 2.66952, 0.960, 106.4975, and in week 10 2.872620, 0.954 and 105.9954. These observations are used as starting values for most empirical analysis in this book.

Table DA.10. *Quarterly unemployment in Germany,*
1962.1–1991.4

Year	Not seasonally adjusted				Seasonally adjusted			
	Q1	Q2	Q3	Q4	Q1	Q2	Q3	Q4
1962	1.1	0.5	0.4	0.7	0.6	0.7	0.7	0.8
1963	1.6	0.6	0.5	0.7	0.9	0.8	0.8	0.8
1964	1.3	0.6	0.5	0.7	0.7	0.8	0.8	0.7
1965	1.2	0.5	0.4	0.6	0.6	0.6	0.7	0.7
1966	0.9	0.5	0.5	1.1	0.5	0.6	0.8	1.2
1967	2.9	2.1	1.7	2.0	2.0	2.4	2.3	2.1
1968	2.7	1.3	0.9	1.0	1.9	1.6	1.3	1.1
1969	1.6	0.6	0.5	0.7	0.9	0.8	0.8	0.7
1970	1.1	0.5	0.5	0.6	0.7	0.7	0.7	0.7
1971	1.2	0.7	0.7	1.0	0.7	0.8	0.9	1.0
1972	1.5	1.0	0.9	1.1	1.0	1.2	1.2	1.1
1973	1.5	1.0	1.0	1.6	1.0	1.1	1.3	1.6
1974	2.6	2.1	2.3	3.6	2.0	2.3	2.8	3.5
1975	5.0	4.5	4.5	4.9	4.2	4.9	5.1	5.0
1976	5.7	4.3	4.0	4.4	4.8	4.6	4.5	4.4
1977	5.2	4.3	4.2	4.5	4.4	4.6	4.6	4.5
1978	5.2	4.1	3.9	4.1	4.5	4.4	4.3	4.2
1979	4.8	3.5	3.4	3.5	4.0	3.8	3.7	3.6
1980	4.2	3.4	3.6	4.3	3.5	3.7	4.0	4.3
1981	5.5	4.8	5.4	6.5	4.7	5.2	5.8	6.6
1982	8.0	7.0	7.4	8.5	7.0	7.4	7.8	8.6
1983	10.1	8.9	8.8	9.0	9.1	9.4	9.2	9.1
1984	10.0	8.7	8.8	8.9	9.0	9.1	9.2	9.2
1985	10.4	8.9	8.9	9.0	9.3	9.3	9.3	9.2
1986	10.2	8.6	8.4	8.4	9.2	9.0	8.8	8.7
1987	9.9	8.5	8.6	8.7	8.9	8.9	8.9	8.9
1988	9.8	8.6	8.4	8.2	8.9	8.9	8.7	8.4
1989	8.8	7.6	7.5	7.6	8.0	8.0	7.7	7.7
1990	8.1	7.1	6.9	6.6	7.5	7.3	7.1	6.7
1991	6.8	6.0	6.2	6.2	6.3	6.3	6.4	6.3

Source: OECD Macroeconomic Indicators.

Table DA.11. *Dow-Jones index (week 1 in 1980 to week 39 in 1994)*

Observation					
1	824.5600	850.0900	865.1900	877.5600	881.9100
6	881.8300	903.8400	886.8600	855.1300	844.8800
11	819.5500	800.9400	762.1300	787.8000	785.9200
16	771.2500	789.2500	817.0600	821.2500	819.6300
21	831.0600	860.3100	858.0200	872.7000	881.9100
26	887.5500	876.0200	897.2700	904.4400	928.5800
31	936.1900	938.2300	949.2300	945.3100	943.0900
36	953.1600	938.4800	961.2700	964.7700	939.4200
41	963.9800	972.4400	955.1300	929.1900	953.1600
46	964.9400	991.0500	989.6900	972.2700	916.2000
51	928.5000	963.0500	963.9800	980.8900	966.4700
56	946.2500	942.5800	941.9800	942.4800	947.0900
61	954.4100	971.4400	967.6700	994.0600	1015.220
66	1014.140	993.4400	1001.700	1007.020	1004.310
71	973.3400	967.7700	976.8600	993.1400	989.7000
76	993.8800	1006.560	999.3300	967.6600	953.4800
81	954.1600	924.6600	937.4100	953.5800	945.2000
86	926.4500	899.2700	884.2300	853.8800	851.5900
91	840.9400	849.9800	868.7200	850.6600	851.0300
96	837.6100	866.8100	857.1300	844.0800	878.1400
101	882.6100	888.2200	868.7200	869.6700	873.0900
106	861.0200	838.9500	845.8900	842.6600	845.0300
111	836.6600	827.6300	826.7700	815.1600	804.8900
116	795.8400	823.3400	822.7700	836.8400	838.0900
121	843.4200	852.6400	854.4500	865.7700	835.9100
126	828.7700	816.8800	795.5600	796.9100	813.1700
131	811.9400	799.6600	828.3900	832.1900	811.8300
136	803.4500	777.2000	829.4400	884.8900	895.0500
141	915.7500	930.4500	927.6100	906.2700	944.2700
146	1015.080	1034.130	1006.340	1065.480	1044.520
151	1027.500	1000.000	1031.090	1047.090	992.6400
156	1035.050	1059.590	1044.890	1083.610	1068.060
161	1037.980	1062.640	1067.420	1087.440	1096.940
166	1135.060	1132.640	1116.000	1140.880	1143.300
171	1113.480	1156.640	1191.470	1208.410	1212.660
176	1219.720	1203.560	1229.020	1202.200	1185.500
181	1237.280	1245.690	1213.840	1220.660	1197.810
186	1227.860	1230.470	1197.810	1175.980	1206.500
191	1184.250	1216.160	1244.110	1229.470	1243.300
196	1241.970	1250.200	1259.660	1246.750	1243.800
201	1237.300	1232.520	1251.310	1275.610	1276.020
206	1273.780	1246.660	1254.980	1263.200	1269.050

Table DA.11. (*cont.*)

Observation					
211	1277.310	1269.380	1231.890	1212.310	1156.300
216	1158.700	1134.200	1154.630	1143.630	1166.050
221	1170.840	1174.630	1148.560	1130.970	1156.520
226	1163.530	1186.560	1165.520	1153.160	1113.800
231	1102.590	1133.840	1110.530	1131.630	1116.720
236	1134.280	1108.550	1111.640	1096.950	1134.610
241	1196.110	1198.980	1231.780	1226.920	1209.030
246	1200.310	1213.020	1212.120	1182.860	1177.230
251	1195.890	1216.440	1207.380	1233.220	1206.940
256	1201.520	1205.390	1171.590	1175.130	1208.050
261	1208.920	1198.880	1202.730	1230.690	1274.730
266	1287.880	1280.590	1297.920	1283.130	1281.030
271	1280.370	1261.700	1265.240	1264.910	1258.060
276	1259.940	1272.310	1278.490	1242.050	1249.780
281	1273.520	1303.760	1302.980	1320.560	1306.340
286	1297.380	1323.810	1326.390	1332.890	1357.970
291	1348.900	1347.450	1325.040	1316.980	1329.530
296	1331.090	1326.720	1319.440	1300.400	1312.050
301	1333.670	1326.720	1368.500	1367.160	1375.570
306	1403.440	1427.750	1439.220	1475.690	1484.400
311	1511.700	1542.430	1519.150	1546.670	1526.610
316	1527.290	1502.290	1558.940	1593.120	1629.930
321	1658.260	1696.900	1686.660	1745.450	1787.950
326	1810.700	1795.260	1778.620	1847.970	1829.610
331	1783.980	1775.300	1808.280	1775.170	1878.280
336	1863.290	1846.070	1868.940	1885.050	1909.030
341	1826.070	1774.180	1798.370	1779.390	1779.530
346	1844.490	1881.330	1904.530	1881.330	1879.500
351	1769.400	1803.290	1782.900	1803.850	1831.690
356	1808.350	1851.800	1899.040	1893.700	1826.630
361	1916.760	1947.270	1932.930	1918.310	1926.880
366	1895.950	1993.950	2035.010	2094.070	2163.390
371	2191.230	2171.960	2237.630	2226.240	2257.450
376	2268.980	2286.930	2363.490	2316.050	2372.160
381	2282.950	2285.940	2254.260	2342.190	2329.680
386	2215.870	2295.810	2320.690	2353.610	2407.350
391	2428.410	2409.760	2463.970	2483.740	2470.180
396	2539.540	2566.650	2669.320	2665.820	2701.850
401	2602.040	2549.270	2530.190	2585.670	2596.280
406	2551.080	2412.700	2027.850	1846.820	1945.290
411	1899.200	1939.160	1946.950	1848.970	1902.520
416	1974.470	2005.640	1950.100	2037.800	1924.730

Table DA.11. (*cont.*)

Observation					
421	1879.140	1911.140	1924.570	1962.040	2000.990
426	2039.950	2071.290	2074.270	2064.320	2067.640
431	1978.120	2061.670	2107.100	1985.410	2047.910
436	2036.310	1965.850	1951.090	1961.370	2064.010
441	2102.950	2131.400	2152.200	2121.980	2130.160
446	2104.370	2110.600	2053.700	2134.070	2034.140
451	2025.960	2026.670	2031.650	2065.790	2100.640
456	2090.500	2085.530	2106.510	2126.240	2137.270
461	2165.180	2156.830	2118.240	2038.580	2092.280
466	2114.510	2153.630	2134.250	2164.640	2166.430
471	2177.680	2206.430	2238.750	2265.890	2338.210
476	2343.210	2303.930	2283.930	2243.040	2295.540
481	2320.540	2263.210	2281.520	2304.800	2319.650
486	2386.910	2389.110	2393.700	2374.450	2462.430
491	2483.870	2480.150	2512.320	2503.360	2464.910
496	2504.740	2456.560	2532.630	2584.410	2613.050
501	2657.440	2686.080	2693.290	2678.110	2728.150
506	2719.790	2679.520	2683.890	2673.060	2771.090
511	2773.360	2643.650	2653.280	2645.900	2623.360
516	2632.580	2656.780	2688.780	2736.770	2761.090
521	2687.930	2724.400	2809.730	2750.640	2659.130
526	2604.500	2590.540	2640.090	2624.320	2583.560
531	2627.250	2669.590	2687.840	2727.930	2743.690
536	2719.370	2729.730	2732.880	2666.440	2689.640
541	2732.880	2819.680	2856.260	2878.560	2911.650
546	2929.950	2895.300	2862.130	2911.630	2932.670
551	2981.680	2930.940	2899.260	2734.900	2748.270
556	2560.150	2632.430	2628.220	2625.740	2557.430
561	2459.650	2489.360	2407.920	2387.870	2504.210
566	2442.330	2440.840	2559.650	2539.360	2535.150
571	2610.400	2622.280	2626.730	2637.130	2610.640
576	2470.300	2508.910	2619.060	2713.120	2830.940
581	2909.160	2899.010	2889.110	2973.270	2955.200
586	2872.030	2917.570	2926.730	2874.500	3004.460
591	2949.500	2930.200	2930.900	2865.380	2910.330
596	2969.590	3005.370	2961.990	2955.500	2913.010
601	2934.700	2944.770	2978.760	2966.230	3024.820
606	3026.610	3005.370	3001.790	3055.230	3008.500
611	2987.030	3017.890	3021.020	3012.520	2946.330
616	3061.720	3040.920	3071.780	3038.460	3065.300
621	2930.010	2900.040	2911.670	2865.380	2908.090
626	3050.980	3168.830	3203.940	3258.500	3255.810

Table DA.11. (*cont.*)

Observation					
631	3224.960	3257.600	3276.830	3230.320	3283.320
636	3268.560	3208.630	3254.250	3259.390	3249.330
641	3181.350	3353.760	3338.770	3333.180	3369.410
646	3391.980	3393.840	3370.440	3406.990	3343.220
651	3287.760	3290.700	3354.100	3293.280	3345.420
656	3277.610	3379.190	3365.140	3320.830	3307.060
661	3246.810	3290.310	3271.390	3319.210	3278.690
666	3271.660	3152.250	3195.480	3187.100	3251.400
671	3223.040	3240.330	3207.370	3266.260	3286.250
676	3323.810	3255.180	3313.540	3321.100	3305.160
681	3263.560	3241.950	3291.390	3373.790	3412.420
686	3312.190	3356.500	3404.040	3478.340	3426.740
691	3445.380	3435.110	3397.020	3455.650	3439.440
696	3413.500	3449.100	3482.310	3500.030	3540.160
701	3553.450	3511.930	3511.650	3466.810	3516.080
706	3475.670	3542.550	3555.400	3553.450	3552.050
711	3583.350	3604.860	3652.090	3645.100	3588.930
716	3633.650	3547.020	3566.300	3598.990	3603.190
721	3645.100	3664.660	3661.870	3663.550	3704.350
726	3687.580	3697.080	3734.530	3716.920	3762.190
731	3794.330	3798.820	3848.630	3884.370	3908.000
736	3975.540	3931.920	3937.270	3891.680	3831.740
741	3853.410	3848.150	3869.460	3626.750	3679.730
746	3661.470	3598.710	3699.540	3697.750	3629.040
751	3732.890	3755.300	3760.830	3749.450	3790.410
756	3724.770	3667.050	3674.500	3704.280	3727.270
761	3720.470	3792.660	3766.760	3776.480	3846.730
766	3913.420	3886.250	3895.330	3851.600	3878.180

Note:
The weekly data correspond with the Wednesday quotes.

Table DA.12. *Television rights for Olympic Games for USA networks (in millions of dollars)*

Year	City	Network	Rights
1960	Rome	CBS	0.394
1964	Tokyo	NBC	1.5
1968	Mexico-City	ABC	4.5
1972	Munich	ABC	7.5
1976	Montreal	ABC	25.0
1980	Moskou	NBC	87.0
1984	Los Angeles	ABC	225.0
1988	Seoul	NBC	300.0
1992	Barcelona	NBC	401.0
1996	Atlanta	NBC	456.0

References

Abraham, B. and J. Ledolter (1983), *Statistical Methods for Forecasting*, New York: Wiley.

Abraham, B. and N. Yatawara (1988), A Score Test for Detection of Time Series Outliers, *Journal of Time Series Analysis*, 9, 109–119.

Agiakloglou, C. and P. Newbold (1992), Empirical Evidence on Dickey–Fuller Type Tests, *Journal of Time Series Analysis*, 13, 471–483.

Akaike, H. (1974), A New Look at the Statistical Model Identification, *IEEE Transactions on Automatic Control*, AC-19, 716–723.

Anderson, H. and F. Vahid (1998), Testing Multiple Equation Systems for Common Nonlinear Components, *Journal of Econometrics*, 84, 1–36.

Anderson, T.W. (1971), *The Statistical Analysis of Time Series*, New York: Wiley.

Baillie, R. T. (1996), Long Memory Processes and Fractional Integration in Econometrics, *Journal of Econometrics*, 73, 5–60.

Balke, N.S. and T. Fomby (1997), Threshold Cointegration, *International Economic Review*, 38, 627–646.

Banerjee, A., J. Dolado, J.W. Galbraith, and D.F. Hendry (1993), *Cointegration, Error Correction, and the Econometric Analysis of Nonstationary Data*, Oxford: Oxford University Press.

Banerjee, A., R. Lumsdaine, and J.H. Stock (1992), Recursive and Sequential Tests for a Unit Root: Theory and International Evidence, *Journal of Business and Economic Statistics*, 10, 271–287.

Beaulieu, J.J. and J.A. Miron (1993), Seasonal Unit Roots in Aggregate US Data, *Journal of Econometrics*, 55, 305–328.

Bell, W.R. (1987), A Note on Overdifferencing and the Equivalence of Seasonal Time Series Models With Monthly Means and Models With $(0,1,1)_{12}$ Seasonal Parts When $\theta = 1$, *Journal of Business and Economic Statistics*, 5, 383–387.

Bell, W.R. and S.C. Hillmer (1984), Issues Involved with the Seasonal Adjustment of Economic Time Series (with discussion), *Journal of Business and Economic Statistics*, 2, 291–320.

Bera, A.K. and M.L. Higgins (1993), ARCH Models: Properties, Estimation and Testing, *Journal of Economic Surveys*, 7, 305–366.

Bera, A.K. and C.M. Jarque (1982), Model Specification Tests: A Simultaneous Approach, *Journal of Econometrics*, 20, 59–82.

261

Beran, J. (1995), Maximum Likelihood Estimation of the Differencing Parameter for Invertible Short and Long Memory Autoregressive Integrated Moving Average Models, *Journal of the Royal Statistical Society* B, 57, 654–672.

Bernardo, J.M. and A.F.M. Smith (1994), *Bayesian Theory*, New York: Wiley.

Bierens, H.J. (1987), ARMAX Model Specification Testing, With an Application to Unemployment in The Netherlands, *Journal of Econometrics*, 35, 61–90.

Birchenhall, C.R., R.C. Bladen-Hovell, A.P.L. Chui, D.R. Osborn, and J.P. Smith (1989), A Seasonal Model of Consumption, *Economic Journal*, 99, 837–843.

Bishop, C.M. (1995), *Neural Networks for Pattern Recognition*, Oxford: Oxford University Press.

Blattberg, R.C., R. Briesch, and E.J. Fox (1995), How Promotions Work, *Marketing Science*, 14, G123–G132.

Bollerslev, T. (1986), Generalized Autoregressive Conditional Heteroskedasticity, *Journal of Econometrics*, 31, 307–327.

(1987), A Conditionally Heteroskedastic Time Series Model for Speculative Prices and Rates of Return, *Review of Economics and Statistics*, 69, 542–547.

(1988), On the Correlation Structure for the Generalized ARCH Process, *Journal of Time Series Analysis*, 9, 121–131.

Bollerslev, T., R. Chou, and K. Kroner (1992), ARCH Modeling in Finance: A Review of the Theory and Empirical Evidence, *Journal of Econometrics*, 52, 5–59.

Bollerslev, T. and R.F. Engle (1993), Common Persistence in Conditional Variance, *Econometrica*, 61, 166–187.

Bollerslev, T., R.F. Engle, and D.B. Nelson (1994), ARCH Models, in R.F. Engle and D.L. McFadden (eds.), *Handbook of Econometrics*, Volume IV, Amsterdam: Elsevier.

Boswijk, H.P. (1994), Testing for an Unstable Root in Conditional and Structural Error Correction Models, *Journal of Econometrics*, 63, 37–60.

(1998), *Asymptotic Theory for Integrated Processes*, Oxford: Oxford University Press, to appear.

Boswijk, H.P. and P.H. Franses (1995), Periodic Cointegration: Representation and Inference, *Review of Economics and Statistics*, 77, 436–454.

(1996), Unit Roots in Periodic Autoregressions, *Journal of Time Series Analysis*, 17, 221–245.

Bowerman, B.L., A.B. Koehler, and D.J. Pack (1990), Forecasting Time Series with Increasing Seasonal Variation, *Journal of Forecasting*, 9, 419–436.

Box, G.E.P. and G.M. Jenkins (1970), *Time Series Analysis, Forecasting and Control*, San Francisco: Holden–Day.

Box, G.E.P, G.M. Jenkins, and G.C. Reinsel (1994), *Time Series Analysis, Forecasting and Control* (third edition), Englewood Cliffs: Prentice Hall.

Box, G.E.P. and G.C. Tiao (1975), Intervention Analysis with Application to Economic and Environmental Problems, *Journal of the American Statistical Association*, 70, 70–79.

Breitung, J. (1994), Some Simple Tests of the Moving-Average Unit Root Hypothesis, *Journal of Time Series Analysis*, 15, 351–370.

Bustos, O.H. and V.J. Yohai (1986), Robust Estimates for ARMA Models, *Journal of the American Statistical Association*, 81, 155–168.

Campbell, J.Y. and P. Perron (1991), Pitfalls and Opportunities: What Macroeconomists Should Know about Unit Roots, in O.J. Blanchard and S. Fisher (eds.), *NBER Macroeconomics Annual* 1991, Boston: MIT Press.

Canova, F. and B.E. Hansen (1995), Are Seasonal Patterns Constant over Time?, A Test for Seasonal Stability, *Journal of Business and Economic Statistics*, 13, 237–252.

Chatfield, C. and D.L. Prothero (1973), Box-Jenkins Seasonal Forecasting: Problems in a Case Study, *Journal of the Royal Statistical Society*, A, 136, 295–336.

Chen, C. and L.-M. Liu (1993), Joint Estimation of Model Parameters and Outlier Effects in Time Series, *Journal of the American Statistical Association*, 88, 284–297.

Cheung, Y-W. (1993), Long Memory in Foreign Exchange Rates, *Journal of Business and Economic Statistics*, 11, 93–101.

Chow, G.C. (1993), Capital Formation and Economic Growth in China, *Quarterly Journal of Economics*, 103, 809–842.

Clements, M.P. and D.F. Hendry (1993), On the Limitations of Comparing Mean Square Forecast Errors (with discussion), *Journal of Forecasting*, 12, 617–676.

(1995), Forecasting in Cointegrated Systems, *Journal of Applied Econometrics*, 10, 127–146.

(1997), An Empirical Study of Seasonal Unit Roots in Forecasting, *International Journal of Forecasting*, 13, 341–355.

Crato, N. and B.K. Ray (1996), Model Selection and Forecasting for Long-Range Dependent Processes, *Journal of Forecasting*, 15, 107–125.

Day, T. and C. Lewis (1992), Stock Market Volatility and the Information Content of Stock Index Options, *Journal of Econometrics*, 52, 267–287.

De Gooijer, J.G., B. Abraham, A. Gould, and L. Robinson (1985), Methods for Determining the Order of an Autoregressive-Moving Average Process: A Survey, *International Statistical Review*, 85, 301–329.

De Gooijer, J.G. and K. Kumar (1992), Some Recent Developments in Non-linear Time Series Modelling, Testing, and Forecasting, *International Journal of Forecasting*, 8, 135–156.

Denby, L. and R.D. Martin (1979), Robust Estimation of the First-Order Autoregressive Parameter, *Journal of the American Statistical Association*, 74, 140–146.

De Ruyter van Steveninck, M.A. (1996), *The Impact of Capital Imports; Argentina 1970–1989*, Amsterdam: Thesis Publishers.

Dhrymes, P.J. (1981), *Distributed Lags, Problems of Estimation and Formulation* (Second Revised Edition), Amsterdam: North-Holland.

Dickey, D.A. and W.A. Fuller (1979), Distribution of the Estimators for Autoregressive Time Series With a Unit Root, *Journal of the American Statistical Association*, 74, 427–431.

(1981), Likelihood Ratio Statistics for Autoregressive Time Series with a Unit Root, *Econometrica*, 49, 1057–1072.

Dickey, D.A., D.P. Hasza, and W.A. Fuller (1984), Testing for Unit Roots in Seasonal Time Series, *Journal of the American Statistical Association*, 79, 355–367.

Dickey, D.A. and S.G. Pantula (1987), Determining the Order of Differencing in Autoregressive Processes, *Journal of Business and Economic Statistics*, 5, 455–461.

Diebold, F.X. and R.S. Mariano (1995), Comparing Predictive Accuracy, *Journal of Business and Economic Statistics*, 13, 253–263.

Eitrheim, O. and T. Teräsvirta (1996), Testing the Adequacy of Smooth Transition Autoregressive Models, *Journal of Econometrics*, 74, 59–76.

Engle, R.F. (1982), Autoregressive Conditional Heteroskedasticity with Estimates of the Variance of UK Inflation, *Econometrica*, 50, 987–1008.

Engle, R.F. ed. (1995), *ARCH, Selected Readings*, Oxford: Oxford University Press.

Engle, R.F. and C.W.J. Granger (1987), Co-integration and Error Correction: Representation, Estimation, and Testing, *Econometrica*, 55, 251–276.

Engle, R.F., C.W.J. Granger, S. Hylleberg, and H.S. Lee (1993), Seasonal Cointegration: The Japanese Consumption Function, *Journal of Econometrics*, 55, 275–298.

Engle, R.F., D.F. Hendry, and J.-F. Richard (1983), Exogeneity, *Econometrica*, 55, 251–276.

Engle, R.F. and S. Hylleberg (1996), Common Seasonal Features: Global Unemployment, *Oxford Bulletin of Economics and Statistics*, 58, 615–630.

Engle, R.F. and S. Kozicki (1993), Testing for Common Features (with discussion), *Journal of Business and Economic Statistics*, 11, 369–395.

Engle, R.F., D.M. Lilien, and R.P. Robins (1987), Estimating Time-Varying Risk Premia in the Term Structure: The ARCH-M Model, *Econometrica*, 55, 391–407.

Engle, R.F. and V. Ng (1993), Measuring and Testing the Impact of News on Volatility, *Journal of Finance*, 48, 1749–1778.

Engle, R.F., V. Ng, and M. Rothschild (1990), Asset Pricing with a Factor ARCH Covariance Structure: Empirical Estimates for Treasury Bills, *Journal of Econometrics*, 45, 213–238.

Engle, R.F. and B.S. Yoo (1987), Forecasting and Testing in Cointegrated Systems, *Journal of Econometrics*, 35, 143–159.

Ermini, L. and D. Chang (1996), Testing the Joint Hypothesis of Rationality and Neutrality Under Seasonal Cointegration: The Case of Korea, *Journal of Econometrics*, 74, 363–386.

Fan, J. and I. Gijbels (1996), *Local Polynomial Modelling and Its Applications*, London: Chapman and Hall.

Fox, A.J. (1972), Outliers in Time Series, *Journal of the Royal Statistical Society* B, 34, 350–363.

Franses, P.H. (1991a), Seasonality, Nonstationarity and the Forecasting of Monthly Time Series, *International Journal of Forecasting*, 7, 199–208.

(1991b), Primary Demand for Beer in The Netherlands: An Application of ARMAX Model Specification, *Journal of Marketing Research*, 28, 240–245.

(1994), A Method to Select Between Gompertz and Logistic Trend Curves, *Technological Forecasting and Social Change*, 46, 45–49.

(1995), A Differencing Test, *Econometric Reviews*, 14, 183–193.

(1996), *Periodicity and Stochastic Trends in Economic Time Series*, Oxford: Oxford University Press.

Franses, P.H. and G. Draisma (1997), Recognizing Changing Seasonal Patterns Using Artificial Neural Networks, *Journal of Econometrics*, 81, 273–280.

Franses, P.H. and N. Haldrup (1994), The Effects of Additive Outliers on Tests for Unit Roots and Cointegration, *Journal of Business and Economic Statistics*, 12, 471–478.

Franses, P.H. and B. Hobijn (1997), Critical Values for Unit Root Tests in Seasonal Time Series, *Journal of Applied Statistics*, 24, 25–47.

Franses, P.H., S. Hylleberg, and H.S. Lee (1995), Spurious Deterministic Seasonality, *Economics Letters*, 48, 249–256.

Franses, P.H. and F. Kleibergen (1996), Unit Roots in the Nelson–Plosser Data: Do They Matter for Forecasting?, *International Journal of Forecasting*, 12, 283–288.

Franses, P.H. and A.B. Koehler (1998), Model Selection Strategies for Time Series with Increasing Seasonal Variation, *International Journal of Forecasting*, to appear.

Franses, P.H. and R.M. Kunst (1997), On the Role of Seasonal Intercepts in Seasonal Cointegration, Research Report, Institute for Advanced Studies, Vienna.

Franses, P.H. and A. Lucas (1998), Outlier Detection in Cointegration Analysis, *Journal of Business and Economic Studies*, to appear.

Franses, P.H. and R. Paap (1998), Does Seasonal Adjustment Change Inference from Markov Switching Models?, *Journal of Macroeconomics*, to appear.

Franses, P.H. and J.D. Van der Nol (1997), Selecting Between Gompertz and Logistic Growth Curves, Rotterdam Institute for Business Economic Studies Report 9701/M, Erasmus University Rotterdam.

Franses, P.H. and D. Van Dijk (1996), Forecasting Stock Market Volatility Using (Non-linear) GARCH Models, *Journal of Forecasting*, 15, 229–235.

Franses, P.H. and P. Van Homelen (1998), On Forecasting Exchange Rates Using Neural Networks, *Applied Financial Economics*, to appear.

Franses, P.H. and T.J. Vogelsang (1998), On Seasonal Cycles, Unit Roots and Mean Shifts, *Review of Economics and Statistics*, to appear.

Fuller, W.A. (1976), *Introduction to Statistical Time Series*, New York: Wiley.

Gençay, R. (1996), Non-linear Prediction of Security Returns with Moving Average Rules, *Journal of Forecasting*, 15, 165–174.

Ghysels, E. (1994), On the Economics and Econometrics of Seasonality, in C.A. Sims (ed.), *Advances in Econometrics, Sixth World Congress of the Econometric Society*, Cambridge: Cambridge University Press.

Ghysels, E., C.W.J. Granger, and P.L. Siklos (1996), Is Seasonal Adjustment a Linear or Nonlinear Data-Filtering Process? (with discussion), *Journal of Business and Economic Statistics*, 14, 374–397.

Ghysels, E., H.S. Lee, and J. Noh (1994), Testing for Unit Roots in Seasonal Time Series, *Journal of Econometrics*, 62, 415–442.

Ghysels, E. and P. Perron (1993), The Effect of Seasonal Adjustment Filters on Tests for a Unit Root, *Journal of Econometrics*, 55, 57–98.

Glosten, L., R. Jagannathan, and D. Runkle (1992), On the Relation Between the Expected Value and the Volatility of Nominal Excess Returns on Stocks, *Journal of Finance*, 46, 1779–1801.

Godfrey, L.G. (1979), Testing the Adequacy of a Time Series Model, *Biometrika*, 66, 67–72.

Gonzalo, J. and C.W.J. Granger (1995), Estimation of Common Long-Memory Components in Cointegrated Systems, *Journal of Business and Economic Statistics*, 13, 27–36.

Granger, C.W.J. (1966), The Typical Spectral Shape of an Economic Variable, *Econometrica*, 34, 150–161.

(1969), Investigating Causal Relations by Econometric Models and Cross-Spectral Methods, *Econometrica*, 37, 424–438.

Granger, C.W.J. and A.P. Andersen (1978), *Introduction to Bilinear Time Series Models*, Goettingen: Vandenhoeck and Ruprecht.

Granger, C.W.J. and R. Joyeux (1980), An Introduction to Long-Memory Time Series Models and Fractional Differencing, *Journal of Time Series Analysis*, 1, 15–39.

Granger, C.W.J., M.L. King, and H. White (1995), Comments on Testing Economic Theories and the Use of Model Selection Criteria, *Journal of Econometrics* 678, 173–188.

Granger, C.W.J. and P. Newbold (1974), Spurious Regressions in Econometrics, *Journal of Econometrics*, 2, 111–120

(1976), Forecasting Transformed Time Series, *Journal of the Royal Statistical Society* B, 38, 189–203.

(1986), *Forecasting Economic Time Series*, 2nd Edition, San Diego: Academic Press.

Granger, C.W.J. and N.R. Swanson (1997), An Introduction to Stochastic Unit Root Processes, *Journal of Econometrics*, 80, 35–62.

Granger, C.W.J. and T. Teräsvirta (1993), *Modelling Nonlinear Economic Relationships*, Oxford: Oxford University Press.

Grether, D.M. and M. Nerlove (1970), Some Properties of Optimal Seasonal Adjustment, *Econometrica*, 38, 682–703.

Haggan, V. and T. Ozaki (1981), Modelling Non-linear Vibrations using an Amplitude-Dependent Autoregressive Time Series Model, *Biometrika*, 68, 189–196.

Haldrup, N. (1994), Semi-parametric Tests for Double Unit Roots, *Journal of Business and Economic Statistics*, 12, 109–122.

(1996), Mirror Image Distributions and the Dickey–Fuller Regression with a Maintained Trend, *Journal of Econometrics*, 72, 301–312.

Hall, A. (1994), Testing for a Unit Root in Time Series With Pretest Data-Based Model Selection, *Journal of Business and Economic Statistics*, 12, 461–470.

Hall, A.D. and M. McAleer (1989), A Monte Carlo Study of Some Tests of Model Adequacy in Time Series Analysis, *Journal of Business and Economic Statistics*, 7, 95–106.

Hamilton, J.D. (1989), A New Approach to the Econometric Analysis of Nonstationary Time Series and Business Cycles, *Econometrica*, 57, 357–384.

(1990), Analysis of Time Series Subject to Changes in Regime, *Journal of Econometrics*, 45, 39–70.

(1994), *Time Series Analysis*, Princeton: Princeton University Press.

Hannan, E.J. (1970), *Multiple Time Series*, New York: Wiley.

Hansen, L.P. and T.J. Sargent (1993), Seasonality and Approximation Errors in Rational Expectations Models, *Journal of Econometrics*, 55, 21–56.

Härdle, W., H. Lütkepohl, and R. Chen (1997), A Review of Nonparametric Time Series Analysis, *International Statistical Review*, 65, 49–72.

Harvey, A.C. (1989), *Forecasting, Structural Time Series Models and the Kalman Filter*, Cambridge: Cambridge University Press.

Hassler, U. and J. Wolters (1995), Long Memory in Inflation Rates: International Evidence, *Journal of Business and Economic Statistics*, 13, 37–46.

Hasza, D.P. and W.A. Fuller (1982), Testing for Nonstationary Parameter Specifications in Seasonal Time Series Models, *Annals of Statistics*, 10, 1209–1216.

Hatanaka, M. (1996), *Time-Series-Based Econometrics, Unit Roots and Cointegration*, Oxford: Oxford University Press.

Hendry, D.F. (1995), *Dynamic Econometrics*, Oxford: Oxford University Press.

Hendry, D.F. and A. Neale (1990), The Impact of Structural Breaks on Unit Root Tests, in P. Hackl and A. Westlund (eds.), *Economic Structural Change, Analysis and Forecasting*, Berlin: Springer.

Hosking, J.R.M. (1980), The Multivariate Portmanteau Statistic, *Journal of the American Statistical Association*, 75, 602–608.

(1981), Fractional Differencing, *Biometrika*, 68, 165–176.

Hylleberg, S. (1986), *Seasonality in Regression*, Orlando: Academic Press.

(1994), Modelling Seasonal Variation, in Hargreaves, C.P. (ed.), *Nonstationary Time Series Analysis and Cointegration*, Oxford: Oxford University Press.

(1995), Tests for Seasonal Unit Roots: General to Specific or Specific to General?, *Journal of Econometrics*, 69, 5–25

Hylleberg, S., ed. (1992), *Modelling Seasonality*, Oxford: Oxford University Press.

Hylleberg, S., R.F. Engle, C.W.J. Granger, and B.S. Yoo (1990), Seasonal Integration and Cointegration, *Journal of Econometrics*, 44, 215–238.

Hylleberg, S. and G.E. Mizon (1989a), A Note on the Distribution of the Least Squares Estimator of a Random Walk With Drift, *Economics Letters*, 29, 225–230.

(1989b), Cointegration and Error Correction Mechanisms, *Economic Journal*, 99, 113–125.

Jaeger, A. and R.M. Kunst (1990), Seasonal Adjustment and Measuring Persistence in Output, *Journal of Applied Econometrics*, 5, 47–58.

Johansen, S. (1988), Statistical Analysis of Cointegration Vectors, *Journal of Economic Dynamics and Control*, 12, 231–254.

(1991), Estimation and Hypothesis Testing of Cointegration Vectors in Gaussian Vector Autoregressive Models, *Econometrica*, 59, 1551–1580.

(1992), Cointegration in Partial Systems and the Efficiency of Single-Equation Analysis, *Journal of Econometrics*, 52, 389–402.

(1995), *Likelihood-Based Inference in Cointegrated Vector Autoregressive Models*, Oxford: Oxford University Press.

Johansen, S. and E. Schaumburg (1997), Likelihood Analysis of Seasonal Cointegration, Report ECO 97/16, European University Institute, Florence.

Kuan, C.M. and T. Liu (1995), Forecasting Exchange Rates using Feedforward and Recurrent Neural Networks, *Journal of Applied Econometrics*, 10, 347–364.

Kuan, C.M. and H. White (1994), Artificial Neural Networks: an Econometric Perspective (with discussion), *Econometric Reviews*, 13, 1–91.

Kunst, R.M. (1993), Seasonal Cointegration in Macroeconomic Systems: Case Studies for Small and Large European Countries, *Review of Economics and Statistics*, 75, 325–330.

Kwiatkowski, D., P.C.B. Phillips, P. Schmidt and Y. Shin (1992), Testing the Null Hypothesis of Stationarity Against the Alternative of a Unit Root, *Journal of Econometrics*, 54, 159–178.

Laroque, G. (1977), Analyse d'une Méthode de Désaissonnalisation: le Programme X-11 du Bureau of Census, Version Trimestrielle, *Annales de l'INSEE*, 28, 105–127.

Ledolter, J. (1989), The Effect of Additive Outliers on the Forecasts from ARIMA Models, *International Journal of Forecasting*, 5, 231–240.

Lee, H.S. (1992), Maximum Likelihood Inference on Cointegration and Seasonal Cointegration, *Journal of Econometrics*, 54, 351–365.

Lee, H.S. and P.L. Siklos (1995), A Note on the Critical Values for the Maximum Likelihood (Seasonal) Cointegration Tests, *Economics Letters*, 49, 137–145.

(1997), The Role of Seasonality in Time Series: Reinterpreting Money-Output Causality in US Data, *International Journal of Forecasting*, 13, 301–391.

Lee, J.H.H. (1991), A Lagrange Multiplier Test for GARCH Models, *Economic Letters*, 37, 265–271.

Lee, T.-H. and Y. Tse (1996), Cointegration Tests with Conditional Heteroskedasticity, *Journal of Econometrics*, 73, 401–410.

Leone, R.P. (1987), Forecasting the Effect of an Environmental Change on Market Performance, *International Journal of Forecasting*, 3, 463–478.

Leybourne, S.J. and B.P.M. McCabe (1994), A Consistent Test for a Unit Root, *Journal of Business and Economic Statistics*, 12, 157–166.

Lin, J.-L. and R.S. Tsay (1996), Cointegration Constraints and Forecasting: An Empirical Examination, *Journal of Applied Econometrics*, 11, 519–538.

Ljung, G.M. and G.E.P. Box (1978), On a Measure of Lack of Fit in Time Series Models, *Biometrika*, 65, 297–303.

Lomnicki, Z.A. (1961), Tests for Departure from Normality in the Case of Linear Stochastic Processes, *Metrika*, 4, 27–62.

Lucas, A. (1995), An Outlier Robust Unit Root Test with an Application to the Extended Nelson–Plosser Data, *Journal of Econometrics*, 66, 153–173.

(1996), *Outlier Robust Unit Root Analysis*, Amsterdam: Thesis/Tinbergen Institute.

Lumsdaine, R. (1995), Finite-Sample Properties of the Maximum Likelihood Estimator in GARCH(1,1) and IGARCH(1,1) Models: A Monte Carlo Investigation, *Journal of Business and Economic Statistics*, 13, 1–10.

Lütkepohl, H. (1991), *Introduction to Multiple Time Series Analysis*, Berlin: Springer-Verlag.

Lütkepohl, H. and H.-E. Reimers (1992), Impulse Response Analysis of Cointegrated Systems, *Journal of Economic Dynamics and Control*, 16, 53–78.

Maddala, G.S. and I.-M. Kim (1996), Structural Changes and Unit Roots, *Journal of Statistical Planning and Inference*, 49, 73–103.

Mahajan, V., E. Muller, and F.M. Bass (1993), New-Product Diffusion Models, in J. Eliashberg and G.L. Lilien (eds.), *Handbooks in Operations Research and Management Science, Vol. 5 (Marketing)*, Amsterdam: Elsevier Science.

Makridakis, S., A. Andersen, R. Carbone, R. Fildes, M. Hibon, R. Lewandowski, J. Newton, E. Parzen, and R. Winkler (1982), The Accuracy of Extrapolation (Time Series) Methods: Results of a Forecasting Competition, *Journal of Forecasting*, 1, 111–153.

MacKinnon, J.G. (1991), Critical Values for Co-Integration Tests, in R.F. Engle and C.W.J. Granger (eds.), *Long-Run Economic Relationships*, Oxford: Oxford University Press.

McCabe, B.P.M. and A.R. Tremayne (1995), Testing a Series for Difference Stationarity, *Annals of Statistics*, 23, 1015–1028.

McLeod, A.I. and W.K. Li (1983), Diagnostic Checking ARMA Time Series Models Using Squared Residual Autocorrelations, *Journal of Time Series Analysis*, 4, 269–273.

Meade, N. and T. Islam (1995), Prediction Intervals for Growth Curve Forecasts, *Journal of Forecasting*, 14, 413–430.

Mills, T.C. (1990), *Time Series Techniques for Economists*, Cambridge: Cambridge University Press.

Miron, J.A. (1996), *The Economics of Seasonal Cycles*, Cambridge Massachusetts: MIT Press.

Nankervis, J.C. and N.E. Savin (1987), Finite Sample Distributions of t and F Statistics in an AR(1) Model With an Exogenous Variable, *Econometric Theory*, 3, 387–408.

Neftçi, S.N. (1984), Are Economic Time Series Asymmetric Over the Business Cycle?, *Journal of Political Economy*, 92, 307–328.

Nelson, C.R. (1976), The Interpretation of R^2 in Autoregressive Moving Average Time Series Models, *American Statistician*, 30, 175–180.

Nelson, C.R. and C.I. Plosser (1982), Trends and Random Walks in Macroeconomic Time Series, *Journal of Monetary Economics*, 9, 139–162.

Nelson, D.B. (1990), Stationarity and Persistence in the GARCH(1,1) Model, *Econometric Theory*, 6, 318–334.

Newey, W.K. and K.D. West (1987), A Simple, Positive Semi-Definite, Heteroskedasticity and Autocorrelation Consistent Covariance Matrix, *Econometrica*, 55, 703–708.

Ng, S. and P. Perron (1997), Estimation and Inference in Nearly Unbalanced Nearly Cointegrated Systems, *Journal of Econometrics*, 79, 53–82.

Ooms, M. (1994), *Empirical Vector Autoregressive Modeling*, Berlin: Springer.

Osborn, D.R. (1988), Seasonality and Habit Persistence in a Life-Cycle Model of Consumption, *Journal of Applied Econometrics*, 3, 255–266.

(1990), A Survey of Seasonality in UK Macroeconomic Variables, *International Journal of Forecasting*, 6, 327–336.

Osborn, D.R., A.P.L. Chui, J.P. Smith, and C.R. Birchenhall (1988), Seasonality and the Order of Integration for Consumption, *Oxford Bulletin of Economics and Statistics*, 50, 361–377.

Osborn, D.R. and J.P. Smith (1989), The Performance of Periodic Autoregressive Models in Forecasting Seasonal UK Consumption, *Journal of Business and Economic Statistics*, 7, 117–127.

Osterwald-Lenum, M. (1992), A Note with Quantiles of the Asymptotic Distribution of the Maximum Likelihood Cointegration Rank Test Statistics: Four Cases, *Oxford Bulletin of Economics and Statistics*, 54, 461–472.

Paap, R., P.H. Franses, and H. Hoek (1997), Mean Shifts, Unit Roots and Forecasting Seasonal Time Series, *International Journal of Forecasting*, 13, 357–368.

Pagan, A.R. (1996), The Econometrics of Financial Markets, *Journal of Empirical Finance*, 3, 15–102.

Pagan, A.R. and G.W. Schwert (1990), Alternative Models for Conditional Stock Market Volatility, *Journal of Econometrics*, 45, 267–290.

Paulsen, J. (1984), Order Determination of Multivariate Autoregressive Time Series With Unit Roots, *Journal of Time Series Analysis*, 5, 115–127.

Perron, P. (1989), The Great Crash, the Oil Price Shock, and the Unit Root Hypothesis, *Econometrica*, 57, 1361–1401.

(1990), Testing for a Unit Root in a Time Series With a Changing Mean, *Journal of Business and Economic Statistics*, 8, 153–162.

Perron, P. and T.J. Vogelsang (1992), Nonstationarity and Level Shifts With an Application to Purchasing Power Parity, *Journal of Business and Economic Statistics*, 10, 301–320.

Phillips, P.C.B. (1986), Understanding Spurious Regressions in Econometrics, *Journal of Econometrics*, 33, 311–340.

(1987), Time Series Regression with a Unit Root, *Econometrica*, 55, 277–301.

Phillips, P.C.B. and S. Ouliaris (1990), Asymptotic Properties of Residual Based Tests for Cointegration, *Econometrica*, 58, 165–193.

Phillips, P.C.B. and P. Perron (1988), Testing for a Unit Root in Time Series Regression, *Biometrika*, 75, 335–346.

Plosser, C.I. and G.W. Schwert (1977), Estimation of a Non-invertible Moving Average Process. The Case of Overdifferencing, *Journal of Econometrics*, 6, 199–224.

Poirier, D.J. (1995), *Intermediate Statistics and Econometrics: A Comparative Approach*, Cambridge Massachusetts, MIT Press.

Poskitt, D.S. and A.R. Tremayne (1982), Diagnostic Tests for Multiple Time Series Models, *Annals of Statistics*, 10, 114–120.

Priestley, M.B. (1981), *Spectral Analysis and Time Series*, London: Academic Press.

(1988), *Non-linear and Non-stationary Time Series Analysis*, San Diego: Academic Press.

Rabemananjara, R. and J.M. Zakoian (1993), Threshold ARCH Models and Asymmetries in Volatility, *Journal of Applied Econometrics*, 8, 31–49.

Reimers, H.-E. (1995), Interval Forecasting in Cointegrated Systems, *Statistical Papers*, 36, 349–370.

(1997), Forecasting of Seasonal Cointegrated Processes, *International Journal of Forecasting*, 13, 369–380.

Ripley, B.D. (1994), Neural Networks and Related Methods for Classification, *Journal of the Royal Statistical Society* B, 56, 409–456.

Rissanen, J. (1978), Modeling by Shortest Data Description, *Automatica*, 14, 465–471.

Rudebusch, G.R. (1992), Trends and Random Walks in Macroeconomic Time Series: A Re-examination, *International Economic Review*, 33, 661–680.

Said, S.E. and D.A. Dickey (1984), Testing for Unit Roots in Autoregressive-Moving Average Models of Unknown Order, *Biometrika*, 71, 599–607.

Schotman, P.C. and H.K. van Dijk (1991), On Bayesian Routes to Unit Roots, *Journal of Applied Econometrics*, 6, 387–401.

Schwarz, G. (1978), Estimating the Dimension of a Model, *Annals of Statistics*, 6, 461–464.

Sentana, E. (1995), Quadratic ARCH Models, *Review of Economic Studies*, 62, 639–661.

Shiskin, J. and H. Eisenpress (1957), Seasonal Adjustment by Electronic Computer Methods, *Journal of the American Statistical Association*, 52, 415–449.

Shiskin, J., A.H. Young, and J.C. Musgrave (1967), The X-11 Variant of the Census Method II Seasonal Adjustment Program, Technical Report 15, Bureau of the Census, US Department of Commerce, Washington DC.

Sims, C.A. (1980), Macroeconomics and Reality, *Econometrica*, 48, 1–48.

Sin, C.Y. and H. White (1996), Information Criteria for Selecting Possibly Misspecified Parametric Models, *Journal of Econometrics*, 71, 207–225.

Sowell, F. (1992), Maximum Likelihood Estimation of Stationary Univariate Fractionally Integrated Time Series Models, *Journal of Econometrics*, 53, 165–188.

Stock, J. and M.W. Watson (1989), Testing for Common Trends, *Journal of the American Statistical Association*, 83, 1097–1107.

Swanson, N.R. and H. White (1995), A Model-Selection Approach to Assessing the Information in the Term Structure Using Linear Models and Artificial Neural Networks, *Journal of Business and Economic Statistics*, 13, 265–275.

Taylor, S.J. (1986), *Modelling Financial Time Series*, Chichester: Wiley.

Teräsvirta, T. (1994), Specification, Estimation, and Evaluation of Smooth Transition Autoregressive Models, *Journal of the American Statistical Association*, 89, 208–218.

Teräsvirta, T. and H.M. Anderson (1992), Characterizing Nonlinearities in Business Cycles using Smooth Transition Autoregressive Models, *Journal of Applied Econometrics*, 7, S119–S136.

Teräsvirta, T., C.-F. Lin, and C.W.J. Granger (1993), Power of the Neural Network Linearity Test, *Journal of Time Series Analysis*, 14, 209–220.

Teräsvirta, T., D. Tjøstheim and C.W.J. Granger (1994), Aspects of Modelling Nonlinear Time Series, in R.F. Engle and D.L. McFadden (eds.), *Handbook of Econometrics*, Volume IV, Amsterdam: North-Holland.

Tiao, G.C. and G.E.P. Box (1981), Modelling Multiple Time Series with Applications, *Journal of the American Statistical Association*, 76, 802–816.

Tiao, G.C. and M.R. Grupe (1980), Hidden Periodic Autoregressive-Moving Average Models in Time Series Data, *Biometrika*, 67, 365–373.

Todd, R. (1990), Periodic Linear-Quadratic Methods for Modeling Seasonality, *Journal of Economic Dynamics and Control*, 14, 763–795.

Tong, H. (1983), *Threshold Models in Non-linear Time Series Analysis*, Berlin: Springer.

(1990), *Non-linear Time Series. A Dynamical System Approach*, Oxford: Oxford University Press.

Tsay, R.S. (1987), Conditional Heteroscedastic Time Series Models, *Journal of the American Statistical Association*, 82, 590–604.

(1988), Outliers, Level Shifts, and Variance Changes in Time Series, *Journal of Forecasting*, 7, 1–20.

(1989), Testing and Modeling Threshold Autoregressive Processes, *Journal of the American Statistical Association*, 84, 231–240.

(1993), Testing for Noninvertible Models with Applications, *Journal of Business and Economic Statistics*, 11, 225–233.

Vahid, F. and R.F. Engle (1993), Common Trends and Common Cycles, *Journal of Applied Econometrics*, 8, 341–360.

Van Dijk, D.J.C. and P.H. Franses (1998), Nonlinear Error Correction Models for Interest Rates in The Netherlands, in *Nonlinear Econometric Modelling*, in W. Barnett, D.F. Hendry, S. Hylleberg, and T. Teräsvirta, (eds.), Cambridge: Cambridge University Press, to appear.

Veenstra, A.W. and P.H. Franses (1997), A Cointegration Approach to Forecasting Freight Rates in the Dry Bulk Shipping Sector, *Transportation Research* A, 31, 447–458.

Weiss, A.A. (1986), ARCH and Bilinear Time Series Models: Comparison and Combination, *Journal of Business and Economic Statistics*, 4, 59–70.

Zellner, A. (1962), An Efficient Method of Estimating Seemingly Unrelated Regressions and Tests of Aggregation Bias, *Journal of the American Statistical Association*, 57, 348–368.

(1970), *Bayesian Analysis in Econometrics and Statistics*, Amsterdam: North-Holland.

Zellner, A. and F.C. Palm (1974), Time Series Analysis and Simultaneous Equation Econometric Models, *Journal of Econometrics*, 2, 17–54.

Zivot, E. and D.W.K. Andrews (1992), Further Evidence on the Great Crash, the Oil-Price Shock and the Unit Root Hypothesis, *Journal of Business and Economic Statistics*, 10, 251–270.

Author index

274

Subject index